Antitrust Law

Supplementary Volume

Antitrust Law

Phillip E. Areeda

with contributions from

Herbert Hovenkamp (vols. II–IIA)
John L. Solow (vol. IIA)
Donald F. Turner (vols. I, III–V)

Supplementary Volume
containing

1. Concordance **(vols. II–IIA)**
2. Complete Table of Contents **(vols. I–IX)**
3. Table of Cases **(vols. I–IX)**
4. Index **(vols. I–IX)**

Little, Brown and Company

Boston New York Toronto London

Library of Congress Catalog Card No. 77-15710

ISBN 0-316-05017-2

ICP

Published simultaneously in Canada
by Little, Brown and Company (Canada) Limited

Printed in the United States of America

Special Notice

Revised volume II and new volume IIA incorporate much new material and some changes in organization. One result is substantial renumbering of Paragraphs. The following "concordance" gives the Paragraph number of original Chapter 3, 4, or 5 in the left column and the most closely corresponding Paragraph(s) in the revised edition in the right column. Where appropriate, the references in the left column also include the Supplement, whose Paragraph numbers are designated by either a prime sign (e.g., 316′) or a decimal point (e.g., 316.1).

This concordance should be consulted to obtain corresponding citations whenever a citation to Chapter 3, 4, or 5 is taken from any volume of the Treatise published before 1995; or any judicial decision or citation from another source to the original 1978 edition of Chapter 3, 4, or 5, or to any Supplement 1993 or earlier.

Original Vol. II (1978)	Revised Vols. II, IIA (1995)
300	300
301	301
302	302
303	303
303a	303a
303b	303b
303c	303c
304	304
304a	304a
304b	304b
304c	304c
305	305
305a	305a
305b	305b
305c	305c
305d	305d
305e	305e
305f	305f
305g	305g
306	306
307	307
307a	307a
307b	307b
307c	307c

Original Vol. II (1978)	Revised Vols. II, IIA (1995)
307d	307d
307e	307e
307f	307f
308	310
309	311a
309a	311a1
309b	311a2
309c	311a3
310	311b
310a	311b
310b	311b
311	312d
311a	312d
311b	312d1
311c	312d2
312	312e
312a	312e1
312b	312e2
312c	312e3
312d	312e4
312e	312f
313	312
313a	312
313b	312a
313c	312b
313d	312f
314	320
314a	320a
314b	320b
314c	320c
315	321
315a	321a
315b	321b
315c	321c
315d	321d
315.1	321e
316	322
316a	322a
316b	322b
316c	322c
316d	322c, d, f
316e	323
316.1a	322c
316.1b	322d-i
316.1c	322j
317	323
317a	323a
317b	323b
317c	323c
317d	323c
317e	323d
317′e	323e
318	324a, b, c
318.1	324b
319	330
320	331
320a	331a
320b	331b
320c	331c
320d	331d
321	332
321a	332a
321b	332
322	333
322a	333a
322b	333b
322c	333c
322d	333d
322e	333e
322f	333f
323	334
323a	334a
323b	334b
323b1	334b1

Original Vol. II (1978)	Revised Vols. II, IIA (1995)	Original Vol. II (1978)	Revised Vols. II, IIA (1995)
323b2	334b2	330	348
323b3	334b3	330a	348a
323b4	334b4	330b	348b
323b5	334b5	330c	348c
323c	334c	330d	348d
323d	334d	330e	348e
323e	336	330f	348f
323.1	335	330g	348g
323.1a	335b	331	355
323.1b	335c	331a	355a
323.2	336	331b	355b
323.2a	336a	331c	355c
323.2b	336b	331d	355d
323.2c	336c	332	356
323.2d	336d	332a	356a, d
323.2e	336e	332b	356b
323.2f	336g	332c	346c
323.2g	336f	333	360, a, b
324	337	334	360c
324a	337	334a	360c, g
324b	337a	334b	360c1
324b1	337a1	334c	360c3, 364b, g
324b2	337a2	334d	360d, 362a, 364g
324c	337b		
325	338	334e	360e, f
325a	338a	334f	360h
325b	338b	334.1	360c
325c	338c	334.1a	360a, c2, 364f
325d	338d	334.1b	360d
325e	338f	334.1c	364e
325′f	338e	334.2	362
326	339a, b	334.2a	362a
327	345	334.2b	362b
328	346	334.2c	362c
328a	346a	334.3	362, 363
328b	346b	334.3a	363
329	347	334.3b	363a, c

Original Vol. II (1978)	Revised Vols. II, IIA (1995)	Original Vol. II (1978)	Revised Vols. II, IIA (1995)
334.3c	363b, e	338a	377a
334.3d	364c, d	338b	377b
334.3e	365d	338c	377c
334.3f	365	338d	377d
335	360c5, 365	338e	381a
335a	360c5, 365a	338f	377d3
335b	365a	338′g	337d5
335c	365a, b, d	339a	381a
335d	381	339b	381a
335e	362b	339c	381a
336	378	340	373, 374, 375
336a	378a	340a	373a
336b	378b	340b	373f
336c	378c	340c	373f
336d	378d	340d	373b, c, d
336e	378e	340e	375
337	370	340.1	375
337a	370	340.1a	375c
337b	361	340.1b	375d
337c	371, a, b	340.1c	375e
337d	371c	340.1d	375d
337e	371c, e, h	340.1e	375a
337f	371f, h, j	340.1f	375b
337g	371j	340.2	373
337.1	370	340.2a	373a
337.2	371	340.2b	373d
337.2a	371a	340.2c	373b
337.2b	371d	340.2d	373b, 381a
337.2c	371e	340.2e	381a
337.2d	371f	340.2f	373d2, 373d4, 381a
337.2e	371h		
337.2f	371g	340.2g	373d5
337.2g	371h	340.2h	373e
337.2h	371h	340.2i	381b
337.3	372	340.2j	374
337.4	371i	340.3	382
338	377	340.3a	382a, b, c

Original Vol. II (1978)	Revised Vols. II, IIA (1995)	Original Vol. II (1978)	Revised Vols. II, IIA (1995)
340.3b	382a, b, c	348b	390b
340.3c	382d	348c	390c
340.4	383	349	391
340.4a	383b		
340.4b	383b	401	400, 401
340.4c	383c	402a	402a
340.5	384	402b	402b
341	376	403a	403a
341a	376a	403b	403b
341b	376a	403c	403c
341c	376b	404a	404a
341d	376b3	404b	404b
341e	376b4	404c	404c, d, e, f
341f	376b2	405a	405a
342	380	405b	405b
342.1	379	405c	405c
342.2	385	406a	406a
343	365	406b	406b
344	365b	407a	407a
344a	365b1	407b	407b
344b	365b2	407c	407c
344c	365b3	407d	407d
344d	365b4	408a	408a
344e	365b5	408b	408b
344f	365a	408c	408c
345	362, 365a	408d	408d
346	362, 363	409a	420, 422, 423
346a	373b, c	409b	421
346b	381a	409c	421h
346c	373	409d	421g
347	365c	409e	421b, c
347a	365c1	409f	421e, f
347b	365c2	409g	420
347c	365c3	410	409
347d	365e	411a	412a
348	390	411b	412b
348a	390a	411c	412c

Original Vol. II (1978)	Revised Vols. II, IIA (1995)
412a	413a
412b	413b
412c	413c
413	414
414	415
415	400, 401
500	500
501	501
502a	503, 507, 525
502b	503, 504
503	505
504a	506a, b
504b	506c
505	506d
506	508
507	515
508	516
509	517
510	518
511	519
512a	520a
512b	520b
512c	520a, c
513a	513
513b	513
513c	513
514a	522a
514b	522b, c
514c	522a
515	524
516	526
517	530, 531
518	530, 531
518.1a	533a
518.1b	533b
518.1c	533c
518.1d	533d
518.1e	533e
518.1f	533g
518.1g	533f
518.1h	533g
518.2a	536
518.2b	537
518.2c	537, 538
518.2d	537
518.2e	531
518.3a	532
518.3b	423
518.3c	532
518.3d	572
519a	530c
519b	530c
520	535
521a	534a, b
521b	534c
521c	534d, e, f
522a	550, 551
522b	550b
523a	552a, b
523b	552c
523c	552d, e
523.1a	552e
523.1b	552
523.1c	552
523.1d	534d, 552c
523.1e	536f
523.2	555
523.3	554
524a	553a
524b	553b
524c	553c
524d	553d
525a	562a

Original Vol. II (1978)	Revised Vols. II, IIA (1995)	Original Vol. II (1978)	Revised Vols. II, IIA (1995)
525b	562b	526b	561b, c, d
525c	562d, e, f, g	527a	570a
525d	562d, e	527b	570b, c
525.1a	562e	527c	570d
525.1b	562, 563	527d	570e
525.1c	539	527e	570f
525.1d	539	527f	570g
526.1a	561	527g	570h
526.1b	561d	528a	571a
526a	561a	b	571b

Table of Contents for Volumes I–IX

VOLUME I

PART ONE
Preliminary and Pervasive Issues: Antitrust Goals, Coverage, Procedure, and Economics

CHAPTER 1. Introduction: About This Work and the Objectives of the Antitrust Laws 3

1A. The Nature and Plan of This Work 3

100. Subject Matter and Scope 3
101. Policy and Precedent 4
102. Plan of the Work 5

1B. Objectives of Antitrust Law

103. Introduction: Possible Antitrust Objectives; Consistencies and Inconsistencies 7
104. Economic Objectives Generally Paramount in the Cases 8
105. Governing Principles Summarized 12
106. Inexplicit Statutes and Unilluminating Legislative History 14
107. Economic Efficiency Operates Within Parameters Set by Other Public Policies 16
108. Objectives Affected by Competition but Mainly Achieved in Other Ways 18
    a. Income distribution 18
    b. Economic stabilization 19

109. Other Goals: Fairness, Power Dispersion, and Political Democracy 21
a. Fairness 21
b. "Populist" goals 22
110. Efficiency and Populist Goals Broadly Consistent 23
111. Promoting Populist Goals Over Efficiency Excessively Costly, Futile, or Unadministrable 24
a. Pervasive priority of populist goals unacceptable; implications 25
b. Antitrust efforts to promote populist goals often futile 25
c. Promoting populist goals at the expense of efficiency would impose unacceptable burdens on the courts 27
d. Summary 29
112. Populist Goals Inappropriate as Antitrust Standards Even if No Conflict with Efficiency 29
113. Limitations on the Achievement of Antitrust Economic Objectives 31
a. Limits of economic analysis 31
b. Institutional limits 31
c. Allocation of enforcement resources 32

CHAPTER 2. Antitrust Law Coverage: Jurisdiction and "Exemptions" 35

200. Scope of This Chapter 35

2A. "Political Action" and Other Dealings with Government 36

201. Introduction and Summary 36
202. Anticompetitive Purpose and Burden on Rivals or Rivalry Not Intrinsically Wrongful 37
a. Generally 37
b. Validation by legislation or authorized administrative action 38
c. Good faith efforts to obtain such action permitted 39
203. "Sham" or Bad Faith Action 39
a. *Noerr* principle: legislative context 39

b. "Sham" or bad faith adjudication 41
c. Conclusion 44
204. Improper Means to Influence Government Action 44
a. Introduction 44
b. *Noerr* rationale 45
c. Criteria of impropriety 46
d. Causation problem 49
e. Conclusions 50
1. Legislative context 50
2. Elsewhere 51
205. Unnecessarily Harmful Political Activity 51
206. Government as Buyer, Seller, Lessor, Lessee, Franchisor 52
a. General rule 52
b. Unilateral seller action; government buyer 53
c. Restrictive purchase agreements 53
d. Government lessor or franchisor 54
1. Summary 54
2. Government victimized 54
3. Government chooses monopoly 55
4. Improper means 56

2B. State Law and "State Action" 57
207. Introduction: Problems of Federalism 57

2B-1. Interplay of State Law and Federal Antitrust Law 58
208. Concurrent Authority: Overlapping State and Federal Antitrust Laws 58
209. Federal Preemption 60
210. Areas of Express Primacy for State Law 64
211. Implied Immunity for "State Action": Overview and Summary 66

2B-2. Elaboration of the Implied Immunity for "State Action": The Parker v. Brown Doctrine 67
212. The *Parker* Decision and Its Rationale 67
a. The *Parker* case 67
b. Extension to private parties 69
c. Limitations on *Parker:* a summary 70

213. Proper Immunity Limits I: No *Parker* Immunity Without Adequate Public Supervision 71
- a. Introduction and summary 71
- b. Who decides? 73
- c. How rigorous the supervision? 75
- d. Self-executing statutes 76
- e. Whose initiative? 77
- f. Agency inaction 77

214. Proper Immunity Limits II: No *Parker* Immunity Without Authorized State Action Clearly Intended to Displace Antitrust Law 80
- a. Introduction and summary 80
- b. Determining intent: meaning of participation or approval 83
  - 1. Relative freedom of action 85
  - 2. Agency record 85
  - 3. Parochial outlook 86
  - 4. Central purpose 86
- c. Determining intent: meaning of agency inaction 89
- d. Authority 89
- e. Clear statement required 91

215. Alternative Possible Limitations on *Parker* Immunity 92
- a. Introduction and summary 92
- b. Compulsion 92
  - 1. Compulsion sufficient? 93
  - 2. Compulsion necessary? 94
  - 3. Compulsion relevant as evidence of state purpose 96
- c. Rule of reason approach 97
- d. Limitation to state defendants 99

216. Non-Immunity Without Substantive Antitrust Violation 99
- a. Government as buyer, seller, or franchisor 99
- b. "Reasonableness" defense 100

217. Non-Immunity Without Punitive Sanctions 101
- a. Government officials as defendants 101
  - 1. Equitable remedies only or no liability 102

2. Equitable antitrust relief not always necessary 103
3. Damage liability cases 105
b. Private defendants 108
1. Introduction and summary 108
2. Relevant interests 109
3. Defendant-initiated state involvement 110
4. Reasonable reliance; apparent authority 111
5. State compulsion revisited 114
218. Applicability of *Parker* to Federal Trade Commission Act 114
a. The issue 114
b. Grounds for greater reach of FTC Act 115
c. Conclusion 118

2B-3. Non-Antitrust Limitations on Anticompetitive State Activities 119
219. Unusual Limitations 119
a. Introduction 119
b. First Amendment 119
c. The Due Process Clause and the Civil Rights Act 121
220. Commerce Clause 122
a. Introduction and summary 122
b. Commerce Clause and anticompetitive state laws 124
c. "Significant" burdens on interstate commerce 127
d. Extent of "legitimate" state benefits 130
e. Antitrust liability contrasted with other limitations on state action 131

2C. Exempt and Regulated Sectors 133
221. Antitrust Mandate Qualified 133

2C-1. Regulated Industries Generally 134
222. The Problem; Key Issues Resolving Particular Cases 134
223. Background Considerations 135
a. Summary 135

b. Variations in regulatory powers and premises 137
c. Competitive policy within regulatory framework 139
d. Flexibility in antitrust rules 140
e. Procedure is substance 140
f. Prospective or retroactive remedies 141
g. Non-doctrinal influences 142
h. "Primary" and "exclusive" jurisdiction 144
224. Can Agency Existence or Approval Confer Antitrust Immunity? 144
a. Summary 144
b. Express immunity power 146
c. Implied immunity generally 147
d. Immunity implied by statutory requirements or assumptions 147
e. Immunity implied by agency approval requirement; "pervasive" regulation 153
f. Immunity implied by agency power to control or prevent 157
225. Was Challenged Conduct Administratively Approved? 163
a. Introduction and summary 163
b. Activities before and after approval 163
c. Approval with continuing supervision 164
d. Who decides 167
226. Unapproved Conduct Referred to Agency That Could Have Immunized It? 168
a. The problem; summary 168
b. Injunction sought 168
c. Availability of damage or criminal sanctions 170
d. Relevance of agency judgments 171
e. Silent agencies 174
227. Prior Resort Apart from Immunity 174
a. Recapitulation 174
b. The *Ricci* case 176

2C-2. Particular Exemptions 178
228. Agricultural and Fishermen's Cooperatives 178
a. Statutory provisions; issues 178
b. Organization issues 180

c. Non-exempt practices 182
d. Market power; price enhancement 185
229. Labor Unions 188
a. Introduction and summary 188
b. Statutory basis for the exemption, express and implied 190
c. Who is an "employee" 195
d. Employer restraints 198
e. Collective bargaining agreements limiting other businessmen 202
f. Illegitimate union restraints 211
230. Other Special Provisions 222
a. Export associations 222
b. National defense 224
c. Small business 225
d. Newspapers 225
e. Banks 226
f. Professional sports 227

2D. Interstate Commerce 227
231. Interstate Commerce: The General Requirement 227
232. Sherman Act Reach 228
a. Summary 228
b. Policy impulses 229
c. Initial development; flow of commerce 230
d. Affecting-commerce test 232
e. Conflicting applications 234
233. The "In Commerce" Statutes 241
a. Generally 241
b. Flow of commerce 242
c. Robinson-Patman Act §2(a) 248
d. Robinson-Patman Act §§2(c)-(f) and Clayton Act §3 251
e. Clayton Act §7 252
f. Overlapping statutes; Federal Trade Commission Act §5 253

2E. Foreign Commerce: General Principles 254
234. Introduction 254
a. Statutory provisions 254

b. Essential point; key issues 255
c. Scope of this subchapter 256
235. Jurisdiction, in Personam and in Rem 256
a. General proposition 256
b. Federal vs. international concerns 257
c. Illustrations 258
d. In rem jurisdiction 260
236. Statutory Reach 260
a. Introduction and summary 260
b. Earlier precedents 261
c. Effects test 261
d. Necessary limitations on effects test 262
e. Intention to affect U.S. commerce 263
f. Significant effects on U.S. commerce 264
1. Given an intention to affect U.S. commerce 264
2. Generally 264
g. Restraints affecting U.S. exports 265
237. Appraising Restraints Abroad 267
238. Remedies Limited 269
239. Foreign Government Involvement 271
a. Introduction and summary 271
b. Act of state 272
1. Private inducement 273
2. Agent of foreign government 275
c. Sovereign immunity 276
240. National Adjudication vs. Diplomacy 277

STATUTORY APPENDIX 279

Sherman Act 279
Clayton Act 281
Federal Trade Commission Act 310
Wilson Tariff Act 339
Webb-Pomerene Act 341
Defense Production Act (excerpt) 344
Small Business Act (excerpt) 359
Bank Holding Company Act (excerpt) 362
Bank Merger Act 376
Newspaper Preservation Act 380
Patent Code (excerpts) 382

VOLUME II

CHAPTER 3. The System of Remedies: Basic Issues

300. Introduction 1
301. Caveat on Scope and Depth 2

3A. Antitrust Laws Related to Common Law and to Each Other 2

302. Relationship of Sherman Act and Common Law 2
303. Clayton Act 4
a. Generally 4
b. Impulse to enactment 5
c. Sherman Act compared 6
304. Sherman Act and Clayton Act Standards Coalesce 7
a. Different standards irrational and not compelled by statutes 7
b. Contrary arguments rejected 7
c. Precedent 8
305. Federal Trade Commission Act 10
a. Impulse to enactment 10
b. Compared with Sherman and Clayton Acts 12
c. FTC jurisdiction; intergovernmental coordination 13
d. Adjudication, formal and informal 14
e. Remedies and sanctions 15
f. Judicial review 19
g. Rule-making 20
306. Structure as Such Under Federal Trade Commission Act §5 21
307. Federal Trade Commission Act §5 Standards Related to Sherman and Clayton Act Standards 21
a. Generally 21
b. Critique of *Brown Shoe*'s "incipient" or "policy" violations 22
c. Sanctions 24
d. Rule-making 25
e. Expertness 26
f. Summary 27

3B. Structure of Sanctions: Relation to Liability 28
310. Introduction 28
311. Many Remedies for a Given "Violation" 29
a. Criminal punishment 29
1. Which statutes? 29
2. Frequency; government practice 30
3. Appropriateness of criminalization 32
b. Civil sweep divorced from criminal sanctions 33
312. Differentiating the Offense According to Remedy 34
a. Against differentiation 34
b. Remedy and offense interrelated 35
c. Differentiating criminal offenses; *Gypsum* 36
d. Treble damages: scope, rationale, and punishment 39
1. Government equity suits and criminal proceedings compared 39
2. Illustration: "behavior-less monopoly" 40
e. Government and Private Equity Suits Compared 42
1. Practical differences 42
2. Relevance 43
3. Recognized distinctions under the antitrust laws 44
4. Equitable discretion 45
f. Summary 47

3C. Rule Determination in the Litigation Process 47
320. Per Se Rules and Presumptions, Formal and Informal 47
a. Key points 47
b. General discussion 48
c. Conclusion 53
321. Jury Trial 54
a. Generally 54
b. Which issues? 54
c. Grounds for judicial resolution; distinguishing fact and law 55
d. Contrary arguments rejected 58
e. Relevance of complexity 60

322. Summary Judgment 62
 a. The problem; key point 62
 b. Obstacles to summary judgment 64
 c. No "genuine issue" though facts disputed—major Supreme Court holdings 66
 d. Single issue can resolve or simplify case 72
 e. Exception to per se condemnation 73
 f. Conduct desirable or not 75
 g. Motivation and rationality, especially in conspiracy doctrine 79
 h. Applying the rule of reason 81
 i. Direct vs. circumstantial evidence 82
 j. Expert affidavits in summary judgment 82
323. Pre-Discovery Summary Disposition
 a. Key points 86
 b. Discovery wanted 87
 c. Discovery superfluous 88
 d. Conclusory or more specific claims of law or fact 89
 e. Sanctions for bad faith claims; Rule 11 93
324. Managing Complexity 95
 a. The problem; helpful steps 95
 b. Compulsory arbitration 97
 c. Implications for state jurisdiction 98

3D. Repose in Antitrust Litigation 99
330. The General Problem 99
331. Guidelines, Clearances, and Advisory Opinions 99
 a. Summary 99
 b. Enforcement guidelines 100
 c. Justice Department clearances 100
 d. FTC advisory opinions 102
332. Mistake of Law 103
 a. By private person 103
 b. By government agency 105
333. Change of Law 107
 a. The issue 107
 b. Values at stake 108
 c. The statute 109
 d. Judicial function 110

e. Rewarding successful litigants 111
f. "Innovative" or "avulsive" change 112
334. Res Judicata 116
a. Generally 116
b. Splitting the cause of action 116
1. Basic proposition 116
2. Multiple statutory standards 117
3. Exception for government monopolization suits 118
4. Legal or equitable relief 119
5. Civil-criminal proceedings 119
c. Continuing conduct and changing law or circumstances 120
d. Public and private plaintiffs; different government agencies 121
e. Parties in "privity" 122
335. Res Judicata; Federal and State Antitrust Law 123
a. Issues 123
b. First claim in federal court; second in state court 124
c. First claim in state court; second in federal court 128
1. Issue preclusion 128
2. Claim preclusion; relevance of state preclusion law 128
336. Collateral Estoppel 130
a. Generally 130
b. Non-mutual estoppel 131
c. Present plaintiff could have joined earlier suit 132
d. Comparing issues and procedures in the two suits 134
e. Inconsistent prior judgments 137
f. Change of law 137
g. Administrative proceedings 138
337. Effect of Government Victory on Subsequent Private Suit 139
a. Which prior proceedings? 140
1. FTC orders 140
2. Consent orders 141
b. Scope and effect 141

c. Relation between offensive collateral estoppel and §5(a) 143
338. Statute of Limitation 144
a. Generally 144
b. Accrual of a cause of action 145
c. *Zenith* exception when damages speculative 149
d. Fraudulent concealment 151
e. Prior administrative or judicial proceedings 154
f. Laches 155
339. Government Suit Tolls Statute of Limitation 158
a. Generally 158
b. Administrative proceedings 159

3E. Equitable Relief 161
345. Objectives and Scope 161
346. Private Suits in Equity 164
a. Entitlement to relief 164
b. Scope of relief 165
347. Preliminary Relief 168
348. Consent Decrees 171
a. Nature and significance 171
b. Modification 172
c. Third-party enforcement or use 173
d. Third-party interests 174
e. Intervention 175
f. Third-party interest under 1974 amendments 176
g. Judicial role 176

3F. Private Antitrust Actions Generally 180
355. Statutory Scheme 180
a. Introduction: key issues 180
b. Private and public purposes; policy dilemmas 180
1. Rationale for treble damages 180
2. Negative consequences of treble damages 181
3. Resolutions 182
c. Public injury 182
d. Attorneys' fees 183
356. Class Actions: An Introduction 184
a. Utility and general requisites 184

b. Absent members 185
c. Manageability 187
d. Predominance of common questions under Rule 23(b)(3) 187

3G. "Standing" of Private Plaintiffs 191

3G-1. General Principles 191
360. "Standing" 191
a. Introduction 191
b. Standing doctrine limits equity 193
c. Basic standing requirements summarized 194
1. Injury to "business or property" 195
2. Injury-in-fact "by reason of" the antitrust violation 195
3. Proximity 195
4. "Antitrust injury" 196
5. Cognizable injury and reasonably quantifiable damages 196
d. *Associated General Contractors (AGC)* 196
e. Nature of "standing" inquiry 200
1. Broadly or narrowly defined? 200
2. More than pleading requirement 202
f. To test standing, assume a violation 202
g. Impulses to broaden or narrow standing requirements 204
h. Subsequent discussion summarized 206
361. "Business or Property" 208
362. "Antitrust Injury" 209
a. Development; rationale 209
b. Antitrust injury equally important in private equity actions 213
c. Per se offenses 216
363. Causation and Injury-in-Fact 219
a. "Material" or "substantial" cause 219
b. Independent cause fully accounts for claimed injury 222
c. Insufficient logical connection 223
d. No loss or own mismanagement 225
e. Injury-in-fact but without causation 227

364. Remote, Derivative, Duplicative, or Inferior Plaintiff 227
- a. Introduction 227
- b. Too many links in chain of causation 228
- c. Derivative and genuinely duplicative injuries 229
- d. Derivative but only "quasi-duplicative" injuries 230
- e. Inferior plaintiffs 231
- f. Remote but "inextricably intertwined" plaintiff 233
- g. "Direct" and "target area" tests revisited 236

365. Reasonably Ascertainable Damages 237
- a. Policy dilemma 237
- b. Illustrative damage assessment problems 239
  1. Price-fixing conspiracy (or other illegal prices) 239
  2. Boycotting experienced newcomer; lost profits 240
  3. Boycotting inexperienced newcomer 242
  4. Terminated dealer 243
  5. Foreclosed supplier 244
- c. Inherently offset injuries 245
  1. Tying and the *Fortner* case 245
  2. Tying, price discrimination, and the *Chicken Delight* case 246
  3. In pari delicto situations 248
- d. Nominal damages 250
- e. Conclusion 252

3G-2. Recurring "Standing" Situations *253*

370. Consumers and Other Buyers 253

371. Indirect Purchasers 255
- a. Introduction and summary 255
- b. Innocent middleman's recovery 256
- c. Consumer standing under *Illinois Brick* 257
- d. Equity suits 259
- e. Pre-existing fixed-markup contracts with fixed or variable quantities 260
- f. Middleman direct purchaser owned or controlled by indirect purchaser or defendant 262

g. Indirect sellers 263
h. Vertical restraints or boycott 264
i. State law not preempted 266
j. Critique 267
1. Identifying victims 267
2. Apportioning an overcharge 270
3. Lost profits for middlemen 271
372. "Umbrella" Transactions 272
373. Competitor Suits 275
a. Introduction and summary 275
b. Rivals' price fixing, market division, or merger 276
c. Greater competition or efficiency 277
d. Exclusionary conduct 278
1. Predatory pricing; arguments on competitor standing 278
2. Future predation possibility 280
3. Illegal foreclosure 282
4. Leverage 282
5. Undesirable efficiency 283
e. Would-be or actual member of combination or substitute monopolist 284
1. Plaintiff seeks access to monopoly 284
2. Plaintiff member challenges cartel bylaw 286
f. Identifying "competitors" when intermediaries are involved 287
1. Plaintiff and dealers compete with integrated defendant 287
2. Integrated plaintiff competes with defendant and his dealers 289
3. Predation at component or finished product level 289
4. Neither integrated 290
374. Nascent Firms 292
375. Suppliers 296
a. Introduction and summary 296
b. Buying cartel 297
c. Downstream horizontal merger or other restraint 299

d. Boycott or other injury to plaintiff's customers 302
e. Supplier foreclosed from selling market 303
f. Supplier redundant when customer supplies himself 305
376. Licensors and Landlords 306
a. General rule 306
b. Underlying issues 307
1. Antitrust injury and foreseeability 308
2. Antitrust administration 309
3. Avoiding windfalls via contract 309
4. Locus of major stake 310
c. Restraint in upstream real estate or licensing market 310
377. Employees 311
a. Introduction and summary 311
b. "Business or property" 311
c. Employment market restrained 312
d. Downstream product market restrained 312
1. Post-restraint consolidations 313
2. Employer harmed 313
3. Fewer inputs needed when downstream output illegally restrained 314
4. "Low" wages to monopolize product market 315
5. "Whistleblowers" 316
378. Taxpayers (or Citizens), Creditors, or Shareholders 317
a. Characteristics 317
b. Taxpayer (or citizen) 318
c. Creditor 320
d. Shareholder 320
e. Shareholder derivative action 321
379. Associations 323
a. Association suit on own behalf 323
b. Association suit on members' behalf 325
380. Governments 326
381. Mergers 329
a. Generally 329
b. Tender-offer targets 331

382. Distribution Restraints 333
a. Introduction and summary 333
b. Consumers 334
c. Restrained or terminated dealer 335
d. Sellers of other brands 338
383. Tying and Exclusive Dealing 340
a. Foreclosed suppliers 340
b. Restrained buyers and their customers 340
c. Supplier of tying product to defendant 341
384. Robinson-Patman Act Violations 342
385. Defenses and Declaratory Judgments 344

3H. Plaintiffs with Unclean Hands 345
390. In Pari Delicto: Plaintiff Participant in Defendant's Antitrust Violation 345
a. Issue and summary 345
b. *Kiefer-Stewart* and *Perma Life* cases 346
c. The aftermath 348
391. Plaintiff's Antitrust Violation Defeating His Non-Antitrust Claim 350

VOLUME IIA

CHAPTER 4. The Economic Basis for Antitrust Policy 1
400. Introduction 1
401. The Rationale of Antitrust Policy 1

4A. The Basic Economics of Competition, Monopoly, Oligopoly, and Cartels 2
402. The Nature and Economic Consequences of a Perfectly Competitive Economy 2
a. Perfect competition defined 2
b. Logical consequences 3
1. Operating efficiency 3
2. Allocative efficiency 3
3. Progressiveness 4
403. The Nature and Economic Consequences of Monopoly 5
a. Monopoly defined 5

b. Effect of monopoly pricing on allocative efficiency 5
c. Effect of monopoly on operating efficiency 6

404. Oligopoly: Nature, Economic Consequences, and Measurement 7
a. Oligopoly defined 7
b. Economic consequences of oligopoly output and pricing decisions 7
1. Non-cooperative oligopoly with single market price and perfectly informed sellers and buyers 8
2. Price-coordinating oligopoly with cartel-like results 10
3. Secret price discrimination 11
c. Factors facilitating or impeding oligopoly pricing 12
1. Generally: effective monitoring and matching 12
2. Individual or group maximization; different costs; excess capacity 13
3. Product heterogeneity, non-price competition, and price disguises 13
4. Infrequent or non-comparable transactions 14
5. Severe decline in demand; capital intensity; management attitudes 15
6. Sellers' number; fringe firm expansion 15
7. Buyer power, sophistication 15
8. Imperfect coordination and facilitating practices 16
9. Summary 16
d. Concentration-performance evidence 17
1. Allocative efficiency 17
2. Operating efficiency 19
e. Concentration measures generally 20
f. Concentration measures technically 21
1. *N*-firm concentration ratio 21
2. Herfindahl-Hirschman Index 23

405. Cartels 24
a. Cartel defined; oligopoly compared 24
b. Cartel purposes, problems, variations 24

1. Difficulty of procuring agreement; divergent interests 25
2. "Cheating"; non-price competition; random variations in market share 25
c. Economic effects 26

4B. Departures from the Competitive Model: Implications for Antitrust Policy 27
406. Essential Points 27
a. Departures summarized 27
b. Practical limits to antitrust policy 28
407. Progressiveness 29
a. The problem 29
b. Absolute size and innovative activity 30
c. Market power and innovative activity 32
1. Additional funds 32
2. Security effects 32
3. Larger realizable rewards; less free riding 33
4. Negative effects 34
5. Oligopoly unusually favorable? 34
6. Qualitative empirical evidence 34
7. Quantitative evidence 35
d. Implications for antitrust policy 35
408. Economies of Scale 36
a. The problem 36
b. Nature and varieties 37
c. Impact of scale economies on market concentration 38
1. Plant economies 38
2. Multiplant economies: plant specialization and capacity expansion 39
3. Capital costs 40
4. Procurement costs 40
5. Promotional costs 41
6. Servicing 41
7. Scale economies in the aggregate 42
8. Trends 42
d. Implications for antitrust policy 42
409. Product Differentiation; Monopolistic Competition 43

410. Information Asymmetry 44
411. Agency Problems 45
412. "Second Best" Problems 45
a. Introduction 45
b. The effects of antimonopoly policy when some monopolies are irremediable 46
c. Multiple market imperfections 48
413. Resource Immobility: "Ruinous" Competition 50
a. The problem 50
b. Secular decline 51
c. Cyclical recession 52
414. Externalities 53
415. Collusion 55

4C. Barriers to Entry: Meaning, Identification, and Antitrust Policy Consequences 55
420. Entry Barriers Generally 55
a. Definition; antitrust concerns 55
b. Proving entry conditions 57
c. Entry barriers in economic or antitrust analysis 60
421. Sources of Entry Barriers 63
a. Scale economies 63
b. High initial investment 64
c. Unsalvageable investment; risk 65
d. Low prices 66
e. Access to needed inputs 67
f. Access to customers 68
g. Product reputation and promotion 68
h. Governmental constraints 69
422. Assessing Likelihood and Effectiveness of Entry 71
a. Likelihood of entry 71
b. Timeliness 73
c. Sufficiency 74
d. Interpreting historical entry data 75
1. No historical entry 76
2. Entry during supracompetitive pricing 76
3. Entry in face of predation 77
423. Potential Competition and Market Definition 77

PART TWO

Market Structure Issues

CHAPTER 5. Market Power and Market Definition 83
500. Introduction and Preview 83

5A. Defining Market Power 85
501. Market Power Defined 85
502. The Social Cost of Market Power 87
503. Formal Price-Cost Measure of Market Power: The Theory 90
a. Analysis 91
b. The Lerner Index 93
504. Formal Price-Cost Measure of Market Power: Difficulties 95
a. Uncertain price 95
b. Uncertain marginal cost 96
505. Complex and Changing Power 100
506. Buyer Response and Substitutes Check Market Power 100
a. Generally 100
b. Identical products: expandable output at comparable costs 101
c. Differentiated products 102
d. Power's duration 103
507. Economic Relationship Among Market Power, Elasticity of Demand, and Elasticity of Supply 103
a. Elasticities defined 104
b. Relationship between elasticities and Lerner Index; residual demand 107
508. "Unexercised" Market Power 109

5B. "Alternative," Non-Market-Based Proofs of Market Power 109
515. Introduction: Market Definition and Alternatives 110
516. Excess Returns as Proof of Market Power: Summary 111
517. Persistent Excess Returns 111
518. "Monopoly Profits" vs. "Scarcity Rents" 113

519. Sole or Dominant Producer 115
520. Proving Excess Returns 115
a. Deficiencies in accounting data 116
1. Differences between accounting and economic costs 116
2. Accounting profit higher than in comparable firms 118
3. Accounting profit low 119
b. Cost of capital 120
c. *Alcoa* and *Cellophane* 121
521. Price-Cost Margins and Excess Returns 122
522. Price Discrimination and Market Power 125
a. Definition and significance 125
b. Utility: problems of proof 127
c. Low marginal cost 129
523. Intellectual Property as Proof of Market Power 130
524. Conduct Indicating Market Power 132
a. Thesis and caveats 132
b. Excluding rivals or coordinating prices costly? 133
c. Rigid prices or shares, price leadership, and non-price competition 134
d. Facilitating practices 136
525. Direct estimates of market power from computation of residual demand curves 138
a. Residual demand curve defined 138
b. Relating residual demand to market power 139
c. Market power assessed without market definition 142
d. Determining residual demand in practice 143
e. Firm-specific cost "shocks" 143
f. Availability and historical nature of data 147
g. Limit pricing 148
526. Concluding Comment 149

5C. Market Definition — General Considerations 149
530. Introduction and Preview 149
a. "Market" defined 150
b. A spectrum of power 152
c. Time factor 153
d. Unavoidable approximations 154

e. How small a market 154
f. Aggregating separate markets; materiality 155
531. Functions of Market Definition 156
a. Surrogate for power when direct measure insufficient 156
b. Statutory requirement 157
c. Non-market approaches and single-firm power 157
d. Future vs. present power 158
e. Market structure in analyzing conduct 159
532. Meaning of Market Shares 160
a. Large share 160
b. Low shares; jury role 164
533. "Submarket" Confusion 167
a. Subdividing the inquiry 168
b. Market scope; degrees of constraint 169
c. Only "markets" are relevant 170
d. Price discrimination 173
e. Differentiated products 174
f. Supply vs. demand substitution 174
g. Inconsistencies and other confusions in geographic "submarkets" 175
534. Price Relationships, Purchasing Patterns 177
a. Market scope over- or understated 178
1. Historical prices competitive 178
2. Historical prices monopolistic 179
3. In practice 179
b. No close price relationships among products 180
c. Close price relationships 182
d. Price discrimination and narrower market definitions 183
e. Buying-selling patterns 185
f. Distribution costs 186
535. Measuring Share Within a Given Market 187
a. Revenue vs. units sold 187
b. Sales vs. production 188
1. Orders exceed production 188
2. Production exceeds sales 189
c. Capacity vs. output 189
1. Relevance of capacity 189
2. Capacity caveats 191

d. Unusual events or lumpy sales 192
e. "Captive" output 193
f. Partial inclusion; "one-way market definition" 194
536. Hypothetical Price Increase Methodology to Define Market 195
537. "Significant" Price Increase Required and Defined 198
a. Necessary though arbitrary 198
b. Five percent or 10 percent test 200
c. Varying the test by markets 201
1. Market size 201
2. Relative profitability 201
d. Consumer impact; degrees of proximity 202
538. Predicting Effects of Hypothetical Price Increase 203
a. Objective data 203
b. Subjective evidence 205
c. Government guidelines 206
539. Misleading Cross-Elasticities, Trading Patterns, or Hypothetical Price-Increase Methodology 207
a. The problem 207
b. Possible solutions 209
1. Non-competitive performance or conduct 209
2. If alleged substitutes similarly noncompetitive; market power though not necessarily substantial power? 211

5D. Geographic Market 212
550. Price Relationships and Trading Patterns 213
a. Price relationships 213
b. Trading patterns 215
551. Economics of Geographic Markets 218
552. Transport Costs 222
a. Introduction and summary 222
b. Relationship of transport to other costs 225
c. Transport costs approximate price differences: persistent one-way sales 228
1. Exporting region 229
2. Importing region: export seller cost advantage 229

3. Importing region: capacity deficit; net cost advantage for local producers 229
4. Importing region: non-competitive pricing 231
5. Exporting region's home demand; physical or legal barriers to greater exports 232
6. Product differentiation 233
7. Importing region: summary 234
d. Transport cost exceeds price difference 234
1. No cross-region sales 234
2. Persistent one-way sales 234
3. Persistent or recurring two-way sales 237
e. One market or barriers overcome? 237
553. Customer Convenience and Preference 238
a. Stationary goods; utility vs. cost 238
b. No common sellers 239
c. Significant common sellers 239
d. Limited common sellers 240
e. Information, urgency, and third-party payors 241
554. Government Guidelines 242
555. Foreign Competition 243
a. International trade barriers 244
b. Attitudes toward imports 245
c. Actual imports vs. foreign output 246
556. Geographic Trade Restrained 249

5E. Product Market 251
560. Introduction 251
561. Producer Substitutes 252
a. Perfect interchangeability 252
b. Incomplete interchangeability 255
c. Broaden market, add likely shifters to narrow market, or merely consider conditions of entry 256
d. Government guidelines: narrow product market but include prompt entrants 257
562. User Substitutes 258
a. Generally 258
b. Interchangeable use with large physical and price differences 260
c. Single market notwithstanding price differences 262
d. Closer and more remote substitutes 263

e. Brand preferences, "lock-ins," and other impediments to buyer shifts 263
f. Discrimination against locked-in or strong-preference buyers 264
g. Government guidelines 266
563. Differentiated Products 267
a. General principle 267
b. Branded vs. unbranded class 268
c. Price categories 270
d. Single brand within a product class 270
e. Inclusive product class 271
564. Distribution Modes 274
565. Cluster Markets 275

5F. Special Situations 277
570. Market Definition to Assess Vertical Foreclosure 277
a. Generally 277
b. Foreclosed market 278
1. Usual market: rivals' alternative opportunities 278
2. Occasional market: consumers' buying opportunities 280
c. Same product, different uses 281
d. Producer substitutes 282
e. Some sellers' markets limited 282
1. A testing case analyzed 283
2. A proposed general solution 284
f. "Preferred" sales foreclosed: price discrimination 285
g. "Captive" outlets 286
h. Supply foreclosure 287
1. Geographic market 287
2. Producer substitutes 287
3. Limited supply alternatives to some purchasers 287
571. Mergers Across Market Boundaries 288
a. The problem 288
b. Relevant factors 289
572. Government Regulation and Market Power 290
a. Entry limitations 290

b. Licensing fees, regulatory requirements, and subsidies 292
c. Price control 293
d. Antitrust immunities 295
573. Durable Products 296
a. Market definition 296
b. Leasing practices 298
574. Measuring Monopsony Power 299

VOLUME III

CHAPTER 6. Monopolization 1
600. The Problem 1
a. The basic issue 1
b. Basic issues interdependent 1
601. Definitions 2

6A. Key Monopolization Cases 3
602. Introduction 3
603. *Standard Oil* 3
a. Court's approach and language 3
b. Intention 5
c. Conduct not "usual" or "normal" 6
604. *American Tobacco Trust* 7
605. *American Can* 9
606. *United States Steel* 11
607. *International Harvester* 13
608. *Alcoa* 13
a. Facts 14
b. Court's general formulation 16
c. Application 19
d. Critique 20
e. Expansion as "exclusionary" 20
f. Pre-1912 exclusionary behavior 22
g. Uncertain causation 22
h. Delay 22
i. Prior suit 24
j. More recent behavior 25
k. Implications 26

609. *American Tobacco* 26
610. *Griffith* 27
611. *United Shoe* 29
  a. Facts 29
  b. General formulation 30
  c. Application 31
612. *Grinnell* 32
  a. District Court 32
  b. Supreme Court 33
613. Summary 34

6B. The Dilemma: The Evils of Monopoly vs. Compunctions Against Condemning "Mere Monopoly" 35
614. Introduction and Summary 35
615. Monopoly as the Statutory Concern 36
616. Language of §2 38
617. Legislative History of §2 39
618. Monopoly as Self-Correcting 41
  a. The possibility 41
  b. Problem remains 42
619. Condemning Mere Monopoly Impractical or Wasteful 43
620. Condemning Mere Monopoly Unfair? 44
  a. Definition of "monopoly" arbitrary? 44
  b. Restrictive behavior presumed? 45
  c. Equitable relief unfair? 45
621. Condemnation of Mere Monopoly Futile? 47
  a. "Natural monopoly" 47
  b. Indivisible scarce resources 50
  c. Legal license 53
    1. Franchised monopoly 53
    2. Monopoly created by patents 53
    3. Distinguishing monopoly perpetuated by patents 54
    4. Practical problems 55
    5. Problems with blanket exemption of patent-based monopolies 56
    6. Conclusions 57
  d. Implications 58

622. Condemnation of Mere Monopoly Counterproductive? 59
a. "The successful competitor . . . turned upon. . . ." 59
b. Significance of market structure and market share 60
c. Significant disincentive not certain 60
d. Significant disincentive possible 61
e. Limiting intervention to persistent monopoly reduces any disincentives 62
f. Conclusion 63
623. Conclusion: Persistent and Not-Inevitable Monopoly in Government Equity Proceedings 63
a. Argument summarized; remedy limitation emphasized 63
b. Persistent monopoly and the case precedents 64
c. Relevance of persistency summarized 65
d. Proving persistence 66
e. Proving inevitability 67
624. Conclusion: Monopoly Cases Generally 67
a. Persistence not required 67
b. Behavioral requirement assessed 68
c. Presumptive illegality assessed 68
d. Behavioral requirement preferable 70

6C. The Nature and Definition of "Monopolizing" Conduct: Relation to Remedies 71
625. The Relevance of Conduct 71
a. Generally 71
b. Summary 72
626. General Definition of Monopolizing 23
a. "Purpose," "intent," "willfulness," or "not inevitable" 73
b. "Competition on the merits" not "exclusionary" 77
c. Substantial effects; uncertainty; "exclusionary" conduct defined 78
d. Business torts or unfair methods of competition 79
e. Relationship to other antitrust offenses 81
f. "Abuse" of monopoly power 82
g. Conclusions 83

627. Exclusionary Conduct and Remedies Beyond Injunction 83
- a. The problem 83
- b. Causation essential to extensive equitable relief: contrary rationales rejected 84
  - 1. Deterrence 85
  - 2. Demonstrated propensity for wrongdoing 86
  - 3. Trigger theory 86
  - 4. "Innocent" exclusionary conduct
- c. Partial causation and equitable relief beyond injunction; full feasible relief? 87
  - 1. Undoing an exclusionary act 88
  - 2. "Intermediate" remedies? 89
  - 3. Conclusion 90

628. "Ancient" Exclusionary Acts 90

629. Changing Legal Standards for Exclusionary Conduct 93
- a. Introduction 93
- b. Reliance 94
- c. "Full" relief inappropriate 94
- d. Reliance on "clearances" 95

630. Criminal Sanctions and Treble Damages 95
- a. Introduction 95
- b. Criminal sanctions 96
- c. Treble damages 96
  - 1. Generally 96
  - 2. Analogy to criminal sanctions 97
  - 3. Causation 97

CHAPTER 7. Monopolization: Particular Exclusionary Practices 101

700. Introduction 101

7A. Horizontal Acquisitions and Agreements 101

701. Mergers with Actual or Potential Competitors 101
- a. Generally 101
- b. "Small" acquisition 102
- c. Potential competitor 103

d. Acquired firm in related market 104
e. Acquisition for diversification 105
f. Acquisition for progressiveness 105
g. Justification: acquisition for efficiency 106
h. Failing company acquired 106
i. Scope of equitable relief 108
702. Acquiring Talent 108
a. The problem 108
b. Generally desirable 109
c. Exclusionary circumstances 109
703. Price Fixing, Market Divisions, and Other Noncompetition Arrangements 111
a. Generally 111
b. Ancillary convenants not to compete 111
c. Joint ventures 113

7B. Exclusionary Practices: Patents 114
704. Patent Exclusions Generally 114
a. Sources of confusion 114
b. Patent accumulation 115
c. Solicitude for outside patentee 116
d. Solicitude for the monopolist 116
e. "Acquisitions" from employees 117
705. Patent Acquisition 117
a. Generally 117
b. Dangers to competition 118
c. Monopolist's legitimate interests 119
d. Non-exclusive license solution 120
1. Generally 120
2. Outside patentee's objections 120
3. Monopolist's objections 121
4. Competitive objections 122
e. Grant-backs 123
f. Settlements 123
g. Compulsory licensing alternative 124
h. Scope of equitable relief 125
i. Unrelated technology 126
706. Internally Developed Patents 127
a. Power with virtue 127

b. Exclusionary purpose 128
c. Non-use 129
1. Varieties of non-use 129
2. Market monopoly vs. patent monopoly 131
3. Objections to licensing duty 131
d. Conclusion 133
707. Improprieties in Patent Procurement 133
a. The problem 133
b. Patent invalidity or misuse 134
c. Federal Trade Commission Act §5 136
d. Impropriety in procuring a valid patent not "exclusionary"; misuse distinguished 137
e. Material impropriety in procuring invalid patent exclusionary 138
f. Connection with monopoly power 139
g. Defining impropriety: materiality 140
h. Defining impropriety: "wilful" misrepresentation 141
1. Decisive materiality 141
2. Less than decisive materiality 142
i. Lack of candor 142
1. Disclosure duty 142
2. What was known? 143
j. Prior art representations 143
k. Unrelated patentee 144
l. Scope of equitable remedies 144
708. Infringement Actions 145
709. Restricted Licenses 147

7C. Exploitative, Predatory, and Other Pricing Policies; Related Issues 148
710. Exploitative Pricing 148
711. Predatory Pricing: Preliminaries; Conclusions 150
a. Introduction 150
b. Prerequisites 151
c. Rejected approaches 152
d. Summary of conclusions 153
712. Alternative Measures of Cost 154

713. Profit-Maximizing (or Loss-Minimizing) Pricing 158
714. Full-Cost Pricing 159
 a. Generally 159
 b. Limit pricing 159
 c. Temporary price reduction 161
  1. Problem 161
  2. Control devices 162
 d. Conclusion 163
715. Marginal-Cost Pricing 164
 a. Price at or above marginal cost 164
 b. Prices below marginal cost 168
  1. General rule 168
  2. Price above average cost excepted 169
  3. No other exceptions 172
 c. Defining short-run marginal costs 172
 d. Average variable cost as surrogate 174
716. Promotional Pricing 176
717. Meeting Competition as a Defense 178
718. Predatory Investment in the Monopoly Market 180
 a. Problem; conclusion 180
 b. Identification problems 180
719. Multiple Products; Differential Returns 181
 a. Different rates of return in the short run 181
 b. "Predatory investment" in new product lines 84
720. Price Discrimination 186
 a. Different geographic markets 187
 b. Same geographic market 188
 c. Relevance of Robinson-Patman Act 189
721. "Excessive" Promotional Spending 191
 a. Predatory spending 191
 b. Increased net returns 191
722. "Excessive" Product Variation 192
 a. Generally 192
 b. Multiple product variations 192
 c. Frequent product changes 193

7D. Vertical Arrangements: Integration, Mergers, Restrictions, and Refusal to Deal 194

723. Vertical Integration: Definition and Varieties 194
724. Vertical Integration in the Absence of Market Power 195
    - a. Efficiency 195
    - b. No "unfair" competitive advantages 196
725. Vertical Integration by a Monopolist 197
    - a. Introduction and summary of possible consequences 197
    - b. No "double" monopoly profit 199
    - c. Integration of successive monopolies 200
    - d. Integration economies 201
    - e. Price discrimination: output effects 201
    - f. Integration eliminating input substitution 202
    - g. Possible adverse long-run consequences: less efficiency and progressiveness 204
    - h. Possible adverse long-run consequences: increased or prolonged barriers to entry 204
        1. Successive monopolies 204
        2. "Partial" integration 206
726. Appropriate Rules or Presumptions 208
    - a. Need for presumptions 208
    - b. Per se legality vs. per se illegality 209
    - c. Generally differentiating among various kinds of integration? 211
    - d. Differentiating "no benefit" integrations 212
        1. Plant integration 213
        2. Complex product relationships 213
        3. Integration into distribution 214
        4. Partial integration 214
        5. Natural monopoly 215
        6. Summary 216
    - e. Vertical integration by a franchised regulated monopolist 217
727. Cases on Vertical Integration as Such 220
    - a. Introduction 220
    - b. Early cases 220
        1. *American Tobacco Trust* 220

2. *Corn Products Refining Co.* 221
3. The "*Anthracite*" cases 221

c. *Yellow Cab I; Griffith; Paramount Pictures* 222
1. *Yellow Cab I* 222
2. *Griffith* dictum 223
3. *Paramount Pictures* 224

d. *Columbia Steel* 226

e. Summary and conclusions 227

728. Integrated Monopolist's Price and Supply Policies Toward Non-Integrated Rivals 228
a. Introduction 228
b. Supply squeeze 229
1. "Arbitrary" action 229
2. Shortages 229
3. Second stage monopoly 230
4. "Coercion" 230
c. Price squeeze 231
1. Market price squeeze 232
2. Squeeze on second level monopoly profits 232
3. Efficiency squeeze 233
4. Price discrimination squeeze 233
5. Predatory price squeeze 233

729. Leading Price and Supply Squeeze Cases Compared 234
a. Introduction 234
b. *Colgate* 235
c. *Alcoa* 235
d. *Grand Caillou Packing Co.* 238
e. *Otter Tail Power Co.* 239
f. *Corn Products* 241
g. *Terminal Railroad; Associated Press* 242
h. Summary 244

730. Vertical Acquisitions 244
a. Internal expansion compared 244
b. Other statutory provisions: their relevance to §2 liability and remedies 245
c. §2 treatment of mergers otherwise unlawful 245
d. Scope of equitable remedies 247

731. Quasi-Integration: Contractual or Other Preemption of Supply 247
a. Nature of the problem 247

b. Requirements and output contracts 248
c. Excessive duration 249
d. Excessive purchases 250
e. Express exclusive dealing contract 250
f. Scope of equitable relief 251
g. Internal vertical integration compared 251
h. Vertical merger compared 252

732. Quasi-Integration: Contractual Preemption of Markets 253
a. The problem 253
b. Relevance of illegality under other statutory provisions 253
c. Assessing unreasonable foreclosures 254
1. Shifts 254
2. Middlemen 254
3. Duration 254
4. Justifications 254
5. Substantiality 255
6. Leases 255
7. Leverage 255
d. Liability and scope of equitable relief 256
e. Internal vertical integration compared 256

733. Tying Arrangements 257
a. Forms and variations 257
b. Other statutes: relationship of tying to monopolization 257
c. Monopoly in the tied product 258
d. Price discrimination 259
e. Affecting monopoly in the tying product 259
f. Scope of equitable remedies 260

734. Other Restrictions on Distribution 261
a. Agreements and effects 261
b. Minimum resale price maintenance 261
c. Territorial and customer restrictions on distributors 262
d. Exclusive outlets 262
e. Maximum resale price maintenance 263
f. Scope of equitable remedies 264

735. Lease-Only; Resale Restrictions 264
a. Exclusionary tendencies 264
1. Continuing relations and access 265

2. Less rivalry 265
3. Overall effects 266
b. Possible justifications 266
1. Increased returns 266
2. Research and development 266
3. Goodwill 267
c. Resale restrictions 267
d. Scope of equitable remedies 268
1. Injunctive terms 268
2. Broader relief 269
736. "Arbitrary" Refusal to Deal 270
a. The problem 270
b. Possible legal theories 271
c. Common law precedents 271
d. Antitrust precedents 272
e. Analysis and conclusions 273

7E. Unfair Competition: Harassment of Rivals and Business Torts Generally 276
737. Unfair Competition 276
a. General characteristics 276
b. Torts generally 277
738. Specific Practices 278
a. Misrepresentation to buyers 278
b. Influencing purchaser specifications 279
c. Disparagement of rival 280
d. Compromising rival's employees 281
e. Compromising rival's suppliers 281
f. Industrial espionage 282
g. Payments to buyer's employees 282
h. Monopolist's former employees or trainees permeate customer companies 283
i. Premature delivery dates and exaggerated claims 283
j. Litigation 284
k. Concealment 285
l. Interference with contracts of advantageous relations 285
m. Non-cooperation with rivals 286
739. Concluding Comments 286

CHAPTER 8. Power and the Power-Conduct Relationship in Monopolization and Attempted Monopolization 289

800. Introduction 289

8A. When Is Market Power "Substantial"? 290

801. The Problem 290
802. General Propositions 290
803. Presumptive Proof of Substantial Market Power 291
804. Market Share 291
805. Price-Cost Margins 292
806. Excess Returns on Investments 293
807. Persistent Power 294
808. Levels of Proof 294
809. Relaxation of Definition and Proof of Power 295

8B. Substantial Market Power Ordinarily Required as Prerequisite for Monopolization Offense 295

810. Introduction and Summary 295
811. Statutory "Any Part of . . . Commerce" Refers to Economic Market 296
812. Substantial Market Power Required 298
813. Relaxed Power Component Considered and Mostly Rejected 300
814. Precisely Varying Power Component with Conduct Not Feasible 302
815. Limited Power-Conduct Variations 303

8C. "Exclusionary" Conduct by Firms That Ultimately Acquire Substantial Market Power 304

816. Introduction and General Conclusions 304
817. Horizontal Merger 306
818. Merger with a Potential Competitor 307
819. Patent Acquisition 308
    a. Generally 308
    b. Non-competing patents 308
        1. Acquired by new producer 308
        2. Acquired by one of several existing producers 309
        3. Acquired by leading producer 309
    c. Competing patents 310

8D. Attempt to Monopolize 311
820. Introduction and Summary 311

8D-1. Intent 313
821. The Classic Formulation 313
822. Defining the Requisite Intent 314
a. Intent to prevail by improper means 314
b. Consciousness of wrongdoing relevant? 315
823. Characterizing Ambiguous Conduct 316
824. Intent as a "Safety Valve" 317

8D-2. Conduct 318
825. Overview 318
826. Unconsummated Conduct 319
827. Monopolizing Conduct Recalled 320
828. Conduct Legal for a Monopolist Cannot Be Illegal for One Without Monopoly Power 321
a. Generally 321
b. False advertising and business torts 321
c. Change to self-distribution 323
d. Various restraints on dealers 325
e. Sole outlet 327
f. Acquiring talent 328
g. Conduct on the road to monopoly 328
829. Conduct Illegal for a Monopolist Is Not Necessarily Illegal for One Without Monopoly Power 328
a. Generally 329
b. Lease-only practice 330
c. Minor acquisitions of competitors or patents 330
d. Certain tie-ins and requirements contracts 331
e. Expanded definitions of monopolization and the problem of persistent monopoly 332
830. Conduct in Violation of Other Antitrust Laws 333
a. Generally 333
b. FTC Act §5 333
c. Clayton Act §§2, 3, and 7 334
d. Sherman Act §1 334
e. Monopolization 335

8D-3. Power 335
831. The Classic Formulation 335
832. The Expansionist Impulse 336
833. Arguments for Relaxed Power Component Considered and Mostly Rejected 339
a. The impulse 339
b. Intention sufficient 339
c. Statutory rationale 340
d. Critique 341
834. Alternate Approaches to a Positive Power Requirement 343
a. Varying power with remedy 343
b. A sliding scale 344
c. A mixed approach 345
835. General Rule: Dangerous Probability of Monopoly Necessary for Attempted Monopolization 346
a. Significant market position 346
b. The calculation of market position 347
c. How large a market share is significant? 348
836. Limited Per Se Rule: Attempted Monopolization Without Proof of Power 350
a. Rationale 350
b. Conduct covered 352

8D-4. Sanctions; Conspiracy 355
837. Varying the Content of the Offense with the Remedy Sought 355
838. Remedies for Attempt 356
839. Conspiracy to Monopolize 358

8E. Shared Monopoly as Monopolizing 359
840. Introduction and Conclusion 359
a. The problem: oligopoly with monopoly-like results 359
b. Summary of conclusions 360
841. Insufficient Anticonspiracy or Combination Provisions 361
a. Conspiracy; express collusion; interdependent behavior 361
b. "Combination" 363
c. Non-interdependent exclusionary conduct 363

8E-1. Shared Monopoly and Monopoly Compared *364*
842. The Statute 364
a. Language and legislative history 364
b. Purpose 365
c. Practical reasons in support 366
d. Contrary considerations 366
843. Is Shared Monopoly Less Serious or More Justifiable? 367
a. Alternatives 367
b. Imperfect coordination 367
c. Scale economies 368
d. Rivalry in quality and innovation 369
e. The role of superior skill 370
844. Maintaining Incentives 370
845. Comparison Summarized 371

8E-2. Identifying and Remedying Shared Monopoly *371*
846. General Guidelines 371
847. Structural Tests Inadequate 372
848. Price-Cost and Profit Tests 374
849. Other Performance Tests: Innovation and Superior Skill 376
850. Remedial Problems 377
a. Feasibility 377
b. Effectiveness 377
c. Which firms? 378
851. Official Discretion Indispensable 378
a. Confining intervention to worthy targets 378
b. Rejecting private and criminal actions 379

8E-3. Legitimacy of Judicial Innovation *380*
852. Legislative Action vs. Judicial Interpretation 380
853. Typical Legislative Proposal 381
a. Tribunal; expertness 381
b. Remedies; discretion 381
c. Criteria 381
854. Judicial Approach Compared 381
a. Tribunal and remedies 381
b. Criteria 382

1. Concentration ratios and performance tests 382
2. Significant markets 383
855. The Net Balance 384

8E-4. Exclusionary Conduct by Firms Sharing Monopoly Power as "Monopolizing" 385
856. Introduction 385
857. Exclusionary Conduct and Comprehensive Equitable Remedies 386
858. Private Remedies Against Exclusionary Conduct; Attempted Monopolization Compared 386
859. Self-Defense 387
860. Insignificant Exclusionary Effects 388
861. Market Shares Redistributed 389
862. Summary 390

VOLUME IV

CHAPTER 9. Mergers: Generally and Horizontal 1
900. Introduction to This Volume: Definitions and Prologue 1
901. The Antitrust Concern with Horizontal Mergers 2

9A. General Guides to Interpretation 4
902. A Brief Historical Review 4
a. Sherman Act 4
b. Original Clayton Act §7 6
c. Clayton Act §7 (as amended 1950) 7
903. Legislative History of Amended §7 Summarized 8
904. The Limited Role of Non-Economic Values 11
905. "Simple" Rules: Their Legality, Appeal, Difficulty, and Structure 14
a. Introduction and summary 14
b. Consistent with statute 15
c. The need for simplification 15
d. Excessively or insufficiently prohibitive rules and their costs 16
e. Interdependence of issues 18

f. Alternative methods of curbing excess coverage: a preliminary assessment 18
1. Inclusive rules plus prosecutorial discretion 19
2. Judicial recognition of additional factors in marginal cases 20
3. Liberalizing basic presumptions 21
g. Conclusion 21
906. Congruent Application of Sherman Act §1 to Horizontal Mergers 21
907. Preview of This Chapter; Summary of Analysis; Conclusions 23
a. Preview 23
b. Summary of analysis 23
c. Conclusions 24

9B. Market Shares as Presumptive Proof of Illegality 26
908. The Problem and a Summary 26
909. Judicial and Enforcement Agency Reliance on Market Shares 29
a. Supreme Court cases summarized 29
b. Other recent cases 33
c. Department of Justice merger guidelines 52
910. Relevance of Market Shares to Anticompetitive Effects 54
a. Introduction and summary 54
b. The competitive significance of market concentration 54
c. Number of sellers 56
d. Size disparities 58
e. The relevance of market shares and their "substantiality" 59
911. "Substantiality" in Competitively Structured Markets 60
a. Introduction and summary 60
b. What is the minimum number of sellers to be preserved? 61
c. Efficiency considerations 62
d. Why "pre-threshold" interference? 63
e. Arbitrary results? 65
f. "Substantiality" where merging firms are of dissimilar size 65

912. "Substantiality" in Concentrated Markets 68
a. Introduction and summary 68
b. Permitting "large" mergers merely to reduce size disparities 68
c. Prohibit smaller mergers? 69
d. Future concentration levels 71
e. Offsetting efficiencies 72
f. Tentative conclusions 73
913. Measures of Concentration and Their Utility in Formulating Presumptions Based on Market Shares 74
a. Measures of concentration 74
1. Concentration ratios 75
2. The Herfindahl index 76
b. Use of concentration measures as general tests for mergers 76
1. Concentration ratios 76
2. The Herfindahl index 77
c. Concentration measures as a basis for varying presumptively illegal aggregate shares 78
1. Single "threshold" or continuous variation? 78
2. Which concentration measure? 79
914. Relevance of Concentration Trends 81
915. Summary and Conclusions 83

9C. Market Factors Other Than Seller Shares 84
916. Introduction 84
917. Entry Barriers 85
a. Their effect 85
b. Assessment 86
c. Conclusions 88
918. Buyer Concentration and Related Factors 89
a. Their effect 89
b. Assessment 89
919. Product Heterogeneity 91
a. Its effects 91
b. Assessment 91
920. Cost Structures 93
a. Cost differences 93
b. High fixed costs 94

921. Uncertainties in Market Definition or Market Shares 94
922. Conclusion: Implications of Excluding Market Factors Other Than Seller Concentration 97

9D. Factors Affecting the Competitive Significance of a Particular Firm's Market Share 98

923. Introduction 98
a. Limitations on the significance of market shares 98
b. General considerations in determining whether and to what extent other facts should be taken into account 98
c. Sequence of discussion 99

9D-1. The Failing Company Defense 100

924. The Legislative History 100
925. The Underlying Questions: A Preliminary Analysis 101
a. The relation of "failing company" to competitive effects and presumptions of illegality based on market shares 101
b. The nature and complexities of the private interests involved 103
c. How and to what extent are private interests to be recognized? 104
926. Defining "Failing Company" 106
a. Introduction and summary 106
b. Reorganization prospects generally irrelevant 107
c. Impending insolvency or bankruptcy presumptively necessary 108
d. Impending failure without insolvency or bankruptcy 109
e. "Failing subsidiary" 112
927. Sale to Preferred Purchasers or Reorganization: When Required 113
a. Introduction and summary 113
b. Cases where proof of impending failure should suffice 114

c. Cases where proof of absence of preferred purchasers should and should not suffice 115
d. Probable liquidation conclusive 116
928. Defining "Preferred Purchaser" 117
a. Introduction and summary of conclusions 117
b. Purchaser preferred only where intent to remain in the market 118
c. Preferred purchasers generally 119
d. Alternative acquisition presumptively lawful 119
e. Alternative merger would itself be immune from an alternative purchaser requirement 120
1. Requirement satisfied 120
2. Ranking of purchasers 120
f. Alternative acquisition would itself have been subject to preferred purchaser requirement 121
1. Requirement not necessarily satisfied 121
2. Ranking such purchasers 122
929. The Requisite Diligence in Seeking Preferred Purchasers 123
a. "Full" search not required 123
b. Reasonable number of inquiries required 124
c. Volunteered offers 124
930. Unreasonably Low Offers 126
a. Introduction and summary 126
b. Offer below value to offeror not necessarily "unreasonably low" 127
c. Substantial disparities unlikely or suspect 127
d. Preferred purchaser rules provide substantial protection of private interests 128
e. Difficulties in determining that an offer is "unreasonable" 128
f. Conclusion 129
931. "Piecemeal" Alternative Offers 130
a. The issues 130
b. Partial stock acquisition preferred 130
c. Partial asset offers rejected 130

9D-2. Factors Other Than Failure 131
932. Factors Bearing on Firm Vitality: Generally 131
933. Pre-existing Relationships 132
934. Inadequate Productive or Marketing Resources 132
a. The *Brown Shoe* and *General Dynamics* cases 132
b. The *Amax* case 134
c. Access to exhaustible resources 135
d. Access to supplies generally; the problem of vertical integration 136
e. Access to consuming market 137
935. Financial Difficulties 138
a. The *International Harvester Co. (IHC)* case 138
b. Critique 140
c. Conclusion 141
936. Management Deficiencies 142
937. Factors Indicating That Competitive Significance Is Understated by Past Market Shares 142
938. The Relevance of Purpose or Intent 143
a. Summary 143
b. Intent as a defense 144
c. Anticompetitive intent corroborating or establishing illegality 145

9E. Economies as a Defense to Prima Facie Illegality 146
939. Introduction and Summary 146
940. Economies Defense Appropriate in Principle 148
941. Preliminary Legal Issues: Statute, Legislative History, and Precedent 151
a. Statutory language 151
b. Legislative history; precedent 152
942. "Offsetting" Benefits in a Second Market 154
943. The Case Against an Economies Defense: Generally 157
944. Relation to Presumptive Rules of Prima Facie Illegality 158
945. Relation to the Failing Company Defense 159
946. Alternatives to Merger: Internal Expansion 160
a. Introduction and summary 160
b. Is internal expansion socially preferable? 161
1. Affirmatives 161

2. Negatives 161
3. Conclusion 163
c. Is internal expansion likely to occur? 163
1. Generally 163
2. Capacity effect as a deterrent to internal expansion 163
3. Product differentiation 164
4. Capacity increment relative to market demand; magnitude of cost savings 165
5. Expansion by others 165
6. Other barriers to internal expansion 166
d. Summary of factors bearing on likelihood and preferability of internal expansion: paradoxes 167
e. Conclusions 168
947. Alternatives to Merger: Joint Venture 169
a. Introduction and summary 169
b. Possible disadvantages of joint ventures: transaction costs; legal risks 169
c. Conclusions 171
948. Integration Economies and Other General Proof Issues 172
a. Introduction and summary 172
b. Scale economies and integration economies 172
c. Magnitude of cost savings 173
d. Direct proof of size diseconomies required 174
949. Summary on Appropriateness of a Defense with Respect to Various Specific Scale Economies 175
950. Plant Size Economies 176
951. Plant Specialization Economies Without Product Complementarity 177
952. Plant Specialization Economies Plus Product Complementarity 178
a. Where diseconomies pervasive 178
b. Where diseconomies limited to a small part of output 179
c. Proof problems 180
953. Distribution Economies 181
a. The prerequisites 181
b. Proof problems 184

954. Promotional Economies 185
a. "Wasteful" aspects of promotion an insufficient ground for rejecting an economies defense 185
b. The necessary conditions 186
c. Proof problems 188
955. Economies in Research and Development 189
956. Capital Cost Economies 191
957. Procurement Economies Generally 191
958. "Overhead" Economies 192
959. Complementary Resources 193
a. Generally 193
b. Management superiority 193
c. Other complementarities 194
960. Aggregated Economies 195
961. General Conditions for an Economies Defense: Both Merging Firms Inefficiently Small 196
962. Substantial Economies an Absolute Defense 197
a. Defense absolute: failing company defense compared 197
b. The relevance of *General Dynamics* 198

9F. Horizontal Merger Rules for Buyer Concentration 200
963. Introduction and Summary: The Need for Special Rules 200
964. Asymmetries Between Buyer and Seller Concentration Effects 201
a. Buyer concentration a potential problem only where supply produced at increasing costs 201
b. Buyer collusion less likely than seller collusion 202
c. Efficiency considerations 204
965. Conclusions 205
a. Presumptive rules 205
b. Scope of the failing company defense 206
c. Economies defense 206

CHAPTER 10. Vertical Mergers 207
1000. Introduction 207
a. The general problem 207
b. Vertical integration by internal growth: a summary 209
c. Vertical integration by merger compared 211

1001. Preview and Summary 212
1002. Statutory Language and History 215

10A. Economic Consequences of Vertical Mergers 218
1003. Integration Fallacies and the "Supply Shortage" Question 218
a. Internal transactions at cost 218
b. Recoupment 218
c. "Conglomerate advantages" 219
d. Preferential access to "short" supply 219
1004. The Foreclosure Issue and Its Short and Long Run Implications 221
a. Introduction 221
b. Merged firms not always foreclosed to outsiders 221
c. Self-dealing is not foreclosure in perfectly competitive markets 223
d. Self-dealing may not be harmful even in less competitive markets 224
e. Possibly harmful foreclosures 225
1005. Reduced Competitiveness in Either Market 225
1006. Disruptive Buyer Eliminated 226
a. Introduction and summary 226
b. Second-level market relatively competitive 227
1. Rationale 227
2. Proof 228
c. Supply market capable of behaving non-competitively in the absence of disruptive buyers 229
d. Pre-merger supply market performance more competitive than it might be 229
1. Rationale 229
2. Proof: price discrimination? 229
3. Performance proved or assumed 230
e. Larger buyer(s) disruptive 231
f. Most disruptive buyers eliminated 232
g. Potential future effect 232
1007. Second-Level Concentrated Increased 233
1008. Rivals Deprived of Efficient Scale 236
a. Introduction and summary 236

b. Prerequisites 237
c. Proofs 238
1009. Rivals Destabilized 238
a. Introduction and summary 238
b. Partial backward integration 239
c. Stable user 240
1010. Consumer Choice Reduced 242
1011. Entry Barriers 243
a. Introduction and summary 243
b. Basic mechanism; pre-existing entry barrier a prerequisite to rise in entry barriers from total integration 244
c. Will total integration occur? 245
1. Monopolist 245
2. Other situations 246
d. Two-level entry necessary? 247
e. Market performance impaired when burdensome two-level entry imposed by vertical integration? 247
1. Introduction 247
2. No effects where both markets competitive 248
3. No incremental harm from increasing entry barriers into the more competitive of two markets 249
4. Harm possible from increasing entry barriers into less competitive of two markets 250
f. Total integration a prerequisite? 250
1. Narrowing of outlets or sources—generally 251
2. Total integration of one supply market with one of several purchasing markets 252
g. Conclusions 253
1012. More Competitive Pricing 254
a. Introduction 254
b. Eliminate successive monopoly or oligopoly profits 255
c. Facilitate price discrimination 257
d. Eliminate input substitution 258
e. Obstruct oligopolistic coordination 259

1013. Market Definition; Measuring Foreclosure 260
a. General issues 260
b. Interconnection of supplier and customer market shares 260
1014. Initial and Cumulative Foreclosures; Trends 262
a. Introduction and summary 262
b. Initial merger 263
c. Aggregating one firm's acquisitions 264
d. Cumulative foreclosures 264
1. Implementation; administrability 265
2. Efficiency considerations 266
3. Merger incentive 267
4. Conclusion 267
e. Trends 268
1015. Suggested Presumptions 269
a. Introduction and summary 269
b. High concentration as proof of non-competitive markets 270
c. Substantial entry barriers 271
d. Merging firms' market shares 272
e. Exception for a monopolist's vertical acquisitions 273

10B. Efficiencies, Failing Firms, and Other Defenses 273
1016. Efficiencies Defense to Prima Facie Illegality 273
a. Introduction and summary 273
b. Desirability in principle and under the statute 274
c. Relation to rules of presumptive illegality and to other defenses 274
d. Absolute defense for substantial efficiencies 275
e. Internal expansion alternative 276
f. Which efficiencies 278
g. Proving integration economies 279
1017. Efficiencies Defense Where Merging Firm Already Integrated 281
a. Introduction and summary 281
b. Scale economies 282
c. Integration economies 283
d. Integration economies where both firms partially integrated 287

1018. Failing Firms 288
a. Introduction and summary 288
b. General requirements 289
c. Requiring alternative purchasers or more 289
d. Who is preferred? 290
1019. Firm's Significance Not Reflected by Market Share; Defensive Mergers 292

10C. Applications 296
1020. Precedents Surveyed 296
1021. Precedents Related to Our Proposals 310
1022. Selected Cases 310
a. *Brown Shoe* case 310
b. *Bethlehem Steel* case 314
c. *Fruehauf* case 316

VOLUME V

CHAPTER 11. Conglomerate Mergers 1
1100. Definition and General Approach 1

11A. Merger Motivations and Their Relevance to Tests of Illegality 3
1101. Introduction 3

11A-1. Economies Generally 4
1102. Economies as a Defense 4
1103. Cost Savings as Anticompetitive: The Entrenchment Issue 5
a. The entrenchment concern 5
b. Internal problems with the entrenchment notion 6
1. Why distinguish dominant firms? 6
2. Practical difficulties in establishing prerequisites 7
c. Resource savings desirable 9
d. Certain savings distinguished? 10

11A-2. Particular Cost Savings Motivations Surveyed *11*
1104. Purchasing 11
a. Resource savings, "buying power," and market imperfections 11
1. Monopsony 11
2. Access to competitive market 12
3. Price discrimination 12
b. Policy choices and considerations 12
1. The dilemma 12
2. Other antitrust avenues: the Robinson-Patman Act 13
3. Alternatives for small rivals: joint purchasing arrangements 13
4. Toleration for remaining price discrimination 14
c. Conclusion 14
1105. Capital Cost Savings 14
a. Transaction costs and improved rationing 14
b. Diversification and risk reduction 15
c. Access to another's financial resources: capital, liquidity, cash flow, or unused borrowing power 16
d. Access to wider capital market 18
e. The mere possession of capital 18
f. Conclusion 19
1106. Other Financial Motivations 19
a. Growth appearance and mystique 19
b. Unused tax shields 20
c. Unused capital 20
1107. Buying Needed Resources Faster or Perhaps Cheaper 21
1108. Scale Economies and Other Operational or Management Efficiencies 21
a. Scale economies generally and at plant level 21
b. Research and development 22
1. Diversity 23
2. Internal organization 23
3. Conglomerates as acquirers of technology 24
c. Specialized management and staff 24

d. Better or more accountable management 25
e. Diseconomies 26
f. Summary 27
1109. Marketing Gains 28
a. Advertising and related economies 28
1. Nature and extent 28
2. Appraisal 30
b. Brand recognition and trust: increased returns from each unit of promotional activity 32
1. Possibilities 32
2. Appraisal 33
c. Ancillary services 35
1. Selling or repair services 35
2. Warranty reliability 35
d. Wide-line coverage 36
1. Generally 36
2. Variations and the cases 37
(A) Package selling 37
(B) One-stop service 38
(C) Know customers 39
3. Recapitulation and appraisal 40
(A) Transaction costs 40
(B) Selling and distribution economies 40
(C) Leverage 41
(D) Conclusion 41
e. Summary and conclusion 42

11A-3. Other Merger Motivations 42
1110. Protective Mergers 42
a. Introduction and conclusion 42
b. Failing company 43
c. Decline 43
d. Departing entrepreneur 43
e. Rival's unfair practices or advantages 44
f. Resisting uncongenial takeover 45
g. Conclusion 45
1111. Anticompetitive Reasons 45
1112. Summary: A Free Market 48

11B. Less Competitive Market Structure 48
1113. Structural Alterations Generally 48

11B-1. Cross-Market Mergers 49
1114. Extended Interdependence 49
a. The possibility 49
b. Necessary conditions: general incidence vs. proof in particular cases 51
1. The merged firm and at least one rival must confront each other in two markets, each with some but not rigid oligopolistic performance 51
2. The merged firm and at least one other two-market firm must both be significant in both markets, and both markets must be relatively important to both firms 52
3. To be deterred from a price cut in one market, a firm must be subject to unpleasant sanctions in the second market 53
c. Effect on innovations 56
d. Intermarket and intramarket interdependence compared 57
e. How significant: conclusions, presumptions, and proof burdens 57
1115. Mergers Affecting "Interindustry" Competition 58
a. The problem defined 58
b. Interindustry and horizontal mergers compared; market definition 59
c. Both markets must be non-competitive 60
d. The two-market firm must be able to affect price in both markets 61
e. Two-product firms collectively dominating both markets must occupy roughly symmetrical positions in both 62
f. Effects on innovation 66
g. Conclusion 68

11B-2. Potential Competition 69
1116. Overview: Possible Effects and Key Issues 69
a. The anticompetitive possibilities 69
b. Summary of conclusions 70

1117. Actual Present Competitor Distinguished 73
a. The *El Paso* case 73
b. Relation to market definition 74
1118. Statutory Coverage 74
1119. Market Characteristics I: Non-Competitive Market Prerequisite to Present or Future Effect from Potential Entry 76
a. General rule and summary 76
b. Concentration ratios: precedent 78
c. Other factors: general principle 80
d. Market boundaries 81
e. Stability; trends 83
1. Concentration ratio 83
2. Relative shares 83
f. Entry barriers 85
1. Entry difficult into less concentrated market 85
2. Entry easy into concentrated market 86
g. Oligopolistic coordination impaired 88
1120. Market Characteristics II: Additional Prerequisites for Present Effect from Potential Entry 89
a. Problems previewed 89
b. Limit pricing theory and weaknesses 89
1. General theory illustrated 89
2. Cost advantage 90
3. Reaction to entry 91
4. Ignorance 92
5. Existing competition 93
6. Summary: proof required 94
c. Impact on other aspects of competitive performance 95
d. Proving present effect: structure 96
e. Proving present effect: performance data 97
1. Relatively competitive performance proved 98
2. Causes of relatively competitive performance 98
3. Post-acquisition data 99
f. Proving present effect: subjective evidence 99
g. Conclusion 101

1121. Outside Firm as Probable Future Entrant 102
a. The issue 102
b. Subjective intentions 103
1. Generally 103
2. Bias 103
3. Whose intention 104
4. Meaning 105
5. Initial steps 107
6. Conclusion 107
c. Objective evidence 108
1. Generally 108
2. Entry attractiveness 108
3. Legal barrier 109
4. Entry resources 110
5. Market relationships 113
6. Conclusion 113
d. Significance of defendant's addition to future competition 114
1. Generally 114
2. *Marine Bancorporation* case 114
3. Predicting entry scale 115
4. Significance threshold 116
e. Conclusion; burden of proof 117
1122. Outside Firm as Perceived Potential Entrant 117
a. Prerequisite for present effect 117
b. Evidence about existing firms 118
c. Evidence about defendant 119
d. Conclusion 120
1123. Universe of Potential Entrants 120
a. General principle; summary 120
b. Sufficiently large universe; paradigm situations 122
c. Proving potential entrant universe generally 124
1. "Most likely entrant" 124
2. Proof burden 124
3. Consistency requirement 126
d. Same product elsewhere 126
e. Similar products 128
1. *Clorox* case 128

2. *Penn-Olin* case 129
3. *Ekco* case 132
4. *Wilson* case 132
5. Summary 133
f. Summary by negative example: The *Kennecott* case 134
1124. Non-"Toehold" Acquisitions Forbidden? 138
a. The doctrine and its premises; summary of conclusions 138
b. Would smaller acquisition improve competition significantly? 141
1. Future effect 141
2. Present effect of potential toehold mergers 142
3. Present beneficial effect of actual merger 143
c. Can "toehold" be defined: in principle and practice 145
d. Would toehold merger otherwise have occurred? 146
1. Outside firm 146
2. Would-be toehold firm 147
3. Others' perceptions 148
e. Is the universe of potential acquirers very limited? 148
f. True basis for doctrine? 149
g. Precedent; statutory coverage; conclusion 150
1125. Pro-Competitive Effects Balanced; Toeholds Permitted? 151
a. Need for balancing 151
b. New or improved competition 152
c. Alternative approaches; toeholds permitted? 152
d. Presumptively permissible acquisitions 155
1126. Potential Entry in a Vertical Context 156
a. The problem; paradigm case 156
b. Necessary conditions 157
1. Significant entry probable in fact; potential entry universe irrelevant 157
2. Facilitating entry 158

3. Proof of significant anticompetitive effects 159
c. Waiting and seeing rejected 159

11C. Increased Opportunity for Anticompetitive Behavior 162
1127. Introduction 162

11C-1. Reciprocity 162
1128. Introduction: Definitions and General Issues 162
1129. Competitive Effects of Reciprocity 164
a. Introduction and summary 164
b. Usual concerns 164
c. No imposition on supplier: reciprocity cannot itself increase defendant's power 165
d. Indirect price competition 166
1. Reciprocity for the oligopolist 166
2. Preferable alternative of direct price competition may not occur 168
3. "Unfair advantage" or greater competition? 169
(A) Rival price reductions ineffective 170
(B) Rival price reduction improvident 171
(C) Rivals less efficient 172
4. Summary 172
e. Cost savings through reciprocity 173
f. Transient circumstances: promotion or barter 173
g. Disciplining or destroying rivals 174
1. Preemption 174
2. Predation 175
h. Conclusion 176
1130. Implications for Mergers of Condemning Reciprocity Agreements 177
a. Judicial doctrines 177
b. Scope of prohibition 178
c. Implications for merger law 180
d. Conclusion 180

1131. Likelihood of Reciprocity Occurring 181
a. Introduction and summary 181
b. Defendant can sell to actual or potential suppliers 182
c. Defendant and supplier each can gain 183
1. Generally 183
2. Market competitiveness 183
3. Purchase-sale ratios; user-distributor distinctions; rivals compared 184
4. Summary 185
d. Characteristics of products bought and sold by defendant 186
e. Defendant's policy 187
f. Actual or intended reciprocity 189
1132. Magnitude of the Foreclosure 190
a. General issue; summary 190
b. Post-merger evidence of actual reciprocity 191
c. Pre-reciprocity appraisal 192
1133. Standards for Determining the Substantiality of a Given Foreclosure 194
a. Tying test 195
b. Vertical merger compared 196
c. Some precedents 198
d. Conclusion 201

11C-2. Leverage and Disproportionate Size 202
1134. Transferred Leverage: Possible Tying 202
a. Introduction and summary 202
b. Competitive effects 204
c. Relevance for merger law of prohibiting most tying while not reaching certain "subtle" forms 206
d. Tying potential 208
e. Measuring possible foreclosures 211
f. Substantiality defined 212
1135. Resources as Such 213
a. The general fear 213
b. Entry barriers 216
c. Lower capital costs or other economies 217

d. Improper conduct in markets neither fully competitive nor already non-competitive 217
1136. Predatory Activities 219
a. Definition; minimum conditions 219
b. Cases discussed 220
1. *Clorox* 220
2. *Cupples* 221
3. *Reynolds* 222
c. Probabilities and likelihoods 223
1137. Disciplinary Pricing 225
1138. Other Unfairly Low Prices 227
a. Indifference or ignorance 227
b. "Loss leaders" 227
1139. Price Leadership 230

11D. Asset Aggregation as Such 231
1140. Introduction and Summary 231
1141. The Data and Its Difficulties 232
a. Introduction and summary 232
b. Asset concentration: data and qualifications 233
1. Concern in industrial sector 233
2. Inclusion of non-manufacturing and foreign assets 233
3. Inferences qualified: stability, growth sectors, and shifting memberships 234
c. Value-added data; recent stability 236
d. Role of mergers 237
e. Other indicia 238
f. Future prospects 239
1142. "Overall" Concentration as a Social Problem 241
a. Unmeasurable market effects 241
b. Economic effects apart from market effects 242
c. Political and social effects 244
d. Summary 247
1143. Criteria for Limiting Asset Aggregations as Such 247
a. Introduction; selective vs. general prohibitions 247
b. "Large" firms 248
c. Market leaders, market relationships, prior offenses 249

d. Merger-prone firms 250
e. Qualifications: failing firms, toeholds, efficiencies, and offsetting divestitures 251
1. Failing firm 251
2. Toehold acquisitions 252
3. Other efficiencies 252
4. Offsetting divestitures 252
f. Summary and conclusion 253

11E. Conclusions: Statutory Meaning, Effects, Defenses 254
1144. Introduction 254
1145. Statutory Application: Anticompetitive Market Effects Required 254
a. Clayton Act §7 255
b. Sherman Act 256
c. Federal Trade Commission Act §5 257
1146. Quantum of Required Effects 259
a. Ephemeral possibilities vs. reasonable probabilities 259
b. Sufficiency of low-order effects 259
c. Discretion and ideology 262
d. Conclusion 263
1147. Cumulation of Several Anticompetitive Possibilities 264
a. The problem; summary 264
b. Probability theory and its qualifications 265
c. Cumulated benefits 267
d. Consistent claims 269
e. Rule inclusiveness and nature of shortfall 269
1. Eliminating a competitor 270
2. Foreclosure of rival suppliers 270
3. Disproportionate size 271
4. Cross-market effects 271
5. Potential competition 272
f. Conclusion 273
1148. Redeeming Virtues Generally: Relationship to Intensity of Prohibitory Rules 274
1149. Efficiencies Defense 275
a. Introduction and summary 275
b. Impact of prohibitory rules and toehold toleration; presumptions 276

c. Which efficiencies? 277
d. Less restrictive alternatives 279
e. Must both firms suffer diseconomies? 280
1150. Failing Firms 280
a. Introduction 280
b. Failing company defense reviewed 281
c. Who is failing 281
d. Requiring alternative purchaser or more 282
e. Who is preferred 284
1. Non-competitor whose acquisition would be lawful without regard to the failing firm defense 284
2. Competitors of the failing firm 284
3. Unlawful acquirers generally 286
f. Scope of the required search 287
1151. Weak Firms 288
a. Five approaches 288
b. Weakness notions 289
c. Competitive effects 290
1152. General Caveat on Distinguishing Conglomerate from Horizontal or Vertical Mergers 291

CHAPTER 12. Partial Acquisitions and Post-acquisition Evidence 295
1200. Introduction: Issues 295
1201. "Acquire" 296
a. The problem 296
b. Temporal questions 297
c. Damage and injunction actions 298
d. Pledges and contracts in ordinary course of business 300
1202. Partial Asset Acquisitions 301
a. The problem and its solution 301
b. Merger policy: immediate and durable structural alteration vs. general resource acquisitions 303
c. Supplies and entire inventories 304
d. Another's plant or equipment 305
e. Real property and mineral leases 307
1. Generally 307
2. Rare or unique real property 307

3. Reducing competition in real property market itself 308
4. Mineral leases 308

f. Patents, copyrights, and trademarks 309

1. Trademark 309
2. Copyright 310
3. Patents 311
4. Precedents 312

g. Contracts and contract rights 313

h. Joint ventures 314

i. Caveat and general conclusion 315

1203. Partial Stock Acquisitions 316

a. The problem 316

b. Statutory jurisdiction with or without control 317

c. Anticompetitive threats where control is neither attained nor contemplated 318

d. Substantiality as compared with full acquisitions 320

e. Subsequent change of circumstances 322

1204. Stock Acquisitions "Solely for Investment" 324

a. Introduction and summary 324

b. No exceptions for anticompetitive acquisitions 325

c. Investment intent 328

d. "Solely" 331

e. Post-acquisition developments 332

1205. Post-acquisition Evidence and Appraisal at Time of Suit 333

a. Introduction and summary 333

b. Equitable remedies 335

c. Retroactivity or continuing reexamination rejected 337

1. The situation 337
2. Arguments for continuing reexamination 337
3. Controlling rationale 340

d. Later anticompetitive effects implicit in situation at time of merger 342

1. Generally 342
2. Increased market shares 344

3. Increased concentration 345
4. Unanticipated vertical dealings 346
5. Vertical expansion 347
6. Acquirer had been a potential entrant 348
7. Extended interdependence 349
8. Reciprocity or subtle tying 350
9. Predation or other undesirable pricing 350

e. "Probable" anticompetitive effects fail to materialize 350
1. Generally 350
2. Competition remains healthy 351
3. Decline in market share, concentration, or foreclosure 352
4. Vertical dealings, reciprocity, and subtle tying 353
5. Other entrants 354

f. Early post-merger statistical data 355

g. Consummation date 357
1. Generally 357
2. Announcement or contract vs. actual transfer 357
3. Successive transfers 357

CHAPTER 13. Interlocking Directors 359

1300. Introduction; the Problem 359

1301. Relevant Statutes 360
a. Sherman Act 360
b. Federal Trade Commission Act §5 361
c. Clayton Act §8 362

1302. Horizontal Interlocks 364
a. The per se rule: the *Sears* and *Protectoseal* cases 364
b. "Competitor" defined: parents and subsidiaries 365
c. Potential competitors 367
d. Bank- non-bank interlocks 368
e. Management interlocks 371

1303. Vertical Interlocks 371

1304. Indirect Interlocks 372

1305. Mootness 375

VOLUME VI

PART THREE
Restraints of Trade: Horizontal and Vertical

CHAPTER 14. Conspiracy, Horizontal and Vertical 3

1400. Introduction 3
- a. Statutory requirements 3
- b. Agreement's existence vs. legality 4
- c. Underlying policy questions clarifying cases of doubtful agreement 4
- d. More particular issues and the organization of this chapter 5

14A. Pervasive Issues and Critical Distinctions 6

1401. Preview Highlighting Key Points 6

14A-1. Statutory Rationale and Preliminary Issues 9

1402. Statutory Rationale for Conspiracy Requirement 9
- a. Central concepts 9
  1. Generally 9
  2. Cooperation increases danger 10
  3. Common action creates an anticompetitive restraint not otherwise possible 11
  4. Cooperation increases market power; power aggregation 11
  5. Limiting individual autonomy; restraining freedom of action 11
- b. Non-competitors and non-common action 12
  1. Consultation alone 12
  2. One-sided promise 14
  3. Exchanged undertakings 15
  4. Vertical agreements compared: no common action but restraint not otherwise possible 15

1403. "Combination" Not Distinct from Conspiracy 17

1404. How Much Assent? 18
1405. Proof Criteria and Burden; Judge and Jury 21
1406. Inter-firm Contact as Agreement 23
- a. Meeting vs. agreement to meet; agreement vs. restraint 23
- b. Meeting with planned or unplanned exchange 24
- c. Unsolicited information provided by one firm to another 24
- d. Solicitation unaccepted but "used" 25
- e. Question-response patterns or single instances 25
- f. Important caveats 27

1407. Facilitating Practices 28
- a. Introduction and summary 28
- b. Definition and distinctions 29
  - 1. Generally 29
  - 2. Causation revisited 30
  - 3. Relation to remedy 31
- c. Concerted facilitating practice as equivalent to conspiracy on matter facilitated 32
- d. Concerted facilitating practice as indirect evidence of conspiracy on the matter facilitated; jury question? 33
- e. Concerted facilitating practices as unreasonable restraints of trade 34
- f. Facilitating practices without concerted action 36

1408. "Coerced" Agreements; Acts Motivated by Fear of Another 39
- a. Common situations summarized 39
- b. Summary of relevant factors 42
  - 1. Identifying and controlling anticompetitive effects. Explicitness of return promise 42
  - 2. Justice for party imposing unpleasant consequences 43
  - 3. Justice for threatened party 45
  - 4. Weighing and balancing these factors in particular cases or types of cases 46
- c. Competitor compelled to participate in a cartel 46

d. Customer (or supplier) compelled to agree to restraint 47
e. Uncommitted acquiescence in another's demand 48
f. Non-dealing to avoid unappealing consequences imposed by others 49
1. Avoiding patent infringement suit 49
2. *Arizona Bank* case 51
3. *Eastern States* case 52
4. *Ambook* case 53

14A-2. Steps in Finding Agreement 59
1409. Identify Agreeing Parties and Content of Agreement 59
a. Subject matter: the thing done vs. its possible result 59
b. The conspirators 60
c. Illustration 61
1410. Distinguish Commitment from Interdependence 63
a. Introduction and summary 63
b. Mere oligopolistic interdependence 65
c. Traditional agreement: weak commitment 66
1411. Interdependence I: No Conspiracy Inference from Parallelism Without It 69
1412. Interdependence II: Motivation for Agreement 72
a. Definition and summary 72
b. *Theatre Enterprises* 73
c. Credit denials 74
d. Non-dealing with "troublemakers" 75
e. Tying 77
f. Motivation objective or subjective, hypothetical or actual; burdens of proof 78
g. Judicial recognition: motivation for common action an essential requirement for conspiracy 79
1413. Interdependence III: No Independent Reason for Challenged Behavior 80
1414. Interdependence IV: Benefit from Agreement 83

1415. Interdependence V: Action Against Self-Interest 84
a. Introduction and summary 84
b. Self-interest served without regard to others' acts 85
c. Self-interest depends upon others' behavior 88
d. Rejecting "superior" offer 89
e. Self-interest in long- vs. short-run 92
f. Reluctant behavior avoiding unpleasant consequences 93

14B. Traditional Conspiracy 94
1416. Introduction; Topics Considered 94
1417. Conspiratorial Opportunity, Unexplained Meetings, Furtive Behavior, and Cover-ups 97
a. Introduction and summary 97
b. Mere opportunity 97
c. Unexplained meetings 99
d. Secret meetings and other furtive collaboration 101
e. "Cover-ups" 102
f. Contemporaneous false or incomplete explanations 103
g. Mere parallelism unexplained 105
1418. Discussions and Participant Admissions: Meaning—Facilitating Practice or More—and Reliability 106
a. Introduction and summary 106
b. Participant testimony and its meaning 106
1. Generally; credibility 106
2. Interpretation example 106
3. *Foley* case 108
4. *Champion* case 109
5. Facilitating practices 110
c. Indirect admissions 111
1419. Solicitations: Accepted or Not 113
a. Introduction and summary 113
b. Performance as conspiracy: verbal responses 114

c. Mere solicitation implies ongoing conspiracy? 116
d. Solicitation alone enjoinable or punishable 117
1420. Identical or Sham Bidding; Refusal to Bid 118
a. Identical closed bids 118
b. Deliberately losing or sham bid 120
c. Refusal to bid 121
1. Non-interdependent refusals 121
2. Interdependent refusals distinguished in principle or fact 121
3. Appraising grounds for refusal to bid, standing alone 122
4. Suspicious patterns 122
d. Coordination through recognized interdependence or more 122
1. Legal issue 123
2. Interdependent refusals as evidence of traditional conspiracy 124
1421. Conspiracy or Competition in Other Markets or Times 125
a. Introduction and summary 125
b. Scope of other conspiracy 126
1. Distinct past conspiracy 126
2. Character and credibility 127
3. Continuing conspiracy? 128
4. Adjacent contemporaneous conspiracy 130
c. Conspiracy in "similar" market with "similar" results 130
1. The logical proposition 130
2. Conspiracy's necessity 131
3. Identity or sufficient similarity 131
d. Less competitive performance than elsewhere implies conspiracy? 132
1422. Information or Inquiry as Facilitating Practice or as Evidence of Further Conspiracy—Generally 133
a. Definition and "direct approach" recalled 133
b. Inferring traditional price-related conspiracy 134

1423. Information Exchanges About Customers or Suppliers 135
- a. Introduction and summary 135
- b. Credit data 136
- c. Effectiveness or character information 137
- d. Data about reselling practices 138
- e. Data about purchasing practices 139

1424. Threat to Potential Victim of Concerted Action 140
- a. Introduction and summary 140
- b. *Standard Oil* case 141
- c. *Tose* case 142

1425. "Unnatural Parallelism" Too Close for Coincidence and Unexplainable by Mere Interdependence; Actions Contrary to Self-Interest 143
- a. Introduction and summary 143
- b. Conspiratorial motive prerequisite qualified 146
- c. Incredible simultaneous parallelism 146
- d. Perilous leading and sequential parallelism 150
  1. Generally 150
  2. Prospect that a move will be followed 151
  3. Consequence of unfollowed move: ease of reversal; cost of non-reversal 152
  4. Illustrations 153
- e. Parallelism on unlikely matters, even in oligopoly 156

1426. *Interstate Circuit* Case 158
- a. Facts and conspiracy finding 158
- b. The Court's broader formula 162
- c. Cut back in *Theatre Enterprises* case? 163
- d. Implications for mere interdependent behavior 164

1427. *Masonite* Case 167
- a. Facts 167
- b. Business interpretations 168
- c. Supreme Court holding 170
- d. No horizontal conspiracy holding 171
- e. Summary 173

14C. Parallel Behavior Among Oligopolists 174

1428. Introduction and Summary 174
1429. Basic Oligopoly Model 175
  a. Interdependence 175
  b. Cartel-like results 175
  c. Non-price competition 177
1430. Factors Affecting Likelihood of Oligopolistic Coordination 178
  a. Verbal communication, direct and indirect 178
  b. Non-verbal communication through known, repeated, and standardized transactions 179
  c. Uncertainty compared: infrequent or secret transactions; differentiated products 179
  d. Customary patterns, formulae, or leadership 180
  e. Cost asymmetry, capital intensity, attitude 180
  f. Number of sellers; fringe expansion 181
  g. Substitute products or new entry 182
1431. Appraising Oligopoly Markets 183
  a. Varying degrees of interdependence 183
  b. Observed behavior 184
  c. Economic performance in concentrated markets, individually or generally 186
  d. Self-correcting markets? 189
1432. Tacit Oligopolistic Price Coordination as Conspiracy; Reasons For and Against 190
  a. Introduction and summary 190
  b. Interdependent pricing compared with traditional price-fixing cartel 190
    1. Generally 190
    2. Anticompetitive results 191
    3. Joint profit maximization vs. divergent selfish interests 192
    4. Completeness and precision vs. uncertainty 193
    5. "Cheating"; abandonment 194
    6. Psychological factors 195
    7. Conclusion 196
  c. Statutory language 196
    1. Generally 196
    2. Conspiracy elsewhere in the law 197

d. Avoidable behavior and related questions 197
1. Generally 197
2. Non-marginal-cost pricing reprehensible and identifiable? 198
3. Expecting abnormal behavior? 202
4. Consistency with monopoly rules 202
5. What equitable remedy? 203
e. No punitive (or private?) sanctions 205
f. Selective intervention 206
g. Administering selective remedies against interdependent pricing: §2 alone or a very different kind of "conspiracy" 207
h. Readily avoided and remedied practices—a different issue? 208
1433. What Courts Actually Do: Parallelism Without "Plus Factors" 208
a. Introduction and summary 208
b. *American Tobacco* case 209
c. *Interstate Circuit* case 211
d. *Norfolk Monument* case 211
e. "Plus factors" required 212
1434. Parallelism with "Plus Factors" 213
a. Introduction and summary 213
b. Customary indications of traditional conspiracy 214
c. Conspiratorial motivation and acts against self-interest 214
1. These terms merely restate interdependence? 214
2. Not meant or used to condemn mere interdependence 216
d. Poor economic performance 219
1. Possible rationales 219
2. Identifying socially harmful interdependence 220
3. Proving traditional conspiracy? 220
e. Facilitating practices—generally 221
1435. Collective and Unilateral Facilitating Practices: Business Utilities and Market Effects 221
a. Practices reducing rivals' uncertainty aid tacit coordination but can also serve legitimate purposes 221

b. Collective facilitating practices illustrated generally 224
c. Public speech 225
d. Advance announcement of prices 227
e. Price protection provisions 229
f. Delivered pricing 231
g. Pricing manuals 234
h. Pricing formula from prior conspiracy or ancient custom 235
i. Exclusionary practices 236

1436. Facilitating Practices and Other Interdependence Remediable Under Federal Trade Commission or Sherman Acts 237
a. Introduction and summary 237
b. Oligopoly pricing remedies compared 240
1. Summary 240
2. Collective facilitating practices 241
3. Interdependent pricing or facilitating practices as "agreement" 241
c. Federal Trade Commission Act §5 243
d. Sherman Act 247
e. Appraising a facilitating practice generally 249
f. Price or structural judgments 250
1. Introduction 250
2. Limited precedent 250
3. Actual effects elusive; market structure surrogate 252
4. Conclusion 253
g. How intense the facilitation: connecting a practice with an assumed supra-competitive price 254
h. "Legitimate" business purposes: relevance and criteria 256
1. Generally 256
2. Qualitative distinctions? 256
3. Less restrictive alternatives 257
4. Effects criteria interconnected 259
i. Intention 259
1. Defining relevant intent 259
2. Uncertainty; limited sanctions 260
3. Intention mediating between effects and legitimate purpose? 260

4. Weighting intention impedes marketwide ruling 261
j. Extreme uncertainty and shifting legality; conclusion 261

VOLUME VII

CHAPTER 14. Conspiracy, Horizontal and Vertical (continued) 3

14D. Vertical Agreement and Refusals to Deal 3
1437. Vertical Agreements Generally 3
1438. Preview and Summary 6
a. Suggestions and initial selection of customers 6
b. The policy analysis and possible extended agreement theories 8
c. The *Colgate* case and doctrine and its revitalization in *Monsanto* 10
d. Qualifications of *Colgate* and their present status in light of *Monsanto* 12
e. Termination of a customer after a complaint from its competitor 15
f. Damage and standing questions 20
g. Clayton Act and Federal Trade Commission Act compared to Sherman Act 21

14D-1. Supplier's Refusal to Deal with Those Not Complying with Announced Conditions 23
1439. Degrees of Refusal to Deal 23
1440. Suggested Resale Prices or Other Behavior 25
a. Suggestions without sanctions 25
b. Suggestion vs. threat 27
c. Threat vs. notice 28
1441. Initial Selection and Subsequent Replacement of Dealers (or Suppliers) Without Announced Conditions 29
a. Introduction and summary 29

b. Dealer entitlement or reliance irrelevant? 30
c. Initial selection of congenial dealers simpliciter 31
1. Policy issues 32
2. Initial selection involves no other agreeing party 33
d. "Silent" termination of uncongenial dealers—generally and where manufacturer's desires unknown to dealers 34
e. Manufacturer's desires and termination prospect deduced from terminations (or from selections) 35
1. Generally 35
2. Effects compared with those of announced conditions 35
3. Recognizing legitimate manufacturer choice 36
4. Conclusion 37
f. Unexplained termination of those not complying with suggestions 38
1. Generally 38
2. Mere suggestions vs. suggestion plus termination 39
3. Dealer awareness 39
g. Legal rule favoring silence unfair to dealers? 40
h. Tying and exclusive dealing compared to restricted distribution 41
1. Mandatory package 41
2. Other tying; exclusive dealing 42
1442. Announced Conditions for Future Dealing: Effects Comparable to Express Agreement; Among Whom? 44
a. Introduction and summary 44
b. Similarity of effects from express agreement and from desire enforced by refusal to deal 46
c. Promise implies greater compliance 46
d. Non-promissory compliance reflects mere coincidence of views? 47
1. The possibility 47
2. Probabilities? 47

3. Is announced condition a threat or merely fair notice? Implications 49
e. Proofs or presumptions 50
1. Distribution restraints 50
2. Tying and exclusive dealing 52
f. Queries in fitting the statutory language and identifying the agreeing parties 52
1443. Complying Dealers as Co-Conspirators—Extended Agreement Theory I: Knowing Purchaser Accepts Seller's Announced Conditions 54
a. Introduction and summary 54
b. The theory 55
c. Qualms about the theory 56
1. Generally 56
2. No offer made or acceptance requested 57
3. No acceptance desired 57
4. Term of agreement, if any, only that each will act as he desires 58
5. No acceptance given 59
6. Manufacturer's announcement merely gives fair notice 59
7. Finding agreement unfair to dealer 60
d. Implementation of implied acceptance agreement theory 61
1. What must be proved? 61
2. Avoiding harassment of manufacturers 62
1444. Complying Dealers as Co-Conspirators—Extended Agreement Theory II: Widespread Compliance with Announced Condition Reflects Coercion and Therefore Agreement 65
a. Introduction and summary 65
b. The theory 66
c. Qualms about the theory 67
1. Effects 67
2. Is "agreement" apt? 67
3. Coercion theory sweeps too broadly? 67
4. Inability to identify a particular co-conspirator 69
d. What must be proved? 71
e. Conclusion 72

1445. *Colgate* Case Allows Announced Conditions on Future Dealing 73
- a. Introduction and summary 73
- b. Facts and holding 73
- c. Express rationales 76
  - 1. No alienation restraint 76
  - 2. Manufacturer privilege 77
- d. Possibly reading *Colgate* as consistent with extended agreement theories 78
  - 1. No rejection of unargued theories 78
  - 2. Reconciling manufacturer privilege to choose dealers with extended agreement theories? 78
- e. Implications of adopting this reconciliation 81

1446. The Supreme Court's Revitalization of *Colgate* in *Monsanto* 82
- a. Introduction and summary 82
- b. The Court's policy concerns and formulae 83
- c. The conspiracy finding 86
  - 1. Direct evidence 86
  - 2. Circumstantial evidence 86
- d. Agreement inferable from implemented conditions or coerced compliance? 88
  - 1. Expansive common purpose language 88
  - 2. Implied request and communication 88
  - 3. Weak evidence supports jury verdict 88
  - 4. Coercion as agreement 89
  - 5. Conclusion 90
- e. Complex enforcement of announced conditions as "agreement"? 91
  - 1. Reconciling *Monsanto* with extended theories of agreement? 91
  - 2. *Monsanto* facts show complex enforcement 92
  - 3. Concurrent validation of *Parke Davis* or *Albrecht*? 93
- f. Suggested prices, initial selection, or silent termination alone 94
- g. Preview 94

1447. Individualized "Negotiation" as Traditional Agreement (and More) Under *Monsanto* and *Parke Davis;* Dealer "Admits Agreement" 94
- a. Introduction and summary 94
- b. Individualized dealing as traditional agreement 95
  1. Generally 95
  2. Assurances requested and received 96
  3. Assurances given after implied request 97
  4. Other personalized dealings 97
- c. Individualized dealings weaken reservations to extended agreement theories 98
- d. Individualized dealings exceed manufacturer's "privilege"? 99
- e. Unsuccessful individualized dealings 100
- f. Dealer "admits agreement" 100

1448. Implied Agreements or Firmly Resolute Enforcement Under *Schrader's, Frey, Beech-Nut, Bausch & Lomb,* and *Schwinn* Cases; Status After *Monsanto* 101
- a. Introduction and summary 101
- b. *Schrader's* and *Frey* cases 102
- c. *Beech-Nut* case 103
- d. *Bausch & Lomb* case 104
- e. *Schwinn* case: firm and resolute enforcement 105
  1. As substitute for express agreement? 105
  2. As precondition for condemning express agreement? 106
- f. Dealer complaint as implicit assurance of acquiescence or agreement 107

1449. Using Wholesalers or Other Complex Enforcement of Announced Conditions: Status of *Parke Davis* After *Monsanto* 107
- a. Introduction and summary 107
- b. Facts and holding 109
- c. Critique: complex enforcement rather than distinctive concept of agreement with wholesalers? 111

1. Interpretative options 111
2. Conceptual consistency 112
3. Boycott overtones 113
d. *Parke Davis* might survive *Monsanto* 113
e. "Information conspiracy" with wholesalers 114
1. The argument 114
2. *Monsanto* implications 115
f. Defining complex enforcement 116
g. Note on "combination" 117
1450. Agreements with "Pawns" or Other Third Parties: Status of *Albrecht* After *Monsanto* 117
a. Introduction and summary 117
b. Facts and holding 117
c. Pawns' function critical 119
1. Incident to termination? 119
2. Incident to soliciting assurances? 119
1451. Coerced or Unwilling Compliance by Terminated Dealer or Dealers Generally; Agreements with Consumers: *Albrecht* and Other Pre-*Monsanto* Decisions 120
a. Introduction and summary 120
b. Coercion mainly irrelevant when agreement express 121
c. Coerced compliance in lower courts before *Monsanto* 123
1. Generally 123
2. Character of compulsion; contingent wholesale price 125
d. The *Albrecht* dicta 127
e. Unwilling compliance after *Monsanto* 128
f. Agreements with consumers 130
1452. Termination as Proof of Agreement with Others 130
a. Introduction and summary 130
b. "Perverse" to deny to non-agreeing dealer relief granted to less virtuous dealer 132
c. If announced condition on future dealing establishes agreement, plaintiff's termination may be exemplary; credible threats 133

1. Explicit announcements 133
2. Silent termination equivalent to announced condition? 133
3. Proof or presumptions; intent or suggestions 135
4. Lower courts; *Monsanto* implications 137

d. Is complex enforcement or individualized negotiation relevant and present in plaintiff's termination? Presuming similar behavior toward others? 139

e. Termination irrational unless others comply and agree? 140

14D-2. Customer Complains About Its Rival to Supplier 141

1453. The Problem: Inherent Ambiguities of Complaint, Termination, and Antitrust Policy 141
a. Introduction and summary 141
b. Agreement theories in general 142
c. Policy: vertical in form but horizontal in substance? 143
d. Policy: price or non-price restraint? 145
e. Interpreting the facts: the meaning of a termination triggered by a complaint 147

1454. Supreme Court's *Monsanto* Decision: Conspiracy with Complaining Dealers 149
a. Introduction and summary 149
b. The facts and the Court's approach in summary 151
c. The Court's policy premises 151
d. The test 153

1455. Termination Merely "After" Complaint 154
a. Introduction and summary 154
b. Lower court decisions 154
c. Termination unconnected with complaint 155
1. Independent ground for termination 155
2. Termination for same reason as disclosed in complaint but unconnected to it 156

d. Insufficient in principle but shifts proof burden? 156

1456. Plaintiff Terminated "in Response to" Rival's Complaint Aiding Supplier's Enforcement; Information and Consultation 156
a. Introduction and summary 156
b. Responsiveness usually required but easily inferred 158
c. Information conspiracy and *Parke Davis* analogy 159
d. Critique: *Parke Davis* queries and distinctions 160
1. Generally 160
2. Preliminaries: information or complex enforcement as conspiracy; termination price-related 160
3. Express price maintenance policy obviates complaint's causal relationship to termination and eliminates non-price ambiguities 161
4. Complaint unsolicited, uncoerced, unpreventable, and may rest on different "horizontal" motives 162
e. *Monsanto* implications 164
f. Manufacturer solicitation of dealer views 165
1457. Manufacturer Terminates in Response to Rival's Complaint: Coerced Suppliers 166
a. Introduction and summary 166
b. Coercion of manufacturer anticompetitive and fits extended agreement theories 167
c. Proving coercion of manufacturer 168
1. Not presumed 168
2. Pre-complaint restricted distribution policy? 169
3. Relative bargaining power 171
4. Manufacturer self-interest 172
d. Lower court decisions 173
e. *Monsanto* implications 175
1458. Complaint and Termination as Meeting of Minds 177
a. Introduction and summary 177
b. Different motives: unlawful common scheme? 177

c. Prior agreement or implied assurance by complainer or by manufacturer 178
d. How much additional evidence? 180

14D-3. Damage Issues; Clayton and Federal Trade Commission Acts 180

1459. Damage and Standing Issues 180
- a. Introduction and summary 180
- b. Consumer suits 182
  1. Standing under *Illinois Brick* 182
  2. Standing and causation 183
  3. Damage and causation 185
  4. Dealer liability 186
- c. Dealer suit against manufacturer—generally and compliance with own prior agreement 187
  1. Own prior agreement: causation 187
  2. Damages for participant in unlawful agreement 189
  3. Mitigation 190
- d. Proving damages from termination after non-compliance 191
  1. Generally 191
  2. Relating termination to non-compliance essential but insufficient 191
  3. Relating termination to own (or other) unlawful agreement 193
- e. Is plaintiff's termination causally related to minimum resale price agreements with others? Other agreements distinguished 194
  1. Other agreements make plaintiff's termination feasible? 194
  2. Plaintiff's termination necessary to make other agreements work or even a term of them? 195
  3. Maximum-price, tying, and exclusive dealing agreements distinguished 197

1460. Clayton Act §3 198
- a. Introduction and summary 198
- b. "Condition, agreement, or understanding" 200
  1. Language 201

2. Policy 203
3. Supplier privilege or administrative impracticality? 204
c. Damage and standing issues—generally 205
1. The problem 205
2. Adequate independent grounds for termination 206
d. Conditioned sales to others? 206
1. Explicitly announced program of conditioned sales 206
2. Terminated customer unique or typical? Presumptions 207
3. Termination equivalent to announced condition? 208
4. Termination irrational unless other conditioned sales? 210
e. Causal connection to other conditioned sales? 211
f. Explaining the cases 212
1461. Federal Trade Commission Act §5 215

14E. Intraenterprise Conspiracy: Corporate Affiliates, Employees, Agents, Pawns, Associations, and Joint Ventures 219
1462. The Firm as a Single Actor and the Conspiracy Concept 219
a. Introduction; the topics of this subchapter 219
b. Conspiracy without increased power or connection to alleged restraint? 222
c. "Agreement" vs. direction 223

14E-1. Corporations Wholly Owned in Common 224
1463. Supreme Court Intraenterprise Conspiracy Cases from *Yellow Cab* to *Copperweld* 224
a. Introduction and summary 224
b. *Yellow Cab* case 225
c. *Kiefer-Stewart* case 227
d. *Timken* case 227
e. *Perma Life Mufflers* case 228
f. *Sunkist* case 228

g. *Citizens & Southern* case 230
h. *Copperweld* case 230
1464. Commonly Owned Corporations: Statutory Language and Policy 232
a. Introduction and summary 232
b. Statutory language and legislative history 234
c. Statutory structure 235
d. Connection between restraint and separate incorporation 237
e. Filling a lacuna in statutory coverage? 240
f. Sister corporations and other remaining questions 245
1465. "Holding Out" or Intended Independence 246
a. Pretended independence 246
b. Intended independence 248

14E-2. *Corporations Commonly Controlled Without Completely Common Ownership* 249
1466. Commonly Controlled Corporations Without 100 Percent Common Ownership: Introduction; Relevance of Minority Interest 249
a. Introduction and summary 249
b. Pre-*Copperweld* trends in lower courts 251
c. Similarities to wholly owned subsidiaries 252
d. Duties to minority owners; relevance 252
1. Generally 252
2. Efficient integrated decision-making 253
3. Connection between challenged behavior and minority interest 254
e. Minority interest held by competitor, supplier, or customer 256
1467. Identifying a Single Economic Unit 257
a. Introduction and summary 257
b. Motivation for separate incorporation, connection with restraint, competitive relationship, and holding out 259
c. Formal contract vs. direction or informal coordination 261

d. Common reports, staff, direction, or directors 261
e. Actual degree of integration or exercised control 264
1. Importance emphasized 264
2. Actual but invisible control 264
3. Evidence of conspiracy as evidence of control 265
f. Power to direct and control 266
1. Decisive under *Copperweld* when wholly common ownership 266
2. Majority vs. "substantial" ownership vs. de facto control 267
g. All-factor vs. simple test 270
h. Jury role 273
1468. Agreement in Fact? 274
1469. Broader Criteria of Reasonableness 277
a. Introduction and summary 277
b. Only restraints on outsiders 278
c. Non-competitors 280
d. Internal matters; different standard 280

14E-3. Employees, Divisions, and Agents 282
1470. Employees Generally and Unincorporated Divisions 282
1471. Employee with "Independent" Interest 284
a. Introduction and summary 284
b. The *Greenville* case; theoretical relevance of an independent interest 286
c. Coordination or constriction of one firm by another which has an employee with an interest in the former 288
d. Restraint by one firm whose employee has an independent interest 291
1. The disloyalty problem 291
2. A significant concern? 291
3. Conceptual problems 293
e. Independent interest defined 294
1. Interest in doing job well 294

2. Interest in plaintiff's competitor 294
3. Other selfish interests and policy bias 296
f. Employee disloyalty proved or presumed 298
g. Disloyal employee causes restraint 299
h. Conspiracy between two employees with independent interests 300
1472. Employees Acting Without Authorization 301
1473. Distribution Agents Restrained 304
a. Agents restrained vs. agents or pawns aiding a restraint 304
b. Distribution intermediaries: introduction and summary 305
c. The Supreme Court cases 307
d. Lower courts applying *Simpson* 310
1. Vastness 310
2. "Independence" 311
e. Relevant interests and issues 314
1. Promoting intrabrand competition; dealer autonomy 314
2. Promoting efficient distribution and interbrand competition; owner and employer-like discretion 314
f. Reconciling the relevant interests 315
g. Toward a refined test of "independent businessman": economic risk 317
1474. Agents and "Pawns" Aiding a Restraint 319
a. Introduction and summary 319
b. Criminal conspiracy model; usual antitrust situations contrasted 320
c. Knowledge, purpose, and stake 327
d. Summary by example 332

14E-4. Continuing Conspiracies Among Creators and Members of Enterprises, Associations, and Joint Ventures 334
1475. The Problem and Initial Distinctions 334
a. Preview and key variables 334

b. Statutory and policy relevance of the continuing conspiracy characterization 336

1476. Usual Business Entity: Formation and Later Merger or Cartel 338

a. Formation and subsequent business behavior 338

b. Comparing formation with later merger or collaboration 339

c. Subsequent behavior of post-merger entity and non-merged collaboration 340

d. Partnerships 341

1477. Trade Associations and Concerted Rule-Making 343

1478. Productive Joint Ventures as Single Entity or Continuing Conspiracy 348

a. Definitions and distinctions 348

b. Formation and future re-examination of the joint venture 350

1. Initial appraisal criteria in general; implications of legality 350
2. Mistaken judgment; later events 351
3. Market changes: parents grow to dominance 353
4. Successful ventures; impact on competitors of parents 354

c. Ongoing venture operations not focused on competition among or with the parents 355

d. Joint organizations so intimate as to be one? Sports leagues 357

CHAPTER 15. "Rule of Reason" and "Per Se Rule"—General Issues 361

1500. Why Reasonableness Matters; Uncertain Reality; Preview 361

1501. "Every" Restraint Embraces Only "Unreasonable" Restraint 364

1502. Restraint of Trade Is Restraint on Competition: General Formulae 370

1503. Competitive Evil: Tendency and Magnitude 372
a. Type of threat to competition 372
b. Output effects; market circumstances and shares 374
1504. Legitimate Objectives 377
1505. Restraint Reasonably Necessary for Legitimate Objective: Actual Connection Without Less Restrictive Alternative 383
a. Given a legitimate objective, does restraint promote it? 384
b. Alternatives: equally effective and substantially less restrictive? 385
1506. Role of Intention 389
1507. Balancing, Administrability, and Tentative Presumptions 394
a. Administrative convenience 394
b. Burdens of allegation, introduction of evidence, and persuasion 397
c. Varying proof requirements and the fact-finder's reasoning process 399
1508. Applying Rule of Reason Summarily 403
a. Instantaneous balancing "in the twinkling of an eye" 403
b. "Facial unreasonableness" 404
c. Categorical or presumptive rules within the rule of reason 405
1509. Per Se Rationale: Class Unreasonableness 408
1510. Per Se Rules: Different Meanings; Redeeming Virtue Recognized Through Exceptions or Classification 414
a. Different meanings 414
b. Justifications not previously thought about can be considered; allowing limited exceptions 416
c. Potentially justified conduct classified outside per se domain 421
1511. Collapsing Reasonableness-Per Se Distinction: Single Inquiry with Varying Presumptions? 427

VOLUME VIII

CHAPTER 16. Vertical Distribution Restraints Limiting Intrabrand Competition 1

16A. Pervasive Legal and Economic Issues 2

16A-1. Introduction with Summary of Possible Effects and Analogies 2

1600. Introduction to Distribution Restraints 2
- a. Vertical images and practices 2
- b. Varieties of distribution restraints and their present legal treatment; open questions 4
- c. Ambiguities and analogies 7
  1. Selective distribution and refusals to deal 7
  2. Horizontal-vertical dichotomy 8
  3. Vertical integration and dealer freedom 8
- d. Testing reasonableness: market coverage and justifications 9
- e. Preview 11

1601. Manufacturer's Reasons for Limiting Intrabrand Competition Among His Dealers: Possible Pro- and Anticompetitive Effects 12

1602. Business Alternatives and Crude Connections 23
- a. Introduction: how restraint's alternatives bear on legal permission or prohibition 23
- b. Connecting restraint to legitimate objective 24
- c. Less restrictive alternatives; dealer service illustration 25
- d. Manufacturer choice relevant 29
- e. Lawful alternatives make prohibition futile 32

16A-2. Legal Analogies and Major Harms 33

1603. Vertical Restraint Less Dangerous Than Horizontal Restraint Because Manufacturer Shuns Excess Dealer Profit 33

1604. Intrabrand Restraints Serving Dealer Power 37
- a. Introduction and summary; dealer power and coercion defined 37
- b. Dealer cartels and power in fact 40
- c. Express dealer cartel on single brand 43
  - 1. Anticompetitive objectives 43
  - 2. Legality 44
  - 3. Detecting dealers' agreement on prices or markets 48
  - 4. Detecting conspiratorial dealer coercion of manufacturer 49
- d. Dealer coercion of manufacturers without horizontal agreement 50
  - 1. Interdependence and other informal "quasi-collective" action 50
  - 2. Powerful individual dealers 51
  - 3. Manufacturer choice constrained even with many multi-brand dealers 52
- e. Relevance of identifying dealer power 55
  - 1. Whether a horizontal dealer agreement provable or not 55
  - 2. "Horizontal" characterization of vertical restraint 55
  - 3. Condemnation futile 57
  - 4. Three interrelated inquiries 57
- f. Identifying dealer power: interbrand retail market structure 58
  - 1. Generally 58
  - 2. Brand dominance or other indications of brand power; market definition 59
  - 3. Dealer concentration 61
  - 4. Cumulative market coverage 62
  - 5. Justice Department guidelines compared 62
  - 6. Economic performance as proof or rebuttal 63
  - 7. Dealer service and other impeded coordination rebuttals 64
  - 8. Entry conditions rebuttal 64
- g. Detecting dealer power: manufacturer-dealer relations 65

1. Relative power generally 66
2. Dealer initiatives: possible congruence with manufacturer interest 67
3. Collective dealer initiatives 69
4. Individual dealer initiatives 70
5. Local or general restraint 71
6. Form of restraint 72
7. Intention 72

h. Manufacturer justification as negation or offset 73
i. Summary 74
j. Coerced manufacturer's liability 76
k. Problems in shifting legality according to cumulative use 76
1. Comprehensive or selective condemnation 76
2. Proceedings against single manufacturer 77
3. Fairness 77

1605. Dual Distribution 78
a. Introduction and summary 78
b. The classification game 80
c. Competitive impact of dual distribution restraints generally 82
d. Possibly suspect restraints in dual distribution 86
1. The qualification 86
2. Restraints serving dealer rather than manufacturer interests 87
3. Price discrimination 88
4. Excess dealer level profits not otherwise capturable 89
5. Partial integration 90

1606. Parallel Action by Manufacturers 91
a. Magnifies evils and facilitates manufacturer coordination: introduction and summary 91
b. Horizontal agreement to use vertical restraints 94
c. Reducing backward pressure on coordinating manufacturers 96

d. Reducing utility of wholesale price cut 98
   1. The possibility 98
   2. Indirect retail price cuts 99
   3. Desired services and dealer recruitment 99
e. Increasing visibility and thereby discouraging wholesale price cuts 100
   1. The possibility 100
   2. General visibility without restraint 101
   3. Multi-brand dealers 101
   4. Single brand dealers 102
   5. Widespread retail price cut on one brand 102
   6. Coordinating manufacturers' cost-benefit calculus 103
f. Frequency; explaining industry-wide usage 104
g. Proving (or disproving) connection to horizontal manufacturer coordination 107
   1. Express agreement among manufacturers to adopt vertical restraint 107
   2. Express agreements among manufacturers to fix wholesale prices 108
   3. Concentration; presumptions 109
   4. Rebutting inferences from concentration 110
   5. Market coverage: relevant threshold 111
   6. Market coverage: integrated firms and informal resale price controllers 113
   7. Market definition 114
   8. Single brand dealers only 115
   9. Offsetting benefits 116
   10. Problem: reasonable restraint becomes illegal when rivals adopt it 116
h. Customer and territorial restraints 117
   1. Introduction 117
   2. Resale price maintenance dangers mainly absent 117
   3. Aiding price coordination among manufacturers 119
      (A) The possibility 119

(B) Prerequisite for implementing express but undetected agreement among unconcentrated manufacturers: market coverage 119
(C) Prerequisite for facilitating tacit price coordination among manufacturers: concentration 120
4. Aiding market division among manufacturers 121
(A) Bid rotation scenario 121
(B) Market allocation scenario 122
5. Conclusions 123
1607. Manufacturer Self-Interest or Error 124
a. Introduction and summary 124
b. Identifying error 124
c. Legal implications 126
1608. Vertical Integration Compared 128
a. The analogy 128
b. Competitive effects 129
c. Third party interests and administrative considerations 131
1609. Dealer Freedom Impaired 132
a. The dealer protection impulse: general analysis 132
b. Competitive effects 135
c. Restraints on alienation 136
d. Irreducible axiom 137
e. "Oppression" vs. competitive objectives 139
1610. Distribution Restraint Exchanged for Exclusive Dealing or Tying 143
a. Introduction and summary 143
b. Unreasonable exclusive dealing 145
c. Reasonable or unappraised exclusive dealing 147
d. Other effects of exclusive dealing 148

16A-3. Pro-Competitive Potential of Distribution Restraints *149*
1611. Distribution Restraints Presumptively "Efficient"? General Argument and Qualifications 149
a. Premises 149

b. Inefficient intrabrand competition: illustrative model 151
c. How restraints can improve distributional efficiency and consumer welfare 152
1. Generally 152
2. Prevent free riding 153
3. Assure minimum scale 154
d. Key qualifications 155
e. Desirability of incremental services 156
f. Services actually impaired 157
g. Restraint's effectiveness and alternatives 161
h. Legal issues, market coverage, and preview 163
1612. Dealer Services Efficient or "Excessive"? 165
a. Introduction and summary 165
b. Dealer services undoubtedly useful for some consumers but superfluous for others; limiting consumer choice 165
c. Spurious product differentiation misleading or mutually offsetting 168
1. Injuries 168
2. Desirable process, perception, or quality surrogate 169
d. Dealer services affect entry 171
e. Excessive services legally cognizable? 173
f. Alternative business methods or restraint types 177
1613. Less Tangible Image Service and Free Riders Generally 179
a. Introduction and summary 179
b. Externalities and free riding in society 180
c. Price as brand image 183
d. "Elite" dealers' "certifications" 184
1. Fashion signal 184
2. Quality signal 185
3. Resale price maintenance justified? Queries 186
e. Impact of free riding on reputation building 188

f. Elite dealers' power 191
g. Business alternatives and conclusions 193
1614. Dealer Goodwill or Recommendations 194
a. Introduction and definition 194
b. No free ride; mainly resale price maintenance; goodwill payments competed away 194
c. Dealer recommendations 196
1. Utility to manufacturer and consumers 196
2. Identification 197
d. Stocking and shelf space 198
e. Induce faithful performance 201
1615. Scale Economies of Distribution Protected or Obstructed: Efficiency vs. Concentration or Extensive Availability 203
a. Introduction and summary 203
b. Assuring scale economies 205
c. High-cost distribution reduces dealer concentration 207
d. High-cost distribution increases product availability 208
1616. Intensive Market Penetration, Dealer Specialization, and Price Discrimination 211
a. Introduction and summary 211
b. Intensive market penetration by a wholly integrated manufacturer 213
c. Eliminating duplicative sales efforts 214
d. Customer restrictions protecting specialized dealers 215
e. Limiting dealers to a customer class in order to protect price discrimination 217
1. Fencing in specialized dealers 218
2. Fencing out regular dealers 220
f. Efficient local focus free of "cream-skimming": territorial limitations and sales quotas 222
1617. Promoting New Entry, Expansion, or Survival 227
a. Recruiting dealers to develop market 227
1. The problem 227
2. Pro-competitiveness 228
3. Proof or presumption 229

b. Supporting weak manufacturers; inducing multi-brand dealers to handle product 231
c. Lowering dealers' risk and capital cost 233
1618. Product Quality and Safety 235
a. Divergent interests generally 235
b. Resale price maintenance as a cure 236
c. Territorial restraints 237
d. Customer limitations 238
1619. Loss Leaders 240

16B. Minimum Resale Price Maintenance 243

16B-1. Understanding and Living with the Rule of Per Se Illegality 244
1620. In the Beginning: The *Dr. Miles* Case 244
a. Facts and holding summarized 244
b. The Court's reasoning 246
c. Critique 249
1. The Court's premises 249
2. Categorical propositions erroneous 250
3. As balancing decision 251
4. Rationalizing a per se decision 252
d. Legal implications 254
1621. Agencies and Products Copyrighted or Patented 255
1622. "Resale" Distinguished from Other Prices 259
a. Generally 259
b. Insurer arrangements with service providers 261
c. Dealer involvement in "direct" manufacturer sales to consumer 264
1623. Influencing Resale Prices Without Traditional Agreements: Suggested Prices, Announced Conditions, Coerced Dealers, or Rivals' Complaints, Remedial Problems 267
a. Introduction and summary 267
b. Selective distribution and "silent" termination of non-compliant dealers 269
c. Suggested prices 269

d. Announcing price conditions on future dealing and ceasing to supply non-compliant dealers 272
e. Responding to dealer complaints about another dealer 274
f. Proving injury and connecting it to unlawful agreement 275
1. Terminating price cutter simpliciter 276
2. Terminations unrelated to intrabrand competition; independent explanations generally 276
3. Dealer bound by unlawful agreement 278
4. Generalizing proofs related to one or few dealers 279
5. Linking dealer termination to unlawful agreement with others 279
6. Antitrust injury based on competitive rather than restrained market 280
g. Implications for reforming *Dr. Miles* 283
1624. Price vs. Non-Price Restraint When Explicit Non-Price Agreement 283
a. Introduction and summary 283
b. Price and non-price restraints, similarities and differences 286
c. Price restraint notwithstanding formal non-price restraint; exception for reasonably ancillary price agreements 287
d. Termination of discounter as non-price restraint 288
1. With territorial restraints 289
2. With service obligations 289
3. With sole outlets 290
4. With control of resales to unauthorized discounting dealers 292
e. Relevance of suggested resale prices 293
1625. Price vs. Non-Price Restraint When No Formal Agreement on Either Subject 294
a. Initial questions and the *Business Electronics* decision 294

b. No explicit non-price restraint—relevance 296
c. Proving non-price motivations vs. chilling effect 297
1. Termination of price cutter providing inadequate service 297
2. Termination of price cutter for invading a territory or customer class 301
3. More selective distribution or price control as such 302
4. The Supreme Court's resolution 304
d. Coercion of unwilling manufacturers by powerful dealer 307
e. Implications for the *Dr. Miles* rule 310
1626. Conditional Reimbursements 310
a. Conditions without agreements 311
b. Prices advertised 312
c. Prices charged 314
d. Conditions not related to price 315
1627. Wholesale Price Formula or "Condition" 316
a. Introduction 316
b. Wholesale prices or changes independent of particular dealer's price 317
c. Simple pricing formula related to each dealer's price 318
d. Pricing formulae as functional equivalent of resale price agreement 319
1. Pricing formulae or practices prohibiting all dealer pricing discretion 319
2. Formulae or practices with the effect of limiting dealer discretion 322
e. "Temporary competitive allowance" 322
1. Unconditional temporary allowances 322
2. Varieties of conditional allowances 323
3. Minimum price agreement compared 323
4. Future allowances based on past resale prices 325
5. Withdrawing allowance from non-conforming dealer 326
f. Quantity control 328

16B-2. Reforming the Dr. Miles *Rule of Per Se Illegality* *330*

1628. Reform Impulses; Types and Costs; Positions Summarized 330
   - a. Sources of dissatisfaction 330
   - b. Alternative legal rules and their corresponding costs 331
   - c. Per Se Legality? 334
   - d. Status quo arguments summarized 335
   - e. Reform arguments summarized 336

1629. Stare Decisis; Implications of Repealing Fair Trade Statutes 337
   - a. Introduction and summary 337
   - b. Background: the fair trade enactments 338
   - c. Implications of repealing fair trade laws 341
   - d. Reexamination appropriate though weight still attaches to established rule 344

1630. Asymmetrical Legal Treatment of Non-Price Restraints; Agreement Complications 345
   - a. Introduction and summary 345
   - b. Theoretical coherence: significance of price-non-price differences 345
   - c. Administering the distinction 347
   - d. Per se rule for price restraints exacerbates "agreement" confusions 347

1631. Potential Benefits as an Argument Against Per Se Illegality 349
   - a. "Traditional" justifications 350
     1. Manufacturer goodwill 350
     2. Loss leader 350
     3. Dealer concentration; product availability 351
     4. Dealer goodwill 351
     5. Price stability 352
   - b. Facilitating new entry 352
   - c. Protecting "desirable" dealer services 353
     1. Free riding and other impediments 353
     2. Efficiency of manufacturer-desired services 354
     3. Restraint's connection to desirable services 355

(A) No tangible services; fashion-quality signals; non-service explanations 355
(B) Effectiveness 356
(C) Manufacturer alternatives and their significance 356
d. Proving Justification 357
1. Which justifications 357
2. Substantiality of benefit; effectiveness of restraint 358
3. Generality of a manufacturer's restraint 359
4. Less restrictive alternatives 359
e. Conclusion: a qualified plus for reform 360
1632. Potential Evils as an Argument for Per Se Illegality 360
a. The issues 360
b. Apparent historical experience; consistency with theory 361
c. Evils summarized 364
1. Minor detriments 364
2. Exchanged for second restraint 364
3. Dealer recommendations 365
4. Stultified high-cost distribution 365
5. Major evils: manufacturer coordination and dealer power 366
d. Manufacturer coordination and its proof or presumption 367
1. Generally 367
2. Concentration and market coverage 368
3. Rebutting or offsetting inference or presumption 369
e. "Dealer power" and its proof or presumption 369
1. The danger and how to prove it generally 369
2. Market structure and restraint's coverage 370
(A) Widespread coverage 370
(B) Concentration 371
(C) Brand power 371
3. Dealer power over manufacturer 371

4. Rebutting inferences or presumptions of dealer power 372
f. Conclusion 374
1633. The Alternatives to Per Se Illegality 376
a. Introduction 376
b. Open-ended rule of reason 377
c. Structuring the inquiry into harm 378
1. Identifying adverse factors and their anticompetitive implications 378
2. Who proves presence or absence of adverse factors 380
3. Rebutting anticompetitive inferences 381
(A) Manufacturer coordination 382
(B) Dealer power 382
(C) Deceptive recommendations to consumers; limiting consumer choice 382
(D) Unjustified restraint 383
d. Structuring the inquiry into benefit 383
1. Logical relevance 383
2. Four sub-issues 384
(A) Identifying and proving legitimate functions 384
(B) Substantiality 385
(C) Effectiveness 385
(D) Less restrictive alternatives 386
(E) Summary 386
3. Alternative legal rules 387
e. Conclusions 389
1. Justice Department guidelines compared 389
2. Recommendations 390

16C. Maximum Resale Price Limitations 392
1634. Introduction 392
1635. The *Albrecht* Case 393
1636. The Justification: Limiting Dealer Monopoly 395
a. Key points 395
b. Controlling monopoly power legitimate 396
c. Less restrictive alternatives and sources of dealer power—generally 397
d. "Bargain" with dealers 398

e. Sue the dealers 399
f. Appoint more dealers 399
1. Inevitable monopoly 399
2. Other distribution restraints 400
g. Vertically integrate 402
h. Cap resale prices indirectly 403
1637. Possible Competitive Evils 404
a. Introduction and summary 404
b. Price floor dangers absent 404
c. Disguised minimum price 405
d. Dealer freedom 406
e. Wrong price 407
f. Limiting dealer services 408
g. Limiting number of own or rival dealers 409
h. Predatory pricing 411
i. Dealer exploitation 412
j. Price discrimination 414
1638. The Future of Maximum Resale Price Limitations 417
a. Harm-benefit summary 417
b. Recommendations 419
c. Present status of maximum resale price agreements 420
1639. Indirect or Partial Influences on Maximum Resale Prices Under *Albrecht* 422
a. Sales quota 422
b. General "competitive price" agreements; limits on non-competitive prices or "unfair" practices 423
c. Intrabrand competition, including dual distribution, caps resale price 425
d. Suggested, advertised, pre-ticketed prices 426
e. Future dealing conditioned on obedience to announced maximum prices 426
f. Conditional reimbursements; formulae connecting wholesale and retail prices 427
g. Temporary promotional price 427
1. Variations and summary 427
2. Express agreement requiring pass-on 428
(A) Dangers 428
(B) Less desirable alternatives 429

3. Express agreements requiring more than a pass-on of wholesale price cut 430
4. Informal arrangements 432
h. Wholesale price discounts assisting particular resales 434
1640. Attacking Price Ceilings: Standing and Antitrust Injury 438
a. Introduction and summary 438
b. Injury in fact (and other preliminaries) 440
1. Dealer prevented from charging higher prices 440
2. Rival dealer 442
3. Disobedient dealer terminated 442
c. Antitrust injury concept 444
d. The *Albrecht* rationale 446
1. Dealer choice inviolate 446
2. Ceiling illegal not because, but despite, limitation of supracompetitive dealer pricing 447
3. Administrability and consistency with other damage measures 449

16D. Territorial or Customer Limitations on Dealers 451
1641. Issues Previewed, Restraints Defined, and "Agreement" Recalled 451
a. Overview and preview 452
b. Territorial restraint forms 453
1. Area of primary responsibility; local quota 454
2. Location clause 454
3. Pass-over payments 454
4. Differential pricing or royalty systems 455
5. Closed territory 455
c. Customer restraint forms 455
1. Generally 455
2. Reserving customers to manufacturer 456
3. Limiting sales through unauthorized outlets 456
d. Finding agreement 456

1642. Legal Developments Through *White Motor* and *Schwinn* Cases 457
- a. *White Motor* 458
- b. *Schwinn* 460
- c. Developments under *Schwinn* 463

1643. *Sylvania* 465
- a. Facts and lower court holdings 465
- b. Supreme Court's holding 466
- c. Remand 468
- d. Implications 468

1644. Rejecting Per Se Illegal Price, Boycott, or Horizontal Restraint Characterizations 469
- a. Price effect generally 469
- b. Horizontal restraint 471
  - 1. "Horizontal" price effect 471
  - 2. Dual distribution 473
- c. Boycott 473

1645. Post-*Sylvania* Cases Applying Rule of Reason 478
- a. In brief 478
- b. Market definition and share 479
- c. Share substantiality and other factors 481
- d. Justification, reasonable necessity, and less restrictive alternatives 483
- e. Burden of persuasion 487
- f. Critique and prologue 488

1646. Business Justifications—General Issues 488
- a. Relevance 488
- b. Legitimacy and uncertainty 489
- c. Restraint actually solves real business problem 491
- d. Less restrictive alternatives 492
- e. Surrogates for effects: selective restraint; manufacturer market share 494
- f. Inducing lawful second restraint 495

1647. Particular Business Justifications: Legitimacy and Necessity of Restraint 496
- a. Introduction and summary 496
- b. Point-of-sale services and free riders; more about necessity 498
  - 1. Argument and objections 498
  - 2. Proving services suffer from free riding 499

3. Less restrictive customer and territorial restraints or other alternatives 500

c. Efficient dealer specialization, territorial size, and market penetration 502

1. Summary 502
2. Higher-cost dealers 503
3. Minimum efficient scale 504
4. Market penetration generally 504
5. Price discrimination and market penetration 505
6. Price discrimination and "specialized" dealers 506

d. Product quality and safety 507

1. Summary 507
2. Consumer safety 508
3. Unauthorized dealers or subdealers 509
4. Remoteness; dumping 510

e. New entrants and weak firms 511

f. Dealer goodwill 513

1. Exchanged for faithful dealer performance 513
2. Exchanged for not unreasonable exclusive dealing 513
3. Exchanged for stocking or pushing brand by regular or elite dealers 513

1648. Identifying Anticompetitive Dangers 514

a. Introduction and summary 514

b. Inherent or eschewed effects 517

1. Limiting dealer autonomy, intrabrand competition, or dealer scale 517
2. Manufacturer error and excessive differentiation or services 518
3. Significance in monopoly or elsewhere 518

c. Manufacturer power 520

1. Foreclosing rival manufacturers and other entry barriers 520
2. Winning misleading recommendations from multi-brand dealers 521
3. Price discrimination 522

(A) Generally 522

(B) Typical situations 522

(C) Equivalent lawful discrimination as rebuttal in particular case 524
4. Facilitating coordination among manufacturers 525
d. Dealer power 526
1. Transferring non-competitive manufacturer market structure to dealer level; dealer or manufacturer interests 527
2. Dealer ability to restrict output 529
(A) Relevance; performance data or local market structure 529
(B) Brand power; intrabrand concentration 529
(C) Interbrand concentration, market coverage, integrated firms, and rebuttals 531
3. Dealer ability to extract restraint from unwilling manufacturer 532
(A) Reluctant manufacturer bows to dealer power or market necessity—uncertainty 532
(B) Initiatives; manufacturer testimony 533
(C) Dealer's brand or market share, other brands, and replaceability; cumulative use 535
(D) Dealer ultimatum 537
(E) Selective vs. general restraint 539
(F) Restraint's form or intensity; checked by sales quota 539
4. Intent and legitimate purpose 541
e. De facto price restraint 542
f. Market shares and structures related to theory of anticompetitive effect 543
1. Theory of anticompetitive effect needed 543
2. Manufacturer market shares generally 544
3. Low share and concentration 545
4. High share, concentration, and coverage 547
1649. Structuring the Rule of Reason for Customer and Territorial Restraints 547
a. Traditional order of proof 547

b. Presumptive legality or illegality within rule of reason 549
c. Restraint's detriments 550
1. Adverse factors for prima facie illegality 550
2. Performance, entry conditions, or factors impeding oligopolistic coordination 554
d. Restraint's benefits 555
1. Largely unconnected with detriments 555
2. Prima facie justification 556
3. Less restrictive alternatives; burden of persuasion on justification 557
4. Justification and detriment both proved prima facie 558
e. Justice Department guidelines compared: safe harbors vs. identifying the prima facie case 559

16E. Single Dealer Appointed for Region or Customer Class 560
1650. "Sole" or "Exclusive" Outlet: Introduction and Definitions 560
1651. Intensity of Intrabrand Restraint 562
a. Introduction 562
b. Other dealers in same brand 563
1. Single sole outlet vs. many sole outlets 563
2. Multiple sole outlets insulated from each other 563
c. Minimum sales quota 564
d. Manufacturer's self-distribution 565
e. Duration and availability of other dealers 565
f. Agreed vs. de facto sole outlet 567
g. Summary 568
1652. Related Legal Concepts Compared 568
a. Introduction; refusal to deal 568
b. Not group boycott, price-fixing, or horizontal restraint 569
c. "Exclusion" of would-be dealers 571
1. "Output contract" 571
2. "Essential facility" 573
d. Customer and territorial restraints compared 574

1653. No Concern Without Threat to Market Competition Generally 577
- a. Introduction and *Schwinn* dictum 577
- b. No intrabrand effect: mere substitution of one dealer for another 578
- c. Intrabrand impact insufficient; need threat to market competition 580
- d. Monopoly manufacturer 585
- e. One sole outlet for multiple manufacturers 588
- f. Implications 593

1654. Detriments—Mainly Dealer Power—and Remedies 593
- a. Introduction and summary 593
- b. Other dangers minor 593
- c. Dealer power to exploit consumers 594
  - 1. Sole outlet for multiple manufacturers creates new monopoly 595
  - 2. Sole outlet for single monopoly manufacturer 596
- d. Dealer power to obtain unchecked sole outlet: control of needed distribution resources 597
- e. Dealer's exercise of power as legitimate or monopolization 598
- f. Remedies 600
  - 1. Requiring dealer to buy 600
  - 2. Requiring manufacturer to sell 601
    - (A) Necessity 601
    - (B) In favor of particular would-be dealer 601
  - 3. Damage remedies 602
- g. Prima facie unreasonableness 603
  - 1. Generally 603
  - 2. Interbrand competition: brand power; dealer concentration 604
  - 3. Intensity of restraint 605

1655. Justifications 606
- a. Introduction and summary 606
- b. Exclusivity enhances resource value 607
- c. Objectives other than new entry or great dealer risk 607

d. New entry: typical situations 608
e. Monopoly consistent with new entry 611
f. Appraising need and duration 612
1. Generally; proof burdens 612
2. Risk reallocation 612
3. Judging duration 613
4. Arbitrary time period and burden of persuasion 614
g. Distinguishing dealer control over distribution resources 615
1. Relevance and direct indicators 615
2. Indirect indicators—generally; unhelpful ones 616
3. Dealers collectively demand multiple unchecked sole outlets 616
4. Shifts among dealers 616
5. Selective markets 617
6. Multi-product sole outlet for one manufacturer 617
7. Multi-brand sole outlet 617

VOLUME IX

CHAPTER 17. Tying Arrangements 3
1700. Introduction I: Definitions, Concerns, and Statutory Coverage 4
a. The paradigm 4
b. Linguistic conventions for this Chapter 4
c. Unusual interdependence of issues 5
d. Fundamental concern: "leverage"; different elements 6
1. Foreclosure concentrating tied market 6
2. "Alien" intrusion and "unfair" advantage? 8
3. Buyer choice or oppression? 9
e. Relevant statutes 10
f. All transfers 10
g. Practical effect of foreclosing rivals 11

h. Two products 11
i. Tying "agreement" or "coercion" 11
j. Relation to other possible restraints 13
1. Vertical integration 13
2. Vertical mergers 17
3. Requirements contracts 17
4. Vertical restraints on intrabrand competition compared 18
1701. Introduction II: Capsule History: Patents, Power, Effects, Defenses, and Legal Process 18
a. Initial patent infringement decisions 19
b. "Leverage" seeking monopoly in tied product: the *Motion Picture* case 20
c. Development of tying doctrine: a quick survey 24
1. Expansion 24
2. Retraction? 26
d. The future? 27
e. Preview 29
1702. Introduction III: Black Letter Doctrine 30

17A. Anti- and Pro-Competitive Impact 32
1703. Effects and Motivations Summarized 32
a. Introduction and preview 32
b. Economic reasoning vs. defendant's explanation or intention 35
1. Respective roles 35
2. Exculpations not claimed in actual litigation or subjectively documented 36
c. Alternatives and their relevance 38
1. Counting for or against legality 38
2. Uncertain proof; inferences from defendant's choice 39
d. Threats to vitality of competition in tied and perhaps tying market 39
1. Creating new monopoly (or oligopoly) in tied market 40
2. More tacit coordination among pre-existing oligopolists 42
3. Preconditions: substantial concentration and foreclosure 43

e. Exploitation of pre-existing market power; social costs of monopoly increased? 44
1. Price discrimination 44
2. Limit input substitution 45
3. Evade government (or private) price ceilings 46
4. Relevance of price, with or without output effects 47
f. Additional possible anti-social functions 48
1. Evade price floors 48
2. Conceal true prices 49
3. Cheat upstream supplier 49
4. Obstruct copying 49
5. Block customer autonomy 49
6. "Foreclose" customer access to supplies 50
g. Major beneficial possibilities 50
1. Protect product quality 50
2. Lower costs or raise value 51
3. Increase price competition through indirect or selective price cuts 52
4. Aid entry 53
5. Reward for combination patent 53
h. Minor or doubtful benefits 53
1. Vague or general profit-efficiency claims 54
2. Obscure effects: price discrimination; input substitution 54
3. Non-antitrust domain: evading price floors 54
4. Unnecessary tying: eliminating subsequent monopoly toll; more complete price information 54
5. Non-market paternalism and other oddities 55
1704. Foreclosure Mechanism: Creating Monopoly or Oligopoly in Tied Market 55
a. Introduction and summary 55
b. Impact upon number of efficient rivals 56
1. From mere realignment to substantial foreclosure 56
2. Depriving rivals of needed patronage 57

3. Weakening rivals by transferring market fluctuations to them 58
c. Impact on concentration in tied market 59
1. Tying and tied monopoly 59
2. Tied monopoly without tying monopoly? 60
3. Tying monopoly and tied oligopoly 61
4. Tying and tied oligopoly 62
d. Effect vs. motivation 62
1705. Long-Run Entrenchment and Stagnation 63
a. Introduction and summary 63
b. Stagnation in newly monopolized tied market 65
c. Two-product monopoly impedes entry by forcing two-level entry 65
d. Oligopoly 66
e. Conditions for harmfully inhibiting entry 67
1. Non-competitive tying market 68
2. Substantial foreclosure 68
3. Two-product entry required 68
4. Two-product entry burdensome 69
f. Reinforcing power of tying product by weakening substitute 70
1. Substitute is tied product 70
2. Third product tied 71
3. Inferior substitute 72
1706. Price-Output Effects of New Monopoly or Oligopoly in Tied Market 72
a. Introduction and summary 72
b. Price-output and new monopoly 74
1. Single monopoly profit; fixed proportion case 74
2. Users of second product alone 75
3. Variable proportion tie (rather than second monopoly as such) can affect price-output and output 75
c. Price-output with tying monopoly and tied oligopoly 76
d. Prices-output and oligopoly in each market 76
e. Output of fewer product varieties 77

1707. Facilitating Coordination Among Pre-Existing Oligopolists in Tied Market 78
- a. Introduction and summary 78
- b. Prerequisites generally 79
- c. Narrowed arena for price competition 80
- d. Eliminate disruptive buyer 81
- e. "Competitive-condition" clause 82
  - 1. Buyer relatively indifferent to tie benefiting seller 82
  - 2. Expand sales without discounting 84
  - 3. Monitor and discourage discounting 84
  - 4. Tie unfair to other oligopolists or usefully disruptive? 86

1708. Buyer "Foreclosed" from Competing with Tied (or Tying) Buyer 87
- a. Generally 87
- b. Incentives 88
- c. Exclusive movie exhibition example 89
- d. Limited number of dealers 90

1709. Assessing Foreclosure, Market, and Concentration 92
- a. Introduction 92
- b. Undue concentration 95
  - 1. Importance 95
  - 2. Criteria 95
- c. Identifying relevant markets 96
  - 1. Often unnecessary; general guides 96
  - 2. Usual market: Rivals' selling opportunities 97
  - 3. Occasional market: Region of non-tied buyers 99
  - 4. Which is tying product? 100
  - 5. Tying market at time of agreement 101
- d. Measuring foreclosure 102
  - 1. All tying seller's tied sales 102
  - 2. Cumulating foreclosures: Adding other sellers' actual foreclosures 103
  - 3. Small foreclosure "incipiently" large 104
  - 4. "First step" concept implies further foreclosure 104
  - 5. Tying seller: Additional tying ahead 105

6. Prospective imitating foreclosures of other sellers 105
e. Factors mitigating foreclosure significance 106
1. Caveat: low concentration 106
2. New use 106
3. Duration 106
4. Tied market structure unchanged when tying seller merely buys and resells 107
5. Tying seller lacks economic interest in tied product 108
6. Tied customer is dealer rather than ultimate user; entry conditions 109
7. Buyer choice "voluntary" though constrained 109
8. Significance of a tying product to the foreclosure? 110
1710. Intensified Exploitation of Pre-existing Market Power as Innocent Explanation or as Detriment 111
a. As non-leverage explanation; summary 111
b. Precedent 113
c. Incremental exploitation as detriment 114
1. Administrability 115
2. Income distribution 115
3. Statutory focus on suppressed rivalry; incentives and legitimate rewards 116
4. Conclusion 117
1711. Exploitation of Supplier's Own Tying Product Power Through Price Discrimination 118
a. Introduction and summary 118
1. Relatively harmless non-leverage explanation of tying 118
2. Utility and prerequisites of price discrimination 119
3. Preview and summary 120
b. Intensity of use and risk of non-use 121
1. Usage determines value to customer 121
2. Sharing risk of non-use 121
3. Ties and alternative "metering" devices 122
4. Effects 124
(A) Perfect ("first-degree") discrimination 124

(B) Less perfect ("second-degree") price discrimination 125
c. Independent demand for different downstream uses ("third-degree" discrimination) 126
d. Package pricing when individual demand not identifiable 128
e. Lawful alternatives—relevance 129
1. Summary 129
2. Imply legitimacy? 129
3. Equal to tying? Implications 130
f. Conclusions 131
1. Condemn otherwise harmless restraint? 131
2. Save otherwise harmful restraint? 133
3. Save restraint condemned without proof of adverse effects? 133
g. Robinson-Patman Act not relevant 134
1712. Additional or Disguised Exploitation vs. Efficient Pricing or Proper Reward 136
a. Introduction and summary 136
b. Eliminate exploitative and inefficient successive monopolies 137
c. Limiting substitution of inefficient inputs 138
1. Summary 138
2. Mechanism 138
3. Efficient resource allocation 139
4. Effects on tied customers; alternatives; uncertainty 139
5. Conclusion 141
d. Evade government price ceiling 141
1. The mechanism 141
2. Assessment 142
e. Evade private price ceiling 144
f. Deceptively understate price 144
g. Reward from useful combination patent (as tying product) 146
1713. Supporting New Entry or Weak Firm 148
a. Introduction and summary 148
b. Into tying market 149
1. Relevance 149
2. Higher quality or revenue, lower costs 149
3. Economic necessity 150

c. Into non-competitive tied market 152
1. Issues 152
2. Pro-competitive illustration 152
3. Unfair anticompetitive "process"? 155
d. Application 156
1. Depends on prima facie illegality test 156
2. Share and duration 157
3. Tie's necessity 157
4. Post-entry performance 157
5. Pre-entry performance 158
6. Large foreclosure for very short period 158
7. Tying product monopolist enters "related" market 158
e. Permanent small-foreclosure tie supporting "weak" firm 160
1714. Temporary Promotion in Either Market 161
a. Introduction and summary 161
b. Discount promotes tied product 162
1. The mechanism 162
2. Possible superiority to advertising or general price cut 163
3. Pro-competitive when no substantial foreclosure or other proved detriment 165
4. If substantial foreclosure or other proved detriment 166
c. Tying product promoted. Which is which? 167
d. Duration 167
e. Predation as key concern, regardless of tying 169
1715. Indirect, Selective, or Disguised Price Cuts in Either Market 171
a. Introduction and summary 171
b. Evading regulated price floor on tying product 173
c. Evading private price floor on tying product: oligopoly and resale price maintenance 175
1. Mechanism and motive 175
2. Competitive appraisal 176
3. Identifying characteristics 178

d. Price competition in the tied market 179
1. Tie-in motive 179
2. Appraisal 180
e. Which product is truly discounted and is it, by definition, the tying product? 181
f. More of existing excess profit in tied market 183
1716. Protect Goodwill or Quality of Tying Product 185
a. Introduction and summary 185
1. Illustrations 185
2. The present inquiry; other topics connected 186
3. Preview 187
b. Legitimacy 188
c. Quality self-protecting 189
1. Buyer alone at risk 190
2. Seller also at risk 191
3. Intermediate buyer transferring malfunction risk to others 192
4. Pioneering vs. established products 192
d. Published specifications as an alternative 193
1. The attraction 193
2. Adequate articulation 195
3. Voluntary vs. compulsory compliance 197
4. Cost and effectiveness 198
e. Required use of approved providers 200
1. Utility 200
2. Adequacy and good faith implementation 202
3. Inspection fees 203
4. Access fee 205
5. Number of approvals 207
f. Trade secret dilemmas 207
1. The problem 207
2. Actual and continuing secret 208
3. Royalties 209
4. Conclusion: trade secrets protected 211
g. Tie-in to improve quality of tying (or tied) product 211
1717. Save Costs, Increase Utility, or Please Customers 212
a. Introduction and summary 212

b. The many forms of cost savings 214
1. Supplier savings 214
(A) Generally 214
(B) Scale economies 215
(C) Risk reduction 215
(D) Less restrictive alternatives 216
2. Customer convenience, preference, cost, and utility 216
c. Legitimacy of cost savings generally 218
1. Recognition of cost savings in finding or defending tie 218
2. Which costs? 219
3. Exception for enhanced revenue or guaranteed markets? 220
4. Proving savings 221
d. Customer choice as a less restrictive alternative 221
1. Explanation and appeal 221
2. Practicality 222
3. Package discount vs. amount of cost savings 223
(A) Discount exceeds savings 224
(B) Savings exceed discount 224
(C) Discount insufficient to generate savings 225
(D) Magnitudes uncertain 226
e. Average pricing 226
1. New films 226
2. Old films 228
3. Conclusion 230
f. Additional or elaborated illustrations 231
1. Bundled products or services in vertical integration 231
2. Turnkey franchise 233
3. Package patent or copyright license 236
4. Condominium with management or amenities contract 238
1718. Additional Functions or Effects 239
a. Introduction and summary 239
b. Greater profit or efficiency 241
c. Customer choice 242

d. Equalize customers? 244
e. Cheating upstream supplier 244
f. Limit exposure to tying product 245
g. True prices more transparent 247
h. Packaging without incremental value 249
i. Value-increasing combination 249
j. Charitable paternalism 250
k. Limited purpose separate sale of "tying" product 252

17B. Effects Required for Illegality 253
1719. Overview; One Test Under Several Statutes 253
a. Introduction and preview 253
b. Single effects test under Sherman and Clayton Acts 254
c. Standard under Federal Trade Commission Act 257

17B-1. Effects Required by So-Called Rule of Per Se Illegality 257
1720. The Per Se Rule 257
a. Meaning of this unusual per se rule 258
b. Derivation 259
1. Patent infringement and misuse 259
2. *United Shoe* and *IBM* cases 260
3. *Salt* and *Northern Pacific* cases especially 263
4. *Fortner* and *Jefferson Parish* cases 266
c. Summary: the rule and its rationale 267
1721. Defining Not Insubstantial Volume of Tied Commerce 268
a. Introduction and preview 268
b. Meaning and measurement 268
1. Dollar coverage, not share of defined market 268
2. Relevance to per se concept and antitrust policy 270
3. Adjust for inflation, multi-year tying, intrastate sales, or value added? 271
4. Required volume 273
c. Multiple tied purchasers 275
1. Required 276

2. Counted if actually tied 279
3. Other tying sellers 280
d. Non-foreclosing tied sales 280
1. Zero relevant foreclosure 280
2. Explicit all-purchase tie 281
3. Partial ties 282
(A) The principle 283
(B) Tie proved by coerced purchase or package 283
(C) Incremental purchases allegedly coerced 284

17B-2. *Qualifications When No Potential Foreclosure or Tied Market Power for Tying Seller* 285
1722. "Threshold" to the Per Se Rule: Potential "Anticompetitive Effects" or "Power" in Tied-Product Market 285
a. Introduction and summary 285
b. *Northern Pacific* and *Jefferson Parish* 288
c. Qualitative vs. quantitative effects in lower courts 291
d. "Market power" in market for tied product 294
e. Proof burdens 295
1723. Zero Foreclosure: No Rival Sellers Exist 296
a. The concept 296
b. Illustrative rulings 297
c. Caveat I: What universe of rivals? What market? 302
d. Caveat II: Why no rivals—because of tie? 306
e. Other sellers but of inferior quality 307
1724. Zero Foreclosure: Rivals Not Otherwise Patronized 308
a. Introduction and summary 308
b. Completely unwanted product 309
c. Rival brand would not have been purchased 311

d. Unfinanced or new user 312
1. Financing needed; credit as tying product 312
2. New user 315
1725. Intrinsically Minor, or Even Zero, Foreclosures, Especially of Dealers 316
a. Introduction and summary 316
b. Dealer tie-ins generally 317
c. Full-line force: limited displacement of rivals; procompetitive 319
d. Pro-competitive full-line force vs. dealer ties generally 323
e. Allocations of one item based on sales of another 325
f. Sales quota 327
g. Rewards based on sales 328
h. Temporary promotion 328
i. Fractional requirement 329
j. "Irrelevant" foreclosures that are also small 330
1726. No Relevant Foreclosure: No Financial Interest in Suppliers of Tied Product 330
a. Introduction and summary 330
b. Statutory language 333
c. Precedents; illustrations 334
d. Zero financial interest and tying policy 336
1. Power in tied market 336
2. Bestowing power on strangers 337
(A) General rule 337
(B) Tied product is substitute for tying product 338
(C) Insufficiently complementary products; inadvertence 338
(D) Categorical rules vs. no-interest ties 339
(E) Conclusion 339
3. Price discrimination and other tied-product revenue attributable to power over tying product 340
4. Redeeming virtues 341

e. Approvals, disapprovals, and specifications 342
1. Nearly universal approvals 342
2. Standards and widespread approvals 344
3. Supplier specifically disapproved 344
4. Fewer approvals 346
f. Rule of reason if actual detriments to competition 347
1727. Relevant Foreclosure Tests: Arguable Financial Interests 348
a. Introduction and summary 348
b. Present in tied market though customers free to buy from unrelated firms 349
1. Not typically harmful 349
2. Charade potential 352
c. Debt, partial equity, or "family" interest in tied sales 352
d. Fee from sellers of tied product 354
1. Fee for inspection or license vs. access 354
2. Access fee and tied market's structure-performance 356
(A) Potential impact 356
(B) Policy 356
3. Access fee and rechanneled revenues 358
(A) Potential impact 358
(B) Policy 359
4. Conclusion 360
e. Reselling goods purchased from others 361
f. Exiting from tied market 362
g. General interest, disloyal employee, or fee for service in tied market 364

17B-3. Rule of Reason Applications and Reforms 367
1728. Residual Reasonability Test for Non-Per-Se Ties 368
a. Introduction and summary 368
b. Reasonability test as supplements per se rule 368
c. Justified tie 370
d. No power over tied product 371

e. Insufficient effects for per se illegality 372
f. Rule of reason applications 373
1729. Proving Unreasonable Effects 375
a. Introduction and summary 375
b. Obstruct entry into tying market 379
c. Weaken partial substitute for tying product 381
d. Create monopoly in tied market 382
e. Concentrate tied market 384
1. Concentration threshold 384
2. Foreclosure threshold 386
3. If minimum efficient scale large 391
4. If no non-tied purchasers 392
f. Facilitate oligopolistic coordination 393
1. Preliminary conditions 393
2. Eliminating disruptive buyer 393
3. More effective monitoring 395
g. Implementation: market definition 396
h. Implementation: foreclosure measurement guides 398
i. Incremental social cost and other non-foreclosure effects 401
1. Incremental exploitation, price discrimination, and input substitution 402
2. Disguise prices, evade ceilings or floors, cheat suppliers, deceive customers, or obstruct copying 404
3. Buyer choice and conclusion 406
1730. Per Se Rule Critique; Recommended Reform 406
a. Per se premises unsatisfied 407
b. Social impact of tying's "per se" rule 409
c. Stare decisis 411
d. Conclusion 413

Table of Cases for Volumes I-IX

References are to paragraph numbers.

A-A-A Elec. Co., United States v., 338b

AAA Liquors v. Joseph E. Seagram & Sons, 1451c2, 1639h

A-Abart Elec. Supply v. Emerson Elec. Co., 323d

AAMCO Automatic Transmissions v. Taylor, 1721b3-b4

A. A. Poultry Farms v. Rose Acre Farms, 550b

Aaron E. Levine & Co. v. Calkraft Paper Co., 1467a-b, 1469b, d

Abadir & Co. v. First Miss. Corp., 1605b, 1605d1

Abbott Labs. v. Brennan, 523

Abbott Labs. v. Gardner, 332b

ABC Great States v. Globe Ticket Co., 235a

Abercrombie v. Lum's, 356d

Abex Corp. v. FTC, 305e, 909c

AB Iro v. Otex, 1405

ABMI case, see American Bldg. Maintenance Inds., United States v.

Abney v. United States, 332a

Abraham Constr. Corp. v. Texas Indus., 1459c2

Abrams v. Interco, 356d, 1623c

Abrams v. International Co., 364d

A.B.T. Sightseeing Tours v. Gray Lines N.Y. Tours Corp., 233e

Ace Beer Distribs. v. Kohn, 317e, 1653b

Ackerman-Chillingworth, Div. of Marsh & McLennan v. Pacific Elec. Contractors Assn., 229e, 323d

Acme Precision Prods. v. American Alloys Corp., 832

A. Copeland Enters. v. Guste, 381b

Acqua Flame v. Imperial Fountains, 1721b3-b4

Action Towing & Rental v. U-Haul Intl., 1473d2, f, 1644a

Adams v. Burke, 1621

Adams v. Pan Am. World Airways, 364d, 377d2

Adams Dairy Co. v. St. Louis Dairy Co., 229e

Adams, Ray and Rosenberg v. William Morris Agency, 229b

Adams Tire Co. v. Dunlop Tire & Rubber Corp., 1452b, 1623f2

Addrisi v. Equitable Life Ins. Soc., 210
Addyston Pipe & Steel Co. v. United States, 232c, 604, 703b, 736e, 1501, 1509, 1510a, c
Addyston Pipe & Steel Co., United States v., 302
A.D.M. Corp. v. Sigma Instruments, 381b
Admiral Theatre Corp. v. Douglas Theatre Co., 311a2, 1504
Adolph Coors Co. v. A&S Wholesalers, 1645d
Adolph Coors Co. v. FTC, 1642c
A & D Supermarkets v. United Food and Commercial Workers, 311a1
Advance Business Machines & Supply Co. v. SCM Corp., 835c
Advertising Checking Bureau, 1626b
Aeolian Co. v. Harry H. Juelg Co., 1701a
Affiliated Capital Corp. v. City of Houston, 363a
Afran Transp. Co. v. National Maritime Union, 229e
Agrashell v. Hammons Prods. Co., 832, 835
A. G. Rogers Co. v. Merck & Co., 1455b
A. G. Spalding & Bros. v. FTC, 909c
A. H. Cox & Co. v. Star Mach. Co., 1456f, 1605c, 1652b, 1653c
Air-Fix Corp. v. Aurora Plastics Corp., 345
Air Freight Haulage Co. v. Ryd-Air, 225c
Air Freight Haulage of Puerto Rico v. American Airlines, 225c
Air Passenger Computer Reservation Sys., 533c
A. I. Root Co. v. Computer/Dynamics, 383b
Airweld v. Airco, 1719b
Akron Presform Mold Co. v. McNeil Corp., 338d
Aladdin Oil Co. v. Texaco, 1452c4, 1627e5, 1653b
Alaska v. Standard Oil Co. (Cal.), 371c, e
Alberta Gas Chems., Ltd. v. E. I. du Pont de Nemours & Co., 365b5, 373b, 375e
Albert Levine Assoc. v. Bertoni & Cotti, 235
Albert Pick-Barth v. Mitchell Woodbury Corp., 828b
Albrecht v. Herald Co. (390 U.S. 145), 362c, 365c3, 725c, 734a, e, 1130b, 1403, 1408d, 1449b, c2, f, g, 1450, b, c2, 1451, d, f, 1452b, 1473a, 1474b, 1609a-d, 1630d, 1634, 1635, 1636f1-f2, g, 1637c-g, 1638a, c, 1639, 1640a, b3, d, 1642c
Albrecht v. Herald Co. (452 F.2d 124), 365b4
Albrecht v. Herald Co. (321 F. Supp. 99), 365c3
Alcoa case, see Aluminum Co., United States v. (148 F.2d 416)
Alders v. AFA Corp., 703b
Alexander v. National Farmers' Organization, 356d
Alfred Bell & Co. v. Catalda Fine Arts, 236f

Alfred Dunhill of London v. Cuba, 239b
Al George v. Envirotech Corp., 338b
Allen v. McCurry, 336f
Allen Bradley Co. v. Local 3, IBEW, 229e
Allen-Myland v. IBM, 1721b3
Allied Air Freight v. Pan Am, World Airways, 226d, 227a
Allied Chem. Corp., United States v., 348c
Allis-Chalmers Mfg. Co. v. White Consol. Indus., 347, 536, 1020, 1109d2, 1121a, c2, c4, 1130b, 1131c3, e, 1133c
Alloy Intl. Co. v. Hoover-NSK Bearing Co., 1456d4, 1457d, 1604e2
Allstate Ins. Co. v. Lanier, 213a
Almeda Mall v. Houston Lighting & Power Co., 373e1, 572c
Aloha Airlines v. Hawaiian Airlines, 224f, 226d, 227a
Alpert's Newspaper Delivery v. New York Times Co., 334e
Alpha Distrib. Co. v. Jack Daniels Distillery, 1468, 1469d
Alphin v. Henson (552 F.2d 1033), 355d
Alphin v. Henson (538 F.2d 85), 355d
Alpine Pharmacy v. Chas. Pfizer & Co., 355d
Alstate Constr. Co. v. Durkin, 232a
Aluminum Co. v. Sperry Prods., 391
Aluminum Co. v. United States, 334b3
Aluminum Co., United States v. (377 U.S. 271), 530f, 561a, 562b
Aluminum Co., United States v. (148 F.2d 416), 104, 236c-f, 311b, 333f, 506a, 520c, 521, 522b, 532a, 535e, 555c, 573a, 608, 611b, 613, 615, 621a, 622a, 623b, 626a, 727c3, 729c, h, 731a, 804, 812, 820, 821, 829e, 842a, 854b1, 1020, 1205e3, f, 1710c3
Aluminum Co., United States v. (233 F. Supp. 718), 1135a, 1136b2, 1137
Aluminum Co., United States v. (91 F. Supp. 333), 236c, 345, 621c5, 727a, 1109b
Aluminum Co., United States v. (20 F. Supp. 608), 608i
Aluminum Co., United States v. (19 F. Supp. 374), 608
Aluminum Co., United States v. (41 F.R.D. 342), 348e
Alvord-Polk v. F. Schumacher & Co., 322f
ALW v. United Air Lines, 832
Alyeska Pipeline Serv. Co. v. Wilderness Society, 355d
Amajac v. Northlake Mall, 1609a
Amarel v. Connel, 371g
Amax, United States v., 909c, 934b, c, 937, 1203c, 1404
Ambook Enters. v. Time, 1408f, 1414
AM/COMM Sys. v. AT&T, 356d
Americana Indus. v. Wometco de Puerto Rico, 323a
American Airlines, United States v. (743 F.2d 1114), 1404

American Airlines, United States v. (570 F. Supp. 654), 1407f
American Banana Co. v. United Fruit Co., 236b, c, 239b, b1
American Bldg. Maintenance Ind., United States v., 233a, b, e
American Brake Shoe Co., 917
American Can Co., United States v. (230 F. 859), 421c, 422d2, 605, 606
American Can Co., United States v. (87 F. Supp. 18), 421f, 732c5
American Chinchilla Corp., 305d
American Crystal Sugar Co. v. Mandeville Island Farms, 365b1
American Crystal Sugar Co. v. Cuban-American Sugar Co., 1203b, c, 1204c
American Cyanamid v. FTC, 707c
American Cyanamid Co., United States v., 348e, 1466a
American Family Life Assurance Co. v. Planned Marketing Associates, 210
American Football League v. National Football League, 821
American General Ins. Co., 909c
American Home Prods. Corp. v. FTC, 305f
American Honda Motor Co., United States v., 334b5
American Hosp. Supply Corp. v. Hospital Prods., Ltd., 347
American Mail Line Ltd. v. Federal Maritime Commn., 223b
American Medical Assn. v. United States, 216b, 229c
American Medicorp v. Humana, 909c
American Mfrs. Mut. Ins. Co. v. American Broadcasting-Paramount Theatres, 1441h1, 1701c, 1730a
American Motor Inns v. Holiday Inn, 1456f, 1605c, d5
American News Co. v. FTC, 233d
American Oil Co. v. McMullin, 1440a, 1473d2, f, 1642c
American Oil Co., United States v., 822a, 839
American Safety Equip. Corp. v. J. P. Maguire & Co., 324b
American Sea Green Slate Co. v. O'Halloran, 365b4
American Smelting & Ref. Co. v. Pennzoil United, 555c, 1121b4, c4
American Smelting and Ref. Co., United States v., 320b, 1507c
American Socy. of Mechanical Engrs. v. Hydrolevel, 1471d2, 1472, 1477
American Socy. of Mechanical Engrs., United States v., 348g
American Structures v. Fidelity & Deposit Co., 1412c
American Technical Indus., United States v., 909c, 926b, 929
American Tel. & Tel. Co., see AT&T
American Tobacco case, see American Tobacco Co. v. United States (328 U.S. 781)

American Tobacco Co. v. United States (328 U.S. 781), 333f, 609, 626a, 731d, 734e, 831, 841a, 964b, 1433b, 1434d1, 1435i, 1446b
American Tobacco Co. v. United States (221 U.S. 106), 603c, 604, 626a, 701a, 711a, 727b1, 727e, 738k, 902a
American Tobacco Co., United States v., 1720b2
Americap v. ADJ Co., 1722c
America's Best Cinema Corp. v. Fort Wayne Newspapers, 736a
America West Airlines v. Burnley, 360a
Amerifirst Properties v. FDIC, 383a
Amerinet v. Xerox Corp., 363a, d
Amey v. Gulf Abstract & Tile, 338b, 360d, e1, 370, 1721b4, c1, 1722c, 1726c
Amplex v. Outboard Marine Corp., 1460f
Amtrol v. Vent-Rite Valve Corp., 374
Anaconda Co. v. Crane Co., 1204b, c
Anago v. Tecnol Med. Prods., 381b
Anaya v. Las Cruces Sun News, 1456f
Anderson Foreign Motors v. New England Toyota Distrib., 1701c, 1716d2, 1717f1, 1718d, 1730a
Anderson-Friberg v. Justin R. Clary & Son, 229e
Anheuser-Busch, FTC v., 233c, 305e, 720c
Ansell v. Schmid Labs., 561b
Ansul Co. v. Uniroyal, 338c
Anthracite cases, see Reading Co., United States v.; and Lehigh Valley R. Co., United States v.
Antibiotic Antitrust Actions, 356d
A&P case, see Great Atl. and Pac. Tea Co. v. Cotrell
Apex Hosiery Co. v. Leader, 229b, 232d, 828b
Apollo Air Passenger Computer Reservation Sys., 552a
Appalachian Coals v. United States, 104, 105, 311b, 842a, 1501, 1719b, 1730c
Apperson v. Fleet Carrier Corp., 37d4
Archer-Daniels-Midland Co., United States v., 562b
Arenson v. Board of Trade, 355d
Argus v. Eastman Kodak Co. (801 F.2d 38), 363d
Argus v. Eastman Kodak Co. (552 F. Supp. 589), 336d, 338f
Arizona v. Maricopa County Medical Socy., 1510b-c
Arizona v. Shamrock Foods Co., 371h, 1459b1
Arizona Dairy Prods. Litig., 339a, 372
Ark Dental Supply Co. v. Cavitron Corp., 1456f, 1467b, 1469d, 1653b
Armco Steel Corp. v. North Dakota, 337a2, 371e
Armco Steel Corp. v. United Mine Workers, 229b
Arnett v. Gerber Scientific, 381b

Arnold Pontiac GM v. Budd Baer, 1648d3
Arnold Pontiac-GMC v. General Motors Corp., 1648d3
Arnold, Schwinn & Co., United States v. (388 U.S. 365), 320b, 842a, 1438, 1448e1-e2, 1473b, e1, f, 1505, 1609a, c, 1610a, 1620c2, 1637d, 1642b-c, 1643, 1647e, 1652d, 1653a
Arnold, Schwinn & Co., United States v. (291 F. Supp. 564), 1642c
Arnold, Schwinn & Co., United States v. (237 F. Supp. 323), 1642b
Arnott v. American Oil Co., 1451c1
Arrow-Hart & Hegeman Elec. Co. v. FTC, 902, 1202a
Arthur Murray v. Reserve Plan, 1727c
Arthur S. Langenderfer v. S. E. Johnson Co. (917 F.2d 1413), 532b
Arthur S. Langenderfer v. S. E. Johnson Co. (729 F.2d 1050), 346b
ASCAP, United States v., 348c
A. Schrader's Son, United States v., 1623d
Ash v. IBM, 378d-e
Asheville Tobacco Bd. of Trade v. FTC, 213a, b, 218a
Ash Grove Cement Co., 1020, 1021
Ash Grove Cement Co. v. FTC, 1205e2
Ashley Meadows Farm v. American Horse Show Assn., 1471e1-e2
Aspen Highlands Skiing Corp. v. Aspen Skiing Co., 533g
Aspen Skiing Co. v. Aspen Highlands Skiing Corp., 311b, 320b
Aspen Title & Escrow v. Jeld-Wen, 1721b
Assam Drug Co. v. Miller Brewing Co., 1645b-c
Associated Beverages Co. v. P. Ballantine & Sons, 1460f
Associated Gen. Contractors v. California State Council of Carpenters, 323c, 360c2-c5, d, e1, f, 364d-e, 365a, 375d, 377a, 379a
Associated Gen. Contractors v. Otter Tail Power Co., 379b
Associated Indus. v. Ickes, 223c
Associated Milk Dealers v. Milk Drivers Local 753, 229e
Associated Milk Producers, United States v., 228c, 348e
Associated Press v. Taft-Ingalls Corp., 391
Associated Press v. United States, 703c, 729g, 736d, 1477, 1478b3-b4, 1506, 1508b
Associated Press, United States v., 736d
Associated Radio Serv. Co. v. Page Airways, 535d
Association of Data Processing Serv. Orgs. v. Camp, 362a
Association of Independent T.V. Stations v. College Football Assn., 563e
Atari Games Corp. v. Nintendo of Am., 347
Atlantic City Elec. Co. v. GE, 338d

Atlantic Co. v. Citizen Ice & Cold Storage Co., 233c
Atlantic Heel Co. v. Allied Heel Co., 828b
Atlantic Ref. Co. v. FTC, 305e, 1134c, 1473d2, 1727d2-d3, e
Atlantic Richfield Co. v. Malco Petroleum, 391
Atlantic Richfield Co. v. USA Petroleum Co., 360e1, 362c, 373f1, 382b, d
Atlantic Richfield Co., FTC v., 112b3, 1123d, 1124c
Atlantic Richfield Co., United States v., 331b, 536, 909c, 1121b4, 1123a
Atlas Building Prods. Co. v. Diamond Block & Gravel Co., 233c, 711a
AT&T, United States v. (552 F. Supp. 131), 345
AT&T, United States v. (524 F. Supp. 1336), 336e
AT&T, United States v. (427 F. Supp. 57), 224d, 346b3
AT&T Co., United States v., 224d
AT&T "Foreign Attachment" Tariff Revisions, In the Matter of, 214b4
Austin v. Blue Cross & Blue Shield, 360d
Austin v. House of Vision, 1474c
Automated Bldg. Components v. Trueline Truss Co., 1202f4
Automatic Radio Mfg. Co. v. Ford Motor Co., 1701c, 1730a
Automobile Mfrs. Assn., United States v., 348g
Avnet, 909c, 938, 1205d1
Axis v. Micafil, 363b, 373e1, 381a
Azalea Drive-In Theatre v. Hanft, 336a
Azzarelli Constr. Co., United States v., 312c

Babcock & Wilcox Co. v. United Technologies Corp., 381b, 1020
Bacon v. Texaco Co., 233b
Baer v. Esprit-de-Corp., 1456c, 1623f2
Bahnmiller v. Derwinski, 379b
Bailey v. Glover, 338d
Bailey's Bakery v. Continental Baking Co., 821
Baker v. F. & F. Inv., 338b
Baker Hughes, United States v., 420b, 538b
Bakers Franchise Corp. v. FTC, 721b
Baldwin v. GAF Seelig, 220b, d
Baldwin v. Loew's, 338b
Baldwin Hills Bldg. Materials Co. v. Fibreboard Paper Prods. Corp., 233b, c
Bale v. Glasgow Tobacco Bd. of Trade, 214d
Balfour, L. G., Co. v. FTC, 305e, 731e
Ball v. Paramount Pictures, 1415d, 1425c
Ballard v. Blue Shield of Southern West Virginia, 210, 232e
Ballard's Serv. Ctr. v. Transue, 323e
Ball Memorial Hosp. v. Mutual Hosp. Ins., 420a, 421e
Balmoral Cinema v. Allied Artists Pictures, 375b, 574

Baltimore Luggage Co. v. Samsonite Corp., 336g
Banco Naçional de Cuba v. Sabbatino, 239b
Barber & Ross Co. v. Lifetime Doors, 383b
Bargain Car Wash v. Standard Oil Co. (Ind.), 233b
Barnosky Oils v. Union Oil Co., 338b, 1460f
Barr Labs. v. Abbott Labs., 324a, 564
Barry v. St. Paul Fire & Marine Ins. Co., 210
Barry Wright Corp. v. ITT Grinnell Corp., 421f
Bartlett v. United States, 909c, 1121b4
Bartleys Town and Country Shops v. Dillingham Corp., 1639a
Bascom Launder Corp. v. Telecoin Corp., 828e, 1653d
Basle Theatres v. Warner Bros. Pictures Distrib. Corp., 839, 1421b3
Bass Bros. Enters., FTC v., 538a
Bateman Eichler, Hill Richards v. Berner, 390c
Bates v. State Bar of Arizona, 213a, 214a, b4, e, 215b, 219b
Battle v. Liberty Natl. Life Ins. Co., 1467b
Battle v. Lubrizol Corp., 1456b-c, 1457d
Battle v. Watson, 1456b-c, 1457d
Bauer & Cie v. O'Donnell, 333f, 1606b, 1621
Baughman v. Cooper-Jarrett, 1418, c, 1424c
Bausch & Lomb Optical Co., United States v., 345, 1448, d, 1642
Baxley-deLamar Monuments v. American Cemetery Assn. (938 F.2d 846), 322j, 534a1, 550b
Baxley-deLamar Monuments v. American Cemetery Assn. (843 F.2d 1154), 532b
Bay Guardian Co. v. Chronicle Publishing Co., 208, 346b
B. B. Chem. Co. v. Ellis, 707b, 709
B & B Oil & Chem. Co. v. Franklin Oil Corp., 828b
B.C. Recreational Indus. v. First Natl. Bank of Boston, 1722c, 1723b, 1726c
Beach v. Viking Sewing Mach. Co., 1624d3, 1652b
Beacon Theatres v. Westover, 321a, 322c
Beard v. Parkview Hosp., 1726c
Beatrice Foods, United States v. (493 F.2d 1259), 305e
Beatrice Foods, United States v. (351 F. Supp. 969), 305e
Beatrice Foods Co., 909b, 1020, 1109a, 1119b, d, f2, 1121b4, 1122b, 1123a, 1124b3
Beatrice Foods Co. v. United States, 1420b, 1421d, 1425d4
Beatrice Foods Co., FTC v., 909b
Beaute Craft Supply Co. v. Revlon, 347
Becker v. Safelite Glass Corp., 832
Beckman v. Walter Kidde & Co., 1467b, h, 1468, 1469c

Beckman Instruments v. Chemtronics, 707h1, 707i2, 835c
Becton, Dickinson & Co. v. Sherwood Medical Indus., 707h1
Beech Cinema v. Twentieth Century-Fox Film Corp., 1417f, 1651f, 1653c
Beech-Nut Packing Co., FTC v., 1447b2, 1448, c, 1461
Beef Indus. Antitrust Litig., 371e, f, 372, 375b, 574, 1408c, 1459b1
Beefy Trail v. Beefy King Intl., 1717f2
Belcher Oil Co. v. Florida Fuels, 373c, 375b, e
Belfiore v. New York Times Co., 334e, 1623c
Belk-Avery v. Henry I. Siegel Co., 1455b, 1623c
Bell v. Cherokee Aviation Corp., 1721b3-b4
Bell v. Dow Chem. Co., 338b, 360e1, 375f
Belliston v. Texaco, 233c
Bement v. National Harrow Co., 1620b
Bendix Corp., 1109a, b, d2, 1124a, d1
Bendix Corp. v. Balax, 333a, 835c
Bendix Home Appliances, United States v., 334d, 348d
Bennett v. Behring Corp., 1723b
Bensinger Co., United States v., 232c
Benson & Ford v. Wanda Petroleum Co., 334e
Bergen Drug Co. v. Parke, Davis & Co., 345
Berger v. Columbia Broadcasting Sys., 1467g
Bergjans Farm Dairy Co. v. Sanitary Milk Producers, 228c, 822a
Berkey Photo v. Eastman Kodak Co., 336d, 363a, d, 1432e, 1506, 1713c3
Berkley, United States v., 305e
Berkson v. Del Monte Corp., 338d
Berman v. River Bay Corp., 539b
Bernstein v. Universal Pictures, 229c, 321e
Besser Mfg. Co., United States v., 345
Bessette, Commonwealth of Massachusetts v., 1474b
Betaseed v. U and I, 1716d4
Bethlehem Steel Corp. v. Fischbach & Moore, 338d
Bethlehem Steel Corp., United States v., 552c3, 561b, 909c, 942, 1020, 1021, 1022b, 1147a
B. F. Goodrich Co. (110 F.T.C. 207), 561b
B. F. Goodrich Co. (5 Trade Reg. Rep. ¶22,519), 420c
Bhan v. NME Hosps., 375c
Big Apple BMW v. BMW of North Am., 322f
Bigelow v. RKO Radio Pictures, 365a, b2, 626c
Bigelow v. Unilever, N.V., 362b, 373d4
Bigelow v. Virginia, 212a
Billy Baxter v. Coca-Cola Co., 362a, 364g, 373f4, 376a
Binderup v. Pathe Exchange, 233b
Bituminous Concrete Assn., United States v., 348c
Bitz, United States v., 828e

Black & Decker Mfg. Co., United States v., 926b, 929c, 1109a, 1119b, f1, 1121c4, 1125c, 1204c
Black Gold v. Rockwool Indus., 1440a, 1446d4, 1451e, 1452c4, 1460d3, 1627e5
Blackley v. Farmers Ins. Group, 210
Blackwelder Furniture Co. v. Seilig Mfg. Co., 347
Blaine v. Meineke Discount Shop, 563d
Blankenship v. Hearst Corp., 316d, 1639h
Blankenship v. Herzfeld, 1456d3, 1467h, 1604g2
Blanton v. Mobil Oil Corp., 363a
Bliss v. Brooklyn, 736d
Bliss & Laughlin, United States v., 555c
Blonder-Tongue Laboratories v. University of Illinois Found., 336b
Blue Bell, United States v., 909c, 926b
Blue Chip Stamp Co., United States v., 348d-e
Blue Cross & Blue Shield (Mich.) v. Michigan Assn. Psychotherapy Clinics, 1622b
Bluefields S.S. Co. v. United Fruit Co., 390a
Blue Shield of Va. v. McCready, 360d, e1, 364, d-f, 370
BMI case, see Broadcast Music v. CBS
BNS, United States v., 381b
Board of Regents of the Univ. of Okla. v. NCAA, 563e
Bobbs-Merrill Co. v. Straus, 1621
Bob Maxfield, Inc. v. American Motors Co., 1722c, 1725c-d
Boccardo v. Safeway Stores, 335b
BOC Intl. Ltd. v. FTC, 1119b, 1120f, 1121b5, 1122b, 1123a
Boddicker v. Arizona State Dental Assn. (680), 1723b, 1726c
Boddicker v. Arizona State Dental Assn. (549 F.2d 626, 630), 1452c4
Bodie-Rickett & Assoc. v. Mars, 377d3
Bodine Produce v. United Farm Workers Org. Comm., 229b, e
Bogosian v. Gulf Oil Corp. (561 F.2d 434), 356d, 1403, 1408c, 1412e, g, 1415a, 1433a 1434c, c2
Bogosian v. Gulf Oil Corp. (337 F. Supp. 1234), 323b
Bogus v. American Speech & Hearing Assn., 1701c, 1730a
Boise Cascade Corp. v. FTC, 384, 1436c, f1
Boise Cascade Intl. v. Northern Minn. Pulpwood Producers Assn., 228b
Bolt v. Halifan Hosp. Med. Ctr., 322g
Bolick-Gillman Co. v. Continental Baking Co., 1639h
Bolton Broadcasting v. Meredith Corp., 1473d2, 1653c
Bond Crown & Cork Co. v. FTC, 1425e
BonJorno v. Kaiser Aluminum & Chem. Corp., 1464e

Borden (Realemon), 520a2
Borden v. FTC, 305d
Borden Co., United States v. 223b-d, 224a, f, 334d, 1425d4
Borger v. Yamaha Intl. Corp., 1456f, 1459c3, 1645b
Borg-Warner Corp., 305c
Borman's v. Great Scott Super Markets, 1653c
Boro Hall Corp. v. General Motors Corp., 1642c
Borough of Ellwood City v. Pennsylvania Power Co., 336g
Boshes v. General Motors Corp., 356d, 371c
Bostick Oil Co. v. Michelin Tire Corp., 1456b-c, e, 1457c4, 1457d, 1611f, 1622c
Boston Professional Hockey Assn. v. Cheevers, 229d
Bourns v. Allen Bradley Co., 333a
Bowen v. New York News, 363c, 1652d, 1653b, c
Bowl America v. Fair Lanes, 832
Bowles v. Inland Empire Dairy Assn., 228b
Bowlus v. Alexander & Alexander Servs., 335b
Bowman v. National Football League, 377c
Boyertown Burial Casket Co. v. Walco Natl. Corp., 909c
Boys Market v. Retail Clerks Local 770, 229b
Bracken's Shopping Center v. Ruwe, 738j
Bradley v. Public Utilities Commn., 220a
Brager & Co. v. Leumi Sec. Corp., 1467a-b, e1
Branch v. FTC, 234a
Brandeis Mach. & Supply Corp. v. Barber-Greene Co., 347
Braun v. Berenson, 338b
Bray v. Safeway Stores, 334g, 964b, 1408c, 1417d
Brayman v. Bassett Furniture Indus., 1469a
Breen Air Freight, Ltd. v. Air Cargo, 225c
Brett v. First Fed. Savings & Loan Assn., 232e
Brian Clewer v. Pan Am. World Airways, 375d, 377d2
Briggs Mfg. Co. v. Crane Co., 1204c
Bright v. Bechtel Petroleum, 335b
Bright v. Moss Ambulance Serv., 572d
Brillhart v. Mutual Medical Ins., 1622b
Bristol Bay Alaska Salmon Fishery Antitrust Litigation, 1459b2
Bristol Myers v. FTC, 305d
British Nylon Spinners, Ltd. v. Imperial Chem. Indus., Ltd., 238
British Oxygen Co., 1121c4, 1122b, 1123a
British Oxygen Co., FTC v., 305e, 347, 1119b, f1, 1120f, 1121b5, c2
Broadcasters v. Morristown Broadcasting Corp., 374
Broadcast Music v. CBS, 312c, 320b, 1477, 1478b1, 1503b, 1504, 1510c, 1717f3, 1730a
Broadcast Music v. Moor-Law, 1717f3

Broadway Delivery Corp. v. United Parcel Serv., 532b
Broadway-Hale Stores, 1121b2, 1121c5
Broch, Henry, & Co., FTC v., 305e
Brodrick Copygraph Co. v. Roper, 1701a
Brooke Group v. Brown & Williamson Tobacco Corp., 304c, 311a2, 322c-d, j, 334b2, 373d2, 384, 420b
Brosious v. Pepsi Co., 233b
Brotherhood of R.R. Trainmen v. Chicago River & Ind. R. Co., 229b
Brothers v. Monsanto Co., 1642c
Broussard v. Socony-Mobil Oil Co., 1451c1
Brown v. Bates, 218b
Brown v. Cameron-Brown Co., 1417b
Brown v. Federated Dept. Stores, 335b
Brown v. Our Lady of Lourdes Medical Ctr., 534a1, 550b
Brown v. Parker, see Parker v. Brown
Brown v. Parker-Hannifin Corp., 322j
Brown, United States v., 311a1, 312c
Brown Shoe Co. v. United States, 104, 530d-e, 531b, 533b-c, f, 563c, e, 902c, 903, 904, 941b, 1002, 1008b, 1009e, 1020, 1021, 1022a, 1101, 1103c, 1136c, 1146a, 1609e, 1713c2
Brown Shoe Co., FTC v., 305c, f, 307a-b, 1145b, c, 1301b
Brown Shoe Co., United States v., 903, 911c, 914, 934a
Broyer v. B. F. Goodrich Co., 377a
Bruce Drug v. Hollister, 1456d3
Brunswick-Balke-Collender Co., United States v., 348c, g
Brunswick Corp. v. Pueblo Bowl-O-Mat (429 U.S. 477), 360a, e2, 362a-b, 364f, 365a, 375c, 1135a, 1136b1, 1459c3, 1609e, 1623f6, 1640a, c, d1-2
Brunswick Corp. v. Pueblo Bowl-O-Mat (523 F.2d 268), 362a-b
Brunswick Corp. v. Riegel Textile Corp., 338e, 373e1
Buckley v. Valeo, 219b
Budd Co., 561a, 1119b, f1, 1124c, 1125d
Budd Co., In re, 1105e
Buffalo Broadcasting Co. v. ASCAP, 1477, 1507b
Buffalo Courier-Express v. Buffalo Evening News, 1713d7, 1714b, e
Bulk Popcorn Antitrust Litig., 322f
Bunte Bros., FTC v., 233a
Burbank v. GE, 337a2
Burch v. Goodyear Tire & Rubber Co., 380
Burdett Sound v. Altec Corp., 1625c3, 1653b
Burke v. Ford, 232d, e, 233b
Burkhead v. Phillips Petrol. Co., 346b
Burlington Coat Factory Warehouse Corp. v. Esprit de Corp., 1604d1, 1632b
Burlington Indus. v. Edelman, 381b
Burnup & Sims v. Posner, 381b

Bushie v. Stenocord Corp., 563d, 828c, 832, 835b
Business Aides v. Chesapeake & Potomac Tel. Co., 213f, 214b4
Business Electronics v. Sharp Electronics (108 S. Ct. 1515), 1604e2, g2, 1606h2, 1623a, e, 1624a-b, d1, e, 1625a-b, c4, d, 1644a, b1, c, 1648c4, d3-d3
Business Electronics v. Sharp Electronics (780 F.2d 1212), 1604e2, 1624d3, 1625c3-c4, d
Business Equip. Center v. DeJur-Amsco, 1460f
Business Guides v. Chromatic Communic. Enters., 323e
Butera v. Sun Oil Co., 1451c2, 1627b, f
Button Fastener, 1701a
Byars v. Bluff City News Co., 1507b, 1710b
By-Prod Corp. v. Armen-Berry Co., 335b

Cable Holdings of Ga. v. Home Video, 374, 539a
C. Albert Sauter Co. v. Richard S. Sauter Co., 828b
Calculators Hawaii v. Brandt, 1653c-d
Calderone Enters. Corp. v. United Artists Theatre Circuit, 376a, b2
Cal. Distrib. Co. v. Bay Distributors, 831, 835b, c
Cali v. Eastern Airlines, 316a
California v. American Stores (495 U.S. 271), 312a, e3-e4, 321c, 331d, 346b
California v. American Stores (872 F.2d 837), 348c, 564
California v. ARC Am. Corp., 371i
California v. California & Hawaiian Sugar Co., 335b
California v. Chevron Corp., 335c2
California v. FPC, 223g, 224a, e
California v. Frito-Lay, 380
California v. Standard Oil Co. (Cal.), 372, 1408c
California Computer Prods. v. IBM, 336d
California ex rel. Christensen v. FTC, 212b, 218a
California ex rel. Van de Kamp v. American Stores, 565
California Glazed Prods. v. Burns & Russel Co., 1716d2
California Motor Transp. Co. v. Trucking Unlimited, 202a, 203b-c, 204b-c, 572a
California Packing Corp., 1130a
California-Pac. Utils. Co. v. United States, 348e
California Retail Liquor Dealers Assn. v. Midcal Aluminum, 1715b
Callanan v. United States, 1474b
Call Carl v. B. P. Oil Corp., 235c, 828b, 1467b, 1469c-d, 1473d2
Calmar, United States v., 422c
Calnetics Corp. v. Volkswagen of Am. (532 F.2d 674), 321a, 365b5, 561a, 1020, 1408d
Calnetics Corp. v. Volkswagen of Am. (348 F. Supp. 606), 365b5, 381a, 926c, 929a

Camotex, S.R.L. v. Hunt, 338c
Campbell Distrib. Co. v. Jos. Schlitz Brewing Co., 835c
Campbell-Taggart Assoc. Bakeries, 909c
Campo v. National Football League, 363d, 356b
Canadian American Oil Co. v. Union Oil Co., 1452c4, 1627e5
Cannon Mfg. Co. v. Cudahy Packing Co., 235c
Cantor v. Detroit Edison Co., 212b, 213a, 214a, b, b1, b4, d, e, 215b, b1-3, 215c, 217b3, b4, 220c
Cape Cod Food Prods. v. National Cranberry Assn., 228d, 839
Capital Imaging Assocs. v. Mohawk Valley Medical Assocs., 323e
Capital Temporaries v. Olsten Corp., 1441h1, 1639b
Capitol Serv., United States v., 311a2
Carbon Steel Prods. v. Alan Wood Steel, 1460f
Cargill v. Hardin, 333f
Cargill v. Monfort of Colo. (479 U.S. 104), 360e2, 362a-b, 373b-c, d2, 1623f6, 1640a, c, d1
Cargill v. Monfort of Colo. (761 F.2d 570), 373d2
Cargo Serv. Stations, United States v. 312c
Carilion Health Sys., United States v., 553e
Carlo C. Gelardi Corp. v. Miller Brewing Co., 1456d4
Carlock v. Pillsbury Co., 563d
Carl Sandburg Village Condominium Assn. No. 1 v. First Condominium Dev. Co., 1722d, 1726c, 1726f-g, 1728b, e
Carlson Cos. v. Sperry & Hutchinson Co., 362a
Carlson Mach. Tools v. American Tool, 1440a, 1456f, 1644c, 1645b-c
Carnation Co. v. Pacific Westbound Conf., 213f, 225d, 226c-d, 227a, 338e
Carnivale Bag Co. v. Slide-Rite Mfg. Corp., 371c
Carpa v. Ward Foods, 523, 1713b2, 1716d, d2
Carpenters District Council v. United Contractors Assn., 229c
Carr Elecs. Corp. v. Sony Corp., 1455b
Carrier Corp. v. United Technologies Corp., 1131c2, d, 1131e
Carroll case, see Federation of Musicians v. Carroll
Carrols Dev. Corp., United States v., 348e
Carter v. AT&T Co., 227a
Carterfone v. AT&T, 214b4
Carter Hawley Hale Stores v. Limited, 381b, 538a, 561b
Carter Mountain Transmission Corp., 572a
Cascade Broadcasting Corp. v. KPDQ, 823
Cascade Cabinet Co. v. Western Cabinet & Millwork, 362a
Cascade Natural Gas Corp. v. El Paso Natural Gas Co., 348a, e

Case, J. I., United States v., 1460f
Case-Swayne Co. v. Sunkist Growers, 228b, d, 832
Casey v. Diet Center, 383b, 1459c1, 1710b, 1712d2, 1715b, 1717b1
Cash v. Arctic Circle, 356d
Cass Student Adv. v. National Educ. Adv. Serv., 731e, 1653e
Castelli v. Meadville Med. Center, 1726, 1727g
Catalano v. Target Sales, 1508c, 1510c
Cataphote Corp. v. DeSoto Chem. Coatings, 707h1
Catlin v. Washington Energy Co., 362a, 363d, 365d
Cayman Exploration Corp. v. United Gas Pipeline Corp., 322g, 1622a
CBS v. ASCAP, 1717f3
Cedar Crest Hats v. United Hatters, 229e
C.E.D. Mobilphone Communications v. Harris Corp., 1645b
Cellar Door Prods. v. Kay, 334c
Cellophane case, see du Pont, United States v. (351 U.S. 377)
Celotex Corp. v. Catrett, 322a
Cemar v. Nissan Motor Corp., 1724b-c
Cement Institute, FTC v., 305c, 334d, 841a, 1403, 1420a
Cement Institute, United States v., 334c, 1301b
Cement Mfrs. Protection Assn. v. United States, 1423b
Center Ins. Agency v. Byers, 210
Central Bank of Clayton v. Clayton Bank, 203c
Central Ice Cream Co. v. Golden Rod Ice Cream Co., 233b
Central Natl. Bank v. Rainbolt, 381b
Central State Bank, United States v., 533f
Central Telecommunic. v. TCI Cablevision, 374
Centronics Data Computer Corp. v. Mannesmann, 235c
Century Hardware Corp. v. Powernail Co., 338b
Cernuto v. United Cabinet Corp., 323e, 1453c-d, 1456d3, 1457d, 1510a, 1604e2, 1624d3, 1625c3, d, 1644b1
C. E. Servs. v. Control Data Corp., 562c
Chamber of Commerce v. FTC, 218a
Champion Intl. Corp., United States v., 1418b4, 1420d1, 1425d4
Champion Spark Plug Co. v. Ransburg Electro-Coating Corp., 381a
Chandler Supply Co. v. GAF Corp., 1653b
Chandler Trailer Convoy v. Morgan Drive-Away, 339a
Chapman v. Rudd Paint & Varnish Co., 1470
Charley's Tour & Transp. v. InterIsland Resorts, Ltd., 339a
Charlotte Telecasters v. Jefferson Pilot Corp., 338c
Chas. Pfizer & Co. v. FTC, 204d, 305e, 707e, g
Chas. Pfizer & Co., United States v. (426 F.2d 32), 1434d1

Chas. Pfizer & Co., United States v. (367 F. Supp. 91), 1433a, 1434d1
Chas. Pfizer & Co., United States v. (246 F. Supp. 464), 832
Chas. Pfizer & Co., United States v. (245 F. Supp. 737), 821
Chastain v. AT&T Co., 214b, b4, 317e, 1469b
Chattanooga Foundry and Pipe Works v. Atlanta, 365b1, 380
Checker Motors Corp. v. Chrysler Corp., 1639g2
Chelson v. Oregonian Publishing Co., 360d
Chemetron Corp. v. Crane Co., 909c
Cherney Disposal Co. v. Chicago & Suburban Refuse Disposal Assn., 232e
Cherokee Labs. v. Rotary Drilling Servs., 828e, 1653d, 1655d
Chesapeake & O. Ry. Purchase, 1204d
Chest Hill Co. v. Guttman, 338b
Chevron Oil Co. v. Huson, 333a, d
Chicago Bd. of Trade v. United States, 105, 320b, 410, 626a, 823, 1204d, 1402a5, 1502, 1504, 1505a, 1506, 1609a, 1729i3
Chicago Mercantile Exch. v. Deaktor, 227b
Chicago Professional Sports Ltd. Partnership & WGN v. National Basketball Assn., 364e, 375d
Chicago Title & Trust Co., United States v., 210
Chicago Tribune v. Palermo, 324b
Chicago Tribune-New York News Syndicate, United States v., 828e, 1655b
Chicken Antitrust Litig., 371f
Chicken Delight case, see Siegel v. Chicken Delight
Child World v. South Towne Centre, 1653c, 1655b
Chillicothe Sand & Gravel Co. v. Martin Marietta Corp., 1507a
Chipanno v. Champion Intern. Corp., 339a
Chiropractic Coop. Assn. of Mich. v. A.M.A., 363d
Chisholm Bros. Farm Equip. Co. v. International Harvester Co., 1440a, 1455b, 1623c, 1639h
Chock Full O'Nuts Corp., 1716d2
Christian Schmidt Brewing Co. v. G. Heileman Brewing Co., 347, 362b
Christianson v. Cold Indus. Operating Corp., 563d
Chrysler Corp. v. Fedders Corp., 375c
Chrysler Corp. v. General Motors Corp., 373d5
Chrysler Corp. v. United States, 348b
Chrysler Corp., United States v., 909c
Chrysler Credit Corp. v. J. Truett Payne Co., 362a, 384
Chusid, Frederick, & Co. v. Marshall Leeman & Co., 828b

CIBA Corp., United States v., 348d-e, g
Cincinnati Milk Sales Assn. v. Natl. Farmers' Org., 228c
Cindy's Candle Co. v. WNS, 324b
Cinema-Tex. Ent. v. Santikos Theaters, 365c3
Cinemette Corp. of Am., United States v., 311a2
Cities Service case, see First Natl. Bank of Arizona v. Cities Service Co.
Cities Serv. Co. v. Peerless Co., 220d
Citizens Publishing Co. v. United States, 333f
Citizen Publishing Co. v. United States, 333f, 926b, 929, 1118
Citizen Publishing Co., United States v., 233e
Citizens & Southern Natl. Bank, United States v., 312c, 933, 935a, b, 1121c3, 1463g, 1465a, 1467f2, g, 1468
City of Anaheim v. Southern Cal. Edison Co., 336g, 572c
City of Chanute v. Williams Natl. Gas Co., 322j
City of Cleveland v. Cleveland Elec. Illuminating Co., 336g
City of Columbia & Columbia Outdoor Advertising v. Omni Outdoor Advertising, 378b
City of Detroit v. Grinnell Corp., 336d
City of Kirkwood v. Union Elec. Co., 572c
City of Long Beach v. Standard Oil of Cal., 322f, 335b, 363b
City of Mishawaka v. American Elec. Power Co., 361
City of Mt. Pleasant, Iowa v. Association of Elec. Co-ops., 562b
City of New York v. United States, 348g
City of St. Paul v. FMC Corp., 371i
Clairol v. Boston Discount Center of Berkeley, 1618d, 1641c1, 1645d-e, 1647d2
Clarke v. Amerada Hess Corp., 1609a
Clark Mechanical Contractors, United States v., 311a3
Clark Walter & Sons v. Theo. Hamm Brewing Co., 233d
Class Plaintiffs (Chemical Bank) v. Seattle, 379b
Clayton Mark & Co. v. FTC, 1436c
Clemmer v. North American Van Lines, 1642c
Cleveland Trust Co., United States v., 1204b, 1302b, 1304, 1305
Cliff Food Stores v. Kroger, 233b, 1470
Clorox case, see Procter & Gamble Co., FTC v.
Clough v. Rush, 335c2
Clune v. Publishers' Assn., 229d
Coast v. Hunt Oil Co., 378a
Coastal Neuro-Psychiatric Assocs. v. Onslow County Hosp. Auth., 1722c
Coastal Transfer Co. v. Toyota Motor Sales, 323e
Coca-Cola Bottling Co., 909c, 921, 1134d

Coca-Cola Co., 1615d, 1616f, 1646d, 1651e, 1652d, 1655d, f3
Coca-Cola Co. v. FTC, 1652d
Coca-Cola Co. v. Howard Johnson Co., 831
Coca-Cola Co., FTC v., 534f
Cofinco v. Angola Coffee Co., 235c
Cohen v. Curtis Publishing Co., 374
Cokeley v. Tandy Corp., 1623c
Cole v. Hughes Tool Co., 735b2, c
Coleman Motor Co. v. Chrysler Corp., 365b, 828c, 832, 835c
Colgate & Co., United States v., 320b, 729b, 731a, 736d, 1408a, 1438, 1441a, g, 1442a, 1443a, 1444a, 1445, a-c, 1447b2, 1448e1, 1452c, 1460b3, 1609c, 1623d, 1624e, 1627d1, 1630d, 1652d, 1653a
Colgate-Palmolive Co. v. FTC, 305f
Colgate-Palmolive Co., FTC v., 305e
Collins v. Associated Pathologists, 570b1
Colorado v. Western Paving Constr. Co., 338d
Colorado Pump & Supply Co. v. Febco, 1642c, 1725c
Columbia Metal Culvert Co. v. Kaiser Aluminum & Chem. Corp., 1463f, 1464e, 1469e, 1474c
Columbia Nitrogen Corp. v. Royster Co., 390c, 1459c2
Columbia Pictures Corp., United States v., 1201c, 1202f2, f4
Columbia River Packers Assn. v. Hinton, 228c, d, 229c
Columbia Steamship Co. v. American Mail Line, 832
Columbia Steel Co., United States v., 552c3, 561a, 727a, d, e, 822, 902a, 1000, 1004, 1202a
Comfort Trane Air Conditioning v. Trane Co., 1452c4, 1627e5
Commissioner v. Sunnen, 334c
Commodore Plaza v. Saul J. Morgan Enters., 1722c
Commonwealth v. Wright, 321d
Commonwealth Edison Co. v. Allis-Chalmers Mfg. Co., 337a2, 1408c
Commonwealth of Pennsylvania v. Milk Indus. Management Corp., 338d
Commonwealth of Pennsylvania v. Russell Stover Candies, 380
Community Builders v. City of Phoenix, 1723b, 1723d
Compact v. Metropolitan Government of Nashville & Davidson County, 1504
Compania Petrolera Caribe v. Arco Caribbean, 346b, 362b
Computer Place v. Hewlett-Packard Co., 1456e, 1625c1
Com-Tel v. DuKane Corp., 1644c, 1645d
Concentrated Phosphate Export Assn., United States v., 230a
Conference of Studio Unions v. Loew's, 364g, 377d3
Congress Bldg. Corp. v. Loew's, 367a

Coniglio v. Highwood Servs., 1701c2, 1718c, 1721b4, 1722c, 1723b, d
Conley v. Gibson, 323a
Conley Motor Express v. Russell, 229c
Conmar Corp. v. Mitsui & Co. (U.S.A.), 338d
Connecticut v. General Motors Corp., 1435d
Connecticut Natl. Bank, United States v., 530d, 565, 1121c3, 1123a
Connell Construction Co. v. Plumbers Local 100, 229b, e, 385
Consolidated Farmers Mut. Ins. Co. v. Anchor Savings Assn., 1426d
Consolidated Foods Corp., 1133c, 1135a
Consolidated Foods Corp., FTC v., 1130a, 1131a, c3, 1131e, 1133c, 1205d1, 1700d2
Consolidated Foods Corp., United States v., 909c, 932, 1103a, 1121c4, 1204c
Consolidated Gas Co. of Fla. v. City Gas Co. (880 F.2d 297), 572c
Consolidated Gas Co. of Fla. v. City Gas Co. (665 F. Supp. 1493), 562b
Consolidated Gold Fields, PLC v. Anglo American Corp., 552c5
Consolidated Gold Fields PLC v. Minorca, S.A., 347, 381b
Consolidated Laundries Corp., United States v., 839, 1421b3
Construction Aggregate Transp. v. Florida Rock Indus., 360d
Consumer Federation of America v. FTC, 305f
Consumers Union v. Kissinger, 206c
Container Corp., United States v., 213d, 312c, 420b, 524d, 842a, 917, 1119f2, 1406e, 1506, 1602e, 1606e3
Contico v. Rubbermaid, 561a
Continental Baking Co. v. Dixon, 305e
Continental Cablevision v. American Elec. Power Co., 1412g
Continental Can Co., United States v., 562a, 571a, 909c, 1109d2, 1115b, f, 1205a, e1
Continental Group, United States v., 312c
Continental Oil Co., United States v., 909c
Continental Ore Co. v. Union Carbide, 214d, 217a3, 236c, g, 239b2
Continental Paper Bag Co. v. Eastern Paper Bag Co., 706c3, 736d
Continental Sec. Co. v. Michigan Central R.R. Co., 346b
Continental Trend Resources v. OXY, USA, 322j
Continental T.V. v. GTE Sylvania (433 U.S. 36), 336f, 904, 1134b, 1143f, 1145, 1441h2, 1446b, 1448e1, 1473b, d, e1, f, 1503a, 1505b, 1600b, d, 1604c2, g2, 1609a, 1611f, 1612e, 1620c, 1624a, 1629c, 1630b, 1636f2, 1637d, 1638c,

1640d, 1641b2, 1642c, 1643, 1645a, d-e, 1646d, 1647e, 1648b3, 1649a-b, 1652b, d, 1653a, 1718c
Continental T.V. v. GTE Sylvania (694 F.2d 1132), 1609a, d, 1610a
Continental T.V. v. GTE Sylvania (461 F. Supp. 1046), 1505b, 1643c-d, 1645c
Continental Wall Paper Co. v. Louis Voight & Sons, 391
Continental Wax Corp. v. FTC, 721b
Contractor Utility Sales v. Certain-Teed Products, 1456d4, 1457c4
Contreras v. Grower Shipper Vegetable Assn., 377d3
Control Data Corp. v. IBM, 330c
Cook v. Ralston Purina Co., 1642c
Cooley v. Board of Wardens, 220a
Cooper Corp., United States v., 380
Cooper Liquor v. Adolph Coors Co., 232e, 363d, 1457c3, 1642c
Coordinated Pretrial Proceedings in Antibiotic Antitrust Actions, In re, 337a1, 339b, 380
Coordinated Pretrial Proceedings in Petrol. Prods. Antitrust Litig., 364d
Cooter & Gell P. Hartmarx Corp., 323e
Copperweld Corp. v. Imetal, 381b, 1020
Copperweld Corp. v. Independence Tube Corp., 1446e3, 1462a-c, 1463, b, h, 1464a-e, 1465, 1466a, b, d2, 1467a-b, f1, g, 1469a, 1470
Copy-Data Systems v. Toshiba America, 1605b
Cordova v. Bache & Co., 229d
Corrugated Container Antitrust Litig., 335b
Cortelyou v. Carter's Ink Co., 1701a
Cortelyou v. Lowe, 1701a
Corenco Corp. v. Schiavone & Sons, 1119f2, 1121b2, 1121c5
Corica v. Ragen, 312e4
Corning Glass Works v. Anchor Hocking Glass Corp., 707b
Corn Prods. Ref. Co., United States v., 422d2, 727b2, e, 728c5, 729f
Cornwell Quality Tools Co. v. C.T.S. Co., 832, 1452b
Cosentino v. Carver-Greenfield, 378b
Cotten v. Witco Chem. Corp., 321e
C-O-Two Fire Equip. Co. v. United States, 1417b, 1421b1, 1425e, 1434d1, 1606b
Country Lake Foods, United States v., 421d, 538a-b, 550a
Country Maid v. Haseotes, 233e
Country Natl. Bank of Bennington, United States v., 530e
County of Oakland v. City of Detroit, 360a, 371e
Courant v. International Photographers of Motion Picture Indus. Local 659, 229e
Courshon v. FTC, 1302d
Cowley v. Braden Indus., 1644c, 1645b-e

Cow Palace Ltd. v. Associated Milk Producers, 204e2
Cox, A. H., & Co. v. Star Mach. Co., 1456f
CPC Intl. v. Standard Brands, 707b
Crawford Transport Co. v. Chrysler Corp., 1726c, 1727g
Credit Bureau Reports v. Retail Credit Co., 346b, 911c
Crescent Amusement Co., United States v., 1436b
Crimpers Promotions v. Home Box Office, 375d
Crocker-Anglo Natl. Bank, United States v., 1121c3, 1123a
Crocker Natl. Corp., United States v., 1302d
Cromar Co. v. Nuclear Materials and Equip. Corp., 373f4, 1467b, 1469a
Cromwell v. County of Sac., 334b1
Cromwell, Collier & Macmillan, United States v., 909c, 911c, 1109a, d2, 1119f2, 1121c2, 1123a
Crossland v. Canteen Co., 1722c
Crouse-Hinds, 1436c
Crown Cork & Seal Co. v. Brooklyn Bottle Stopper Co., 1701a
Crown Cork & Seal Co. v. Parker, 338d
Crown Zellerbach Corp. v. FTC, 909c, 926c, 1205d1
Crummer Co. v. du Pont, 338b
C. Tennant & Sons v. New York Terminal Conf., 347
Culberson v. Interstate Elec. Co., 1644c
Cumberland Farms v. Browning Ferris Indus., 356b
Curtis Publishing Co., FTC v. (260 U.S. 568), 305f
Curtis Publishing Co., FTC v. (78 F.T.C. 1472), 305e
Cutters Exch. v. Durkoppwerke, 563d

Dahl v. Roy Cooper Co., 822a, 1412g
Dailey v. Quality School Plan, 323a, 375c, 377b
Dairy Foods v. Dairy Maid Prods. Coop., 361
Dairy Foods v. Farmers Co-operative Creamery, 381a
Dairymen (102 F.T.C. 1151), 538a
Dairymen, United States v., 228c, 533g
Dairy Queen v. Wood, 321a, 322c
Dalmo Sales Co. v. Tyson Corner Regional Shopping Center, 1655b, d
Damon Corp. v. Geheb, 337a2
Danbury Hat case, see Lowe v. Lawlor
Daniels v. All Steel Equip., 1653c
Dart Drug Corp. v. Parke, Davis & Co., 1452c4, 1627e5
Dart Indus. v. Plunkett Co. (Okla.), 1605d3, 1644c, 1645e, 1725c
Datagate v. Hewlett-Packard Co., 373d3, 375d

Data Gen. Corp. v. Grumman Sys. Support Corp., 562f
Data General Corp. Antitrust Litig., 1713b3, 1716b1, c1, f, 1717d, d2, f1
Data Processing Fin. & Gen. Corp. v. IBM, 348c
David E. Thompson, United States v., 337a2
David Orgell v. Geary's Stores, 338b
David R. McGeorge Car Co. v. Leyland Motor Sales, 1700d
Davis v. Marathon Oil Co., 1721c1-c2, d-d2
Davis-Watkins Co. v. Service Merchandise, 1456d3, 1605b, 1644a, c, 1645b-c
Dayco Corp. v. Firestone Tire & Rubber Co., 338d
Dayco Corp. v. Goodyear Tire & Rubber Co., 338d
Dean Foods, 926c, d
Dean Foods Co., FTC v., 305e, 909c
Dean Milk Co. v. City of Madison, 220a, b, d
Dean Milk Co. v. FTC, 233b
de Atucha v. Commodity Exch., 364b
Deem v. Lockheed Corp., 381a
Deep South Pepsi-Cola Bottling Co. v. PepsiCo, 563d
Dehydrating Process Co. v. A. O. Smith Corp., 1133a, 1716d2
DeJong Packing Co. v. United States, 1421b2, 1425c
Delaney, E. J., Corp. v. Bonne Bell, 831, 835c
Delaware Valley Marine Supply Co. v. American Tobacco Co. (297 F.2d 199), 322c, 1433e
Delaware Valley Marine Supply Co. v. American Tobacco Co. (184 F. Supp. 440), 374
Del Rio Distrib. v. Adolph Coors Co., 336f
Delta Theaters v. Paramount Pictures, 338b
Deltec v. Laster, 708
De Luxe Theatre Corp. v. Balaban & Katz Corp., 337a2
Dempster v. Rosehill Cemetery Co., 338f
Denison Mines v. Michigan Chemical Corp., 1204b
Denman v. Franks, 323d
Dennis Paper v. Simpson Paper, 1609a
Denver and Rio Grande Western R.R. v. United States, 1203b
Denver Petroleum Corp. v. Shell Oil Co., 374
Denver Rockets v. All-Pro Management, 213c, 215c, 377c
Deposit Guaranty Natl. Bank of Jackson, United States v., 1121c2, c4, 1124c, 1125c
Determined Productions v. R. Dakin & Co., 1653c
Detroit v. Grinnell Corp., 338d
Detroit City Dairy v. Kowalski Sausage Co., 1721b4
Deutsches Kalisyndikat Gesellschaft, United States v., 239c
DeVoto v. Pacific Fidelity Life Ins. Co., 232e, 362a
Dexter v. Equitable Life Assurance Soc., 210

DFW Metro Line Serv. v. Southwestern Bell Tel. Co., 347
Dial Mfg. Intl. v. McGraw Edison Co., 1467b
Diamond v. World News Corp., 1408f3
Diamond Alkali Co., 909c, 926c, 1121c2
Diamond Intl. Corp. v. Walterhoefer, 832, 835c
Diebold, United States v., 322b
Diehl & Sons v. International Harvester Co., 828c, 831, 832, 835c, 1467b, 1468
Digidyne Corp. v. Data Gen. Corp., 523, 1721b4, c2, d
Dillard v. Merrill Lynch, Pierce, Fenner & Smith, 322g
Dillon Materials Handling v. Albion Indus., 1460f
Dimmitt Agric. Indus. v. CPC Intl., 532b
Direct Sales Co. v. United States, 1474c
Disenos Artisticos E Industriales v. Work (714 F. Supp. 46), 563d
Disenosartisticose Industriales v. Work (676 F. Supp. 1254), 1644c
Diversified Brokerage Serv. v. Greater Des Moines Bd. of Realtors, 232e
Dobbins v. Kawasaki Motors Corp., 235c
Doctors v. Blue Cross of Greater Philadelphia, 210, 232e
Dolgow v. Anderson, 356b
Dolphin Tours v. Pacifico Creative Serv., 362a, 374
Domed Stadium Hotel v. Holiday Inns, 563d
Domestic Air Transp. Antitrust Litig. (141 F.R.D. 534), 356b
Domestic Air Transp. Antitrust Litig. (137 F.R.D. 677), 356d
Donahue v. Pendleton Woolen Mills, 339b, 377d5
Donald B. Rice Tire Co. v. Michelin Tire Corp. (638 F.2d 15), 1605d2, 1611f, 1644b1
Donald B. Rice Tire Co. v. Michelin Tire Corp. (438 F. Supp. 750), 1605b, d2, d5, 1645c-e
Dorey Corp. v. du Pont, 355d
Dorfmann v. Boozer, 312e4
Dougherty v. Continental Oil Co., 1645b, e
Dreibus v. Wilson, 390c
Dreiling v. Peugeot Motors of Am., 322c
Dresser Indus., 909c
Driscoll v. City of New York, 338b
Driskill v. Dallas Cowboys Football Club, 1722c, 1723b
Dr. Miles Medical Co. v. John D. Park & Sons Co., 104, 333f, 1427c, 1445c1, 1446b, 1473b-c, e2, 1600b, c2, 1606b, 1609a, c, e, 1620, 1624a, 1625e, 1628a-b, d-e, 1634, 1635, 1637b, d, 1644a
Droney, O. M., Beverage Co. v. Miller Brewing Co., 1451c2, 1627b, 1639g2
Drs. Steuer & Latham v. National Med. Enters., 1726c, 1727g

Drumm v. Sizeler Realty Co., 338e
Dry v. Methodist Med. Ctr. of Oak Ridge, 375d
Duff v. Kansas City Star Co., 374
Duke & Co. v. Foerster, 216a, 217a3
Dungan v. Morgan Drive-Away, 339a
Dunham Concrete Prods., United States v., 323c
Dunhill, Alfred, of London v. Cuba, 239b
Dunn v. Phoenix Newspapers, 1451f
Dunn & Mavis v. Nu-Car Driveway, 1653b
Duplan Corp. v. Deering Millikin, 1408c
Duplex Co. v. Deering, 229e
du Pont (Titanium Oxide) (96 F.T.C. 653), 535c1
du Pont v. FTC, 307b, 524d, 1407b2, 1422b, 1435a, f, 1436a, b3, c, f2, g, h2
Dupont Glove Forgan v. AT&T, 1469d
du Pont, United States v. (366 U.S. 316), 345, 926, 1203e, 1204c
du Pont, United States v. (353 U.S. 586), 333f, 531b, 533f, 563e, 628, 902, 1203e, 1204c, d, 1205a, c2, 1478b2
du Pont, United States v. (351 U.S. 377), 501, 520c, 524b, 534b, 539a, 628, 804, 811, 812, 833c, 835b, 1407f
du Pont, United States v. (118 F. 127), 711b, 1020, 1021, 1126c
du Pont, United States v. (126 F. Supp. 235), 1204d
Dyer v. MacDougall, 322b
Dyer, Commonwealth of Massachusetts v., 1474b
Dynalectric Co., United States v., 338b

Eagle v. Star-Kist Foods, 379a-b
Earley Ford Tractor v. Hesston Corp., 1713c2, 1721b4
Eastern Air Lines v. Atlantic Richfield Co., 371e
Eastern Auto Distribs. v. Peugeot Motors of Am., 383c
Eastern Coal Corp. v. Disabled Miners Assn. of Southern W. Va., 229b
Eastern Dental Corp. v. Isaac Masel Co., 564
Eastern Pre-Cast Corp. v. Giant Portland Cement Co., 235c
Eastern Publishing & Advertising v. Chesapeake Publishing & Advertising, 373e1
Eastern R.R. Pres. Conf. v. Noerr Motor Freight, 202a, 203a, b, 204b, d, 205, 206a, 215b2, 217b3, 229e, 239b
Eastern Scientific Co. v. Wild HeerbruggInstruments,1453d, 1624c, 1641b4
Eastern States Retail Lumber Dealers' Assn. v. United States, 1408f3
Eastex Aviation v. Sperry and Hutchinson Co., 1642c
Eastman Kodak Co. v. FTC, 1629b

Eastman Kodak Co. v. Home Util. Co., 1629b
Eastman Kodak Co. v. Image Technical Serv., 304c, 322b, f, 373d3, 562f, 563e
Eastman Kodak Co. v. Southern Photo Materials Co., 729e
Eaton Yale & Towne, United States v., 1642c
E. B. Muller Co. v. FTC, 711c
E. C. Knight Co., United States v., 232c, 605
Edelman v. Jordan, 214a, 217a1, 218b
Edward J. Sweeney & Sons v. Texaco, (637 F.2d 105), 1446b, 1452c4, 1455b, 1456d4, 1457c4, d, 1627b
Edward J. Sweeney & Sons v. Texaco (478 F. Supp. 243), 1627e5
Edwin K. Williams & Co. v. Edwin K. Williams & Co.—East, 1642c
Eiberger v. Sony Corp. (622 F.2d 1068), 1602b, 1641b3, 1645b-d, 1647b3
Eiberger v. Sony Corp. (459 F. Supp. 1276), 1611f, 1612b
Eichlin Mfg. Co., 420c, 421c
Eichman v. Fotomat Corp. (880 F.2d 149), 322g, 338b, 363d
Eichman v. Fotomat Corp. (759 F.2d 1434), 335c2
Eisen v. Carlisle & Jacquelin (417 U.S. 156), 356b-d
Eisen v. Carlisle & Jacquelin (391 F.2d 555), 356b
E. J. Delaney Corp. v. Bonne Bell, 831, 835c, 1653c
Ekco Prods. Co. v. FTC, 305e, 1119b, d2, 1121b4, 1135a, 1205d
Elco Corp. v. Microdot, 909c
Elder-Beerman Stores Corp. v. Federated Dept. Stores, 365b3, 1459c3, 1653c
Elders Grain, FTC v., 305e, 362b, 552d2
Electric and Musical Indus., Ltd., In re, 235c
Eli Lilly & Co., United States v. (24 F.R.D. 285), 1421d
Eli Lilly & Co., United States v. (1959 Trade Cas. ¶69,411), 1421d
Elizabeth Arden Sales Corp. v. Gus Blass Co., 233d
Elizabeth Hospital v. Richardson, 232e
Elm Spring Farm v. United States, 228b
El Paso Natural Gas Co., United States v., 224e, 348e, 701c, 929e2, 1117a, 1119b, 1121c4, 1123d, 1123e3
Elrod v. Burns, 219b
Embry-Riddle Aeronautical Univ. v. Ross Aviation, 229e
Emich Motors Corp. v. GM (340 U.S. 558), 337b
Emich Motors Corp. v. GM (229 F.2d 714), 338b
Empire Gas Corp., United States v., 821, 1137
Empire State Pharmaceutical Socy. v. Empire Blue Cross, 323e
Employing Plasterers' Assn., United States v., 229e, 232e

Energex Lighting Indus. v. NAPLC, 532b
Energex Lighting Indus. v. North Am. Philips, 532b
Engbrecht v. Dairy Queen Co., 1623c
Engine Specialties v. Bombardier, 1652b
Erie County Malt Beverage Dist. Assn., United States v., 210
Ernest, Finis P., United States v., 232e, 1420a-b
Esco Corp. v. United States, 348g, 1407d
Esposito v. Mister Softee, 1727d
Essential Communic. Sys. v. AT&T, 572d
Esso Standard Oil Co. v. Secatore's, 1629b
Estate of LeBaron v. Rohm & Haas Co. (506 F.2d 1261), 1434d1
Estate of LeBaron v. Rohm & Haas Co. (441 F.2d 575), 1434d1
Ethyl case, see du Pont v. FTC
Ethyl Corp., 1435a, d, f, 1436a, b3, c, f1-f2, 1621
Ethyl Gasoline Corp. v. United States, 1427c
Eureka Urethane v. Professional Bowlers Assn., 563e
European Sugar Cartel, 1473f
Evans v. S. S. Kresge Co., 1639b
Evans & Assoc. Constr. Co., United States v., 338b, d
Everhart v. United Building Co., 1473d, d2, f
Evers v. General Motors Corp., 322j
E. W. French & Sons v. General Portland, 338d
Exhibitors Serv. v. American Multi-Cinema, 375c
Exploration Co. v. United States, 338d
Exxon Corp. v. Fischer, 336g
Exxon Corp. v. Governor of Md., 335b

Fagan v. Sunbeam Lighting Co., 1642c
Falcone, United States v., 1474b
Fallis v. Pendleton Woolen Mills, 377d5
Falls Church Bratwursthaus v. Bratwursthaus Management Corp., 1713b3, 1721b4, 1727d
Falls City Indus. v. Vanco Beverage, 304c
Falstaff Brewing Corp., United States v., 1118, 1119b, 1120e2, e3, 1121b2, b4, 1121b6, c4, 1122, 1123d
Famous Brands v. David Sherman Corp., 1725c
F. & M. Schaefer Corp. v. C. Schmidt & Sons, 909c, 1201c, 1203c, 1204b
Fanchon & Marco v. Paramount Pictures (215 F.2d 167), 337b, 1415b
Fanchon & Marco v. Paramount Pictures (107 F. Supp. 532), 346b
Farbenfabriken Bayer v. Sterling Drug Co., 338f
Far East Conf. v. United States, 213f, 223b, 226b, c

Far Eastern Coconut Co. v. Sun Ripe Coconut Corp., 1467h
Farmington Dowel Prods. v. Forster Mfg.Co., 337a1, 355d, 365b4
Farm Journal, 926d
Fashion Originators' Guild v. FTC, 213d, 216b, 736e, 836a, 1508c
Faukner Advertising Assocs. v. Nissan Motors Corp., 1700j1
FCC, see under name of other party
Feder v. Martin Marietta Corp., 1305
Federal Baseball Club v. National League, 230f
Federal Co., United States v., 909c
Federal Maritime Bd. v. Isbrandtsen Co., 226b
Federal Maritime Commn. v. Seatrain Lines, 223b, 224b, 332b
Federal Maritime Commn. v. Swedish American Line, 223c
Federal Trade Commn., see under name of other party
Federated Dept. Stores v. Moitie, 335b-c
Federated Nationwide Wholesalers Serv. v. FTC, 305f
Federation of Musicians v. Carroll, 229c, e
Feeney v. Chamberlain Mfg. Co., 377d5, 384
F.E.L. Publications v. Catholic Bishop of Chicago, 1717f3
Ferguson v. Skrupa, 213c
Fields Prod. v. United Artists Corp., 363e, 383c, 1718e
Filco v. Amana Refrigeration, 1456b-c
Filterite Corp. v. Tate Engineering, 706c3
Filtrol Corp. v. Slick Co., 1119b, 1020
Fine v. Barry & Enright Prods., 374, 1413
Fineman v. Armstrong World Indus., 335c2, 561a
Finis P. Ernest, United States v., 232e, 1420a-b
Finnegan v. Campeau Corp., 378d
Firestone Tire & Rubber Co., United States v., 628
First Delaware Valley Citizens Television v. CBS, 374
First Natl. Bancorporation, United States v., 1020
First Natl. Bank of Arizona v. Cities Serv. Co., 322a-c, 1408f2, 1414, 1433d
First Natl. Bank of Maryland, United States v., 1121c2
First Natl. Bank of Sunbury, United States v., 909c
First Natl. Bank & Trust Co. of Lexington, United States v. (376 U.S. 665), 304c, 1202a
First Natl. Bank & Trust Co. of Lexington, United States v. (280 F. Supp. 260), 348e
Fischbach & Moore, United States v., 312c
Fischer v. NWA, 373e1
Fisher v. Balzer, 335c2
Fisher v. Coca-Cola Bottling Co., 1467a, e1, h
Fisher v. Wattles, 371e-f

Fishman v. Estate of Wirtz, 363a, 373e1
Fitzgerald v. General Dairies, 338b
Fleer Corp. v. Topps Chewing Gum, 337c, 374, 1653e, 1655b
Flegel v. Christian Hosp., Northeast-Northwest, 534a1
Fleischmann Distilling Corp. v. Distillers Co., 323d
Fletcher v. Peck, 204d
Flintkote Co. v. Lysfjord, 356b3, 1408f3
FLM Collision Parts v. Ford Motor Co., 1627b, 1639h
F. L. Mendez & Co. v. GM, 334b2
Flood v. Kuhn, 208, 230f
Florence Mfg. Co. v. J. C. Dowd & Co., 626d
Florida Citrus Mutual, 228c
Florida Power Corp. v. Granlund, 1459b1
Florists' Nationwide Tel. Delivery Network v. Florists' Tel. Delivery Assn., 390a
Flowers Indus., 420c
FMC Corp., United States v., 1419b, 1422b, 1435g
Folding Carton Antitrust Litig., 372
Foley, United States v., 312c, 1418b3
Fontana Aviation v. Cessna Aircraft Co., 371h
Food Basket v. Albertson's, 233c
Food Town Stores, FTC v., 347, 909c, 926b
Forbes v. Greater Minneapolis Area Bd. of Realtors, 338d, 356b
Ford Motor Co. v. Webster's Auto Sales, 1641c3
Ford Motor Co. v. United States (405 U.S. 562), 345
Ford Motor Co. v. United States (335 U.S. 303), 348b
Ford Motor Co., United States v., 1118, 1119b, f2
Ford Motor Co., United States v., 1020, 1021, 1121b4, c2, 1123a, 1123c2
Ford Piano Supply Co. v. Steinway & Sons, 563d
Foremost Dairies v. FTC, 233b, 909c
Foremost Intl. Tours v. Qantas Airways Ltd., 224a, 225b, 227a
Foremost-McKesson, United States v., 909c
Forster Mfg. Co. v. FTC, 711c
Fortner Enters. v. U.S. Steel Corp. (429 U.S. 610), 365c1
Fortner Enters. v. U.S. Steel Corp. (Fortner I) (394 U.S. 495), 217a2, 304c, 365c1, 1700d, 1705c, 1707e, 1712d2, 1713c2, 1718c, 1720b4, 1721b, b4, c1-c2, d, 1724d1, 1728b, d-f, 1730a-b
Fortner Enters. v. U.S. Steel Corp. (523 F.2d 961), 365c1
49er Chevrolet v. General Motors Corp., 1622a
Foster v. American Machine & Foundry Co., 736d
Foster v. West Alexandria Props., 1717f4
Foster, State v., 332a
Fox-Keller v. Toyota Motor Sales, U.S.A., 235c

Fox Motors v. Mazda Distribs. (Gulf), 1722c, 1724c, 1725c-e
Fragale & Sons Beverage Co. v. Dill, 1625c3
Franchise Realty Interstate Corp. v. San Francisco Local Joint Exec. Bd. of Culinary Workers, 203c, 323c
Frank Saltz & Sons v. Hart Schaffner & Marx, 538a, 561b
Frantz v. U.S. Powerlifting Fedn., 323e
Frederich Chusid & Co. v. Marshall Leeman & Co., 828b
Fredrickson v. Merrill Lynch, Pierce, Fenner & Smith, 224d
Free v. Bland, 218b, 332b
Freedman v. Philadelphia Terminals Auction Co., 371e
Freeman v. Lester Coggins Trucking, 334e
Frey & Sons v. Cudahy Packing Co., 1448, b
Friedman v. Adams Russell Cable Services, 1723b, d
Friedman v. Kroger Co., 1474c
Friends of Animals v. American Veterinary Medical Assn., 235a, 361
Frost v. Ship Owners & Merchants Tow Boat Co., 390c
Fruehauf Corp. v. FTC., 1000b, 1002, 1003, 1008a, 1020, 1022c
FTC, see under name of other party
FTC Line of Business Report Litigation, 1467d
Fuchs Sugars & Syrups v. Amstar Corp., 346b, 1467h, 1473d2, 1474c, 1622c
GAF Corp. v. Eastman Kodak Co., 336d
Gaetzi v. Carling Brewing Co., 338d
GAF Corp. v. Circle Floor Co., 381b
Gaines v. Carrollton Tobacco Bd. of Trade, 365b2
Gamco v. Providence Fruit & Produce Bldg., 729g
Garelick v. Goerlich's, 338b
Garment District v. Belk Stores Servs., 1625d, 1648d3
Garot Anderson Mktg. v. Blue Cross & Blue Shield of Wis., 375d
Garshman v. Universal Resources Holding, 1622a
Gas-A-Tron v. American Oil Co., 1459b1
Gas Light Co. v. Georgia Power Co., 213a, f, 214b
Gasoline Retailers Assn., United States v., 213d
Gateway Assocs. v. Essex-Costello, 232e
GE v. San Antonio, 337a2, 338d
GE, United States v. (272 U.S. 476), 333f
GE, United States v. (358 F. Supp. 731), 333a, d, 334c
GE, United States v. (115 F. Supp. 835), 345
GE, United States v. (82 F. Supp. 753), 334c
Gelardi, Carlo C., Corp. v. Miller Brewing Co., 1456d4
Gemco Latinoamerica v. Seiko Time Corp., 324b

Gemini Concerts v. Triple-A Baseball Club Assocs., 1653c, 1655d
General Beverage Sales Co. v. East Side Winery, 390
General Business Systems v. North Am. Phillips Corp., 1467a
General Chems. v. Exxon Chem. Co., 1412c
General Cinema Corp. v. Buena Vista Distrib. Co., 1504
General Commns. Engineering v. Motorola Commns. and Elec., 363d, 821, 822a, 828b
General Dynamics Corp. v. AT&T, 336d
General Dynamics Corp., United States v., 320b, 535c1, f, 933, 934a-c, 935a, b, 937, 941b, 961, 962, 962b, 1019, 1119b, c, 1131c3, 1131e, 1132a, c, 1133c, 1202e4, 1205a, e1
General Elec. Co., 1301c
General Elec. Co., United States v. (272 U.S. 467), 1427c, 1473b-c, 1606b, 1609c, 1620b, 1621
General Elec. Co., United States v. (358 F. Supp. 731), 1473d
General Elec. Co., United States v. (115 F. Supp. 835) 237
General Elec. Co., United States v. (82 F. Supp. 753), 236e, 237
General Elec. Co., United States v. (80 F. Supp. 989), 237
General Elec. Co., United States v. (1977 Trade Cas. ¶61,660), 919, 1435e, g
General Foods Corp., 307b, 520a2
General Foods Corp. v. FTC, 533e, 1109a
General Glass Co. v. Globe Glass and Trim Co., 1426d
General Inv. Co. v. Lake Shore Ry., 324c
General Leaseways v. National Truck Leasing Assn., 365b2, 390c
General Mills Corp., 1109a, 1119b, 1122b
General Motors case, see du Pont, United States v. (353 U.S. 586)
General Motors Co. v. Gibson Chem. & Oil Co., 1722c, 1726e1-e2
General Motors Corp. (34 F.T.C. 58), 1716a1, d4
General Motors Corp. (103 F.T.C. 641), 307b
General Motors Corp. v. FTC, 626d
General Motors Corp., United States v. (384 U.S. 127), 1602c, 1604c2, g3, 1611f, 1641c3, 1642c, 1644c
General Motors Corp., United States v. (121 F.2d 376), 1463e, 1464e
General Motors Corp., United States v. (1974 Trade Cas. ¶75,253), 1435d
General Outdoor Advertising Co., United States v., 1301a
Genetic Sys. Corp. v. Abbot Labs., 375c
Genna v. Lady Foot Intl., 1721b4
George R. Whitten, Jr. v. Paddock Pool Builders, 206b, 213a, 214a, b, d, 738b, 828b, 832, 835b, c, 1464e, 1467b

George W. Warner & Co. v. Black & Decker Mfg. Co., 1447b1
Georgia v. Evans, 212a, 217a1, 380
Georgia v. Pennsylvania R. Co., 224a, 225b, 380
Gerli v. Silk Assn., 378c
G. Heileman Brewing Co., United States v., 926b
Giant Food v. FTC, 721b
Giant Paper and Film Corp. v. Albermarle Paper Co., 835c, 839, 1467b
Gibbons, J. T. v. Crawford Fitting Co., 1459c3, 1467b
Gibson v. Berryhill, 212a, 213b, 217a3, 219c
Gibson v. Greater Park City Co., 322c, 1413
Gibson, Herbert R., 1609a
Gilder v. PGA Tour, 347
Gillen, United States v., 312c
Gillette Co. v. White Cross Discount Centers, 1629b
Gillette Co., United States v., 348g
Gilmore v. First Boston Corp., 1413
Gilmour v. Wood, Wire, & Metal Lathers, Local No. 74, 229e
Girard, United States v., 338b
Girardi v. Gates Rubber Co., 1455b, 1456e
Glauser Dodge Co. v. Chrysler Corp., 828c, 1469a
Glaxo Group, United States v., 1642c
Glazer Steel Corp. v. Toyomenka, 338d
Glictronix Corp. v. AT&T, 336e, 356b
GM case, see du Pont, United States v. (353 U.S. 586)
Golden v. Kentile Floors, 1474c
Golden Gate Acceptance Corp. v. General Motors Corp., 1625c3, 1653b
Golden Grain Macaroni Co., 909c, 929, 1203c, 1204b, c, 1205d1, 1205e3
Goldfarb v. Virginia State Bar, 213a, 214a, d, 215b, b1, b3, 217a3, 361, 1477
Gold Fuel Serv. v. Esso Standard Oil Co., 1415b
Goldinger v. Boron Oil Co., 1473d2
Goldlawr v. Shubert, 390a
Goldstein, Sam S., Indus. v. Botany Indus., 832
Golf City v. Wilson Sporting Goods, 1459c3
Gonzalez v. St. Margaret's House Housing Dev. Fund Corp., 1709e5, 1717f1, 1718j, 1721d-d2, 1722c, 1724b, 1726c, 1727e, 1730b
Good Investment Promotions v. Corning Glass Works, 1642c
Goodwin v. First Baptist Church, 338f
Gordon v. Crown Cent. Petrol. Corp., 1609a
Gordon v. New York Stock Exch., 213f, 223b, f, g, 224a, d, e, 323c
Gore, W. L., & Assoc. v. Carlisle Corp., 835c
Gottesman v. GM, 337b, 381a

Gough v. Rossmoor Corp., 1468, 1469c, 1653c
G. & P. Amusement Co. v. Regent Theater Co., 1415b
Graham v. Hudgins, Thompson, Ball and Assocs., 1474c
Grand Caillou Packing Co. case, see La Peyre v. FTC
Grand Jury Investigation of the Shipping Indus., In re, 239c
Grand Union Co., 422c
Graphic Prods. Distribs. v. Itek Corp., 1605b, 1645b-e,
Grappone v. Subaru of America, 235c
Grappone v. Subaru of New England, 523, 1719b, 1728b
Gratz, F.T.C. v., 1720b2, c
Graves v. Cambria Steel Co., 346b
Gray v. Shell Oil Co., 1440a, 1451c1, 1623c
Great Atl. & Pac. Tea Co., 1606e3
Great Atl. and Pac. Tea Co. v. Amalgamated Meat Cutters Local 88, 229e
Great Atl. and Pac. Tea Co. v. Cottrell, 220a, d
Great Atl. & Pac. Tea Co. v. FTC, 312c
Greater Buffalo Press, United States v., 530b, 926b, 929a
Greater Rockford Energy and Technology Corp. v. Shell Oil Co., 363a
Great Northern Ry. v. Sunburst Oil & Refining Co., 333d
Greenbrier Cinemas v. Attorney General, 311a2
Greene v. General Foods Corp., 1452c4, 1473d-e, f, 1622c, 1627e5
Greene, In re, 618a
Greenshaw v. Lubbock County Beverage Assn., 338d, 1406a
Greenstein v. National Skirt & Sportswear Assn., 229c
Greenville Publishing Co. v. Daily Reflector, 822a, 1471b
Gregoris Motors v. Nissan Motor Corp. in USA, 384, 563d
Gregory Mktg. Corp. v. Wakefern Food Corp., 377d5
Greyhound Corp. v. Mt. Hood Stages (437 U.S. 322), 339b
Greyhound Corp. v. Mt. Hood Stages (555 F.2d 687), 339b
Griffith, United States v., 312c, 610, 611b, 613, 626a, e, 727a, c2, c3, 729e, 821, 828d, 1463b, 1713c3
Grinnell Corp., United States v. (384 U.S. 563), 336d, 530f, 531b, 534d, 550a, 562b, 565, 612, 613, 626a, 627b1, 702b, 811, 812, 821, 833c, 1710c3
Grinnell Corp., United States v. (307 F. Supp. 1097), 334b4
Grinnell Corp., United States v. (305 F. Supp. 285), 339a
Grinnell Corp., United States v. (236 F. Supp. 244), 324a, 532, 620b
Grip-Pak v. Illinois Tool Works, 336d, 374
Griswold v. Haven, 1465a
Grossman Dev. Co. v. Detroit Lions, 1723b
Grueninger Intl. Travel v. Air Transport Assn., 225c

Grumman Corp. v. LTV Corp. (665 F.2d 10), 381b
Grumman Corp. v. LTV Corp. (527 F. Supp. 86), 533c
G. S. Suppiger Co. v. Morton Salt Co., 1720b3
GTE Sylvania v. Continental T.V., 104, 1642c, 1643a-b
Guaranty Trust Co. v. United States, 338f, 1205c2
Guidry v. Continental Oil Co., 1451c1
Gulf Coast Shrimpers & Oystermans Assn. v. United States, 228c
Gulf Offshore Co. v. Mobil Oil Corp., 324c
Gulf Oil Corp. v. Copp Paving Co., 232e, 233a, c, d
Gulf States Util. Co. v. FPC, 223c
Gulfstream III Assocs. v. Gulfstream Aerospace Corp., 371e
Gulf & Western Indus. v. Great Atl. & Pac. Tea Co., 909c, 1020, 1203c, 1204b, c
Gurwitz v. Singer, 337a2
Gutor Intl. A.G. v. Raymond Packer Co., 235a, 391
Guzik v. State Bar of Texas, 1409a

Haas, I., Trucking Corp. v. New York Fruit Auction Corp., 835c
Hackett v. General Host Corp., 356d
Haden Co. v. Johns-Manville Sales Corp., 1623c
Haelan Labs. v. Topps Chewing Gum, 1653e, 1655b
Haff v. Jewelmont Corp., 384
Hahn v. Oregon Physicians' Serv., 373b
Hahn, Ernest W. v. Codding, 203b
Hall v. du Pont, 338d
Hallmark Indus. v. Reynolds Metals Co., 828e, 832
Hamilton Glass Co., United States v., 229e
Hamilton Watch Co. v. Benrus Watch Co., 1203b, c, 1204c, d
Hamman v. United States, 391
Hammermill Paper Co., United States v., 1020, 1021, 1204d
Hanover Shoe v. United Shoe Mach. Corp., 338a-b, d, f, 365b1, 370, 371a-c, e, j1, 1459b1
Hanson v. Shell Oil Co., 711d, 1417b, 1440a, 1623c, 1627b, 1639c
Harbor Banana Distribs. v. FTC, 909c
Hardin v. Houston Chronicle Pub. Co., 1473d2, f
Hardin v. Kentucky Util. Co., 233c
Harding v. American Stock Exch., 224d
Hardrives Co. v. East Coast Asphalt Corp., 233b
Hardwick v. Nu-Way Oil Co., 1473d, d2, f
Hardy Salt Co. v. Illinois, 337a2, 339a
Harkins Amusement Enter. v. Harry Nace Co., 334c
Harley-Davidson Motor Co., 1713c2
Harman v. Valley Natl. Bank, 204c

Harnischfeger Corp. v. Paccor, 909c, 1020
Harper Plastics v. Amoco Chem. Corp., 335a
Harris v. Air King Prods. Co., 707d
Harrison v. Paramount Pictures, 376a
Harrison v. Prather, 838b
Harriss, United States v., 311a2
Harron v. United Hospital Center, 323d
Hartford-Empire Co. v. United States, 345
Harvey v. Fearless Farris Wholesale, 1467a
Harwell v. Growth Programs, 224d
Hasbrouck v. Texaco (842 F.2d 1034), 384
Hasbrouck v. Texaco (631 F. Supp. 258), 355d
Hassan v. Independent Practice Assocs., 375b
Hastings Mfg. Co., 305d
Hatley v. American Quarter Horse Assn., 1470
Hawaii v. Standard Oil Co. (Cal.), 323c, 360b, 361, 380
Hayashi v. Sunshine Garden Prods., 235c
Hayden v. Bardes Corp., 381b
Hayden Publishing Co. v. Cox Broadcasting Corp., 532b
Hayes v. Solomon, 374
Hazeltine Research v. Zenith Radio Corp., 236g
Hazeltine Research v. Zenith Radio Corp. (388 F.2d 25), 365b2
Hazeltine Research v. Zenith Radio Corp. (239 F. Supp. 51), 365b2
H & B Equip. Co. v. International Harvester Co., 1468, 1470, 1471e1, 1605b
Head v. New Mexico, 219b
Health Corp. v. New Jersey Dental Assn., 374
Healthco, United States v., 909c, 917, 921, 1205d1
Heart of Atlanta Motel v. United States, 232a
Heater v. FTC, 305e
Heath v. Aspen Skiing Corp., 206d3
Heaton Peninsula Button Fastening Co. v. Eureka Specialty Co., 1701a
Heatransfer Corp. v. Volkswagenwerk (553 F.2d 964), 563d, 570d, 1725c
Heatransfer Corp. v. Volkswagenwerk A.G. (1975) Trade Cas.), 235c, 1020, 1021, 1469a
Hecht v. Pro-football, 206d2, d3, 214d, 216a, 374
Hecht Co. v. Bowles, 346b
Heilemen, G., Brewing Co., United States v., 926b
Helicopter Support Systems v. Hughes Helicopter, 322g, 1603
Helix Milling Co. v. Terminal Flour Mills Co., 363c, 381a, 1201b, 1205e3
Henderson Broadcasting Corp. v. Houston Sports Assn., 563e
Hendricks Music Co. v. Steinway, 563e

Henke Enters. v. Hy-Vee Food Stores, 373c
Hennegan v. Pacifico Creative Serv., 338b
Henry v. A. B. Dick Co., 1701a, 1720b
Henry v. Chloride, 384
Henry Broch & Co., FTC v. (368 U.S. 360), 305e
Henry Broch & Co., FTC v. (363 U.S. 166), 384
Herbert R. Gibson, 1609a
Herbold Lab v. United States, 305e
H. E. Reeves v. Laredo Ready Mix, 1417b
Hershey Chocolate Corp. v. FTC, 828e, 1653e
Hess v. Inland Asphalt Co., 374
H.F. & S. Co. v. American Standard, 829d
H. H. Robertson Co. v. Guardian Indus. Corp., 381b
Higgins v. New York Stock Exch., 338e
Highland Supply Corp. v. Reynolds Metals Co., 381a
High Technology Careers v. San Jose Mercury News, 322c
Hiland Dairy v. Kroger Co., 320b, 822a, 835c
Hill v. A-T-O, 1701c
Hills Condominium Assoc. m-1 v. Corley, 1722c
Hines v. Davidowitz, 209
Hirsh v. Martindale-Hubbell, 1710b, 1716a, 1718c, i
H.J. v. Flygt Corp., 355d
H.J. v. International Tel. & Tel. Corp., 533b-c
H. L. Hayden Co. of New York v. Siemens Medical Sys., 322c
H. L. Moore Drug Exch. v. Eli Lilly Co., 1446b, 1456d3, 1459d2, 1609a
Hobart Bros. Co. v. Malcolm T. Gilliland, 1605b, 1642c
Hoffman Motors Corp. v. Alfa Romeo S.A., 235c
Holloway v. Bristol-Myers Corp., 305e
Holly Farms Poultry Indus. v. Kleindienst, 331c
Holmberg v. Armbrecht, 338d
Holter v. Moore and Co., 1473d2, f
Home Placement Serv. v. Providence Journal, 355d, 365d
Homeware v. Rexair, 1639c
Homewood Theatre v. Loew's, 337a2
Hood v. Tenneco Texas Life Ins. Co., 1464f
Hood, H. P., & Sons v. DuMond, 220a, b, d
Hoopes v. Union Oil Co., 338b, 364g
Hoover v. Ronwin, 572a
Hopkins v. State, 332a
Hopkins v. United States, 1501
Hospital Building Co. v. Trustees of Rex Hospital, 232e
Hospital Corp. of Am. (106 F.T.C. 207), 550b
Hospital Corp. of Am. v. FTC (481 U.S. 1038), 572a
Hospital Corp. of Am. v. FTC (807 F.2d 1381), 553e
Hotel Telephone Charges, In re, 356d

Household Goods Carriers' Bureau v. Terrell, 365b2
Houston, E. & W. Tex. Ry. v. United States, 218b
H. P. Hood & Sons v. DuMond, 220a, b, d
Hughes v. United States, 348b
Hughes Tool Co. v. TWA, 224f, 225c
Hughes Tool Co., United States v., 348a, 1119e1, 1123a
Human Resources Inst. v. Blue Cross (Va.), 1409c
Humboldt Bay Municipal Water Dist. v. Louisiana-Pacific Corp., 1622a
Humphrey's Executor v. United States, 305c
Hunt v. Crumboch, 229e
Hunt v. Mobil Oil Corp., 235c, 239b1
Hunt v. Washington State Apple Advertising Commn., 379b
Hunt-Wesson Foods v. Ragu Foods, 532b, 1467b, e1
Huron Portland Cement Co. v. City of Detroit, 212a
Huron Valley Hosp. v. City of Pontiac (666 F.2d 1029), 374
Huron Valley Hosp. v. City of Pontiac (612 F. Supp. 654), 338e
Huron Valley Publishing Co. v. Booth Newspapers, 824, 832
Hutcheson, United States v., 229b, e
Hyde v. Jefferson Parish Hosp. Dist. No. 2, 1716e2, 1717f1
Hydro Air (Conn.) v. Versa Technologies, 1645c
Hydrolevel case, see American Socy. of Mechanical Engrs. v. Hydrolevel
HyPoint Technology v. Hewlett-Packard Co. (949 F.2d 874), 375f
HyPoint Technology v. Hewlett-Packard Co. (1990-1 Trade Cas. ¶69,090), 562f

IBM v. United States, 563e, 733a, 1460e, 1701c, 171163, 1716a1, b, c1, d, 1720b2, b4, 1721b, 1726e2, 1730a
ICI case, see Imperial Chem. Indus. Ltd., United States v.
ICM Realty v. Cabot, Cabot & Forbes Land Trust, 909c
Idaho First Natl. Bank, United States v., 530e, 1121c3, 1125c
I. Haas Trucking Corp. v. New York Fruit Auction Corp., 835c, 1721b3-b4
ILC Peripherals Leasing Corp. v. IBM Corp., 321e
Illinois v. Borg, 371e
Illinois v. General Paving Co., 337c
Illinois v. Sperry Rand Corp., 338d
Illinois Brick Co. v. Illinois, 371a, c, e-f, 372, 380, 1459b1
Illinois Corporate Travel v. American Airlines, 1652b
Illinois ex rel. Burris v. Panhandle E. Pipe Line Co., 371e
Illinois ex rel. Hartigan v. Panhandle E. Pipe Line Co., 550b, 572c

Imperial Chem. Indus. Ltd., United States v., 238
Imperial Point Colonnades Condominium v. Mangurian, 338b
Implement Workers of Am. v. Brock, 379b
Impro Prods. v. Herrick, 1409a
Independent Iron Works v. US Steel, 821, 822a, 832, 1413
Indiana Fedn. of Dentists, FTC v., 305f, 307a, 320b, 530b, 1643d, 1728a
Indiana Grocery v. Super Valu Stores, 362c, 423, 535c2
Indium Corp. of Am. v. Semi-Alloys, 360d
Industrial Bldg. Materials v. Interchemical Corp., 832
Industrial Commns. Systems v. Pacific Tel. & Tel. Co., 213f
Industrial Gas Antitrust Litig., 360e1, 377d5
Industrial Inv. Dev. Corp. v. Mitsui & Co., 360e1
Information Resources v. A.C. Neilsen Co., 1722c
Ingersoll-Rand Co., United States v., 1105e, 1109d2, 1131c3, 1131d, 1133c
Inland Container Corp., 909c
Inryco, United States v., 338b
Instant Delivery Corp. v. Cities Stores Co., 320b
Insurance Antitrust Litig., 364e
Interamerican Ref. Corp. v. Texaco Maracaibo, 239b
Interborough News Co. v. Curtis Publishing Co., 320b, 1653e
Inter City Oil Co. v. Murphy Oil Corp., 223b
Intercontinental Transp. Corp. v. New York Shipping Assn., 229e
Intermountain Ford Tractor Sales Co. v. Massey-Ferguson Ltd., 235c
International Air Indus. v. American Excelsior Co., 711d
International Assn. of Heat and Frost Insulators v. United Contractors Assn., 229c, 361, 377d4, 379a
International Boxing Club v. United States, 563e
International Business Mach. Co., see IBM
International Distrib. Ctrs. v. Walsh Trucking Co., 532b
International Harvester Co. v. United States, 1713c2
International Harvester Co., United States v., 607, 909c, 934e, 935a-b
International Logistics Group v. Chrysler Corp., 563d
International Minerals & Chem. Corp., United States v., 332a
International Rys. of Central America v. United Brands Co., 364g, 736a
International Salt Co. v. United States, 304c, 727c2, 733b, 1133a, 1134c, 1146b 1701c, 1707e, e3-e4, 1716c1, d, d2-d3, 1719b, 1720b3-b4, c, 1721b-b4, c2, d, 1726e2, 1730a
International Shoe Co. v. FTC, 333f, 904, 924, 926, 926a, 925c, 926a, b, 927d, 1002, 1145a
International Shoe Co. v. Washington, 235a, b

International Shoe Mach. Corp. v. United Shoe Mach. Corp., 337b
International Tel. case, see IT&T Corp. v. General Tel. & Elec. Corp.
International Tel. & Tel. Co., see IT&T
International Travel Arrangers v. Western Air Lines, 224f, 227a, 1474b
International Union, United Automobile, Aerospace & Agric.
Interphoto Corp. v. Minolta Corp., 832, 1605b
Interstate Circuit v. United States, 841a, 1402b1, 1417g, 1426, a-b, d, 1427d, 1433c, 1448d
Investigation of World Arrangements, In re, 239c
Iowa v. Union Asphalt & Roadoils, Inc., 356b, 380
I.P.C. Distribs. v. Chicago Moving Picture Machine Operators, 229c
Irvin Indus. v. Goodyear Aerospace Corp. (974 F.2d 241), 363c
Irvin Indus. v. Goodyear Aerospace Corp. (803 F. Supp. 951), 363c
Irvin Indus. v. Goodyear Aerospace Corp. (774 F. Supp. 849), 363c
Isakson v. Vermont Castings, 382c, 1623f6
Isidor Weinstein Inv. Co. v. Hearst Corp., 381a
Island Tobacco Co. v. R. J. Reynolds Indus., 1467e1
Israel v. Baxter Labs, 203b
IT&T v. General Tel. & Elec. Corp. (518 F.2d 913), 338f, 346b, 355d, 1205c2
IT&T v. General Tel. & Elec. Corp. (369 F. Supp. 316), 334b4
IT&T v. General Tel. & Elec. Corp. (296 F. Supp. 920), 338f, 1020, 1021
IT&T v. United Tel. Co. (550 F.2d 287), 203b
ITT Continental Baking Co. (18 F.T.C. 1021), 305d
ITT Continental Baking Co., United States v. (1972 Trade Cas. ¶73,993), 305e, 1205c2
IT&T (Grinnell), United States v. (1971 Trade Cas. ¶73,665), 348a, 1020, 1108c, 1109a, 1109d2
IT&T, United States v. (349 F. Supp. 22), 348d-e, g, 909c
IT&T, United States v. (324 F. Supp. 19), 1020, 1105e, 1131c3, d, e, 1132c, 1133c
IT&T, United States v. (306 F. Supp. 766), 1133c, 1135a, 1141f
Ivaco, United States v., 565

Jack Faucett Assoc. v. AT&T, 336d
Jackshaw Pontiac v. Cleveland Press Publishing Co., 356b
Jack Walters & Sons Corp. v. Morton Buildings, 382c, 1440a, 1451c2, 1627e5, 1639g3, 1640b1, b3, 1645b, 1716d2

Jacobi v. Bache & Co., 223d, 226d, 356b, d
Jacob Siegel Co. v. FTC, 305e
Jade Aircraft Sales v. City of Bridgeport, 374
James v. United States, 333d
James B. Beam Distilling Co. v. Georgia, 333a
Janel Sales Corp. v. Lanvin Parfums, 1629b, 1642c
Janich Bros. v. American Distilling Co., 1711g
Janush v. U-Haul Co., 1467a, e1
Japanese Elec. Prods. Antitrust Litigation, 321e, 1433a, 1434c2, 1443d2
Javelin Corp. v. Uniroyal, 235c, 390c, 1459c2
Jayco Systems v. Savin Bus. Mach. Corp., 1644c, 1645b
Jays Foods v. Frito-Lay, 334b2
JBL Enterprises v. Jhirmack Enterprises (698 F.2d 1011, 1013-15, 1018-19), 565, 1624d1, 1645b-c
JBL Enterprises v. Jhirmack Enters. (509 F. Supp. 357), 564, 1725h
Jefferson Parish Hospital District No. 2 v. Hyde (104 S. Ct. 1551), 1510a
Jefferson Parish Hosp. Dist. No. 2 v. Hyde (466 U.S. 2), 304c, 320b, 375d, 523, 1700d, j1, 1701c2-d, 1710a-b, 1712d2, f, 1715b, 1716a1, d, e2, 1718c, 1719b, 1720, b, b2-b4, c1, 1721d-d2, 1722a-c, 1723a-b, 1724a, d1, 1725a, f, i, 1726a, c, e2, 1727g, 1728b-d, f, 1729g, i1, 1730a-d
Jeffrey v. Southwestern Bell Tel. Co., 360b, 370
Jennings Oil Co. v. Mobil Oil Corp., 563d
Jerrold Elec. Corp. v. Westcoast Broadcasting Co., 832
Jerrold Elec. Corp., United States v., 320b, 733c, 735b3, 822a, 829d, 1020, 1021, 1133a, 1204c, d, 1508c, 1510b, 1713b3, 1716a1, c2, c4, 1717f1, 1730a
Jeter v. Credit Bureau, 305e
Jewel Cos. v. FTC, 305d
Jewel Tea case, see Local 189, Amalgamated Meat Cutters v. Jewel Tea Co.
Jewish Hosp. Assn. v. Stewart Mech. Enter., 371e-g
J. F. Feeser v. Serv-A-Portion, 384
J. H. Westerbeke Corp. v. Onan Corp., 561a
Jicarilla Apache Tribe v. Supron Energy Corp., 1435e
J. I. Case, United States v., 1460f
Jim Walter Corp., 909c
J&J Furniture and Sleep Shop v. Sealy Southwest, 1425d4
Joe Requeira v. American Distilling Co., 1457c4
John Lenore & Co. v. Olympia Brewing Co., 360e1, 375c
Johns-Manville Corp., United States v., 206b, 832, 835c
Johnson v. Con-Vey/Keystone, 378d
Johnson v. Mobil Oil Co., 1473d2
Johnson v. Nationwide Indus., 1717f4

Johnson v. Pacific Lighting Land Co., 375c, 1640d3
Johnson v. Soundview Apartments Housing Dev. Fund Co., 1721b4, d-d2
Joint-Traffic Assn., United States v., 1501
Jones v. General Tire & Rubber Co., 335b
Jones v. 247 East Chestnut Props., 1717f4
Joseph E. Seagram & Sons v. Hawaiian Oke and Liquors, Ltd., 828e, 1457, 1468, 1470, 1653b
Jos. Schlitz Brewing Co., United States v., 909c, 926b, 1204c, d
JST Properties v. First Natl. Bank of Glencoe, 383a
J. T. Gibbons v. Crawford Fitting Co., 1459c3, 1467b
J. Truett Payne Co. v. Chrysler Motors Corp., 360e1, 362b, 384, 1613f
Julien v. Society of Stage Directors and Choreographers, 229c
Julius M. Ames Co. v. Bostitch, 346b
Julius Nasso Concrete Corp. v. D.I.C. Concrete Corp., 1205c2
Juster Assocs. v. City of Rutland, 362a

Kaiser v. General Motors Corp., 1642c
Kaiser Aluminum & Chemical Corp., 909c
Kaiser Aluminum & Chem. Corp. v. FTC, 533e-f, 561a
Kaiser Aluminum & Chem. Sales v. Avondale Shipyards, 338f
Kaiser Cement Corp. v. Fishback & Moore, 363b
Kaiser Steel Corp. v. Mullins, 385
Kallen v. Nexus Corp., 232e
Kansas City Star Co. v. United States, 338a, 822a, 831
Kansas & Missouri v. Utilicorp United, 371c, e, 380
Kansas Power and Light Co. v. FPC, 224e
Kaplan v. Burroughs Corp., 363d
Kapp v. National Football League, 229d
Karseal Corp. v. Richfield Oil Corp., 373f4
Kartell v. Blue Shield (Mass.), 375b, 411, 574, 1622b
Katinsky v. Radio Shack Division of Tandy Corp., 1437d2
Kauffman v. Dreyfus Fund, 378d
Kaw Valley Elec. Coop. v. Kansas Elec. Power, 338b
Kearney & Trecker Corp. v. Cincinnati Milacron, 361
Kearney & Trecker Corp. v. Giddings & Lewis, 821, 832
Keco Indus. v. Borg-Warner Corp., 821
Keeler v. Standard Fold. Bed Co., 1621
Keener v. Sizzler Family Steak Houses, 1609a, 1709e5, 1726c
Kelco Disposal v. Browning-Ferris Indus. of Vt., 421b

Kellam Energy v. Duncan, 1627b
Kelly v. Kosuga, 391
Kennecott Copper Corp., 1003
Kennecott Copper Corp. v. Curtiss-Wright Corp., 921, 1203c, 1302b
Kennecott Copper Corp. v. FTC, 1119b, 1122b, 1123f, 1124a, c, g, 1135a
Kennecott Copper Corp., United States v., 909c, 1020, 1021, 1121c5
Kentucky Fried Chicken Corp. v. Diversified Packaging Corp., 1716e2, 1726c, 1727b1
Kershaw v. Kershaw Mfg. Co., 390a
Kestenbaum v. Falstaff Brewing Corp., 1609a, 1637f, 1645b-c
Key Enter. of Del. v. Venice Hosp., 375e
Key Fin. Planning Corp. v. ITT Life Ins. Corp., 563e
KFC Corp. v. Marion-Kay Co., 338b
Khedivial Lines, S.A.E. v. Seafarer's Intl. Union, 229b
Kiefer-Stewart Co. v. Joseph E. Seagram & Sons, 390b, 1436b, 1446e3, 1465a, 1604c2, 1609a, 1634, 1635, 1637d
Kimberly-Clark Corp., United States v., 1020, 1021, 1204c
King v. Idaho Funeral Serv. Assn., 363d
Kingsport Motors v. Chrysler Motors Corp., 1721c1-c2, d2
Kirihara v. Bendix Corp., 381a
Kirk-Mayer v. Pac Ord, 335b
Kirkpatrick, United States v., 338f
Klamath-Lake Pharmaceutical Assn. v. Klamath Medical Serv. Bureau, 362a
Klearflax Linen Looms, United States v., 822a, 1616e2
Klebanow v. New York Prod. Exch., 378a
Klein v. American Luggage Works, 365b4, 1623c
Kline v. Coldwell, Banker & Co., 356d
Klor's v. Broadway-Hale Stores, 232d, 355c, 1408f, 1644c
Klo-Zik Co. v. General Motors Co., 1722c
Knight, E. C., Co., United States v., 232c, 605
Knuth v. Erie-Crawford Dairy Cooperative Assn., 228c
Knutson v. Daily Review (548 F.2d 795), 824, 828c, 832, 1451c2, 1452c4, 1459c1, 1466b, 1467a, d, g-h, 1469d
Knutson v. Daily Review (468 F. Supp. 226), 365d, 1640d1-d2
Knutson v. Daily Review (383 F. Supp. 1346), 1642c
Kobe v. Dempsey Pump Co., 361, 708
Kodak, 1473f
Koefoot v. American College of Surgeons, 1722c
Koerner & Assoc. v. Aspen Labs, 1460f
Kolb v. Chrysler Corp., 378d
Kolb v. Pacific Maritime Assn., 229b
Koufakis v. Carvel, 1467a

Kowalski v. Chicago Tribune Co., 347
Kramer Motors v. British Leyland Motors, 1623c
Kreager v. GE, 398d
Krehl v. Baskin-Robbins Ice Cream Co. (664 F. 2d 1348), 1605c, d5, 1645d
Krehl v. Baskin-Robbins Ice Cream Co. (1979 Trade Cas. ¶62,806), 1605c
Kremer v. Chemical Constr. Corp., 335c2
Kreuzer v. American Academy of Periodontology, 1405, 1413, 1417b
Kroger v. FTC, 1606e3
Kurek v. Pleasure Driveway and Park District, 214a
Kypta v. McDonald's Corp., 383b, 1459c1, 1717f2

L. A. Draper & Son v. Wheelabrator-Frye, 534a1, 556
Ladue Local Lines v. Bi-State Dev. Agency, 206d3, 216a
Lafayette v. Louisiana Power & Light Co., 217a2, a3
Laidlaw Acquisition Corp. v. Mayflower Group, 381b, 562b
Laitram Corp. v. Deepsouth Packing Co., 339b
Lake Asphalt & Petroleum Co., United States v., 348c
Lamb Enters. v. Toledo Blade Co., 822a
Lamb's Patio Theatre v. Universal Film Exch., 1415d, 1417f
Lamp Liquors v. Adolph Coors Co., 363b, 374
Lancaster Colony Corp., FTC v., 305e, 909c
Landmark Dev. Corp. v. Chambers Corp., 1624d3
Langenderfer v. S. E. Johnson Co., 346b
Langsam v. Beam, 375e
Lanier Business Prods. v. Graymar Co., 390c, 391
La Peyre v. FTC, 729d, h, 736d, e
LaSalvia v. United Dairymen of Ariz., 338b
Las Vegas Drive-In Theatre v. National General Theatres, 1467a-b
Las Vegas Merchant Plumbers Assn. v. United States, 232c
Las Vegas Sun v. Summa Corp., 1467a, h, 1469d
Latin American Pacific Coast Steamship Conf. v. Federal Maritime Commn., 223c
Lau v. Travellers Indemnity Co., 323b
Laurel Sand & Gravel v. CSX Transp., 371h
Laveson v. TWA, 226d, 227a
Lawlor v. National Screen Serv. Corp., 334b5, c, 828e, 1653e, 1655d
Lawyers Title Co. v. St. Paul Title Ins. Corp., 210
L.C.L. Theatres v. Columbia Pictures Inds., 363c
Leader Theatre Corp. v. Randforce Amusement Corp., 335b
Lear v. Adkins, 209, 220b
Learner, United States v., 236g
Lear Siegler, 1301c

Lee-Moore Oil Co. v. Union Oil Co., 362c, 1459c3
Lefrak v. Arabian American Oil Co., 371c
Leh v. General Petroleum Corp., 339a
Lehigh Valley R. Co., United States v., 727b3, e, 811, 833c
Lehrman v. Gulf Oil Corp. (500 F.2d 659), 365a
Lehrman v. Gulf Oil Corp. (464 F.2d 26), 232e, 365b4, 1451c1-c2, 1452c2-c3, 1606c, 1627e5, 1639h
Leimer v. Woods, 321a
Lektro-Vend Corp. v. Vendo Co., 835c
Lemke v. Farmer Grain Co., 220c
Lenox v. FTC, 305f
Les Shockley Racing Co. v. National Hot Rod Assn., 323e
Lessig v. Tidewater Oil Co., 365b1, b4, 1451c1
Lever Brothers Co., United States v., 1202f1, f4
Levine, Aaron E., & Co. v. Calkraft Paper Co., 1467a-b, 1469b, d
Levi Strauss & Co. v. Federal Pants Co., 1623c
Levitch v. Columbia Broadcasting System, 1433a
Lewis v. Pennington, 229e
Lewis v. Seanor Coal Co., 391
Lewis v. Shell Oil Co., 233b
Lewis Serv. Center v. Mack Trucks, 1451c2, 1627e3, 1639h
L. G. Balfour Co. v. FTC, 305e, 731e, 1653e
Lieberthal v. North Country Lanes, 363c
Liggett & Meyers, 909c
Liggett & Myers v. FTC, 533e
Lilly, Eli, & Co., United States v. (24 F.R.D. 285), 1421d
Lilly, Eli, & Co., United States v., (1959 Trade Cas. ¶69,411), 1421d
Lindy Bros. Builders v. American Radiator & Standard Sanitary Corp., 355d
Ling-Temco Elec., United States v., 909c
Ling-Temco-Vought, United States v., 348g
Link v. Mercedes-Benz of North Am., 371h
Linkletter v. Walker, 333d
Lippa's v. Lenox, 339b
Lipson v. Socony-Vaccuum Corp., 233b
Liquid Carbonic Corp. v. United States, 348b
Little v. Blue Goose Motor Co., 336a
Littlejohn v. Shell Oil Co., 233c
Litton Indus., 909c, 937
Litton Sys. v. AT&T, 336e
Litton Sys. v. Southwestern Bell Tel. Co., 213f
Local 36 Intl. Fishermen v. United States, 228c
Local 167 Intl. Bd. of Teamsters v. United States, 334b5
Local 189, Amalgamated Meat Cutters v. Jewel Tea Co., 229b, e
Local Beauty Supply v. Lamaur, 360e1, 382c, 1623f6

Locker v. American Tobacco Co., 1653e
Loeb v. Eastman Kodak Co., 378c-d
Loew's, United States v., 304c, 345, 733b, 842a, 1134c, 1441h1, 1460b1, 1701c, 1708c, 1717c1-c4, e2, 1719b, 1721b, b3-b4
Lomar Wholesale Grocery v. Dieter's Gourmet Foods, 338b, 421b, 1652b, 1653e
Long Island Lighting Co. v. Standard Oil Co. (Cal.), 371c
Lorain Journal Co. v. FCC, 1705f1
Lorain Journal Co. v. United States (342 U.S. 143), 732c7, 825, 829d, 1134a
Los Angeles Land Co. v. Brunswick Corp., 532a
Los Angeles Meat and Provision Drivers v. United States, 229c
Los Angeles Mem. Coliseum Commn. v. National Football League, 373e2
Louisiana-Pacific Corp., United States v. 305d
Lovett v. General Motors Corp. (975 F.2d 518), 378d
Lovett v. General Motors Corp. (1993 Trade Cas. ¶70,292), 322f
Lowe v. Lawlor, 229b
Lower Lake Erie Iron Ore Antitrust Litig. (998 F.2d 1144), 371h, 372
Lower Lake Erie Iron Ore Antitrust Litig. (1993-1 Trade Cas. ¶70,249), 338b, 364e
Lucas v. Bechtel Corp., 377d4
Luckett v. Bethlehem Steel Broadcasting System, 1467g
Luckett v. Bethlehem Steel Corp., 322j
Lukens Steel Co., FTC v., 1415b
Lunkenheimer Co. v. Condec Corp., 909c
Luria Bros. v. FTC, 909c
Luria Steel and Trading Corp. v. Ogden Corp., 339b
Lyons v. Westinghouse Elec. Corp., 333a

McAlpine v. AAMCO Automobile Transmissions, 1721b3-b4
McBeath v. Inter-American Citizens for Decency Comm., 232e
McCabe's Furniture v. La-Z-Boy Chair Co., 1624e, 1625c1
McCaw Personal Communic. v. Pacific Telesis Group, 373d2
McClure v. Undersea Indus., 1459c3
McCormack v. National Collegiate Athletic Assn., 364e
McCormack v. Theo. Hamm Brewing Co., 832
McCullough Tool Co. v. Well Surveys, 1441h1
McDaniel v. Greensboro News Co., 1645c-d
McDonald v. Johnson & Johnson, 375c
McElhenney Co. v. Western Auto Supply Co., 1460f
McElhinney v. Medical Protective Co., 1471e2
McGeorge Car Co. v. Leyland Motor Sales, 1713c2, 1725c

McGlinchy v. Shell Chem. Co., 365b2
McGuire v. Times Mirror Co., 828b
McKesson & Robbins, United States v., 1605b, 1629b
Mackey v. National Football League, 229b, d
McLean Trucking Co. v. United States, 223c
McLeod v. J. E. Dilworth Co., 220b
McMorris v. Williamsport Hospital, 1471e2, g
McNeil v. National Football League, 377c
McQuade Tours v. Consolidated Air Tour Manual Commn., 320b, 729g
Madsen v. Chrysler Corp., 832, 835b
Mailand v. Powerine Oil Co., 233c
Malamud v. Sinclair Oil Corp., 362a
Malcolm v. Marathon Oil Co., 1459c3
Malone v. Crown Cent. Petrol. Corp., 1623c, 1639a
Manaka v. Monterey Sardine Indus., 228c
Mandeville Island Farms v. American Crystal Sugar Co., 231, 232d, e, 375b, 964b
Mans v. Sunray DX Oil Co., 377d3
Mansfield Journal Co. v. United States, 1705f1
Manufacturers' Assn. of the Relocatable Building. Ind., United States v., 321c
Manufacturer's Hanover Trust Co., United States v., 909c
Maple Flooring Mfrs. Assn. v. United States, 410, 1417b
Mapp v. Ohio, 333d
Marathon Oil Co. v. Mobil Corp., 381b, 550a, 1606c
Maricopa case, see Arizona v. Maricopa County Medical Socy.
Maricopa County v. American Pipe and Constr. Co., 338f, 339a
Marin County Bd. of Realtors v. Palson, 335a
Marine Bancorporation, United States v., 530f, 1118, 1119a, c, 1120b6, g, 1121c3, d2-3, 1122b, 1124b, d, g
Marine Cooks and Stewards v. Panama S.S. Co., 229b
Marine Firemen's Union v. Owen-Corning Fiberglass Corp., 339a
Marino v. Ramapo, 218b
Mark Aero v. TWA, 224f, 225d, 226d, 227a
Markel v. Scovill Mfg. Co., 375c
Marketing Assistance Plan v. Associated Milk Producers, 228c
Marks v. San Francisco Real Estate Boards, 356d
Marnell v. United Parcel Serv., 1653e
Marquette Cement Mfg. Co. v. Andreas, 1020, 1021, 1304
Marrese v. American Acad. of Orthopaedic Surgeons (470 U.S. 373), 335b, 335c2

Marrese v. American Acad. of Orthopaedic Surgeons (726 F.2d 1150), 335c2
Marrese v. American Acad. of Orthopaedic Surgeons (628 F. Supp. 918), 335c2
Marston v. Ann Arbor Property Managers Assn., 232e
Martin v. Phillips Petroleum Co., 374
Martindell v. News Group Publications, 1627e5
Martino v. McDonald's Sys. (625 F. Supp. 356), 1710b, 1712g, 1726c, 1727g
Martino v. McDonald's Sys. (1985-2 Trade Cas.), 1716d2
Martino v. McDonald's Sys. (86 F.R.D. 145), 522c
Martin Process Co. v. Lee Co., 1467b
Marty's Floor Covering Co. v. GAF Corp., 1473d2, 1622c
Maryland Baking Co. v. FTC, 711a, c
Maryland Cas. Co. v. American Gen. Ins. Co., 210
Maryland Cooperative Milk Producers, United States v., 228d
Maryland & Va. Milk Producers Assn. v. United States, 228c-d, 345
Maryland & Va. Milk Producers Assn., United States v. (167 F. Supp. 799), 228b, 320b, 926c, 1020, 1021
Masonite Corp., United States v., 1427 a-d
Massachusetts Brewers Assn. v. P. Ballantine & Sons Co., 233c
Massey-Harris-Ferguson, Ltd. v. Boyd, 235c
Master Key Antitrust Litigation, In re, 371c
Material Handling Inds. v. Eaton Corp., 338b
Matsuhita Elec. Indus. Co. v. Zenith Radio Corp., 321e, 322c, f-g, i, 360e1, 373b-c, 1625c1, 1626b
Mayer Paving and Asphalt Co. v. General Dynamics Corp., 233c
MCI Communic. Corp. v. ATT, 312d, 363a, 365b, 572c
MDC Data Centers v. IBM, 1723e
Mechanical Contractors Bid Depository v. Christiansen, 365b4
Mechanical Mfg. Co., 1130a
Mechanical Rubber & Supply Co. v. American Saw & Mfg. Co., 335b
Medical Arts Pharmacy of Stamford v. Blue Cross & Blue Shield (Conn.), 1622b
Meetinghouse Assoc. v. Warwick Township, 338b
Meicler v. Aetna Cas. Ins. Co., 210
Melrose Realty Co. v. Loew's, 376a
Mendelovitz v. Adolph Coors Co., 336f, 1644c, 1645b, e
Mendez, F. L., & Co. v. GM, 232b2
Mendoza, United States v., 336f
Mercedes-Benz, 1716d2
Mercedes-Benz of North America, United States v., 1716d, 1716e2, 1721c2

Meredith v. Mid-Atlantic Coca-Cola Bottling Co., 356b
Merican v. Caterpillar Tractor Co., 360d, 371e
Merit Motors v. Chrysler Corp., 322j, 832
Mesa Petroleum Co. v. Aztec Oil and Gas Co., 909c
Mesirow v. Pepperidge Farm (703 F.2d 339), 1440a, 1473d2, f, 1605b, 1622c, 1623c
Mesirow v. Pepperidge Farm (1981-2 Trade Cas. ¶64,292), 1645b-c
Metrix Warehouse v. Daimler-Benz Aktiengesellschaft (828 F.2d 1033), 336d, 365b2, 1716c1, d4, e2
Metrix Warehouse v. Daimler-Benz Aktiengesellschaft (716 F.2d 245), 384
Metrix Warehouse v. Mercedes-Benz of N. Am., 523
Metro Cable Co. v. CATV of Rockford, 204c, 214d, 216a
Metro-Goldwyn-Mayer v. Transamerica Corp., 1201c
Metro Mobile CTS v. NewVector Communic., 572a
Metropolitan Enter., United States v., 312c
Michaels Bldg. Co. v. Ameritrust Co., N.A., 323e
Michelman v. Clark-Schwebel Fiber Glass Corp., 1412c, g, 1423b
Michigan v. Morton Salt Co., 337a2, b, 339a
Mid-America ICEE v. John E. Mitchell Co., 1711b3, f2
Mid-American Dairymen, United States v., 228c
Mid Atlantic Coca-Cola Co. v. Allegheny Beverage Corp., 336a
Mid-Atlantic Toyota Antitrust Litigation, 371h, 1459a, 1604d1
Midcon, 552a
Midcon Corp. v. Freeport McMoran, 381b
Mid-South Grizzlies v. National Football League, 373e1
Mid-Texas Communic. Sys. v. AT&T, 572c
Midway Ent. v. Petroleum Mkt. Corp., 364g
Midwest Milk Monopolization Litigation, 228d, 371e, h, 1459b1
Mid-West Paper Prods. Co. v. Continental Group, 364d, 371c, e-f, 372, 1408c, 1459b2
Midwest Radio Co. v. Forum Publishing Co. (942 F.2d 1294), 322b
Midwest Radio Co. v. Forum Publishing Co. (1989-2 Trade Cas. ¶68,675), 539a
Midwestern Waffles v. Waffle House, 338b, 360d, 383b, 1459c1, 1605b, 1645b, 1726c
Milavetz v. Northwestern Bell Tel. Co., 212b
Milgram v. Loew's, 322c, 1415d, 1421b1, 1425c, 1426c
Milk and Ice Cream Can Inst. v. FTC, 1425e
Milk Control Bd. v. Eisenberg Farm Prods., 220c, d
Milk Wagon Drivers' Union v. Lake Valley Farm Prod., 229b

Miller v. Granados, 1717f4
Miller v. International Dairy, 1653c, 1716e, 1726e1
Miller Insituform v. Insituform of North America, 1722c
Miller Motors v. Ford Motor Co., 835b, 1460f, 1725c, 1726c, 1727g
Milner, W. J., & Co. v. IBEW, 229e
Milsen Co. v. Southland Corp., 1727g
Milwaukee v. Activated Sludge, 706c3, 736d
Milwaukee County v. M. E. White Co., 235b
Minersville Coal Co. v. Anthracite Export Assn., 373f4
Minielli Cement Contracting v. Richter Concrete Corp., 356b
Minnesota v. Barber, 220b
Minnesota v. Northern Sec. Co., 312e2
Minnesota v. US Steel Corp., 380
Minnesota Mining & Mfg. Co. v. New Jersey Wood Finishing Co., 337a1, 339b
Minnesota Mining & Mfg. Co., United States v., 230a, 236g, 237, 1118
Minpeco v. Conticommodity Servs., 1474d
Minpeco v. Hunt, 532a
Mir v. Litte Co. of Mary Hosp., 338b
Mississippi River Corp. v. FTC, 1020, 1021
Missouri Portland Cement Co. v. Cargill, 1109a, 1124c
Mitchell v. Gibbons, 229c
Mitsubishi Motors Corp. v. Soler Chrysler-Plymouth (473 U.S. 614), 324b
Mitsubishi Motors Corp. v. Soler Chrysler-Plymouth (814 F.2d 844), 334b2
M&M Medical Supplies and Serv. v. Pleasant Valley Hosp., 322j
Mobil Phone v. Commonwealth Tel. Co., 214b
Modern Home Institute v. Hartford Accident and Indemnity Co., 1415b
Mohawk Refining Co. v. FTC, 626d
Moitie v. Federated Dept. Stores (611 F.2d 1267), 335b
Molinas v. National Basketball Assn., 320b
Momand v. Universal Film Exch., 338a
Monona Shores v. US Steel Corp., 338c
Monsanto Co. v. Spray-Rite Serv. Corp., 322c, f, 1408a, 1441a, g, 1442a, 1444a, 1446, b, c1-c2, d1, d4-d5, e2, f, 1448, f, 1449, d, e2, 1450, 1451, e, 1452c, 1453a, d, 1454, b-d, 1455a-b, d, 1456a, c, 1457a, d2, 1458a-c, 1459a, d2-d3, e2, 1460b3, 1463b, 1604d1, g2, 1620c2, 1623, 1624a, e, 1625c1, 1626a, 1627d1, e5, 1630d
Montana v. SuperAmerica, 1415b
Monticello Tobacco Co. v. American Tobacco Co., 337b
Montreal Trading v. AMAX, 370
Moog Indus. v. FTC, 305e

Moore v. Jas. H. Matthews & Co., 832, 833b, 1710b, 1716d2, d4, 1718c, 1721b4, c2, 1726c, 1727d, e
Moore v. Mead's Fine Breads, 233c, d, 711a, c
Moore, H. L., Drug Exch. v. Eli Lilly & Co., 1446b, 1456d3, 1459d2
Morgan, United States v., 320b, 324a
Morgan, Strand, Wheeler & Biggs v. Radiology, Ltd., 534a1, 563e
Morning Pioneer v. Bismarck Tribune Co., 829a, 831, 835c
Morrison v. Murray Biscuit Co., 382c, 1622c, 1624d1, 1645b-c
Morrison v. Nissan Motor Co., 1623c
Morristown Block & Concrete v. General Shale Prods. Corp., 322c
Morse v. Nintendo of Am., 335b
Mortensen v. First Fed. Sav. & Loan Assn., 232e
Morton Buildings of Nebraska v. Morton Buildings, 363b, 1471e3, 1472, 1474c
Morton Salt Co. v. G. S. Suppiger Co., 391, 707b, 709, 1720b, c
Morton Salt Co., FTC v., 384, 828c, 1006e
Morton Salt Co., United States v. (235 F.2d 573), 1419c, 1420a, 1433e
Morton Salt Co., United States v. (1964 Trade Cas. ¶71,304), 1420a
Moss, Samuel H. v. FTC, 720c
Motion Picture Adv. Serv. Co., FTC v., 304c, 305c, 334b3, 732c5, 1301b
Motion Picture Patents Co. v. Universal Film Mfg. Co., 735b3, 1701b-c, 1720b, b4, 1730a
Motive Parts Warehouse v. Facet Enter., 363a
Mount Hood Stages v. Greyhound Corp., 225b, 338e
Movidyn, United States, Corp. v. Hercules, 707d
Movie 1 & 2 v. United Artists Communic., 311a2
Moviecolor Ltd. v. Eastman Kodak Co., 338a
Mowery v. Standard Oil Co. (Ohio), 1451c2, 1639g4
Mozart Co. v. Mercedes-Benz of North America, 336d, 523, 1716d4, e, 1719b
M.P.M., United States v., 909c, 917, 926b, 1205e2
Mr. Furniture Warehouse v. Barclays Am./Commercial, 370
Mrs. Smith's Pie Co., United States v., 909c
Mt. Lebanon Motors v. Chrysler Corp., 828b, 832
Mt. Vernon Sundat v. Nissan Motor Corp., 1626b
Muenster Butane v. Stewart Co., 1645b, d-e
Muller, E. B., Co. v. FTC, 711c
Mullis v. Arco Petroleum Corp., 835b, c
Multidistrict Vehicle Air Pollution, In re, 364b

Multidistrict Vehicle Air Pollution v. General Motors Corp., 338b
Multiflex v. Samuel Moore & Co., 365b, 373d1
Mulvey v. Samuel Goldwyn Prods., 363e, 364g, 383c, 1718e
Municipality of Anchorage v. Hitachi Cable, 336d
Murdaugh Volkswagen v. First Natl. Bank of South Carolina, 1425c
Murdock v. City of Jacksonville, 206d3, 214d, 216a
Murphy Tugboat Co. v. Crowley, 365b2, 1469b
Murphy Tugboat Co. v. Shipowners & Merchants Towboat Co., 1467h, 1469b, d
Murray v. Toyota Motor Distribs., 1466b, 1467h
Murrow Furniture Galleries v. Thomasville Furniture, 563e
Mutual Fund Investors v. Putnam Management Co., 1467h, 1468, 1469a, d, 1653c

Nabisco v. FTC, 305d
Nader v. Allegheny Airlines, 224a, f, 227a
Nagler v. Admiral Corp., 323a
Nanavati v. Burdette Tomlin Memorial Hosp., 335c2
NASD case, see National Assn. of Sec. Dealers, United States v.
Nash v. United States, 311a3
Nash Cty. Bd. of Educ. v. Biltmore Co., 335c2
Nashville Milk Co. v. Carnation Co., 312d, d1, 355a
National Assn. of Pharmaceutical Mfrs. v. Ayerst Labs. (850 F.2d 904), 563d
National Assn. of Pharmaceutical Mfrs. v. Ayerst Labs. (1987-1 Trade Cas. ¶67,573), 379b
National Assn. of Real Estate Boards, United States v., 229c, 334b5
National Assn. of Realtors v. National Real Estate Assn., 379b
National Assn. of Sec. Dealers, United States v., 213f, 223f, 224a, c-f
National Assn. of Women's and Children's Apparel Salesmen v. FTC, 229c
National Auto Brokers Corp. v. General Motors Corp., 1644c
National Bancard Corp. v. VISA U.S.A., 312c, 563d
National Broiler Mktg. Assn., United States v., 228b, 1463f
National Cas. Co., FTC v., 210
National City Lines, United States v., 334b5, 839
National Collegiate Athletic Assn. v. Board of Regents of the Univ. of Oklahoma, 320b, 373e2, 1500, 1502, 1503b, 1504, 1505a-b, 1508a, 1510c, 1511, 1643d, 1728a
National Dairy Prods. Corp. v. Milk Drivers Local 680, 229e
National Dairy Prods. Corp., United States v., 312d1, 711c

National Lead Co., United States v., 237, 345, 620c
National Macaroni Mfrs. v. FTC, 574
National Malleable Steel Castings Co., United States v., 1421b1
National Music Ctrs. of Am. v. Kimball Intl., 338d
National Petroleum Refiners Assn. v. FTC, 218b, 305g
National Securities, SEC v., 210
National Society of Professional Engineers v. United States, 1145b, 1477, 1502, 1504, 1508c, 1511, 1718j
National Souvenir Ctr. v. Historic Figures, 338b
National Supply Co. v. Hillman, 1203b
National Tea Co., FTC v., 305e, 909c
Nationwide Auto Appraiser Serv. v. Association of Casualty and Surety Cos., 376a
Nationwide Mut. Ins. Co. v. Automotive Serv. Councils of Del., 335c1, 336d
NBO Indus. Treadway Cos. v. Brunswick Corp., 345, 346b, 1135a, 1136b1
Nelligan v. Ford Motor Co., 1726c, 1727g
Nelson v. Monroe Regional Medical Ctr., 370
Nelson Radio & Supply Co. v. Motorola, 1460f, 1470
Nerney v. New York, 736d
Neumann v. Reinforced Earth Co., 374
Newberry v. Washington Post Co., 1451c2, 1627d1, 1645c-d
New England Liquor Sales Co. v. General Beverage Co., 336g
New Jersey v. Morton Salt Co., 339a
Newman v. Universal Pictures, 362c
New Mexico v. American Petrofina, 216a1, 217a3
New Mexico Natural Gas Antitrust Litigation, 371e, 1426d
New Orleans Chapter, Associated Gen. Contractors, United States v. (382 U.S. 17), 338f
New Orleans Chapter, Associated Gen. Contractors, United States v. (238 F. Supp. 273), 331c
New Orleans Ins. Exch., United States v., 210
Newport Components v. NEC Home Elecs., 563d
Newspaper Drivers Local 372 v. Detroit Newspaper Publishers Assn., 229d
Newspaper Drivers Local 372 v. NLRB, 229d
Newspaper Guild v. Levi, 230d
New York v. Dairylea Cooperative, 1459b1
New York Citizens Comm. v. Manhattan Cable TV, 572a
New York ex rel. Abrams v. Kraft General Foods, 347
New York Great Atl. & Pac. Tea Co., United States v., 727e
Nichols v. Mobile Bd. of Realtors, 356d

Nichols v. Spencer Intl. Press, 229d, 377c, 1469d
Nifty Food Corp. v. Great Atl. & Pac. Tea Co., 563d, 1400a
Nissan Antitrust Litigation, 336c, 356b, 1440a, 1623c, 1626b
Nissan Corp., 1408c
Nissan Motor Corp. Antitrust Litig., 336c, 356b
Nobel Scientific Indus. v. Beckman Instruments, 539a, 563d
Noble v. McClatchey Newspapers, 355b2
Noerr case, see Eastern R.R. Pres. Conf. v. Noerr Motor Freight
Nordenfelt v. Maxim Nordenfelt Guns and Ammunition Co., 1501
Norfolk Monument Co. v. Woodlawn Memorial Gardens, 322c, 1433d
Norman's on the Waterfront v. Wheatley, 213a, f
Norman Tobacco & Candy Co. v. Gillette Safety Razor Co., 338b
North Am. Corp. v. Men's Intl. Professional Tennis Council, 373e2
North American Soccer League v. National Football League, 1478d
North Carolina v. Chas. Pfizer & Co., 1433a
North Carolina Elect. Membership Corp. v. CP&L, 338c
North Carolina Utilities Commn. v. FCC, 214b4
Northern v. McGraw-Edison Co., 1701c, 1717b2, f2, 1730a
Northern Assurance Co. v. Grand View Bldg. Assn., 338b
Northern Cal. Pharmacists Assn. v. United States, 233b
Northern Cal. Supermarkets v. Central Cal. Lettuce Producers Cooperative, 228b, d
Northern Improvement Co., United States v., 338b
Northern Pac. Ry. Co. v. United States, 304c, 524d, 905, 1133a, 1134c, d, 1502, 1642a, 1643b, 1700a, d, 1701c, d, 1707e, e3-e4, 1715b, d2, 1719b, 1720b3-b4, 1721b, b3, d, 1722a-c, 1725c, 1728c, 1730a
Northern Sec. Co. v. United States, 209, 212c, 213a, 214a, 232c, 345, 902a, 1403, 1463b, 1466d2
North Penn. Oil & Tire Co. v. Phillips Petrol. Co., 1415b
North Texas Producers Assn. v. Metzger Dairies, 228c
North Texas Producers Assn. v. Young, 374
Northwest Indus., United States v., 133c, 909c
Northwest Publishing v. Crumb, 362a, 382c, 1459c1, 1640b1
Northwest Wholesale Stationers v. Pacific Stationery & Printing Co., 320b, 1644c, 1652b
Nurse Midwifery Assocs. v. Hibbett, 1471e2, f
N.W. Controls v. Outboard Marine Corp., 822b

Oak Distrib. Co. v. Miller Brewing Co., 835c, 1653c

Oberweis Dairy v. Associated Milk Producers, 336d

Obron v. Union Camp Corp., 337a2

Occidental Petroleum Corp. v. Buttes Gas & Oil Co., 239b1

Occidental Petroleum Corp., FTC v., 535c1, 555c

Ocean State Physicians Health Plan v. Blue Cross, 365d

Oetiker v. Jurid Werke, 836b

Official Publications v. Kable News Co., 323e

Ogden Food Serv. Corp. v. Mitchell, 1441h1

Ogilvie v. Fotomat Corp., 1466b, 1467a, d, h

Ohio-Sealy Mattress Mfg. Co. v. Sealy, 1622c, 1641b3, 1709e4, 1716e4, 1722a, c, 1726c, 1727d-d1

Ohio Valley Elec. Corp. v. GE, 338d, 365b1, 1419c

OKC Corp., 1020, 1021

Oklahoma v. Allied Materials Corp., 337b

Old Dearborn Distrib. Co. v. Seagram-Distillers Corp., 1629b

Oldham, R. P., Co., United States v., 236e

Olin Corp., 555c, 562a

Oliver case, see Teamsters Union v. Oliver

Olmstead v. Amoco Oil Co., 1727g

Oltz v. St. Peter's Community Hosp., 570b2

Olympia Equip. Leasing v. Western Union Tel. Co., 365b2, 1727f

Olympia Food Market v. Sheffield Farms Co., 233b

Olympia Provision & Baking Co., United States v., 229c

O. M. Droney Beverage Co. v. Miller Brewing Co., 1627b, 1639g2

Omni Outdoor Advertising v. Columbia Outdoor Advertising, 563e

O. M. Scott & Sons, United States v., 1623c, 1639b

O'Neill v. Coca-Cola Co., 360f, 370, 381a

Optivision v. Syracuse Shopping Center Assocs., 1653c, 1655d

Orange Front Paint Supply v. Pur-All Paint Prods. Co., 1653c

Orbo Theatre Corp. v. Loew's, 337b, 1415b

Oreck Corp. v. Whirlpool Corp. (639 F. 2d 75), 1604g2

Oreck Corp. v. Whirlpool Corp. (579 F.2d 126), 1456d4, 1457c3, d, 1604f4, 1644a, c, 1645b-c, e

Original Appalachian Artworks v. Granada Elec., 382c, 1623f6

Orion Pictures Distrib. Corp. v. Syufy Enters., 375b

O'Riordan v. Long Island Bd. of Realtors, 1722c, 1723b, 1724b

Orthopedic & Sports Injury Clinic v. Wang Labs., 322j

Osborn v. Sinclair Ref. Co., 365b1, 365b4
O.S.C. Corp. v. Apple Computer (792 F.2d 1464), 1645b, d-e
O.S.C. Corp. v. Apple Computer (601 F. Supp. 1274), 1625c1, 1645b-c
O.S.C. Corp. v. Apple Computer (1983-2 Trade Cas. ¶65,493), 1625c1
O.S.C. Corp. v. Toshiba American, 235c
Ostrofe v. H. S. Crocker Co., 377d5
Otter Tail Power Co. v. United States, 223b, 224d, 572c, 726e, 729e
Otto Milk Co. v. United Dairy Farmers Cooperative Assn., 228c, 1408f3
Outboard, Marine & Mfg. Co., 1461
Outlet Communications v. King World Prods., 1721c2, d2
Overhead Door Corp. v. Nordpal Corp., 1473d2, 1622c
Overseas Motors v. Import Motors Ltd., 1417b
Ovitron Corp. v. GM, 363c, 822a
Owens-Illinois, 421c, 533c, 561d
Owens-Illinois, FTC v., 563e

Pabst Brewing Co., United States v., 530f, 902c, 909c, 914, 926b, 929a, 930a, 1205f
Pace Indus. v. Three Phoenix Co., 338b-c
Pacific & Arctic Ry. & Nav. Co., United States v., 236b
Pacific Coast Agric. Exp. Assn. v. Sunkist Growers, 228c, 236g, 832, 1653d
Pacific Dunlop Holdings, United States v., 348a
Pacific Eng. & Prod. Co. v. Kerr-McGee Corp., 711d, 831
Pacific Express v. United Airlines, 373c
Pacific Seafarers v. Pacific Far East Line, 236c, f2
Pacific Southwest Airlines, United States v., 215b, b2
Pacific Tobacco Co. v. American Tobacco Co., 1413, 1415e
Pacific W. Cable Co. v. City of Sacramento, 312e4
Package Shop v. Anheuser-Busch, 563d
Packard Motor Car Co. v. Webster Motor Car Co., 1652d, 1653c
Padgett v. Louisville & Jefferson City Air Bd., 214d, 216a
Page v. Work, 232e, 233e
Paine Lumber Co. v. Neal, 312e2
Palermo v. First Natl. Bank & Trust Co. of Okla. City, 383a
Palmer v. BRG of Ga. (111 S. Ct. 401), 322e-g, i
Palmer v. BRG of Ga. (874 F.2d 1417), 322e
Pan Am. World Airways v. United States, 224a, f, 225c, 226b, c, d, 305e, 703c
Pan Am. World Airways, United States v., 348g
Pandola v. Texaco, 375c
Panotex Pipe Line Co. v. Phillips Petroleum Co., 831, 835c
Papercraft Corp., 926b, 936

Paramount Famous Lasky Corp. v. United States, 213d, 216b, 836a
Paramount Pictures Corp. v. Baldwin-Montrose Chemical Co., 1301c, 1302b, 1303, 1304
Paramount Pictures, United States v. (334 U.S. 131), 345, 563e, 672b1, 727a, c3, e, 1408d, 1433c, 1717c1, e1, 1720b3, 1720c, 1726c
Paramount Pictures, United States v. (333 F. Supp. 1100), 348e
Paramount Pictures, United States v. (85 F. Supp. 881), 710
Pargas v. Empire Gas Corp., 909c, 1201b
Parke, Davis and Co., United States v., 734a, 841b, 1403, 1447b2, 1448c, 1449, b, d, 1450b, 1456a, 1460f, 1623d, 1630d
Parker v. Brown, 207, 209, 211, 212, 213a-f; 214a, b, b1, b2, b4, d; 215c, d; 216a, b; 217a3, b3, b4, b5; 218a-c; 219a, c; 228a-c
Parklane Hosiery Co. v. Shore, 336b-d
Parks v. Watson, 356d
Parmelee Transp. Co. v. Keeshin, 822a
Parsons v. Paramount Film Distrib. Co., 1415b
Parts and Elec. Motors v. Sterling Elec., 562f, 1722d, 1729g
Paschall v. Kansas City Star, 320b, 1639c
Pastor v. AT&T, 374
Patten, United States v., 609
Patterson v. United States, 1470
Patterson Dental Co. v. McGaughey, 1721b4, 1724b, d1
Paul v. Pulitzer Publishing Co., 1623c
Paul M. Harrod Co. v. A. B. Dick Co., 348c
Pavelic & Leflore v. Marvel Entertainment, 323e
Pay Less Drug Stores Northwest v. City Prods. Corp., 1653c
Payne, J. Truett, Co. v. Chrysler Motors Corp., 1613f
Pearl Brewing Co. v. Anheuser-Busch, 346c, 1451c2, 1639g4
Pearl Brewing Co. v. Jos. Schlitz Brewing Co., 365c3, 390c
Peck v. General Motors Corp., 378d
Peerless Prods. v. FTC, 218a
Peller v. International Boxing Club, 374
Penick & Ford, United States v., 133c
Penn Central Sec. Litigation, 1305, 1467h, 1468, 1469b, d
Pennington case, see United Mine Workers v. Pennington
Penn-Olin Chem. Co., United States v., 304c, 1118, 1119b, 1121b2, 3, 4, 6, c4, 1123d, 1123e2, 1125a, 1202h, 1478b2
Pennsalt Chem. Corp., United States v., 338e
Pennsylvania v. Pepsico, 1644c, 1652b
Pennsylvania Dental Assn. v. Medical Serv. Assn. (Pa.), 338b, 370, 1471g

Pennsylvania Railroad case, see Georgia v. Pennsylvania R. Co.
Pennsylvania Refuse Removal Assn., United States v., 233b
Pennsylvania R.R. v. ICC, 1204b, c
Pennzoil Co., United States v., 965a, 1204c
Pensiero v. Linogle, 323e
People v. Lauria, 1474c
People v. McLaughlin, 1474c
PepsiCo., FTC v., 909c, 911c
Performed Lines Prods. Co. v. Fanner Mfg. Co., 391
Perkasie Indus. Corp. v. Advance Transformer, 322b
Perkins v. Standard Oil Co., 360g
Perma Life Mufflers v. International Parts Corp., 365c3, 390b, c, 1403, 1408d, 1451b, e, 1459c2, 1463e, 1464e
Permanente Cement Co., 909c
Perpetual Fed. Savings & Loan Assn., 1302d
Perryton Wholesale v. Pioneer Distrib. Co., 828b
Person v. New York Post Corp., 1415b
Peter v. Union Oil Co., 333a, d
Petroleum for Contractors v. Mobil Oil Corp., 1721d2
Petroleum Prods. Antitrust Litigation, 322b-c, e-f, i, 1459b1
Petruzzi's IGA Supermarkets v. Darling-Delaware Co., 322g, i, 574
Pevely Dairy Co. v. United States, 233b
Pfizer v. India, 380
Pfizer v. Lord, 380
Pfizer, Chas., & Co. v. FTC, 305e, 707e, g
Pfizer, Chas., & Co., United States v. (426 F.2d 32), 1434d1
Pfizer, Chas., & Co., United States v. (367 F. Supp. 91), 1433a, 1434d1
Pfizer, Chas., & Co., United States v. (246 F. Supp. 464), 832
Pfizer, Chas., & Co., United States v. (245 F. Supp. 737), 821
Phelps Dodge, United States v., 1418b5
Phi Delta Theta Fraternity v. J. A. Buchroeder & Co., 1467a
Philadelphia v. American Oil Co., 356d, 380
Philadelphia v. Morton Salt Co., 235a
Philadelphia Bank, United States v., 214e, 223b, c, 224a, f, 322f, 534c, 535e, 902c, 909c, 942, 1006e, 1135d, 1147a
Philadelphia Elec. Co. v. Anaconda Am. Brass Co. (47 F.R.D. 557), 356a
Philadelphia Elec. Co. v. Anaconda Am. Brass Co. (43 F.R.D. 452), 356c
Philadelphia Housing Auth. v. American Radiator & Standard Sanitary Corp. (309 F. Supp. 1057), 380
Philadelphia Housing Auth. v. American Radiator & Standard Sanitary Corp. (50 F.R.D. 13), 371j1
Philadelphia Natl. Bank, United States v., 333f, 530d-e, 539b2, 565

Philadelphia Record Co. v. Manufacturing Photo-Engravers Assn., 229e
Philadelphia World Hockey Club v. Philadelphia Hockey Club, 229d
Philco Corp. v. RCA, 338d
Phillips v. Crown Central Petroleum Corp. (602 F.2d 616), 371e, 1419c, 1451c2, 1627d2
Phillips v. Crown Central Petroleum Corp. (426 F. Supp. 1156), 365b1
Phillipsburg Natl. Bank, United States v., 530e, 565, 909c, 942
Phillips Petrol. Co., United States v., 926b, 931c, 1119b, f1, 1125c, 1205e3
Phonetele v. AT&T (664 F.2d 716), 572c
Phonetele v. AT&T (1984-1 Trade Cas. ¶65,921), 336d, f
Phosphate Export Assn., 42 F.T.C. 555 (1946), 230a
Phototron Corp. v. Eastman Kodak, 347, 362b, 373d2, d4
Photovest Corp. v. Fotomat Corp., 523, 533e, 1467a-b, d, h, 1717f2, 1727e
Pick Mfg. Co. v. General Motors Corp. (80 F.2d 641), 1716a1, d4, 1720b2
Pierce v. Commercial Warehouse, 323e
Pierucci v. Continental Cas. Co., 210
Pike v. Bruce Church, 220a, d
Pillsbury Co., 909c, 911c, 935a
Pink Supply Corp. v. Hiebert, 1624e, 1625c1
Pinney Dock & Transp. Co. v. Penn. Cent. Co., 338d
Pioneer Co. v. Talon, 338b
Pitchford v. PEPI, 1605b, 1725c
Pittsburgh v. FPC, 223c
Pittsburgh Corning Europe, 1473f
Pittsburgh Plate Glass Co. v. United States, 1433e
Plastic Packaging Materials v. Dow Chemical Co., 1455b, 1642c
Plekowski v. Ralston Purina Co., 356d
Plumbers & Steamfitters Local 598 v. Morris, 379a
Pogue v. International Indus., 365c3, 1473d2
Polar Ice Cream & Creamery Co. v. Andrews, 220b, d
Pollack & Riley v. Pearl Brewing Co., 355b2, 365b4
Poller v. CBS, 322b-c, 1470, 1473a, 1474b
Pollock v. Citrus Assocs. of the New York Cotton Exch., 372
Polytechnic Data Corp. v. Xerox Corp., 1716e2
Pontius v. Children's Hospital, 1471e1
Pope v. Mississippi Real Estate Commn., 373b
Poque v. International Indus., 365c3
Porto Rican American Tobacco Co. v. American Tobacco Co., 711a, c
Port Terminal & Warehousing Co. v. John S. James Co., 363a
Posa v. Miller Brewing Co., 1726c, e3-e4, 1727b1

Poster Exchange v. National Screen Serv. Corp., 336b, 338b-c, 1653e
Potter's Photographic Applications Co. v. Ealing Corp., 828e, 1653b, c, d
Power Draulic-Nielson v. Libbey-Owens-Ford Co., 382c
Power Test Petroleum Distrib. v. Calcu Gas, 1722c
PPG Indus., FTC v., 561b
Practice Perfect v. Hamilton Cty. Pharmaceutical, 374
Precision Air Parts v. Avco Corp., 336d
Preformed Line Prods. Co. v. Fanner Mfg. Co., 707b, 709, 1460f
Premier Elec. Const. Co. v. Miller-Davis Co., 390c
Premier Elec. Constr. Co. v. NECA, 336c, 361
Prepmore Apparel v. Amalgamated Clothing Workers of America, 229b
Price v. TWA, 226d, 227a
Principe v. McDonald's Corp., 1701c2, 1711b3, 1717f2, 1730a
Procter v. State Farm Mut. Auto Ins. Co., 210, 1622b
Procter & Gamble Co., FTC v., 104, 373d5, 421g, 941b, 1103a, 1109a, 1118, 1119b, d, 1120b6, 1121b4, c4, 1123a, c, d, e1, 1134d, 1135a, b, 1136b1, 1137, 1139, 1205c2
Productive Inventions v. Trico Prods. Corp., 376a
Professional Engineers case, see National Socy. of Professional Engrs. v. United States
Professional Real Estate Investors v. Columbia Pictures Indus., 323c
Protectoseal Co. v. Barancik, 1302a
Provident Natl. Bank, United States v., 909c
Province v. Cleveland Press Publishing Co., 377d3
Provision Salesmen & Distrib. Local 629 v. United States, 229c
Public Serv. Co. v. GE, 338d
Public Util. Commn. v. United States, 218b
Pullman Co., United States v., 338a, f, 726d5
Purex Corp. v. General Foods Corp., 390c
Purex Corp. v. Procter & Gamble Co., 1136b1
Purex Corp. v. Procter & Gamble Co. (664 F.2d 1105), 373d5
Purex Corp. v. Procter & Gamble Co. (596 F.2d 881), 373d2, d5
Purex Corp. v. Procter & Gamble Co. (453 F.2d 288), 337a1, 373d5
Purex Corp. v. Procter & Gamble Co. (419 F. Supp. 931), 1136b1

Quality Auto Body v. Allstate Ins. Co., 1433a, 1622b
Quality Mercury v. Ford Motor Co., 1651f, 1653c
Quinn v. Mobil Oil Co., 1440a, 1451c1, 1452b, 1457c4

Quinonez v. National Assn. Sec. Dealers, 377c

Rader v. Balfour, 339b
Radiant Burners v. Peoples Gas, Light & Coke Co. (364 U.S. 656), 360g
Radiant Burners v. Peoples Gas, Light & Coke Co. (273 F.2d 196), 355c
Radio City Music Hall Corp. v. United States, 322b
Radio Corporation of America, see RCA
Radovich v. National Football League, 360g, 377c
Ragar v. J. T. Raney & Sons, 378b
Railing v. United Mine Workers, 338c
Raitport v. Chase Manhattan Capital Corp., 1412, 1412g
Raladam Co., FTC v., 334c
Ramsey v. United Mine Workers, 229e
Randustrial Corp. v. Union Rubber Co., 336a
Rangen v. Sterling Nelson & Sons, 206d4, 233c
Rasmussen v. American Dairy Assn., 232e
Ratino v. Medical Serv. (D.C.), 1457c4
Rayco Mfg. v. Dunn, 1467a, h
Raymond Bros.-Clark Co., FTC v., 829d
RCA, United States v. (358 U.S. 334), 223b, 224a, e, 338f
RCA, United States v. (46 F. Supp. 654), 348g
R.C. Bigelow v. Unilever, N.V., 347
R. C. Dick Geothermal Corp. v. Thermogenics, 367a
Rea v. Ford Motor Co., 828c, 832, 1622c
Reading Co., United States v., 727b3, 727c, e
Reading Indus. v. Kennecott Copper Corp., 372, 1434c2
REA Express, 1469b
REA Express v. Alabama Great S. R.R., 1469b
Realty Multi-List, United States v., 1508a
Reazin v. Blue Cross & Blue Shield of Kan., 375d-e, 421e
Rebel Oil Co. v. Atlantic Richfield (133 F.R.D. 41), 324a
Rebel Oil Co. v. Atlantic Richfield (1993-2 Trade Cas. ¶70,308), 324a
Reborn Enter. v. Fine Child (754 F.2d 1072), 1625c1
Reborn Enter. v. Fine Child (590 F. Supp. 1423), 1623c, 1624e
Recommendations for Pacific Forest Indus. (40 F.T.C. 843), 230a
Redd v. Shell Oil Co., 1448e2, 1642c, 1716d2
Red Diamond Supply v. Liquid Carbonic Corp., 1605d1, 1645c-e
Redmond v. Missouri W. State College, 563e
Redwood Theatres v. Festival Enters., 335b
Reed Bros. v. Monsanto Co., 1642c

Reed Roller Bit Co., United States v., 909c, 926b, 929
Reeves, H. E. v. Laredo Ready Mix, 1417b
Regency Oldsmobile v. General Motors Corp., 563d
Regina Corp. v. FTC, 1623c
Region Properties v. Appalachian Power Co., 213f
Reibert v. Atlantic Richfield Co., 362a, 375c, 377d1
Reichhold Chemicals, 909c
Reid Bros. Logging Co. v. Ketchikan Pulp Co., 574
Reifer v. Sonotone Corp., 1459b1
Reisner v. General Motors Corp., 1466d3, 1468, 1469d, 1718k, 1721c1
Reiter v. Sonotone (442 U.S. 330), 361, 370, 377b
Reiter v. Sonotone (579 F.2d 1077), 361
Reiter v. Sonotone (486 F. Supp. 115), 371h
Reliable Tire Distribs. v. Kelley Springfield Tire Co., 1400a
Reliable Volkswagen v. World-Wide Auto, 1460f
Remington Prods. v. North Am. Phillips Corp. (755 F. Supp. 52), 373d4
Remington Prods. v. North Am. Phillips Corp. (717 F. Supp. 36), 373c, 533f
Removatron Intl. Corp. v. FTC, 305e
Republic Prods. v. American Federation of Musicians, 229b
Republic Steel Corp., United States v., 727a
Requeira, Joe, v. American Distilling Co., 1457c4
Response of Carolina v. Leasco Response, 363b, 1448e2, 1641b, 1642c
Return on Inv. Sys. v. Translogic Corp., 375f
Revlon, United States v., 1642c
Reynolds Metals Co. v. FTC, 711a, 1135a, 1136b3, 1137, 1205d1
R & G Affiliates v. Knoll Intl., 1460f, 1721b3, d2, 1722c
Ricci v. Chicago Mercantile Exch., 213f, 227a, b
Rice, Donald B., Tire Co. v. Michelin Tire Corp. (638 F.2d 15), 1605d2, 1611f, 1644b1
Rice, Donald B., Tire Co. v. Michelin Tire Corp. (438 F. Supp. 750), 1605b, d2, d5, 1645c-e
Richards v. Neilsen Freight Lines, 322f-g
Richard Short Oil Co. v. Texaco, 384
Richter Concrete Corp. v. Hilltop Basic Resources, 1507a
Rickards v. Canine Eye Registration Found., 1409c, 1726c
Ring v. Spina, 390a
Ringtown Wilbert Vault Works v. Schuylkill Mem. Park, 1721b3-b4, 1727e
Rip Side Prods. v. Jam Prods., Ltd., 323e
Rite Aid Corp. v. Borden Pharmacy, 219c
Roberts v. Elaine Powers Figure Salons, 1726c, 1727d
Roberts v. Exxon Corp., 1473d2

Roberts Co., 1461
Robert's Waikiki Rent-A-Car v. Budget Rent-A-Car, 1714c, 1715e, 1717b1, 1726c, 1727g
Robertson v. National Basketball Assn., 229d
Robinson v. Intergraph, 563d
Robinson v. Magovern, 1471e2, g
Rockford Memorial Corp., United States v. (898 F.2d 1278), 304c, 553e
Rockford Memorial Corp., United States v. (717 F. Supp. 1251), 550b, 563e
Rodgers v. FTC, 305d
Rodrigue v. Chrysler Corp., 1726c
Roesch v. Star Cooler Corp., 1455b, 1456c
Rogers v. American Can Co., 378e
Rogers, A. G., Co. v. Merck & Co., 1455b
Roland Mach. Co. v. Dresser Indus., 362b, 421f, 1449f
Rome Cable case, see Aluminum Co., United States v. (377 U.S. 271)
Ron Tonkin Gran Turismo v. Fiat Distribs., 1460f, 1604f4, 1644c, 1645b-c, 1652b, 1653c
Roosevelt Sav. Bank v. Eveready Maintenance Supply Co., 384
Rosebrough Monument Co. v. Memorial Park Cemetery, 365d, 1713c2, 1716d2, 1721b3
Rosefielde v. Falcon Jet Corp., 322g
Roseland v. Phister Mfg. Co., 377b
Rosenberg v. Cleary, Gottlieb, Steen & Hamilton, 376c
Ross v. Bernhard, 321a
Rothery Storage & Van Co. v. Atlas Van Lines, 533c, 1604c2, 1645c-d
Roth Office Equip. Co. v. G.F. Business Equip. Co., 1653b
Royal Drug Co. v. Group Life & Health Ins. Co., 1412g, 1426d, 1622b
Royal Oil Corp. v. FTC, 218a
Royal Printing Co. v. Kimberly-Clark Corp., 371f
Royal Serv. v. Goody Prods., 362a
R. P. Oldham Co., United States v., 236e
RSR Corp. v. FTC, 533e, 909c
Rubberoid Co., FTC v., 305e
Rush-Hampton Indus. v. Home Ventilating Institute, 204c
Russell Stover Candies, 1461
Russell Stover Candies v. FTC, 1451c1, 1461
Russ Togs v. Grinnell Corp., 339a
Rutman Wine Co. v. E. & J. Gallo Winery, 1652b, 1653c
Ryko Mfg. Co. v. Eden Serv., 570b1, 1622c, 1645c, 1652b, 1721c1, d-d2

Sabre Shipping Corp. v. American President Lines, Ltd., 236e
Sacramento Valley Chapter of NECA v. IBEW, Local 340, 364e, 379a
Saenz v. University Interscholastic League, 216a

Sahm v. V-1 Oil Co., 1452b
Salco Corp. v. GM, 839, 1642c
Salveson v. Western States Bankcard Assn., 335b
Sam Fox Publishing Co. v. United States, 334d, 348g
Sam S. Goldstein Indus. v. Botany Indus., 832
Samuel H. Moss v. FTC, 720c
Sander Bros. Radio Station, FCC v., 223c
Sandura Co., 1461
Sandura Co. v. FTC, 1617b, 1648c2
Sandy River Nursing Care v. Aetna Casualty, 572c
Sanitary Milk Producers v. Bergjans Farm Dairy, 373f4
Santa Clara Valley Distrib. Co. v. Pabst Brewing Co., 1627b
Sapp v. Jacobs, 232e
Sargent Elec. Co., United States v., 312c
Satellite Financial Planning Corp. v. First National Bank (Wilmington), 1622a
Saunders v. National Basketball Assn., 338b, 377c
Sausalito Pharmacy v. Blue Shield, 1425c, 1622b
Sauter, C. Albert, Co. v. Richard S. Sauter Co., 828b
Savon Gas Stations Number Six v. Shell Oil Co., 1653c
Scanlan v. Anheuser-Busch, 1653b, 1713c2, 1725c
Schaben v. Samuel Moore & Co., 1468, 1469d
Schaefer, F. & M., Corp. v. C. Schmidt & Sons, 909b, 1201c, 1203c, 1204b
Schenley Indus. v. New Jersey Wine & Spirit Wholesalers' Assn., 214a, d
Schine Chain Theatres v. United States, 345, 627b1, 1463b
Schnapps Shop v. H. W. Wright & Co., 1623c
Schofield v. Lake Shore & Michigan S. Ry. Co., 552b
Schrader's, A., Son, United States v., 1623d
Schoenkopf v. Brown & Williamson Tobacco Corp., 362b, 1413
Schrader's Son, United States v., 1448, b
Schwartz v. Broadcast Music, 378a
Schwegmann Bros. v. Calvert Distillers Corp., 209, 212c, 213a, b, 215b1, 1629b
Schwimmer v. Sony Corp. (America), 1452c4, 1455c1, 1456d3, 1470, 1623f2, 1625c2, 1627e5
Schwinn, Arnold, & Co., United States v., 842a, 1438, 1448e1-e2, 1473b, e1, f, 1505
Sciambra v. Graham News, 365d
SCM Corp. v. FTC, 1304, 1305
SCM Corp. v. RCA, 376a, 707b, 707h1, 707i1, 835c
SCM Corp. v. Xerox Corp., 339a, 533e, 1202f3, f4, 1205c3, 1506, 1655e
Scooper Dooper v. Kraftco Corp., 229d
Scophony Corp., United States v., 235a, b, c
Scott, O. M., & Sons, United States v., 1623c, 1639b

Scott Paper Co., 1020
Scott Publishing Co. v. Columbia Basin Publishers, 822b
Scoville Mfg. Co. v. Skaggs Pay Less Drug Stores, 1629b
Scranton Constr. Co. v. Litton Inds. Leasing Corp., 232e, 233b
Scriptomatic v. Agfa-Geraert, 235c
Scroggins v. Air Cargo, 225c
S.D. Collectibles v. Plough, 375f
SDI Reading Concrete v. Hilltop Basic Resources, 371e
Seaboard Air Line Ry. v. Blackwell, 220a
Seaboard Supply Co. v. Congoleum Corp., 384
Seago v. North Carolina Theatres, 1415b
Sealy, United States v., 954a, 1604c2, 1605d2
Sears, Roebuck & Co. v. Stiffel Co., 209, 220b, 1508c, 1613b, 1718f
Sears, Roebuck & Co., United States v., 1301, 1302a
Seasongood v. K & K Ins. Agency, 210
Seatrain case, see Federal Maritime Commn. v. Seatrain
Seattle Totems Hockey Club v. National Hockey League, 373e1
SEC, see under name of other party
Second Report on CATV Regulation, 572a
Securities and Exch. Commn., see under name of other party
Security Fire Door Co. v. Los Angeles County, 738b
Seeburg Corp. v. FTC, 305e, 909c
Selectron v. AT&T, 336d
Seligson v. Plum Tree, 356b, d
Semler v. Dental Examiners, 219b
Serta Assocs., United States v., 1626b
Service Merchandise Co. v. Boyd Corp., 1455b
Service & Training v. Data Gen. Co., 562f
Seven Gables Corp. v. SRO Co., 532b
Seville Indus. Mach. Corp., United States v., 312c
Sewell Plastics v. Coca-Cola Co., 375f
Shaeffer v. Collins, 1726b-c
Sharon Steel Corp. v. Chase Manhattan Bank, 1504
Sharp v. United Airlines, 377d2
Shearson/American Express v. McMahon, 324b
Shell Oil Co. v. FTC, 1609d, 1727d2
Shell Oil Co. v. Younger, 208
Sherman v. British Leyland Motors, 1644c, 1645c
Shimazaki Communic. v. AT&T, 338d
Shoaf v. Triangle Publications, 391
Shoenberg Farms v. Denver Milk Producers, 228d
Shop & Save Food Markets v. Pneumo Co., 1722c
Shreveport Macaroni Mfg. Co. v. FTC, 233d

Shulton v. Optel Corp., 1645e
Sibley v. Federal Land Bank of New Orleans, 1726c
Siegel v. Chicken Delight (448 F.2d 43), 365c2, 522c, 1134d, 1640a, 1711b3, 1713b3, 1716a1, d2, 1727e
Siegel v. Chicken Delight (271 F. Supp. 722), 356d
Sierra Wine & Liquor Co. v. Heublein, 1468
Silver v. New York Stock Exch., 223b, 244a, d, e, 1477
Simeon Management Corp, FTC v., 233f
Simmonds Precision Prods., United States v., 348d, e
Simpson [I] v. Union Oil Co. (377 U.S. 13), 333a, d, f, 1427c, 1451b, 1473a, c, d1, f, 1609c-d, 1621, 1622c, 1642b
Simpson [II] v. Union Oil Co. (396 U.S. 13), 333a, d, f
Sinclair Ref. Co., F.T.C. v., 1720b2-b3, c
Singer Mfg. Co., United States v., 1403
Sisal Sales Corp., United States v., 236b, 239b1
Sitkin Smelting & Ref. Co. v. FMC Corp., 1400a, 1622a
SJ Advanced Tech. & Mfg. Corp. v. Edward Junkunc, 338b
SKF Indus., 909c, 1652b
Skinner v. US Steel Corp., 233c
Skyview Distrib. v. Miller Brewing Co., 1653b
Slaughter v. Southern Talc Co., 322j
Smith v. Denny's Restaurant, 1716e2
Smith v. Pro-Football, 229d, 377c
Smith v. Staso Milling Co., 312e4
Smith v. Underwood Memorial Hosp., 563d
SmithKline Corp. v. Eli Lilly Co., 732a, 1725g
Smith Mach. Co. v. Hesston Corp., 1713c2, 1725c
Smith-Victor Corp. v. Sylvania Elec. Prods., 835c
Snow Crest Beverages v. Recipe Foods, 373f4
Snyder v. Howard Johnson's Motor Lodges, 322f
Socony-Vacuum Oil Co., United States v., 104, 206c, 213d, 217b4, 320b, 331c, 841a, 1404, 1451b, 1509, 1510a, 1639g2, 1644a
Solar Fuel Co. v. United Mine Workers, 229e
Sollenbarger v. Mountain States Tel. & Tel. Co., 356b, d
Solomon v. Houston Corrugated Box Co., 1408c, 1415b
Sorisio v. Lenox, 322b
Sound v. AT&T, 572d
Sound Ship Building Corp. v. Bethlehem Steel Co., 323c, 363c
South Carolina Council of Milk Producers v. Newton, 373f4
South Carolina State Highway Dept. v. Barnwell Bros., 220a
South-East Coal Co. v. Consolidation Coal Co., 229e, 390c
South-Eastern Underwriters Assn., United States v., 210, 231, 232a

Southern Concrete Co. v. United States Steel Corp., 839, 1201c
Southern Land Co. v. Malone & Hyde, 360d, 376a
Southern Pac. Co. v. Arizona, 220c
Southern Pac. Co., United States v., 902
Southern Pac. Communic. Co. v. AT&T (740 F.2d 1011), 336d-e, 572c
Southern Pac. Communic. Co. v. AT&T (567 F. Supp. 326), 336g
Southern Pac. Communic. Co. v. AT&T (556 F. Supp. 825), 365b2
Southern Pac. R.R. v. United States, 336a
South Florida Asphalt Co., United States v., 233b
Southland Reship v. Flegel, 828b
Southway Theatres v. Georgia Theatre Co., 1405, 1413, 1457c4
Southwest Airlines Co. v. Texas Intl. Airlines, 334e
Southwestern Brush Elec. Light & Power Co. v. Louisiana Elec. Light Co., 736d
Southwestern Cable Co., United States v., 572a
Southwestern Greyhound Lines, United States v., 729g
Southwest Suburban Bd. of Realtors v. Beverly Area Planning Assn., 364e, 379b
Spartan Grain & Mill Co. v. Ayers, 1719b
Spears Free Clinic v. Cleere, 232e
Special Equip. Co. v. Coe, 706c3
Spectrofuge Corp. v. Beckman Instruments, 1470
Spectrum Sports v. McQuillan, 323d, 523, 531b
Sperry & Hutchinson Co., FTC v., 218b, 305c, f, 307a, 1145c, 1301b
Sperry Rand Corp., United States v., 1467f2
Sports Center v. Riddell, 1645c-e
S.S.W. v. Air Transport Assn., 226d, 227a
Staley Mfg. Co., FTC v., 312c
Standard Oil Co., 1301c
Standard Oil Co. v. Brown, 1006e
Standard Oil Co. v. FTC, 103
Standard Oil Co. v. United States (221 U.S. 1), 302, 303a, 304a, 320b, 345, 531b, 603, 615, 618a, 626a, 710, 711a, b, 811, 830d, 902a, 1136c, 1464b, 1500, 1501, 1506, 1509, 1719b
Standard Oil Co., United States v. (253 F. Supp. 196), 421b
Standard Oil Co. (Cal.) v. Moore, 1412d, 1423a, 1424b, 1425c, 1606c
Standard Oil Co. (Cal.) v. United States (337 U.S. 293), 304c, 333f, 421f, 854b1, 902c, 1002, 1022a, 1145a, 1473c, 1507a, 1509, 1701c-c2, 1716d, 1720b3, 1721b3, 1728c, 1730a
Standard Oil Co. (Cal.), United States v. (362 F. Supp. 1331), 732a

Standard Oil Co. (Cal.), United States v. (1959 Trade Cas.), 348g
Standard Oil Co. (Ind.) v. FTC, 233b
Standard Oil Co. (Ind.), United States v., 1020, 1021
Standard Oil Co. (N.J.), United States v., 727a, 1020, 1119b, 1121c2, 4
Standard Oil Co., United States v. (316 F.2d 884), 1417g
Standard Stations case, see Standard Oil Co. (Cal.) v. United States (337 U.S. 293)
Stanley Works, 1121b4
Stanley Works v. FTC, 909c, 911c, 937
Stan Togut Corp. v. Hobart Mfg. Co., 1642c
Stanton v. Texaco, 355b3
Starview Outdoor Theatre v. Paramount Film Distrib. Corp., 338d
State v. Foster, 332a
State v. Striggles, 332a
State of New York v. Anheuser-Busch, 1645c
State of New York v. Cedar Park Concrete Corp., 380
State of New York v. Hendrickson Bros., 338d
State of New York v. Salem Sanitary Carting Corp., 335c2
Stauffer Chem. Co., United States v., 336f
Stearns v. Genrad, 1725c
Steele v. Bulova Watch Co., 236c
Steiner v. Twentieth Century-Fox Film Corp., 338b, 376c
Sterling Drug v. FTC, 305e
Sterling Drug Co., 909c, 1121b6, 1123a
Stern v. Lucy Webb Hayes Natl. Training School for Deaconnesses and Missionaries, 364e
Stiffel case, see Sears, Roebuck & Co. v. Stiffel Co.
Stone v. William Beaumont Hospital, 1471g
Story Parchment Co. v. Paterson Parchment Paper Co., 365a, b1
Stover, Russell, Candies, 1461
Stover, Russell, Candies v. FTC, 1451c1, 1461
St. Paul Fire & Marine Ins. Co. v. Barry, 1510c
Straus v. Victor Talking Machine Co., 1621
Strax v. Commodity Exch., 372
Streiffer v. Seafarers Sea Chest Corp., 229c
Striggles, State v., 332a
Strobl v. New York Mercantile Exch., 1425c
Suckow Borax Mines v. Borax Consolidated, 338d
Sugar Indus. Antitrust Litig., 371f
Sugar Instit. v. United States, 1435d-e
Sullivan, Commonwealth v., 321d
Sulmeyer v. Seven-Up Co., 1467a, e1
Sun-Drop Bottling Co. v. Coca-Cola Bottling Co. Consol., 1725c
Sun Dun v. Coca-Cola (770 F. Supp. 285), 322j

Sun Dun of Wash. v. Coca-Cola Co. (740 F. Supp. 381), 563d
Sunkist Growers v. Winckler & Smith Citrus Prods. Co., 228b, 1463f
Sun Oil Co. v. FTC, 1451c2, 1639g4
Sun Oil, FTC v., 1606c
Sunshine Books v. Temple Univ., 504b
Sunshine Cellular v. Vanguard Cellular Sys., 562f
Sun Valley Disposal Co. v. Silver State Disposal Co., 206d3, 216a, 232e
Superior Bedding Co. v. Serta Assoc., 1692b, 1642c, 1647b3
Superior Beverage Co. v. Owens-Illinois, 356d
Superior Premium Ice Cream Distrib. Antitrust Litig., 563e
SuperTurf v. Monsanto Co., 533c
Surety Title Ins. Agency v. Virginia State Bar, 213a
Susser v. Carvel Corp., 1623c, 1716d2
Sweeney v. Athens Regional Medical Ctr., 373d1
Sweeney, Edward J., & Sons v. Texaco, 1446b, 1452c4, 1455b, 1456d4, 1457c4, d, 1627c
Swenson's Ice Cream Co. v. Corsair Corp., 324b
Swettlen v. Wagoner Gas & Oil Co., 1451c2, 1606c, 1627e4
Swift & Co. v. FTC, 1204c
Swift & Co. v. United States, 232c, 233b, 820, 821, 831
Swift & Co., United States v. (286 U.S. 106), 104, 348b, g, 608b
Swift & Co., United States v. (189 F. Supp. 885), 348b
Swift & Co., United States v. (1971 Trade Cas. ¶73,760), 348b
Swine Flu Immunization Prods. Liability Litig., 335b
Swingline, United States v., 305e
Swiss Watch case, see Watchmakers of Switzerland Information Center, United States v.
Switzer Bros. v. Locklin, 363a
Sybron Corp., United States v., 1020, 1021
Sylvania, see GTE Sylvania
Sylvania case, see Continental T.V. v. GTE Sylvania (433 U.S. 36)
Syntex Labs. v. Norwich Pharmacal Co., 703b
Syracuse Broadcasting Corp. v. Newhouse, 1469d
Syufy Enterps. v. American Multicinema, 362a, 532b, 1653e
Syufy Enters., United States v. (903 F.2d 659), 421d, 422d
Syufy Enters., United States v. (712 F. Supp. 1386), 539a

Taggart v. Rutledge, 1721c1
T'ai Corp. v. Kalso Systems, 1451c2, 1642c
Tamaron Distrib. Corp. v. Weiner, 1474d
Tampa Elec. Co. v. Nashville Coal Co., 304c, 534a1, 570b1, 732c5, 1709c2-c3

Tapeswitch Corp. v. Recora Corp., 1471e1
Tarabishi v. McAlester Regional Hosp., 532a
Tasty Baking Co. v. Ralston Purina, 373d4
Taterka v. Wisconsin Tel. Co., 229d
Taxi Weekly v. Metropolitan Taxicab Board of Trade, 1425c
Taylor v. Local No. 7 Intl. Union of Journeymen Horseshoers, 229c
Teamsters Union v. Oliver, 229c, e
Technical Learning Collective v. Daimler-Benz, 371h, 1459b1
Technical Tape Corp. v. Minnesota Mining & Mfg. Co., 1460f
Telecommunications Research v. Allnet Communic., 379b
Teleflex Indus. Prods. v. Brunswick Corp., 1716d4
Telerant Leasing Corp., In the Matter of, 214b4
Telerate Sys. v. Caro, 1721b4
Telex Corp. v. IBM (510 F.2d 894), 561a, 714d, 738j, 834b
Telex Corp. v. IBM (367 F. Supp. 258), 312d, 714d, 834b
Tenneco, 533d, 534f, 561b
Tenneco, FTC v., 1119b, f1
Tennessean Truckstop v. NTS, 375b
Tennessee Consolidated Coal Co. v. United Mine Workers, 229e
Terminal R.R. Assn., United States v., 729g, 1478b4
Terre Du Lac Assn. v. Terre Du Lac, 379b, 1715d2, 1727f
Terrell v. Household Goods Carriers' Bureau, 365a
Texaco v. FTC, 305d
Texaco v. Hasbrouck, 1716e3
Texaco, FTC v., 1134c, 1727d1-d3, 1727e
Texas v. Allan Constr. Co., 338d
Texas v. Insurance Servs. Office, 335b
Texasgulf v. Canada Develop. Corp., 1121c4, 1204d
Texas Indus. v. Radcliffe Materials, 372, 1459b4, c2
Texas Utils. Co. v. Santa Fe Indus., 338c
T. Harris Young v. Marquette Elecs., 534a1
Theatre Enter. v. Paramount Films Distrib. Corp., 323d, 1412b, 1425c, 1426c
Theatre Investment Co. v. RKO Radio Pictures, 345
Theatre Party Assn. v. Schubert Organization, 563d
The Flintkote Co. v. United States, 312d
305 East 24th Owners Corp. v. Parman Co., 1721b4, c1
Thi-Hawaii v. First Commercial Financial Corp., 390c, 1459c2
Thill Sec. Corp. v. New York Stock Exch., 224d
Third Natl. Bank in Nashville, United States v., 224e, 230e, 909c, 926c, 936
Thomas v. Amarada Hess Corp., 1413
Thomason v. Mitsubishi Elec. Sales Am., 377d5

Thompson v. Metropolitan Multi-List, 379a, 1726c
Thomsen v. Cayser, 236b
Thomsen v. Western Elec. Co., 1467a, e1, 1469b, d
Thomson Newspapers v. Toledo Typographical Union No. 53, 229c
Three J Farms v. Alton Box Board Co., 335b
Three Movies of Tarzana v. Pacific Theatres, 375e, 1644b1
Thurman Indus. v. Pay 'N' Pak Stores (875 F.2d 1369), 532b, 565
Thurman Indus. v. Pay 'N' Pak Stores (1987-1 Trade Cas. ¶67,591), 532b
Ticor Title Ins. Co., FTC v., 572c
Tic-X-Press v. Omni Promotions Co., 355d, 1721b4
Tidewater Marine Serv., United States v., 555c, 909c, 917, 921
Timberlane Lumber Co. v. Bank of America, 236f2, 239b
Times Mirror Co., United States v., 909c, 1135b
Times-Picayune Publishing Co. v. United States, 304c, 331c, 733e, 822b, 1700d, 1717c2, 1719b, 1720b3
Timken Roller Bearing Co. v. FTC, 1460f
Timken Roller Bearing Co. v. United States, 237, 345, 1463d, 1467c
Timken Roller Bearing Co., United States v., 1463d
Tire Sales Corp. v. Cities Service Oil Co., 835b, 839, 1460f, 1709e4, 1727e
Tobman v. Cottage Woodcraft Shop, 1474d
T.O.C. v. United Artists Theatre Circuit, 335b
Todhunter-Mitchell & Co. v. Anheuser-Busch, 236g, 1642c
Todorov v. DCH Healthcare Auth., 373e1
Togur, Stan, Corp. v. Hobart Mfg. Co., 1642c
Toilet Seat Antitrust Litig., 371f
Tomac v. Coca-Cola Co., 321c, 363c, 382c
Tominga v. Shepherd, 523
Tonkin, Ron, Gran Turismo v. Fiat Distribs., 1460f
Toolson v. New York Yankees, 230f
Toomer v. Witsell, 220b
Top-All Varieties v. Hallmark Cards., Inc., 828e, 1653c
Topco Assoc., United States v., 213c, 215c, 218b, 954a, 1503, 1507a, 1509, 1604c2, 1605d2
Tose v. First Penn. Bank, 1424c, 1470
Totem Ocean Trailer Express v. Sea-Land Serv., 227a
Tower Tire and Auto Center v. Atlantic Richfield Co., 828b
Town of Concord v. Boston Edison Co. (915 F.2d 17), 518, 572c
Town of Concord v. Boston Edison Co. (721 F. Supp. 1456), 550b
Town Sound & Custom Tops v. Chrysler Motors Corp. (959 F.2d 468), 322j, 563d
Town Sound & Custom Tops v. Chrysler Motors Corp. (743 F. Supp. 353), 523

Toye Bros. Yellow Cab. v. Irby, 220c
T. P. Laboratories v. Huge, 209
Tracinda Inv. Corp., United States v., 1204b, c
Transamerica Computer Co. v. IBM, 1507a
Transamerica Corp. v. McCabe, 305d
Trans-Missouri Freight Assn., United States v., 1501, 1509
Transocean Tender Offer Sec. Litig., 336c
Trans World Assoc. v. Denver, 212b, 214d, 216a
Travelers Health Assn., FTC v., 210
Travelers Ins. Co. v. Blue Cross, 214a, 572c, 822a
Treasurer v. Philadelphia Natl. Bank, 373d2
Treasure Valley Potato Bargaining Assn. v. Ore-Ida Foods, 228b, d
Trenton Potteries Co., United States v., 710, 736e, 1509, 1510a
Triangle Conduit & Cable Co. v. FTC, 1436c
Triangle Conduit and Cable Co. v. Wheeling Steel Corp., 385
Tri-Continental Fin. Corp. v. Tropical Marine Enter., 703b
Trident Neuro-Imaging Lab. v. Blue Cross (S.C.), 1402b1
Triebwasser & Katz v. AT&T Co., 347, 1467e1, e3
Tripoli Co. v. Wella Corp., 1618d, 1641c1, 1642c, 1647d2
Tripper Corp. v. Chrysler Corp., 1413, 1645b, d
Tri-R Sys. v. Friedman & Son, 1408f3
Trist v. First Fed. Sav. & Loan Assn., 1417e, 1425d4
Trixler Brokerage Co. v. Ralston Purina Co., 832
TRW, 1301c, 1305
Tubular Rivet & Stud Co. v. O'Brien, 1701a
Tugboat v. Mobile Towing Co., 361, 377d4, 379a
Tulsa Oil case, 318
Tunis Bros. Co. v. Ford Motor Co. (952 F.2d 715), 556, 563d
Tunis Bros. Co. v. Ford Motor Co. (823 F.2d 49), 1609a
Tunis Bros. Co. v. Ford Motor Co. (763 F.2d 1482), 322c, 1468
Turner v. Johnson & Johnson, 375c
TV Signal Co. v. AT&T (462 F.2d 1256), 831, 1466b, 1467b
TV Signal Co. v. AT&T (1981 Trade Cas. ¶63,944), 1467a, e1
TWA v. Hughes, 225c, 355d, 365b2
T.W. Elec. Serv. v. PECA, 322c
Twentieth Century-Fox Film Corp., United States v., 1415b
Twin City Sportservice v. Charles O. Finley & Co. (676 F.2d 1291), 421f
Twin City Sportservice v. Charles O. Finley & Co. (512 F.2d 1264), 338b, 832
Twin City Sportservice v. Charles O. Finley & Co. (364 F. Supp. 233), 365b1
2361 State Corp. v. Sealy, 338b

United States Football League v. National Football League (842 F.2d 1376), 365d
United States Football League v. National Football League (794 F. Supp. 474), 365d
United States Football League v. National Football League (644 F. Supp. 1040), 365b2, d, 533b
United States Football League v. National Football League (634 F. Supp. 1155), 563e
United States Gypsum Co., United States v. (438 U.S. 422), 312c, 1606e3
United States Gypsum Co., United States v. (51 F. Supp. 613), 334b5
United States Movidyn Corp. v. Hercules, 707d
United States Steel Corp. v. FTC, 421b
Universal Brands v. Phillip Morris, 323c, 375c, 1202f1
Universal Lite Distribs. v. Northwest Indus., 1435d, 1467h, 1468, 1469d, 1623c
Universal-Rundle Corp., FTC v., 305e
University Health, FTC v., 347
Univis Lens Co., United States v., 1621
Upjohn Co. v. Charles Labs, 1629b
Uranium Antitrust Litig., 372
USA Petrol. Co. v. Atlantic Richfield, 1640a, d1-d3
US Steel Corp., 742 F.T.C. 1270 (1968), 926b
US Steel Corp. v. Fortner Enters. (Fortner II), 1134d, 1135a, 1715b, 1719b, 1720b4, 1724d, 1728d, f, 1730a-b
US Steel Corp. v. Fraternal Assn. of Steelhaulers, 229c
US Steel Corp. v. FTC, 1003, 1020, 1021
US Steel Corp., United States v. (251 U.S. 417), 104, 603a, 606, 607, 902a
US Steel Corp., United States v. (223 F. 55), 727a
Utah v. American Pipe and Constr. Co., 356c
Utah Pie Co. v. Continental Baking Co., 720c
Utah Pub. Serv. Commn. v. El Paso Nat. Gas Co., 345, 348e

Valley Liquors v. Renfield Importers (822 F.2d 656), 532b, 1645b-c
Valley Liquors v. Renfield Importers (678 F.2d 742) 1456d4, 1457c4, 1611f, 1625c3, 1644a, 1645b, e
Vanadium Corp. v. Susquehanna Corp., 909c, 1203a
Vandervelde v. Put and Call Brokers and Dealers Assn., 377b
Van Dyke Ford v. Ford Motor Co., 828b
Varney v. Coleman Co., 831, 832, 835c
Vasiliow Co. v. Anheuser-Busch, 356d
Vendo Co. v. Lektro-Vend Corp., 203b
Venture Technology v. National Fuel Gas Co., 1405

Venzie Corp. v. United States Mineral Prods., 1412g, 1434c2, 1708a, d, 1722a, 1726c, d1
Vermont v. Cayuga Rock Salt Co., 339a
Viacom Intl. v. Tandem Prods., 391
Video Intl. Prods. v. Warner-Amex Cable Communic., 365d
Viking Theatre Corp. v. Paramount Film Distrib. Corp., 311a2
Village of Bolingbrook v. Citizens Util. Co. of Ill., 324c
Vincent v. Reynolds Memorial Hosp., 338b
Virginia Academy of Clinical Psychologists v. Blue Shield (Va.), 364e-f, 375d, 1402b1, 1468
Virginia Pharmacy case, see Virginia State Board of Pharmacy v. Virginia Citizens Consumer Council
Virginia State Board of Pharmacy v. Virginia Citizens Consumer Council, 218a, 219b, 1435c
Virtual Maintenance v. Prime Computer, 562f
Vitamin Technologists v. Wisconsin Alumni Research Found., 706c3, 736d
Vitarroz Corp. v. Borden, 335b
Viterbo v. Dow Chem. Co., 322j
V. & L. Cicione v. C. Schmidt & Sons, 1653c
Vogue Ring Creations v. Hardman, 836b
Volasco Prods. Co. v. Lloyd A. Fry Roofing Co., 365b1, 373f4, 835c
Von's Grocery Co., United States v., 902c, 909c, 914, 917, 1205f

Wachovia Corp., United States v., 1121b2, c4
Wainwright v. National Dairy Prods. Corp., 212b
Walder v. Paramount Publix Corp., 373d3
Waldron v. British Petroleum Co., 235c, 374
Walker v. Providence Journal Co., 835c, 1470
Walker Distrib. Co. v. Lucky Lager Brewing Co., 378d
Walker Oil Co. v. Hudson Oil Co., 233e
Walker Process Equip. v. Food Mach. and Chem. Corp., 204c, 523, 707e, 831, 836a
Walling v. Jacksonville Paper Co., 233b
Wall Prods. Co. v. National Gypsum Co., 365b1, 1408c
Walovsky v. Carlton, 1467g
Walters, Jack, & Sons Corp. v. Morton Bldgs., 1440a, 1451c2
Ward Baking Co., United States v., 348g
Warner Communic., FTC v., 305e
Warner, George W., & Co. v. Black & Decker Mfg. Co., 1447b1
Warner-Lambert Co., 909c

Warner-Lambert Co. v. FTC, 305e
Warner Mgt. Consultants v. Data Gen. Corp., 1726d4, 1727d
Warriner Hermetics v. Copeland Refrig., 1716d2, 1717f1
Warth v. Seldin, 379b
Washington v. Automobile Mfrs. Assn., 345
Washington Crab Assn., 228c
Washington Gas Light Co. v. Virginia Elec. and Power Co., 213f, 214b, 217b4
Washington Mutual Sav. Bank v. Federal Deposit Ins. Corp., 1121c2, 1124c, 1125c
Washington Professional Basketball Corp. v. National Basketball Assn., 374
Waste Management, United States v., 422c, 423, 550b
Watchmakers of Switzerland Information Center, United States v., 235c, 238
Waugh Equip. Co., 1130a
Webb v. Bladen, 229e
Weber v. Consumer's Digest, 338b
Weber v. Wynne, 711d
Webster County Memorial Hospital v. United Mine Workers, 323d, 1478c
Weeks Dredging & Contracting Co. v. American Dredging Co., 909c
Weight Watchers (Rocky Mountain) v. Weight Watchers Intl., 1609a, 1639b
Weiman Co. v. Kroehler Mfg. Co., 363a
Weinberg v. Federated Dept. Stores, 335b
Weinstein v. Norman W. Morris Corp., 235c
Weir v. Chicago Plastering Inst., 229e
Weiss v. York Hospital, 356b, 1471b, e2, h
Weit v. Continental Ill. Bank, 1417b, 1433a
Wells Real Estate v. Greater Lowell Bd. of Realtors, 383b, 1722c, 1723b, d, 1724b
Wendkos v. ABC Consol. Corp., 377a1
Weniger v. United States, 1402a2
Westchester Radiological Assocs. v. Empire Blue Cross & Blue Shield (707 F. Supp. 708), 364e, 375b
Westchester Radiological Assocs. v. Empire Blue Cross & Blue Shield (659 F. Supp. 132), 364e
West Coast Theater Corp. v. City of Portland, 323e
Western Elec. Co., United States v. (592 F. Supp. 846), 348g
Western Elec. Co., United States v. (1968 Trade Cas. ¶72,415), 348e
Western Geophysical Co. v. Bolt Assoc., 1202f4
Western Liquid Asphalt Cases, In re, 232e, 233c, 1408c
Western Meat Co., FTC v., 1205c2
Western Shoe Gallery v. Duty Free Shoppers, 338b

Western Wholesale Liquor Co. v. Gibson Wine Co., 1652d, 1713c2, 1725c
Westgo Indus. v. W. J. King Co., 1627c
Westinghouse Elec. Corp. v. Burlington, 338d
Westinghouse Elec. Corp. v. Pacific Gas & Elec. Co., 338d
Westinghouse Elec. Corp., United States v., 348e
Westman Commn. Co. v. Hobart Intl., 565
Westor Theatres v. Warner Bros. Pictures, 346b
Westpoint Pepperell v. Rea, 1644c
West Virginia v. Chas. Pfizer & Co. (440 F.2d 1079), 371c
West Virginia v. Chas. Pfizer & Co. (314 F. Supp. 710), 312d, 356d
Weyerhaeuser Co., 420c
Weyerhaeuser Co., FTC v., 305e
W.H. Brady Co. v. Lem Prods., 532b, 1721c1
Wheat v. Mass, 323d
Wheat Rail Freight Rate Antitrust Litig. (759 F.2d 1305), 336g
Wheat Rail Freight Rate Antitrust Litig. (759 F. Supp. 510), 336g
Whims Appliance v. GMC, 1460f, 1623c
White v. Hearst Corp., 1467a, d, 1469a
White v. Rockingham Radiologists, 1726c, 1727g
White Bear Theatre Corp. v. State Theatre Corp., 1470
White Motor Co. v. United States, 1510b, 1602c, 1630b, 1642a, 1643a, 1646d, 1647b3, 1648d4
White Motor Co., United States v., 1637j, 1642a
White & White v. American Hospital Supply, 533g, 1460f
Whitlock v. Under Sea Indus., 364d
Whitten, George R., Jr. v. Paddock Pool Builders, 206b, 213a, 214a, b, d, 738b, 828b, 832, 835b, c, 1464e, 1467b
Wickard v. Filburn, 232a
Wiggins, E. W., Airways v. Massachusetts Port Authority, 206d3, 214d, 216a
Wilcox v. First Interstate Bank of Or., N.A., 322c
Wilcox v. Jeffery, 1402a2
Wilder Ent. v. Allied Artists Corp., 1415b
Wilk v. American Medical Assn. (815 F.2d 352), 532a
Wilk v. American Medical Assn. (735 F.2d 217), 1409c, 1426d
Wilk v. American Medical Assn. (672 F. Supp. 1465), 562e
Wilkerson v. McCarthy, 322c
Will v. Comprehensive Accounting Corp., 1722d
Willard Dairy Corp. v. National Dairy Prods. Corp., 233c
William Goldman Theatres v. Loew's, 365b3
William Inglis & Sons Baking Co. v. ITT Continental Baking Co. (668 F.2d 1014), 504b, 522a, 535c2, 1464d, 1467b, e1, e3, 1507a

William Inglis & Sons Baking Co. v. ITT Continental Baking Co. (526 F.2d 86), 347
Williams v. Cannon, 235c
Williams v. Independent News Co., 828e, 1474c, 1653c
Williams v. Kleaveland, 1471e2, f
Williams v. United States, 1402a2
Williams, Edwin K., & Co. v. Edwin K. Williams & Co. — East, 1642c
Williamson v. Columbia Gas & Elec. Corp., 334b2
Williamson v. Lee Optical Co., 219b
Willmar Poultry Co. v. Morton-Norwich Prods., 338d
Wilson v. Ringsby Truck Lines, 377d3
Wilson Chem. Co., United States v., 305e
Wilson Indus. v. Chronicle Broadcasting Co., 362a
Wilson Sporting Goods Co., United States v., 347, 1109a, 1109b, 1119b, d, 1121b4, 1121c2, 1122c, 1123a, 1123e4, 1134d, 1135a, 1139, 1204c
Winchester Theatre Co. v. Paramount Film Distrib. Corp., 1415b
Windham v. American Brands, 356d
Windsor Theatre Co. v. Walbrook Amusement Co., 1467a
Winn v. Edna Hibel Corp., 322g
Winther v. DEC Intl., 377d5
Wirebound Boxes Antitrust Litig., 356d
Wiring Device Antitrust Litig., 335b
Wisdom Rubber Indus. v. Johns-Manville Sales Corp., 323c, 363d
Wise, United States v., 311a1
WIXT Television v. Meredith Corp., 1469d
W. J. Milner & Co. v. IBEW, 229e
W. L. Gore & Assoc. v. Carlisle Corp., 835c
Wobb v. Ford Motor Co., 378d
Wolf v. Wagner Spray Tech Corp., 338b
Women's Sportwear Mfrs. Assn., United States v., 229c, 232e
Wood v. Carpenter, 338d
Woodbury Daily Times Co. v. Los Angeles Times-Washington Post News Serv., 1655b
Woods Exploration & Producing Co. v. Aluminum Co., 204c, 214a, d, 335b, 832
Woolen v. Surtran Taxicabs, 338b
Workers' Compensation Ins., 572c
Workman v. State Farm Mut. Auto Ins. Co., 1418b2
World of Sleep v. La-Z-Boy Chair Co., 1625c4
World of Sleep v. Stearns & Foster Co., 1642c
Wright v. Hardrives Co., 233b
Wright, Commonwealth v., 321d
W. T. Grant Co., United States v., 1304, 1305

Yachts Am. v. United States, 336d

Yamaha Intl. Corp. v. ABC Intl. Traders, 563d

Yamaha Motor Co. v. FTC, 305c

Yellow Cab Co. v. Cab Employers, 232c

Yellow Cab Co., United States v. (Yellow Cab I, 332 U.S. 218), 232e, 233b, 727a, b3, c1, c3, e, 531b, 811, 833c, 1463

Yellow Cab Co., United States v. (Yellow Cab II, 338 U.S. 338), 727c, c3, e, 1010, 1463b

Yellow Pages Cost Consultants v. GTE Directories, 373d1, 375f

Yentsch v. Texaco, 1440a, 1451c1, 1623c, 1721b4, c2, 1722c, 1724b, d2

Yoder Bros. v. California-Florida Plant Corp., 339a, 363c, 371e, 831, 835c

Young, Ex Parte, 218b

Young v. Lehigh Corp., 360a

Y & Y Popcorn Supply Co. v. ABC Vending Corp., 337a1

Zaslaw v. MCA Distrib. Corp., 1413

Zdanok v. Glidden, 323e

Zell-Aire of New England v. Zell-Aire Corp., 1624b

Zelson v. Phoenix Mut. Life Ins. Co., 210

Zenith Radio Corp. v. Hazeltine Research (401 U.S. 321), 334b4, 338b-c, 339a

Zenith Radio Corp. v. Hazeltine Research (395 U.S. 100), 346b, 363a, 365a, b2

Zidell Explorations v. Conval Intl., 1624d3, 1625c1, c3, 1644b1

Zimmerman v. National Football League, 363c

Zinser v. Continental Grain Co., 371g

Zinser v. Rose, 375b

Index for Volumes I-IX

References are to paragraph numbers. Always consult detailed Table of Contents.

ACT OF STATE. *See* FOREIGN COMMERCE

ADMINISTRATIVE AGENCIES. *See* FEDERAL TRADE COMMISSION; REGULATED INDUSTRIES; STATE ACTION

ADMINISTRATIVE PROCEEDINGS. *See* FEDERAL TRADE COMMISSION; LITIGATION; POLITICAL ACTION; REGULATED INDUSTRIES; STATE ACTION

ADVANCE ANNOUNCEMENT OF PRICE. *See* FACILITATING PRACTICE

ADVERTISING. *See also* DIFFERENTIATED PRODUCTS; DISTRIBUTION RESTRAINTS GENERALLY
- State restraints, 213d, 219b
- "Wastefulness," 954a, 1109a

ADVISORY OPINIONS, 331

AFFILIATED FIRMS. *See* CONSPIRACY, INTRAENTERPRISE

AGENT. *See* COLLABORATION AMONG COMPETITORS; DISTRIBUTION RESTRAINT GENERALLY
- Conspiracy with principal. *See* CONSPIRACY, INTRAENTERPRISE

AGREEMENT. *See* all CONSPIRACY titles

AGRICULTURAL COOPERATIVES, 228
- Conspiracy within or among, 1463f. *See also* CONSPIRACY, INTRAENTERPRISE
- Executive Branch powers, 228a
- Mergers, 228b, d, 1463f
- Monopolization by, 228d
- Organization, 228b
- Prohibited practices, 228c

ALIENATION RESTRAINT. *See* CONSPIRACY, VERTICAL; DISTRIBUTION RESTRAINTS GENERALLY

ALTERNATIVES (To a restraint). *See also* particular restraints
- Ground for illegality, 1505, 1602, 1703c, 1711e

ALTERNATIVES (*continued*)
Ground for legality, 1602e, 1703c, 1711e
ANTITRUST GOALS. *See* PUBLIC POLICIES GENERALLY
ANTITRUST INJURY
Brunswick case and basic doctrine, 360, 362, 365, 373, 381a, 1623f, 1640c
Dealer challenging resale price fix, 1623f6, 1640
Resale price ceiling, 1459c, 1640
Resale price floor, 1459c, 1623f
Tying, 1705f3
ANTITRUST LAWS GENERALLY. *See also* CLAYTON ACT GENERALLY; FEDERAL TRADE COMMISSION GENERALLY; PUBLIC POLICIES; RULE OF REASON; SHERMAN ACT GENERALLY
Texts, *Appendix A*
ARBITRATION
Required by state law, 213d, 216b
ASSET CONCENTRATION, 109b. *See also* MERGERS, CONGLOMERATE
ATTEMPTED MONOPOLIZATION. *See also* MARKET POWER; MONOPOLIZATION; Specific practices (e.g., SOLE OUTLET; TYING)
Basic issues, 829
Classic formulations, 820, 821, 131
Conduct, generally, Ch. 7, 825-830
antedating monopoly, 828g
broadened definitions, 829e
classic view, 821
monopolization compared
generally, 827
permissible for monopolist, 828
wrongful for monopolist, 829
other antitrust statutes violated, 830
unconsummated, 826
General rule, 835
Harassment of rivals, 737-738
Intent, 821-824
defined, 822
indicating reasonableness, 824
safety valve, 824
substitute for power, 833b
to appraise conduct, 823
Leveraging, 1134a; also 725
Per se rule, limited, 836
Power requirement, 831-836
alternate approaches, 834
amount of power, 835
calculation, 835
classic view, 831
expansionist tendencies, 832-833, 837
critique, 833d
inherent limits, 833d
general rule, 835, 837
limited per se rule, 836
monopolization compared, 835b
reduced power arguments, 833

significance quantified, 835c
Sanctions
bearing on offense content, 834a, 837
relief scope, 838
Solicitation to unlawful agreement, as, 1407f, 1419
Statutes, other antitrust, relevance of, 830
Summary, 820
Unfair competition, 737-738
Unfair tactics illustrated, 738
ATTORNEY'S FEES, 331d

BANKS. *See also* REGULATED INDUSTRIES
Special statutory provisions, 230e
BARRIERS TO ENTRY. *See* ENTRY BARRIERS
BASING POINT PRICES, 404b3, c, 1435f, 1436c. *See also* CONSPIRACY, GENERALLY; FACILITATING PRACTICE
BID-RIGGING, 1420. *See also* CONSPIRACY, GENERALLY; PER SE RULE; RULE OF REASON
BIG CASE, 324
BLOCK BOOKING. *See* TYING
BOYCOTT. *See* CONCERTED REFUSAL TO DEAL; CONSPIRACY, GENERALLY; CONSPIRACY, VERTICAL; CUSTOMER AND TERRITORIAL RESTRAINT, VERTICAL; REFUSAL TO DEAL; SOLE OUTLET
BURDEN OF PROOF OR ALLEGATION. *See* all CONSPIRACY titles; RULE OF REASON; more particular titles
BUSINESS OR PROPERTY (CLAYTON ACT §4). *See* STANDING
BUSINESS TORTS. *See* UNFAIR COMPETITION
BUYER COLLABORATION, 411c, 964b. *See also* DEALER POWER
BUYING SPECIFICATIONS INFLUENCED
Government purchasers, 206, 216a
Monopolization, 738b, h

CAPACITY TO CONSPIRE. *See* CONSPIRACY, INTRAENTERPRISE
CAPITAL MARKETS. *See* ENTRY BARRIERS
CAPPER-VOLSTEAD ACT. *See* AGRICULTURAL COOPERATIVES
CARTELS. *See* PRICE FIXING
CEASE AND DESIST ORDERS. *See* FEDERAL TRADE COMMISSION
CHANGE OF LAW DEFENSE
Criminal proceedings, 333a
no liability for acts previously thought lawful, 333a, c

CHANGE OF LAW DEFENSE (*continued*)
Generally, 333a
Innovative or avulsive changes of law, 333f
identifying such changes, 333f
narrow definition, 333f
Prospective-only effect of changes of law
consistency with statute, 333c
consistency with the judicial function, 333d
effect on development of the antitrust law, 333e
generally, 333b
problem of rewarding successful plaintiffs, 333e
Retroactive effect of changes of law, 333a, d
Unequal treatment of similar actors, 333d-e
Values served by protecting reasonable reliance, 333b
Various change of law situations, 333a
CIVIL RIGHTS ACT, 219c
CLAIM PRECLUSION. *See* RES JUDICATA AND COLLATERAL ESTOPPEL
CLASS ACTIONS
Absent class members, 356b
notice, 356b
Appropriateness of class action liability, 356d
Class representative
interests consistent with class interests, 356b
Common questions, 356d
damage issue, 356d
injury, 356d
predominance of, 356d
Efficiency of, 356c
Franchisee class actions, 356d
Fluid class action, 356d
Generally, 356
Manageability, 356c
Parens patriae suits, 356d
Requisites, 356a
Tying arrangements, 356d
Utility of, 356a
CLAYTON ACT GENERALLY. *See also* more specific topics (e.g., CONSPIRACY, VERTICAL; MERGER; TYING)
Historical background, 303b
Relation to Federal Trade Commission Act, 305b, 1719c
Relation to Sherman Act, 304, 902a, 906, 1145b, 1460, 1719b
Text, *Appendix A*
CLEARANCES, 331
COERCION. *See* CONSPIRACY, COERCED; CONSPIRACY, VERTICAL; particular offenses
COLLABORATION AMONG COMPETITORS. *See* BUYER COLLABORATION; CONCERTED REFUSAL TO DEAL; CONSPIRACY, GENERALLY; FOREIGN COMMERCE; JOINT VENTURES; LITIGATION; MERGER; OLIGOPOLY; PATENTS;

PER SE RULE; POLITICAL ACTION; PRICE FIXING; RULE OF REASON; STATE ACTION; TRADE ASSOCIATION
Dealers boycott suppliers not limiting resales,
Generally, 1604. *See also* DEALER POWER
Customer and territorial restraints, 1648d
Resale price maintenance, 1632e
Suppliers restrain their dealers' resales,
Generally, 1606
Customer and territorial restraints,1606h,1648c4
Express horizontal agreement, 1606b
Resale price maintenance, 1632d
COLLATERAL ESTOPPEL
Clayton Act §5(a), 337
plaintiff's use of findings adverse to defendant in prior government suit, 337
prima facie effect, 337b
relation to collateral estoppel, 337c
Defensive collateral estoppel, 336b
Generally, 336a
"Necessary" to earlier suit requirement, 336b
Non-mutual estoppel, 336b
Offensive collateral estoppel, 336b
administrative proceedings, 336g
change of law, 336f
defendant did not fully litigate issue in earlier suit, 336d
different rules of law, 336f
inconsistent prior judgments, 336e
plaintiff could have joined earlier suit, 336c
COLLECTIVE BARGAINING. *See* LABOR UNIONS
COLLUSION. *See* all CONSPIRACY titles
COMBINATION, 841b, 1403, 1449g. *See also* all CONSPIRACY titles
COMMERCE. *See* FOREIGN COMMERCE; INTERSTATE COMMERCE
COMMERCE CLAUSE (Of the Constitution), 220
COMMON CARRIERS. *See* REGULATED INDUSTRIES
COMMON LAW
Alienation restraint, 1620c1, 1642b
Duty to deal, 736c
Sherman Act, relation to, 302, 1501
COMPETITION. *See also* CONCENTRATION; all CONSPIRACY titles; EFFICIENCIES; MARKET POWER; all MERGER titles; MONOPOLIZATION; OLIGOPOLY; PER SE RULE, PUBLIC POLICIES; RULE OF REASON
Cutthroat, 413

COMPETITION (*continued*)
De-emphasized as an antitrust objective, 107-108, 221-230
Defined, 402
Departures from, 406a
collusion, 415
differentiated products, 409
entry barriers, 420-423
externalities, 414
policy implications, 406b
research, 407
scale economies, 408
second best, 412
Economic and social objectives served, 103-113
Effects generally, 1431
Efficiencies
allocative, 402b1
operating, 402b2
Exemptions from competitive regime, 221-230
Fair, 109a. *See also* Process
Goal of antitrust policy, as a, 401, 1710c
Imperfections improving economic performance, 412c
Innovations, 402, 407
Interdependent parallelism as conspiracy. *See* same
Intrabrand. *See* DISTRIBUTION RESTRAINTS GENERALLY; particular restraints
Meaning, 1710c
Non-price, 407, 409
Perfect competition
necessary conditions, 402
necessary long-run results, 402
Process, as, 1707e4, 1713c3, 1717f
Ruinous, 413
Workable competition, 406b, 407b, 843-845

COMPLAINT AGAINST RIVAL (Usually by dealer to supplier who then refuses to deal with complained-against dealer; CONSPIRACY INFERENCES). *See also* CONSPIRACY, COERCED; CONSPIRACY, GENERALLY; CONSPIRACY, VERTICAL
After it, refusal to deal, 1455, 1623a, d, 1624d3, 1625c3, 1644b
affects proof burden, 1455d
as proof of agreement, 1623a, d
Business Electronics case, 1623a, d, 1625a, c3, 1648d3c
prohibition of mail orders, 1625c1
relevance, 1455a-b
Agreement
Monsanto case, 1454, 1623e
theories determine significance, 1453b
what content, 1453a-b
Causes refusal to deal
coerces supplier, 1453c, 1457, 1624d3, 1625c3-d, 1644b-c

independent reason, if, 1455c1
information provided, 1455c2, 1456
Coerced supplier. *See also* DEALER POWER
bargaining power dealer vs. supplier, 1457c3, 1604g, 1632e3-4, 1648d3, 1655g
coerced dealer compared, 1457b, e
congruent interests with dealer, 1457b
extended agreement theories apply, 1457c
Monsanto case implications, 1457e
precedent, 1457d-e
presuming coercion, 1457c1
proving coercion, 1457c
summary, 1457a
supplier coercion of dealer compared
agreement concepts, 1457e
anticompetitive effects, 1457b
supplier self-interest, 1457c4
Dealer power. *See* same title
Express price maintenance policy before complaint, relevance, 1456d3, 1457c2
Horizontal aspects, 1453c, 1454c, 1604e2, 1644b1, c
Implicit assurance of complainer's agreement or acquiescence, 1448f, 1458c
Information
complex enforcement involved, 1456d2
connection to refusal to deal, 1455c2, 1456b-c
conspiracy created, 1456c-e
Monsanto case implications, 1456e
Parke Davis case compared, 1456c-d
policies concerning, 1454c
solicited by supplier from dealer, 1456f
subject matter of agreement, as, 1456c-e
summary, 1456a
unsolicited by supplier, 1454c, 1456d4
In response to, refusal to deal. *See* coerced supplier; Information
meaning, 1456a
Interpreting complaint or termination, 1453e
Monsanto case, 1454, 1455-1458
Motives of supplier and complainer
congruent, 1457b
differ, relevance of, 1456d4, 1457b, 1458b
explained, 1453e
Non-price subject matter, 1453d
Policies, 1454c, 1457e
Precedes refusal to deal, 1455

COMPLAINT AGAINST RIVAL (*continued*)
Price or non-price subject matter, 1453d, 1454c, 1624-1625
Prior agreement, evidence of, 1458c, 1623c
Supplier coerced. *See* Coerced supplier
CONCENTRATION. *See also* COMPETITION; DISTRIBUTION RESTRAINTS GENERALLY (and related titles); EFFICIENCIES; MARKET POWER; all MERGER titles; MONOPOLIZATION; MONOPOLY SHARED; OLIGOPOLY; TYING
Generally, 404d
Herfindahl index, 404f, 931a2, b2
Interdependent parallelism as conspiracy. *See* same
Market, Chs. 4-11
Measures, 913
"Overall," 1141-1142
Ratios, 913a1, b1
CONCERTED REFUSAL TO DEAL. *See also* PER SE RULE; RULE OF REASON
Agreement or conspiracy
between competitors. *See* CONSPIRACY, GENERALLY
between supplier and dealer. *See* COMPLAINT AGAINST RIVAL; CONSPIRACY, VERTICAL
Credit data or denial, 1412c, 1423b
Ventures excluding rivals, 736, 1478
Vertical distribution restraints as, 1625c-d, 1644c, 1652b
CONSCIOUS PARALLELISM. *See* CONSPIRACY, GENERALLY; INTERDEPENDENT PARALLELISM AS CONSPIRACY; OLIGOPOLY; MONOPOLY SHARED
CONSENT DECREE OR ORDER
Intervention, 348e
Judicial role, 348g
Legislation (1974), 348f-g
Modification, 348b
Subsequent use in private suit, 337a
Third-party
enforcement, 348c
interests, 348d, f
use, 348c, 337a
CONSIGNMENT. *See* CONSPIRACY, INTRAENTERPRISE
CONSPIRACY COERCED (Unwilling behavior as conspiracy with party compelling it). *See also* COMPLAINT AGAINST RIVAL; CONSPIRACY, GENERALLY; CONSPIRACY, VERTICAL; DEALER POWER
Acquiescence with demand or condition, 1408e, f

avoiding patent infringement suit, 1408f1
avoiding refusal to deal generally, 1408f3-4. *See also* CONSPIRACY, VERTICAL
avoiding suits generally, 1408f2
Agreement with competitor, 1408c
Agreement with supplier or customer, 1408d
Cartel formation, 1408b-c
Common situations, 1408a
Equities, 1408b-c, 1459b4
Express agreements distinguished, 1408a
Factors relevant, 1408b
Generally, 1408a, 1415f, 1444a, 1451
Interpreting a situation, 1408a, e
Policies, 1408b
Restricted distribution, tying, and exclusive dealing. See generally this title; CONSPIRACY, VERTICAL
Self-interest, 1408a, e, 1415f
Summary, 1408a
CONSPIRACY, GENERALLY (Including horizontal conspiracy). *See also* COMPLAINT AGAINST RIVAL; CONSPIRACY, COERCED; CONSPIRACY, INTRAENTERPRISE; CONSPIRACY, VERTICAL; FACILITATING PRACTICE; INTERDEPENDENT PARALLELISM AS CONSPIRACY
Abandonment, 1421b3
Adherence by rivals to another's plan, 1426-1427
Admissions
credibility, 1418b1
indirect, 1418c
interpretation, 1418b
Affiliated corporations. *See* CONSPIRACY, INTRAENTERPRISE
Agreement as synonym, 1400
Agreement to act (e.g., to meet) vs. agreement to do that which becomes more likely (e.g., fix price), 1406-1407. *See also* Discussion; Information; Meeting; FACILITATING PRACTICE
Assent, degree of, 1404. *See also* generally this title
Attempt to form illegal agreement, 1407f, 1419
Autonomy limited, 1402a5
Benefit from conspiracy. *See also* Interdependence
absence negates conspiracy, 1414
conspiracy motivation or interdependence, equivalent to, 1414
presence does not prove traditional conspiracy, 1414, 1434c
Bidding
deliberately losing, 1420b

CONSPIRACY, GENERALLY (*continued*)
interdependent pricing compared, 1420a, c2, d1
refusal to bid, 1418c4, 1420c-d
rotation, 1425d4
secret parallel, 1420a, 1425c, 1434b
sham, 1420b
suspicious patterns, 1420a, c4
Boycott, 1412c-e
Burden of proof, 1405, 1417g
Cartel results through recognized interdependence alone, 1429b. *See also* Interdependence; Leadership; Parallelism; INTERDEPENDENT PARALLELISM AS CONSPIRACY
Circumstantial evidence, 1425; also, 1417-1427. *See also* generally this title
Clayton Act compared, 1400a, 1460
Coerced behavior as conspiracy with coercing party. *See* CONSPIRACY, COERCED; CONSPIRACY, VERTICAL
Coercion and express agreement, 1451b
Combination, 1403, 1449g
Commitment
as essential element, 1404, 1410
facilitating practice distinguished, 1407
interdependence distinguished, 1410
weak, 1410c
Common law, 1402a1-2, 1464b, 1474a-b
Competition endangered, 1402
Competition in "similar" market or at other time, 1421a, d
Concept, 1402
Connection between agreement and feared result, 1400a, 1407b, 1436e-j
Conspiracy in "similar" market or at other time, 1421a-c
Consultation as conspiracy, 1402b, 1406. *See also* Discussion; Information; Meeting
Cooperation. *See* this title generally, esp. Tacit coordination
Coordination, reasons for statutory concern, 1402a. *See also* generally this title, esp. Tacit coordination
Cover-up, 1417e
Credit data or denial, 1412c, 1423b
Danger, 1402
Defined, 1402, 1405, 1409-1410
Discussion, 1410c, 1418-1419. *See also* Information; Meetings; Solicitation

Distribution, in, 1412a. *See also* CONSPIRACY, VERTICAL
Employees, with. *See* CONSPIRACY, INTRAENTERPRISE
Existence vs. legality, 1400b, 1402
Explanation, innocent, and. *See also* Independent reason; Interdependence; Leadership; Parallelism
  facilitating practice. *See* same
  false, 1417f
  generally, 1413, 1417-1427
  interdependence, 1410
  motivation, 1412
  self-interest, 1415
Express agreement obviates
  coercion, 1451b
  firm enforcement, 1448e2
  interdependence, 1425b
  motivation, 1425b
Facilitating practice. *See* same
Fact finding, 321, 323, 1405, 1446c-d, 1467g-h
False explanation, 1417f
Federal Trade Commission Act. *See* same
Film distribution, 1412b, 1415b, d, 1425d, 1426
Firm enforcement and express agreement, 1448e2
Furtive behavior, 1417d
Health care situations, 1402b, 1406f, 1409c, 1426d, 1471b, d-h
Horizontal
  generally, 1402a
  vertical compared, 1402b4
"Hub and spoke," 1426a
Independent reason (for each's act), 1413; also 1412, 1415, 1425. *See also* Interdependence; Motivation; Parallelism; Self-interest
Inference prerequisites, 1410a; also 1401, 1405, 1411, 1416. *See also* generally this title
Information. *See also* Meetings; COMPLAINT AGAINST RIVAL; CONSPIRACY, VERTICAL; FACILITATING PRACTICE
  acquisition privileged, 1402b, 1406f
  conspiracy on subject matter of information, 1406a, 1407b-c, 1422b
  conspiracy to exchange, 1406, 1422
  credit data, 1423b
  customer, about, 1423
  dealer, about, 1423b-e
  dealer supplies about own rival, 1456
  exchanged, 1404b, 1406, 1417, 1418b2-4
  facilitating practice, 1407a, e. *See also* same
  solicited, 1402b, 1422
  solicited by supplier from dealer, 1456f
  source's rivals, about, 1402b

CONSPIRACY, GENERALLY (*continued*)

supplier, about, 1422
unsolicited, 1406c, 1456d4
Innocent explanation, defined, 1417c. *See also* Independent reason
Inquiry. *See* Information
Insurer and providers
consultation, 1402b, 1406f, 1409
contracts, 1426d
Interdependence. *See also* Self-interest, action against; INTERDEPENDENT PARALLELISM AS CONSPIRACY; OLIGOPOLY
absence negates conspiracy inference, 1411; also 1412-1415
benefit from conspiracy compared, 1414
bidding situations, 1420
commitment distinguished, 1410
defined, 1407b, 1410b, 1411-1415, 1429a
degrees, 1412f, 1431a
generally, 1407b, 1410, 1428
independent reasons for action compared, 1413
motivation for conspiracy compared, 1412
necessity for conspiracy inference, 1411, 1412a, g, 1413-1415
not for express agreement, 1411, 1425b
non-price matters, 1429c
objectively defined, 1411, 1412f, 1425a
oligopoly model, 1429
parallelism resulting from interdependence alone
no, 1418b4, 1425d, 1429c, 1431
yes, 1407b, 1410, 1418b4, 1428
plus factor, as, 1434a, c
presence does not prove traditional agreement, 1411, 1412-1415, 1434c
self-interest, actions against, compared, 1415, 1425d
subjectively defined, 1412f
sufficiency for conspiracy inference, 1411, 1412a, 1425, 1433a, 1434a, c
traditional conspiracy, as evidence of, 1420d2
Interdependent parallelism as conspiracy. *See* same
Interstate Circuit case
broad formula, 1426b; also 1402b1, 1433c
implications and applications, 1426d, 1433c
traditional conspiracy, 1425d, 1426a, 1433c
Intraenterprise. *See* CONSPIRACY, INTRAENTERPRISE
Jury role, 1405, 1407e, 1410a. *See also* generally this title; other

CONSPIRACY titles; FACILITATING PRACTICE; INTERDEPENDENT PARALLELISM AS CONSPIRACY
Key points highlighted, 1401
Leadership (and competitors follow). *See also* INTERDEPENDENT PARALLELISM AS CONSPIRACY; OLIGOPOLY
  cartel-like results, 1429b
  following, likelihood of, 1425d2
  interdependence explains, 1410b
  non-price matters, 1425e, 1429c
  not followed, cost of, 1425d3
  oligopoly model, 1429
  perilous without advance agreement, 1425d
  reversal, ease of, 1425d3
  risks for leaders or early followers, 1425d
  uncertainty, 1425d, 1430c
Legality vs. existence, 1400b, 1402
Market division, 1425d4
Market power increased, 1402a4
Masonite case, 1427
Meeting. *See also* Discussion; Information; Solicitation; FACILITATING PRACTICE
  before secret bid, 1418c4, 1420d
  conspiracy on subject matter of, 1406a, 1407b-c
  conspiracy to meet, 1406
  facilitating practice, as, 1407a, e, 1418
  interpretation, 1418b
  opportunity to conspire, 1417a-b
  secret, 1417d
  unexplained, 1417c
Motivation for common action. *See also* Interdependence
  absence negates conspiracy inference, 1412a
  generally, 1412
  illustrations, 1412
  presence does not prove traditional conspiracy, 1412a, 1434c
Non-competitors, agreement with and statutory concern, 1402b, 1437
Oligopoly, in. *See* Interdependence; Leadership; Parallelism; INTERDEPENDENT PARALLELISM AS CONSPIRACY
One-sided promise, 1402b2
Opportunity to conspire, 1417. *See also* Information; Meeting
Parallelism. *See also* Interdependence; Leadership; FACILITATING PRACTICE; INTERDEPENDENT

CONSPIRACY, GENERALLY (*continued*)
PARALLELISM AS CONSPIRACY; OLIGOPOLY
advance understanding aids, 1418b2-4, 1425
business risks, 1425d
coincidence, 1411-1415, 1425
implies traditional conspiracy, 1416-1427, esp. 1425
inexplicable without conspiracy, 1425c
interdependence explains, 323d, 841, 1410, 1411-1415, 1420c2, 1425, 1429-1430. *See also* INTERDEPENDENT PARALLELISM AS CONSPIRACY
interdependence not an explanation for, 1425, esp. c-d
leadership. *See* Leadership
non-price matters, 1425e, 1429c
not interdependent, 1411-1415
oligopoly model, 1429
perilous without conspiracy, 1415, 1425d
prerequisites to inferring any conspiracy, 1411-1415
prima facie case, 1417g
sequential, 1425d
simultaneous, 1425c
unlikely matters, 1425e
unnatural, 1425a
Parties, need to identify, 1409b-c
Plus factors, 1434
Price. *See also* Interdependence; Leadership; Parallelism; INTERDEPENDENT PARALLELISM AS CONSPIRACY
discrimination, 323d
idiosyncratic, 1425d4
manual, 1406c, 1435g. *See also* FACILITATING PRACTICE
Product uniformity, 1425e, 1429c
Proof criteria and burden, 1401, 1405, 1410, 1425a. *See also* generally this title
Purpose, statutory, of conspiracy requirement, 1402. *See also* Unilateral behavior
Question-response as agreement, 1406e
Quid pro quo, necessity for, 1402b3, 1437, 1453
Rationale for requiring, 1402
Reciprocity context, 1130b
Refusal to bid. *See* Bidding
Refusal to deal and
horizontal agreement, 1412-1415
vertical agreement. *See* CONSPIRACY, COERCED; CONSPIRACY, VERTICAL; DISTRIBUTION RE-

STRAINT GENERALLY (and related titles)
Request for, rejected, 1419
Requirement in statute, 1400a
Sale contract, ordinary, 1400b, 1437
Secret bids. *See* Bidding
Secret meeting, 1417d
Self-interest, action against. *See also* Interdependence; Leadership; Motivation; Parallelism
  coerced action, 1415f. *See also* CONSPIRACY, COERCED
  defined, 1415a
  generally, 1415a, 1425a
  immediate vs. ultimate interest, 1415e
  other's behavior irrelevant, 1415b
  other's behavior relevant, 1415c
  perilous leading, 1425d
  plus factor, as, 1415, 1425, 1434c
  reversible action, 1425d3
  short-run vs. long-run, 1415e
  superior offer rejected, 1415d
  unnatural following, 1425
Sequential parallelism, 1425d
Solicitation
  attempted monopolization, 1407f
  creates conspiracy, 1419b
  facilitates anticompetitive parallelism, 1419d
  reflects conspiracy, 1419c
  responses interpreted, 1419
  unaccepted, 1406d, 1407f
Statutory policies and requirement, 1400a, c, 1402. *See also* Unilateral behavior; CONSPIRACY, COERCED
Statutory rationale, 1402. *See also* Unilateral behavior
Subject matter, need to specify, 1409a, c
Summary, 1401, 1409-1410, 1428
Summary disposition, 322. *See also* generally this title; Fact finding
Superior offer rejected, 1415d
Tacit coordination. *See also* INTERDEPENDENT PARALLELISM AS CONSPIRACY
  commitment compared, 1410
  factors impeding, 1430
  Interstate Circuit formula, 1426
  traditional agreement compared, 1432b
Theatre Enterprises case, 1412b, 1426c
Threats of concerted action, 1424
To injure rival (*Pick-Barth* rule), 828b
Traditional conspiracy. *See also* particular topics
  commitment element, 1410
  defined, 1410, 1416

CONSPIRACY, GENERALLY (*continued*)
generally, 1416
inferred, 1416-1427
interdependence contrasted, 1410
parties, 1409
subject matter, 1407c, 1409
Tying context
suppliers, among, 1412e
vertical. *See* CONSPIRACY, VERTICAL
Unilateral behavior (statutory policies concerning compared), 1402, 1432c, 1437, 1462, 1463c, e, 1475. *See also* CONSPIRACY, VERTICAL
Unwilling behavior. *See* CONSPIRACY, COERCED
Vertical agreement
generally. *See* CONSPIRACY, VERTICAL
participation with knowledge of rival's participation, 1426-1427
CONSPIRACY, HORIZONTAL. *See* CONSPIRACY, GENERALLY
CONSPIRACY, INTRAENTERPRISE (Capacity to conspire of affiliated persons)
Administrability, 1467g
Agency agreement distinguished from restraint, 1473a
Agents, distribution, restrained, 1473
aiding restraint distinguished, 1473a
autonomy of intermediary, 1473e1
business risks, 1473b, c, d2
compensation, 1473d2
consignment. *See* generally this subtitle
economic risk as key element, 1473g, 1622c
efficient distribution, 1473e2
employee compared, 1473a, d2
European Economic Community, 1473g
food brokers, 1473d2
handling goods vs. taking orders, 1473d2, 1622c
independence, degree of, 1473d2, f, g. *See also* this subtitle generally
intrabrand competition, 1473e1, f
investments, 1473d2, g
legitimate objective, 1473d2, e2
market power, 1473c, d1
polar illustrations, 1473b
policy issues, 1473e-f
real estate broker, 1473d2
risk of loss of goods or capital, 1473b, c, d2, f-g
substantive illegality rules qualified, 1473b, c, d2, e2, f
summary, 1473b

Supreme Court cases, 1473a-c
taxes, 1473c, d2
title to goods, 1473c, d2, 1622c, 1642b
"vast" number of intermediaries, 1473c, d1
vertical integration alternative, 1473c, e1, f
wholesaler, 1473d2
Agents pawns aiding a restraint, 1474
act aided independently unlawful, 1474b
agent restrained distinguished, 1473a
aid itself restrains trade, 1474b
banks and pension fund administrators, 1474c
benefit from restraint, 1474c
common law conspiracy, 1474b
criminal law generally compared, 1474b
employee compared, 1473a
illustrations, 1474a-d
intent to restrain trade, 1474b-c
knowledge, purpose, and stake, 1474c
lenders, 1474c
market power increased, 1474b
material contribution, 1474b
monitor of dealer resale prices, 1449f, 1474
pawn defined, 1473a
policy issues, 1474a
summary, 1474a
Supreme Court cases, 1474b-c
unilateral distinction obscured, 1474b
Agreement
as evidence of integration, 1467e2-3
distinguished from direction, 1462c, 1467c
in fact, 1468
Common law, 1402a1-2, 1464b, 1474a-b
Competitive relationship of affiliated persons, 1467b, 1469c
Competitors, rule making bodies for, 1477-1478. *See also* Trade association
Connection between business form and alleged restraint, 1462b, 1464d, 1467c
Consignment. *See* Agents, distribution
Conspiracy among related parties fills gap between Sherman Act §§1-2, 1464e, 1476a
Conspiratorial capacity distinguished from conspiracy in fact, 1468
Contacts among related persons not necessarily conspiracy, 1468

CONSPIRACY, INTRAENTERPRISE (*continued*)
Continuing conspiracy among creators or members of firms, associations, and joint ventures, 1475-1478. *See also* those topics in this title
factors, 1475a
not governed by usual substantive rules, 1477
policy and practical relevance, 1475a
Contract compared to direction, 1467c
Cooperatives, 1463f
Corporation, single. *See* Enterprise
Corporations owned partially in common. *See also* Corporations wholly owned in common; this title generally
alter ego test, 1467f2
control, de facto, 1463g, 1467f2
control, de jure, 1467f2
control, exercised vs. power to, 1467e
factors, 1467
generally, 1466a
government practice, 1466a, 1467f
jury question, 1467g-h
majority ownership, 1467f
merger policy compared, 1466d2
minority interest held by competitor, supplier, or customer, 1466e
minority interest, relevance of, 1466d
policies, 1464
precedents, 1466b, 1467
simple test vs. all-factor test, 1467g
wholly owned corporations compared, 1466c
Corporations owned wholly in common. *See also* Enterprise; this title generally
Copperweld case, 1463h, 1464
earlier Supreme Court decisions, 1463b-g
policies, 1464
sister corporations, 1464f
subsidiary corporations, 1463h
Creators of firms, trade associations, and joint ventures, continuing conspiracy among, 1475-1478. *See also* those topics in this title
Defined, 1462
Direction distinguished from agreement, 1462c, 1467c
Directors in common, 1467d, 1471b-c
Distribution intermediaries. *See* Agents, distribution, restrained
Divisions within a corporation, 1470

Employee conspires with employer, 1470-1473
  administrability problems, 1471d3-g
  causes restraint, 1471g
  conceptual difficulties, 1471d1, 3
  conduit between independent firms, 1471b-c
  connected to restraint, 1470, 1471d, g
  disloyalty reflecting independent interest
    explained, 1471d1
    incremental incentive for anticompetitive act, 1471b, d
    policy relevance, 1471d2
    presumed or proved, 1471d2, f
    prevalence, 1471d2
  distribution restraint, 1471c
  employment contract itself, 1470
  generally, 1470
  hospital and medical staff, 1471b, d-g
  independent interest implying disloyalty
    competitive with employer, 1471b
    connected to restraint, 1471g
    defined, 1471b, e
    magnitude, 1471e2
    policy relevance, 1471a, b, d
  predation, 1471c
  price fixing among competitors, 1471c
  second firm coordinated or constricted through common employee, 1471b-c
  status in firm, 1471c, g
  unauthorized act, 1472
Employees conspire among themselves, 1471h
Employees in common, 1467d, 1471b-c
Enterprise. *See also* Single enterprise; generally this title
  alliance vs. single entity, 1476c
  by-law limits shareholder's investments elsewhere, 1476a
  creation as conspiracy, 1464c, 1475, 1476a
  integration index, 1476c
  merger compared with creation, 1464c, 1476b
    loose-knit collaboration, 1476c
  operation not continuing conspiracy of creators, 1475, 1476a
  post-merger operation as continuing conspiracy of pre-merger firms, 1203-1204, 1476c
Estoppel, 1465a
Fact or law question, 1467g-h
Gaps (unilateral anticompetitive behavior not involving monopoly), 1464e
Generally, 1462
Holding out firms as unrelated, 1465, 1467b

CONSPIRACY, INTRAENTERPRISE (*continued*)
Integrated operations, 1467c-e, 1476c. *See also* Enterprise; Joint venture
Intended to act as if unrelated, 1465
Internal matters, 1469d. *See also* Joint venture; Trade association
Intracorporate relations, 1462
Joint venture, single entity or continuing conspiracy, 1475, 1478
  classification significance, 1462a
  definition, 1478a
  different kinds, 1478a
  excesses controlled though ordinary operations not continuing conspiracy, 1478b2-4
  factors, 1475a
  formation, 1478b
  integration, degree of, 1478b2, d
  on-going operations not focused on parent's competition, 1478c
  reappraisal after error, success, or market changes, 1478b2-4
  rules governing members' own market operations, 1477, 1478c-d
  summary, 1478a
Jury role, 1405, 1467g-h
Legislative history, 1464b
Members of trade associations and joint ventures, continuing conspiracy among, 1475, 1477-1478. *See also* those topics in this title
Motivation for separate incorporation, 1467b
Natural persons, 1462
Officers in common, 1467d, 1471b-c
Offices in common, 1467d
Ownership, degree of, 1466d-e, 1467f
Partnership. *See also* Enterprise
  formation, 1476d
  operation as continuing conspiracy, 1476d
Policies generally, 1462, 1464, 1475
Power increased, as criterion, 1462b, 1464c
Pretended separateness, 1465a, 1467b
Reasonableness
  criteria different for agreements among related parties, 1469
  obviates concern for defining two parties, 1462, 1464a, c
Rule-making bodies, 1477-1478. *See also* Joint venture; Trade association
Single enterprise. *See* generally this title

behavior relevant under Sherman Act, 1462b, 1464b-c, e
conspiracy in creation or operation. *See* Enterprise
consultation evidences integration in fact, 1467e3
control exercised vs. control power, 1467e
criteria, 1464, 1467. *See also* this title generally
directive power, 1467e-f
employees, officers, or directors in common, 1467d
generally, 1463h, 1467a
joint ventures, 1475, 1478. *See also* Joint venture
jury role, 1467g-h
partnership, 1476d
records and reports in common, 1467c
relevant unit for antitrust purposes, as, 1462
simple vs. all-factor test, 1467g
sports league, 1478d
trade association, 1475, 1477. *See also* Trade association
Sports league, 1478d. *See also* Continuing conspiracy; Joint venture
Statutory language, 1464b
Summary, 1462
Tax returns in common, 1467d
Trade association, 1475, 1477
formation, 1477
member's liability, 1477
own liability, 1477
own operation as conspiracy, 1477
rules governing members, 1477
Two parties. *See* generally this title
in-between situations, 1462
relevance of, 1462, 1464c
"Unilateral" behavior
analysis obscured by conspiracy characterization, 1464e
covered by Sherman Act only when monopoly involved, 1462a, 1464c-e
CONSPIRACY TO MONOPOLIZE, 839
CONSPIRACY, VERTICAL (based on supplier's refusal to deal with customers reselling or purchasing contrary to supplier's desire, suggestion, or condition; or based on rival customer's complaint; or based on customer's refusal to deal with supplier dealing with rival buyer). *See also* COMPLAINT AGAINST RIVAL; CONSPIRACY, COERCED; CONSPIRACY, GENERALLY. Note: all Ch. 14 subtitles summarized, 1438
Admitted by dealer, meaning, 1447e

CONSPIRACY, VERTICAL (*continued*)

Agents aiding enforcement. *See* Pawn
Albrecht case, 1450-1451
Announced condition on future dealing. *See* generally this title
Assent, degree of, 1404, 1443-1444, 1446b
Attempt to form agreement, 1407f, 1419
Causally connected to injury of terminated dealer plaintiff. *See also* ANTITRUST INJURY
- independent reason for termination, 1413, 1459d2, 1460c2
- mitigation, 1459c3
- non-complying plaintiff, 1459d, 1623f, 1640b
- plaintiff's own prior agreement, 1459c-d, 1640b
- summary, 1459a
- supplier's agreements with rival dealers, 1459e
- tying and exclusive dealing distinguished from resale price maintenance, 1459e3, 1460

Ceasing to deal. *See* this title generally; Termination
Clayton Act §3
- conditioned sales
  - causally connected to non-purchasing plaintiff, 1460e
  - inferred, 1460d
- damage and standing issues, 1460c
- non-sales to plaintiff and conditioned sales to others, 1460d-e
  - precedent, 1460f
- statutory language broader than Sherman Act, 1460b
- statutory policy, 1460b3

Coerced agreement theory. *See also* Coerced compliance;CONSPIRACY, COERCED
- aptness, 1444c2
- dealers, fairness to, 1443c7
- harassment of suppliers, 1443d2
- implications broad, 1444c3
- objections, 1444c
- parties unknown, 1442d, 1444c4, 1459b2
- precedent, 1445-1452, esp. 1451; 1457
- prerequisities, 1444d
- stated, 1444b
- summarized, 1444a, e
- supplier coerced, 1457

Coerced compliance
- *Albrecht, Parke Davis,* and other pre-*Monsanto* cases, 1451c-d, 1623d, 1624a, 1630d
- defined, 1451a
- express agreements, and, 1451b
- *Monsanto* case, 1446d, 1451e, 1623d, 1630d
- one instance implies others, 1452d
- summary, 1444a, 1451a

supplier coerced by customer, 1457, 1625d
theory of agreement, 1444
Coercion theory implications, 1627d1
Colgate case. *See also* generally this title
consistency with extended agreement theories, 1445d, e, 1630d
facts and holding, 1445b
limited by subsequent cases, 1448-1451, 1630d
present status, 1446b, e
rationale, 1445c
revived by *Monsanto* case, 1446b, e, 1623d, 1630d
traditional agreement involved, 1445b
Combination, 1403, 1449g
Competitive policy, relation to, 1437. *See also* generally this title
Complaint against rival (usually to supplier by dealer). *See* same
Complex enforcement (of announced conditions)
complaints by rival dealers, 1456d2
defined and distinguished from simple enforcement, 1449f; also 1445d2, 1446e, 1449c-d, 1450-1451
one instance implies others, 1452d
reconciles the cases, 1445d, 1446e, 1449c-d
relevance, 1445d2
Compliance reflecting dealer's preference, 1442d, 1443d1, 1444c4, 1459b2
Conditions on future dealing. *See* generally this title
Congenial dealers selected, 1441c-e, 1623b, 1630d
Consumer
agreement with supplier
controlling retailer, 1451f
generally, 1437
damages or standing, 1459b
Customer restraints. *See* this title generally
Damages for consumers or terminated dealers, 1459. *See also* DAMAGES
Dealer disobedient, consequences, 1439
Distribution restraints. *See* this title generally
Effects of announced conditions on future dealing compared with express agreements
differences, 1442c-d
generally, 1442
presumptions or proofs, 1442e
similarities, 1442b, 1630d
summary, 1442a
tying and exclusive dealing, distinguished, 1442e2
Exclusive dealing. *See* Tying and exclusive dealing

CONSPIRACY, VERTICAL (*continued*)

Express contract compared with announced condition on future dealing, 1442
Extended agreement theories. *See* Coerced agreement theory; Implied agreement theory
Federal Trade Commission Act §5, decisions under, 1461
"Firm and resolute enforcement" of announced conditions
  express agreement, and, 1448e2
  implying agreement, 1448e1
Generally, 1402b4, 1437, 1453
Horizontal agreement, recharacterized as, 1604e2, 1625c4, 1644b
Implied agreement theory
  acceptance requested, desired, or given, 1443c2-3, 5
  dealers, fairness to, 1443c7
  harassment of suppliers, 1443d2
  implications, 1627d1
  objections, 1443c
  offer, 1443c2
  parties unknown, 1444c4, 1459b2
  precedent, 1445-1452. *See also* this title generally
  prerequisites, 1442e, 1443d1
  stated, 1443b
  summarized, 1443a
  terms, 1443c4
Independent reasons (other than claimed restraint) for non-dealing, 1413, 1443d2, 1459d2, 1460c2, 1623f2, 1624-1625
Individualized dealings. *See* Negotiation
Information provided by third parties, 1449e, 1456
Intent of supplier, 1452c3
Intermediate distributors
  complex enforcement of supplier's announced condition on future dealing with retailers, 1448c, d, 1449
  conspire with supplier controlling retailer, 1449
  Monsanto case, 1449d
  Parke Davis case, 1449
  supplying information about retailers, 1449e, 1456
  utilized by supplier to control retailer, 1439, 1448c, d, 1449
Jury role, 1405, 1442e, 1446b-d
Monitoring dealer's resale prices, 1449e-f
Monsanto case. *See also* COMPLAINT AGAINST RIVAL
  Albrecht case, and, 1450, 1451
  Colgate case, and, 1446b, e

complex enforcement, 1446e
consistency with extended agreement theories, 1446e
dealer acquiescence as agreement, 1446b, d
earlier cases, implications for, 1446e, 1447-1452, 1454-1458
facts and holding on announced conditions, 1446b-c
facts and holding on agreement with complaining dealers, 1454
Parke Davis case, and, 1446e3, 1449d, e2
summary, 1446a
Negotiation (and other individualized dealings)
complex enforcement of announced condition, 1447c-d, 1449f
implications for extended agreement theories, 1447c-d
one instance implies others, 1452d
traditional agreement, 1447b; also 1445b, 1446c1, 1448c
unsuccessful, 1447e
varieties and meaning, 1447a-b
Notice to dealers, announced condition as, 1440c, 1441g, 1442d3, 1443c6
Parke Davis case, 1449; also 1450b, 1451, 1456c-d. *See also* Intermediate distributors
Parties, possible, 1442f
Pawn aiding enforcement of announced conditions on future dealing. *See also* Complex enforcement; CONSPIRACY, INTRAENTERPRISE
Albrecht case, 1450b
defined, 1474
monitoring resale price, 1449e-f
providing information, 1449f
soliciting assurances, incident to, 1450c2
terminating dealer, incident to 1450c1
Persuasion without coercion, 1440b
Precedent in Supreme Court
Albrecht case, 1450-1451
Colgate case, 1445
Monsanto case, 1446
Other post-*Colgate* pre-*Monsanto* cases, 1448
Parke Davis case, 1449
Proof. *See also* Termination; generally this title
burdens generally, 1405
ceasing to deal implies previous agreement with former customer, 1452e, 1459c-d

CONSPIRACY, VERTICAL
(*continued*)
depends on whether extended agreement theories adopted, 1459
illustrative evidence, as in *Monsanto* case, 1446c
independent reasons (other than claimed restraint) for non-dealing. *See* Independent reasons.
one instance of threats, individualized negotiation, or complex enforcement implies others, 1452d
refusal to deal with customer implies agreement with other customers, 1452, esp. d-e
Pyramided inferences controlled, 1443d2, 1452d
Refusal to deal. *See* Termination; generally this title
Resale prices, customers, or territories. *See* this title generally
Sales contract, ordinary, 1437
Selection, initial, of "congenial" customers (or suppliers), standing alone, 1441c, 1446f
Silent termination (without announced condition or explanation), 1441d-h, 1623b
dealer inferences, 1441d-f
effects compared with announced conditions, 1441e2
equivalence to announced condition, 1441e, 1452c
initial selection compared, 1442b
intended as message to others, 1441e, 1452a, c3
legitimate objectives, 1441e3
pyramided inferences, 1443d2, 1452d
status after *Monsanto* case, 1446f
suggestions, after, 1441f
summary, 1441a
tying and exclusive dealing compared with restricted distribution, 1441h
Simple enforcement (of announced conditions). *See* Complex enforcement
Standing for consumers or terminated dealers, 1459, 1623f, 1640. *See also* STANDING
Statutory concepts, 1402, 1437, 1442f, 1443-1444, 1462, 1464c, e
Subject matter
boycott, 1644c, 1652b
non-resale price, 1622
price vs. non-price, 1624-1625, 1644a, 1652b
Suggested resale price or other behavior

agreement concepts, 1440a, 1623c
effects, 1440a
justifications, 1440a
termination for non-compliance, 1441f, 1446f, 1623a
threats or notice compared, 1440b-c, 1441g, 1623c-d
without sanctions, 1440a, 1446f, 1623c-d, 1630d
Supplier coerced by customer, 1457, 1625d
Summary, general, 1437-1438
Termination. *See also* Silent termination; Subject matter; Suggested price; generally this title
agreement with continuing customers implied, 1452d-e, 1624-1625
agreement with terminated customer implied, 1459c-d
cause. *See* Independent reason
caused by agreement with others, 1459e
dealer's
expectation or reliance, 1441b
fairness claim, 1452b
exemplary, 1440b, 1441e, f3, 1452c, 1627e
irrational without agreement with others, 1452e
message to other customers, as, 1441e, f3, 1452c
pyramided inferences
caveat, 1443d2, 1452d
summary, 1452a
Territorial restraints. *See* this title generally
Theories of agreement. *See* Coerced agreement theory; Implied agreement theory
Third parties used to implement announced condition on future dealing. *See* Intermediate distributors; Pawns
Threats, unsuccessful, as
attempt to form illegal agreement, 1407f, 1419
attempt to monopolize, 826
Traditional agreement often present, 1445b, 1446c1, 1447, 1448c, 1449b
Tying and exclusive dealing. *See also* this title generally; Clayton Act §3; Federal Trade Commission Act §5
effects of express agreements compared, 1442, esp. e2
package sale as agreement, 1441h1
silent termination of non-complying customers, 1441h
Unwilling compliance. *See* Coerced compliance
Wholesale price formula as, 1627d1
Wholesalers. *See* Intermediate distributors

CONSPIRATORIAL CAPACITY. *See* CONSPIRACY, INTRAENTERPRISE
CONTRACT. *See* CONSPIRACY, GENERALLY
CONTRACTING WITH GOVERNMENT. *See* POLITICAL ACTION; STATE ACTION
CONTRIBUTION, 1459b
COOPERATIVES (Including fishermen's cooperatives). *See* AGRICULTURAL COOPERATIVES
COPYING, 209, 735, 829b, 1508c, 1613b, 1718f
COPYRIGHT. *See also* TYING
- Acquired, 1202f
- Resale price restrained, 1621
  - *Bobbs-Merrill* case, 1621
  - free riding prevented, 1613b

COUNTERCLAIM, 391
COVENANTS AGAINST COMPETITION. *See also* PER SE RULE; RULE OF REASON
- Monopolization, 703b

CRIMINAL SANCTIONS. *See also* CHANGE OF LAW; MISTAKE OF LAW; REGULATED INDUSTRIES; STATE ACTION
- Appropriateness, 311a3
- Burdens of proof, 311b
- Effect on content of particular offenses
  - generally, 311b, 312
  - monopolization, 623, 630a-b
  - oligopolistic interdependence, 1432e
  - shared monopoly, 851
- Effect on statutory development, 311a3
- Fairness, 309c, 311b
- Frequency of use, 311a2
- Good faith, relevance of, 311b
- Government practice, 311a2
- Offenses, 311a1
- Penalties, 309a
- Statutes relevant, 309a
- System of sanctions, 310

CROSS-ELASTICITY. *See* MARKET POWER, Market definition
CUSTOMER AND TERRITORIAL RESTRAINT, VERTICAL. *See also* DEALER POWER; DISTRIBUTION RESTRAINTS GENERALLY; RESALE PRICE MINIMUM; SOLE OUTLET
- Agreement, 1641d
- Analogies to other restraints, 1624b, 1642
- Ancillary to price-fixing scheme, 1642
- Area of primary responsibility, 1641b1
- Burden of persuasion, 1645e, 1646d, 1649a
- Burden of proof, 1645a, 1646d, 1649a
- Closed territory, 1641b5, 1646d. *See also* Intensity of restraint
- Customer needing distinctive services, 1641c1
- Customer restraint forms, 1641c

Customers reserved to manufacturer, 1641c2, 1648c4
Dangers of, 1648. *See also* Evils
Dealer power. *See* same
Dealer services, 1611-1614, 1646b, 1647b
De facto price restraints, 1648e
Defined, 1641b-c
Dual distribution, 1605, 1641c2, 1644b2, 1649c
Easy vs. hard sales, 1616f
Entry facilitation, 1617
Effects, 1630b, 1646-1649
Evils, 1648
  burden of proof, 1649c
  cream skimming, 1648c3B
  efficient dealers restrained, 1648b1
  high-cost dealers protected, 1648b1
  intrabrand competition curtailed, 1648b1
  introduction and summary, 1648a
  manufacturer concentration transferred to dealer, 1648d1
  manufacturer coordination facilitated, 1604h, 1648c4, e
  manufacturer error, 1607, 1648b2
  misleading dealer recommendations, 1614c, 1648c2
  monopoly exacerbates, 1648b3
  multibrand dealers favored, 1648c2
  price discrimination, 1648c3
  rule of reason in addressing, 1648b3, 1649
Exchanged for second restraint, 1610, 1646f, 1648c1
Fencing dealers in, 1616e1,f
Fencing dealers out, 1616e2,f
Free riding prevented, 1611, 1647b, 1648b
Horizontal characterization, 1604e2, 1644
Intensity of restraint, 1641b-c, 1648d3F, 1651
Intention to affect price irrelevant, 1624-1625, 1644a
Intrabrand competition continued, 1616f
Justifications, generally, 1645-1647
Legitimacy, 1646-1649
Less restrictive alternatives, 1602, 1645d, 1647
Local promotion, 1645d
Local quota, 1641b1
Location clause, 1641b2, 1643c
Manufacturer objective in imposing, 1646-1648
Market definitions, 570, 1645b-c
Market shares, 1645b-c, 1649c
  Related to theory of anticompetitive effect, 1648f
Minimum distributor costs, 1645d

CUSTOMER AND TERRITORIAL RESTRAINT, VERTICAL (*continued*)
Multi-brand dealers, 1646h
Pass over payments, 1641b3, 1642a, 1645d, 1646d
de facto closed territories, danger of, 1641b3
defined, 1641b3
promotion and services costs, 1641b3
royalty, compared, 1641b4
Per se theories, 1641a, 1644, 1646a
Presumptions, 1641a, 1649
Product quality, 1618, 1645d
Product safety, 1618, 1645d
Quality protected, 1618, 1645d
Rule of reason, and, 1642a, 1643-44, 1645a, 1646a, 1649
Sales quota, 1648d3F. *See also* Intensity of restraint
Schwinn doctrine, 1642b-c
agency and consignment arrangments, 1642b-c
developments under, 1642c
facts and holding, 1642b
overruled by *Sylvania*, 1643
per se rule, and, 1642b
rationale, 1642b
rule of reason, and, 1642b
sale-non-sale distinction, 1642b-c, 1643b
transfer of title important, 1642b
Scope and intensity of restraint, 1648d2, 1648d3B, F
Selective v. general restraint, 1648d3E, 1649c
Sole outlet. *See* same
Sole outlet compared, 1652d
Summary judgment, 1641a, 1649
Sylvania case, 1630b, 1643, 1644-1645. *See also* this title generally
developments following, 1643d, 1645
distinguishing among types of restraints, 1646d
Termination, 1641d, 1644c
boycotts, characterization as, 1644c
non-compliance, 1641d, 1644c
Theory of anticompetitive effect and market share, 1648f
Treatment by courts, 1641a, 1644-1645
Tying compared, 1700j4
Unauthorized dealers limited, 1641c3, 1645d
Undifferentiated product, 1649c
Vertical price-fixing compared, 1624-1625, 1630, 1641a, 1644
White Motor case, 1642a

DAMAGES *See also* ANTITRUST INJURY; CHANGE OF LAW; MISTAKE OF LAW; PRIVATE ACTIONS; REGULATED IN-

DUSTRIES; STANDING; STATE ACTION
Appropriateness, 312, 355, 365, 623, 851
Approximations, 365
Based on competitive price, 1640
Boycott victims, 365b. *See also* Terminated dealer
Causation. *See also* generally this title
- generally, 363, 364
- consumers and resale price maintenance, 1459b3
- terminated dealer, 1459c-e

Clayton Act §7, 335d, 345-346
Compensatory rationale, 362, 363, 365
Consumer suit
- dealer liability for resale price maintenance, 1459b4
- indirect purchaser from price-fixer, 370, 371
- generally, 370
- resale price maintenance, 1459b

Creditors, 378c
Dealers terminated, 365b4, 381a, 382c, 1640a
Deterrence rationale, 312d, 355
Doubtful, inherently, 360c5, 365
Effect on content of particular offenses
- generally, 312
- monopolization, 623, 630c
- monopoly shared, 851
- oligopolistic parallelism, 1432e

Effects absent notwithstanding statutory violation, 362, 1640c-d
Employees, 377
Governmental plaintiffs, 380
Illinois Brick doctrine, 370-372, 1459b
Indirect purchasers, 370-372
Injuries not within rationale of offense, 360, 362, 363
Landlords, 376
Licensors, 376
Merger victims
- competitors, 373b, 381a, 1640c
- customers, 630c3
- dealers, 381a, 1640c
- suppliers (etc.), 365b5, 375
- takeover target, 381b

Mitigation, 1459c3
Monopolization cases, 630c
New business, 374
Non-profit plaintiffs, 370
Offset by plaintiff's gains
- *in pari delicto* situations, 365c3, 390, 1459c2
- tying situations, 365c1, 2

"Otherwise prevailing price," 1640d3
Passing-on
- defensive use, 371
- offensive use, 371a

Patent accumulations, 630c3
Price-fixing victims, 370. *See also* Consumer suit
Remoteness and denial of standing, 364
Shared monopoly cases, 851, 858

DAMAGES (*continued*)
Shareholders, 378d, e
Standing, related to, 360c, 365
Suppliers, 365b5
Takeover target, 381b
Taxpayers, 378b
Terminated dealer and
Clayton Act §3, 1460c-f
mitigation, 1459c3
non-compliance with condition, 1459d
own prior illegal agreement, 365c3, 1459c1
supplier's illegal agreements with other dealers, 1459e
tying and exclusive dealing distinguished from resale price maintenance, 1459e3
Trebling mandatory, 331b, 630c1
jury informed, 355b
Tying, 365c
Umbrella theories, 1459b2
Unestablished business, 344c
Vertical price ceiling, 1640
Vertical price floors, 1623f3-4
DANGEROUS PROBABILITY STANDARD. *See* ATTEMPTED MONOPOLIZATION
DATA DISSEMINATION. *See* COMPLAINT AGAINST RIVAL; CONCERTED REFUSAL TO DEAL; CONSPIRACY, GENERALLY; CONSPIRACY, VERTICAL; FACILITATING PRACTICE; RULE OF REASON
DEALER AUTONOMY, 1609, 1632c1, 1637d, 1640d1, 1648b, 1651c. *See also* DISTRIBUTION RESTRAINTS GENERALLY; TYING, Autonomy; particular restraints
Advertising, 1609a
Agency, 1473
Alienation restraint, 1473, 1609c
Bargaining power inequality, 1609e
Colgate doctrine, 1445, 1609c
Competition, surrogate for, 1609b
Competitive effects, 1609b
Concern about, 1609
Efficiency values, 1609c, e
Ethics, 1609a, 1639h
Fairness, 1609e
Freedom to contract, 1609d-e, 1637d
Function, 1609a
Hours, 1609a
Inventories, 1609a
Limitations per se lawful, 1609a
Location, 1609a, Ch.16-D
Oppressed class, 1609e
Preference of dealer, 1609e
Premises, 1609a
Producer in own right, 1609d
Rationale for concern, 1609
Resale price ceilings, rationale for opposing, 1637d, 1640d2
Schwinn doctrine, 1609e, 1637d, 1642b

Services, 1609a
State statutes, 1609e
Transfers, 1609a,e
Warehouses, 1609a
DEALER CARTEL. *See* DEALER POWER
DEALER POWER 1604, 1613, 1614, 1632e, 1633c1, 1648d, 1649c1, 1653e, 1654c-g. *See also* DISTRIBUTION RESTRAINTS GENERALLY; particular distribution restraints
Ambiguity, 1648d3A
Arbitrary thresholds, 1604f1
Bargaining power defined, 1648d3A, 1654d, 1655g1
Bargaining power re manufacturer, 1604g, 1632e3, 1648d3, 1652d
Brand dominance, 1604f2, 1632e, 1648d2
Brand loyalty, 1604f2, 1631e
Brand power, 1604f2, 1632e, 1633c1, 1648d2, 1648d3, 1654g2
Burdens of proof, 1604i, 1632d-e, 1633c, e
Ceiling prices justified by, 1636a
Characterization as horizontal, 1453, 1457, 1604e2
Coercion defined, 1604a, g, 1648d3A
Concentration threshold, 1604f3, 1632e, 1633c1, 1648c4, d, 1649c, 1654g2
Dealer association, 1604b-c, f2, g2, 1632b,e1, 1648d3B
Dealer complaint. *See* Dealer initiative
Dealer concentration, 1604f3, 1632e2, 1633c1,c3,d2, 1648d, 1654g2
Dealer initiatives, 1604g2-4, 1632e3-4, 1633c, 1648d3B, 1649c, 1655g3
Dealer intent, 1648d4
Dealer profit, 1604f6
Dealer profit excessive
exchanged for dealer goodwill, 1647f
exclusive dealing exchange, 1610, 1632c2, 1647f
good performance hostage, 1614e, 1647f, 1648d
manufacturer interest, 1603
Dealer pushing, 1614c, 1632c, 1647f
Dealer replacement, ease of, 1604g, 1648d3, 1655g4
Dealer services
absent, 1604b, f7, 1632e4
rebuttal, 1604f7, 1632e4
restraint futile, 1604f7, 1632e4
Dealer shelf space, 1614d
Dealer shifting brands, ease of, 1604d3, g1; 1648d3C
Defined, 1604a, f1, 1648d3A
Detectability. *See also* Extent of restraint; Intensity of restraint; Measures
cartel, 1604c2
dealer profit, 1604f6

DEALER POWER (*continued*)
manufacturer justification, 1604h
tacit coordination, 1604c,d1
Distribution resources controlled, 1655g
Dr. Miles rule, and, 1620c4
Economic performance measures, 1604f6
Effects, 1604a-c. *See also* Intensity of restraint; Measures after abandonment, 1604b
Efficient dealers restrained, 1604b-c
Elite dealers, 1613f
Entry conditions, 1604f8, 1632c2, e2 .
Examples, 1604b,d3
Express agreement, 1604e1
Extent of restraint, 1604g5
Fashion certification, 1613d-f
Foreign countries, in, 1604b
Form of restraint, 1604g6
Futility of condemnation, 1604e3
Generality of restraint, 1604g5
Government guidelines, 1604c2, f3-5
Horizontal terminology, 1604e2
Identified. *See* Detectability
Indicators. *See* Measures
Individual action, 1604d2-3. *See also* Initiatives
Individual dealer power, 1604d2, 1646d, 1654
Inevitable monopoly, 1636f1
Informal coordination, 1604d1. *See also* Dealer concentration
Intensity of restraint, 1604g6, 1648d3F, 1651
Interdependent action, 1604d1. *See also* Dealer concentration
Justice Department guidelines, 1604c2, f3-5, 1632e2
Legality of cartel, 1604c2
Localized restraint, 1604g5
Manufacturer choice constrained, 1604d3
Manufacturer interest compared, 1603. *See also* Manufacturer justification
Manufacturer justification, 1604h, 1632e4, 1633d, 1647f, 1648d4, 1649
Many dealers, 1604d3, 1614c-e
Market coverage, 1604b,f4. *See also* Measures
Market necessity contested, 1648d3A, 1655g1
Market necessity distinguishable?, 1648d3A
Market power indicators, 1604f. *See also* Measures
Market share of manufacturer, 1604f2, 4. *See also* Measures
Market structure indicators, 1604f, 1632c3, e2, e4, f, 1648d2A-B. *See also* Measures

Measures, 1604f-g, 1632e, 1633c, 1648d, 1649c, 1655g
Multi-brand dealers, 1604d3, g1, 1637b, 1648d3C, f3, 1649c2, 1655g7
Objective: restraint vs. lower wholesale price, 1604b
Parallel non-interdependent action, 1604d1
Presumptive indicators. *See* Measures
Product differentiation, 1604f
Product homogeneity, 1633c1, c3
Relevant market, 1648d2A-B
Rent vs. monopoly return, 1613f, 1614c-d
Rule formulation, 1633
Shelf space, 1614d, 1631a4
Sole outlets, danger of, 1654
Summary, 1604i
Type of restraint, 1604g6

DECLARATORY JUDGMENTS
Antitrust standing not required, 385

DECREE. *See* CONSENT DECREE; EQUITABLE RELIEF

DEFENSE TO NON-ANTITRUST CLAIM, 391

DELIVERED PRICING, 1435f, 1436c. *See also* FACILITATING PRACTICE

DIFFERENTIATED PRODUCTS. *See also* MERGERS; MARKET POWER; PRODUCT VARIATIONS; PROMOTIONAL ACTIVITIES
Departure from perfect combination, 409
Distributions restraints. *See* same
Entry barrier, 1612d
Market definition, 525
Non-price competition in oligopoly, 404c, 919, 1425, 1429c

DISCIPLINARY PRICING. *See* PRICE DISCIPLINE

DISCOVERY
Bearing on summary disposition, 323c
Importance, 323

DISCRIMINATION IN PRICE OR SERVICE. *See* CUSTOMER AND TERRITORIAL RESTRAINT VERTICAL; DISTRIBUTION RESTRAINTS GENERALLY; MARKET POWER; PRICE DISCRIMINATION; PRICE PREDATION; ROBINSON-PATMAN ACT; TYING; VERTICAL INTEGRATION

DISPARAGEMENT OF RIVALS
Attempted monopolization, 828b
Monopolization, 738c

DISSOLUTION OR DIVESTITURE. *See also* EQUITABLE RELIEF
After change of law, 629c
Attempted monopolization, 837

DISSOLUTION OR DIVESTITURE (*continued*)
Content of offense, bearing on
attempted monopolization, 837
generally, 312e, 346a
monopolization, 627
In specific situations. *See* specific offenses
Monopolization, 623, 627
Oligopolistic markets, 1432d5
Power of court, 312e, 346a
Private actions, 346a
Shared monopoly, 850
DISTRIBUTION RESTRAINTS GENERALLY (limiting intrabrand competition). *See also* CUSTOMER AND TERRITORIAL RESTRAINT VERTICAL; DEALER AUTONOMY; DEALER POWER; RESALE PRICE MAXIMUM; RESALE PRICE MINIMUM; SOLE OUTLET
Abandonment, consequences, 1602c, e, 1604b
Advertising, 1609a
Agents, 1473, 1621, 1622c. *See also* CONSPIRACY, INTRAENTERPRISE
Agreement, 1600c1, 1623. *See also* COMPLAINT AGAINST RIVAL; CONSPIRACY, VERTICAL
Alienation restraints, 1473, 1609c, 1620c1. *See also* DEALER AUTONOMY
Alternatives to, 1613g, 1613. *See also* generally this title
contractual requirements, 1602
generally, 1602, 1611g, 1612f, 1613g, 1631c3, d4, 1645d, 1647d3, 1649d3
inferior?, 1602d, 1611g, 1633d, 1649d3
limiting supply, 1616e1
relevance, 1602a, h
types, 1602, 1611g
varying product, 1616e1
varying wholesale price, 1616e1
vertical integration, 1608, 1612e
Attempted monopolization, 828d
Autonomy of dealers. *See* DEALER AUTONOMY
Availability of product, 1615b, d, 1617a, 1631a3, 1633d2, 1648f3
Bidding for dealer talent, as, 1613f, 1614c-d
Brand-specific costs, 1613e, 1614c
Bribing dealers, 1614c1, 1632c3
Bulk sales, 1616e
Burdens of persuasion or proof, 1633, 1649, 1655
Buyer-seller price, 1622a

Combination. *See* Agreement
Competitive price agreements, 1639b. *See also* RESALE PRICE MAXIMUM
Conditional reimbursement. *See* RESALE PRICE MINIMUM
Conditioning of future supply. *See* Agreement
Conspiracy. *See* Agreement
Consumer surplus defined, 1612b, 1616e1
Consumer welfare, 1611c, 1612, 1632b. *See also generally* this title
Cream skimming, 1616a, f, 1648c3
Cumulative use. *See* Widespread use
Customer needs distinctive service, 1616a, d; 1641c1
Customer reserved to manufacturer, 1606h, 1616e, 1641c2
Customer restraint. *See* CUSTOMER AND TERRITORIAL RE-STRAINT VERTICAL
Damages, 365b4, 365c, 1459, 1623f, 1640
Dangerous product, 1618c-d, 1647d
De facto price restraint, as, 1648e
Dealer associations. *See* DEALER POWER
Dealer autonomy. *See* same
Dealer capital costs, 1617c
Dealer cartel. *See* DEALER POWER
Dealer coercion, 1648d3
Dealer complaint, against rival dealer, 1604g2-4, 1624-1625. *See also* COMPLAINT AGAINST RIVAL; DEALER POWER
Dealer concentration
  measured, 1604f3, 1648f3
  prevented, 1615c, 1631a3, 1632, 1633c1, c3
  relevance, 1604f3
Dealer concentration in assigned territory, 1616a, f; 1648f; 1649c1
Dealer creates value, 1613d
Dealer density, 1615d, 1616
Dealer efficiency effect, 1615, 1615a
Dealer freedom impaired. *See* DEALER AUTONOMY
Dealer goodwill, 1614, 1631a4, 1632b, 1647f
Dealer investments, 1617, 1631b, 1647e. *See also* Entry Facilitation
Dealer power. *See* same
Dealer predation, 1615b
Dealer preferences, 1604, 1609. *See also* Dealer goodwill
Dealer profits excessive
  manufacturer seeks, 1614e, 1646f
  manufacturer shuns, 1603, 1620c2
  market necessity compared, 1648d3A

DISTRIBUTION RESTRAINTS GENERALLY (*continued*)
Dealer pushing, 1614
Dealer recommendation, 1614c; 1632c3; 1648c2, f. *See also* DEALER POWER
Dealer quality, reputation of, 1613d-e
Dealer services
adequate despite free riding, 1611f, 1613e, 1647b2
consumer choice restricted, 1612b
consumer surplus affected, 1611c, 1612b
consumer welfare, 1611c, 1612, 1632b
convenience goods 1612f, 1631a3,c3,d1, 1633d2, 1647b2,d3
dealer knows right amount, 1612e, 1637f
dealer profits related, 1620c2
desirability summarized, 1611c-e, 1612, 1631c1
efficient, 1611c-d, 1612, 1631c2
encouraged by restraint, 1611c, 1631a4, c1-2, 1632b
entry barriers increased, 1612d, 1631c2
excessiveness, 1612, 1631c2, 1647b
fashion certification, 1613d, 1631a1, c3, 1632c1, 1633d2
free riding impairs, 1611c, 1632e4, 1633d2, 1647b1-2, 1649d1
manufacturer profit, 1632b
manufacturer-provided services compared, 1602c, 1612e
marginal buyers, 1612b
no-frill substitutes, 1612b, 1637f
non-marginal buyers, 1612b
not subject to free riding, 1611f, 1631c3
product configuration compared, 1612e
product differentiation
entry barrier, 1612d, 1631c2
innovative process, 1612c2
quality surrogate, 1612c2, 1631c2
spurious, 1612c, 1631c2, 1632c1
value perception, 1612c2, 1614c, 1631c2
product specific, 1613e
promotional, 1647b2
proof of presumption, 1611f, 1631d, 1649d
purchased separately, 1647b2
quality certification, 1613d-g, 1631a1, c3, 1632c1
recommendations by dealers. *See* Dealer recommendation

resale price maintenance justified by need for, 1631d1
resources wasted, 1612b-c, 1631c2, 1632c1, 1647c2
restraints don't stop free riding, 1611g
shelf-space, 1614d, 1631a4
shopping goods, 1611g, 1612f, 1647b2
stocking, 1614d, 1647f3
superfluous, 1612b
types of service, 1612, 1631, 1637f

Dealer shelf-space, 1614d
Dealer size effect, 1615
Dealer specialization, 1616b-e, 1647c, 1648c3
Dealers preserved, 1615, 1631a3. *See also* Dealer specialization
Dealer stocking, 1614d, 1647f3
De facto price restraint, as, 1648c
Defined, 1600a-b
Demand curve slopes up, 1613c
Desirable dealers, rival manufacturers foreclosed from, 1648c1
Differential services as price discrimination, 1616f
Distribution scale economies, 1615b
Distribution varieties, 1600b
Dual distribution, 1605, 1636g, 1639c, 1641c2, 1644b2
Dumping in another territory, 1618c, 1647d4
Duplicative sales efforts, 1616c
Duration, 1600d
Easy vs. hard sales, 1616e1, f
Effects
actual, 734a, 1600d, 1630b, 1646a
surrogates for, 1600d, 1633, 1646e, 1649, 1655

Efficiency, 1649d1. *See also* generally this title
dealer power. *See* DEALER POWER
distribution restraint promotes, 1611b-d
free riding impairs, 1611b-d
manufacturer cartel or coordination, 1606
manufacturer error, 1607
manufacturer profit related, 1611a, d
model illustration, 1611b-c
premises, 1611a
qualifications summarized, 1611d

Efficient dealer replaces inefficient, 1615b
Efficient dealers restrained, 1648b1
Eliminating backward pressure on non-competitive manufacturers, 1606c
Elite dealers, 1613d-f, 1631c3, 1632b, c1, 1633d2, 1637b, 1647f3

DISTRIBUTION RESTRAINTS GENERALLY (*continued*)
Entry barriers
restraint overcomes, 1617, 1631b
restraint raises, 1612d; 1631c2; 1632c1; 1648c1, c4
Entry facilitation, 1617, 1631b, 1647e
duration of restraint, 1617a3
expansion compared, 1617a1-2
identifying, 1617a3, 1647e
legitimacy, 1617a2
market development expense defined, 1617a1
new entry defined, 1617a1, 3
presumptions, 1617a3
proof, 1617a3
restraint types compared, 1617a3
Essential facility, 1652c2
Ethical practices required, 1609e
Excess dealer margins competed away, 1614b
Excess dealer profit desired, 1614e, 1632c4-5, 1636b-c, 1647f
Excess margins not competed away, 1618b
Excess service, 1612, 1631c2, 1632c1, 1648b
Exclusive dealing accompanies, 1610b-c, 1646f, 1647d3, f2, 1648c1, 1649c1
Extensive representation, 1615, 1616a
Externalities, 1613b
Fairness to dealers, 1609e
Fair trade legislation, 1604b, 1629b-c, 1632e1
Faithful performance inducement, 1614e, 1647f1
Fashion signal, 1613, 1631c3, 1632b, 1633d2. *See also* Quality signal
Foreign countries, in, 1604b
Free rides,
Free riding, 1611b-c, 1612, 1624b, 1631c3, d4, 1647b, 1655c
absent, 1611f, 1613d-e
alternatives to distribution restraints, 1602c, 1611g
amount, 1611f, 1633d, 1649d
brand-specific costs, 1613d-e
corrected by restraint, 1611c, g
defined, 1611b
degree, 1611f
distribution restraint affects, 1611c
efficiency impaired, 1611b
fashion-quality certifications, 1613d
frequency or likelihood, 1611f, 1613d-3
generally in the economy, 1613b
information, 1613b, d, e

interbrand competition, by, 1611g, 1616b
intrabrand, 1611-1613
legally encouraged, 1613b
non-brand specific costs, 1613e
notwithstanding distribution restraint, 1611g, 1612f
potential for, 1611f, 1613g
restraint types' relative effectiveness, 1611c, g; 1612f
seriousness, 1611f
sometimes impossible, 1611f
Goodwill, 1614, 1631a1, a4, 1647f
Government guidelines, 1604c2, f3-5, 1606g3-6, 1633e, 1649e
High cost dealers needed, 1615d, 1647c2, 1648b1
High cost dealers preserved, 1615c-d, 1647c2, 1648b1
Higher prices increase demand, 1613c
Homogeneous products, 1604f2, 1633
Horizontal agreement
among dealers, 1604b-d; 1632c5, f. *See also* DEALER POWER
among manufacturers, 1604b, 1606, 1632d, f, 1648c4
compared with vertical, 1600c, 1603
Horizontal characterization of vertical restraint, 1456, 1600c, 1603, 1604e2, 1605, 1625d, 1644b
Hostage for faithful performance, 1614e
Hours, 1609a
Image enhancement, 1613, 1620c3, 1647d3
Inefficiently sized dealer protected, 1615-16
Intensity of restraint, 1604g5-6, 1648d3E-F, 1651
Intensive market development, 1615-1616, 1631a3, 1647c
below-cost sales, 1616f
dealer density, 1615d, 1616f, 1616a
dealer specialization, 1616d
integrated manufacturer, 1616b
numerous dealers, 1616, 1616fB, 1616a
price discrimination, 1616f
sales quota, 1616f
Interbrand competition. *See* generally this title
Interbrand free riding, 1616b
Intrabrand competition. *See* generally this title
Introduction, 1600
Inventories, 1609a
Jury role, 1633d2, 1649d4
Justice Department guidelines. *See* Government guidelines

DISTRIBUTION RESTRAINTS GENERALLY (*continued*)
Justifications, 1611-1619, 1631, 1633d, 1646-1647, 1649d, 1655
Legality per se?, 1610b, 1628a, c, e
Location restraint. *See* CUSTOMER AND TERRITORIAL RESTRAINT, VERTICAL
Loss leaders, generally, 1619, 1631a2, 1633d2
 advertising compared, 1619
 aggressive competition, vehicle for, 1619
 brand image, 1619
 consumer welfare, 1619
 dangers of, 1619
 dealer objectives, 1619
 predatory price, compared, 1619
 regulation by state law, 1619
 resale price maintenance, and, 1620c2, 1630b
Low-cost dealer preserved, 1615b
Mail order services limited, 1624c, 1625c1, 1647c2
Manufacturer allowance compared, 1602c, 1611g, 1614b, 1626-1627
Manufacturer cartel. *See* Manufacturer coordination
Manufacturer choice, relevance, 1602d, 1613g
Manufacturer choices restrained, 1600b, 1650
Manufacturer coordination, express or tacit, 1606, 1632c, 1648c4
 backward pressure eliminated, 1606c
 concentrated market, 1606g3, 1633c1, 1649c
 costly vehicle, 1606e6
 customer restraint, 1606h
 facilitation mechanisms, 1606c-f, h3-4,
 disruptive uncertainty, 1606e5, 1648c4
 market coverage, 1606g5
 relevant market, 1606g5
 resale prices, and, 1606; 1632c5, d, f
 "substantiality" defined, 1606g5
 territorial restraint, 1606h
 visibility of wholesale price cut, 1606e
 wholesale price cut futile, 1606d
Manufacturer-dealer interests
 converge, 1604c1-2, g2
 diverge, 1611b, 1615, 1618
Manufacturer-dealer profit sharing, 1636d
Manufacturer desire, restraint outlives, 1614c
Manufacturer error, 1607, 1632c4, 1648b2

Manufacturer interest, 1603, 1611. *See also* generally this title
Manufacturer self-distribution, 1602, 1605, 1608, 1651d, 1652c2
Manufacturer self-interest. *See* Manufacturer interest
Market coverage, 1600d, 1604f3, 1606g5, 1614c2, 1633c1-3, 1649c1
Market penetration, 1616, 1647c4-5
Market share, 1600d, 1604f2, g4, 1617, 1633c, 1645, 1648d3, f, 1649c-d, 1653, 1655g2
Monitoring dealer performance, 1602c, 1614e, 1618c-d, 1633d2
Monopolization. *See also* Market share; CUSTOMER AND TERRITORIAL RESTRAINT, VERTICAL; RESALE PRICE MAXIMUM; RESALE PRICE MINIMUM; SOLE OUTLET
  customer and territorial restraint, 734c, 1648b3
  resale price maximum, 734e
  resale price minimum, 734b
  sole outlet, 1653d-e
Monopoly profit for dealer protected, 1603, 1604, 1614, 1616f, 1616a, 1647f
New entry facilitation. *See* Entry facilitation
Non-price restraint
  generally, Chs. 16D-E
  characterized as price restraint, 1624b, 1644a, 1652b
  defined, 1624a
  intention to affect price irrelevant, 1644a
  price restraint ancillary, 1624c
  price restraint distinguished, 1600b, 1624-1625, 1630
Non-resale prices, 1622
Non-restraints, 1600b, 1622a-b
Numerous high-cost dealers protected, 1615c-d, 1616d-e
Obsolete but continued, 1604d3, 1607, 1614c
Oligopolistic manufacturers, 1606. *See also* Market share
Oppression of dealers, 1609e
Outline, 1600e, 1601
Parallel manufacturer use, 1600d, 1604f4, 1606, 1614c, 1632d2, e2, 1633c1, 1648c4, d2C, 1649c1, 1653e, 1654g
Pioneering dealers, 1617a, 1647e, 1649d1. *See also* entry facilitation
Premise design, 1609a
Presumptions recommended, 1633, 1638c, 1649, 1654g
Price ceiling. *See* RESALE PRICE MAXIMUM

DISTRIBUTION RESTRAINTS GENERALLY (*continued*)
Price cut by manufacturer compared, 1614b
Price discrimination, 1616e-f, 1618d, 1627e, 1637j, 1639h, 1646b, 1647c5-6, 1648c3
Price effects, 1603, 1604b, 16111619
Price floor. *See* RESALE PRICE MINIMUM
Price-non-price compared. *See* Non-price restraint
Price suggested, 1440, 1623c, 1630d
 absence of sanctions, 1440, 1623a
 alternative to ceiling price, 1636h, 1639d
 discipline of non-complying dealers, 1440, 1623a, 1624e
 manufacturer statement of non-binding nature, 1623c
 minimum-maximum effects compared, 1637a
 Monsanto case, and, 1623a
Product class, defined, 1650
Product concentration. *See* Dealer concentration; Market share
Product differentiation, 1612. *See also* Brand power; Dealer services
Product quality, 1618, 1631c2, 1645d, 1647d, 1649d
 dumping, 1647d4
 proof, 1647d1
 remoteness related to, 1647d4
 summary, 1647d1
 unauthorized dealer, 1647d1
Product safety, 1618, 1645d, 1647d, 1649d1
Quality degradation. *See* Product quality
Quality signal, 1613, 1631c3, 1632d
Quantity control, 1627f
Recommendations, 1633, 1638b, 1649, 1654g
Refusal to deal, 1600c1, 1623d, 1650-1654. *See also* CONSPIRACY, VERTICAL
Rent for dealer talent, as, 1614c
Resale price maintenance. *See* RESALE PRICE MINIMUM
Restraint's intensity. *See* Intensity of restraint
Rule of reason generally, 1600d, 1633, 1649. *See also* same title
Sales quota, 1654f5
Sales quota minimum
 ameliorating distribution restraint, 1616f, 1648d3F, 1650, 1651a, c
 ceiling price, as, 1616f, 1636g, 1639a
Scale economies, 1615-1616
Scale economies in distribution,

1615-1616, 1636f, 1647c, 1655c
Selective distribution, 1600c1, 1623b, 1624d3, 1650. *See also* CONSPIRACY, VERTICAL
Selective vs. general restraint, 1604g5, 1633c, 1648d3, 1649c
Services. *See* Dealer services
Shelf-space, 1614d, 1631a4
Sole outlet, *See* same title
Specialized dealers
  encouraging investment, 1616d
  fenced in or out, 1616e
  fleet buyers illustration, 1647c6
  free riders, 1616d
  incompetent rivals, 1616d
  price discrimination, 1616e, 1647c1, c6
  protected from other dealers, 1616d, e2
  scale economies, 1616d, 1647c1
  summary, 1647c1
Summary, general, 1601
Temporary allowances. *See* RESALE PRICE MINIMUM
Temporary promotional price. *See* RESALE PRICE MAXIMUM
Territorial restraint. *See* CUSTOMER AND TERRITORIAL RESTRAINT VERTICAL
Theories of anti-competitive effect, 1648f
Tying
  accompanies. *See* Exclusive dealing accompanies
  compared, 1700j4
Unauthorized dealers, 1645d, 1647d3
Varieties, 1600b
Vertical defined, 1600c2, 1604e2, 1605, 1625d, 1644, 1653
Vertical integration compared, 1608, 1616f, 1647c5, 1651d. *See also* VERTICAL INTEGRATION
Warehouses, 1609a
Weak manufacturers, 1613f, 1614d, 1617b, 1647e, 1655d-g
Wholesale price cut alternative, 1614b
Wholesale price formula, 1627, 1639f-h
Widespread use
  discriminatory condemnation, 1604k, 1606g10
  relevance, 1604f4, 1606g5-6, 1614c2, 1633c, 1649c. *See also* Manufacturer coordination; DEALER POWER
DIVESTITURE. *See* DISSOLUTION OR DIVESTITURE
DIVIDING MARKETS
  Among competitors. *See* TERRITORIAL DIVISION BY COMPETITORS

DIVIDING MARKETS (*continued*)
- Among dealers by supplier. *See* DISTRIBUTION RESTRAINTS; CONSPIRACY, VERTICAL
- With monopolist, 703

ECONOMICS, BASIC, 400-415. *See also* specific topics

ECONOMIES DEFENSE. *See also* particular offenses
- Absolute defense, 962
- Aggregating small economies, 960
- Alternative merger partner, 961
- Both firms inefficient, 946c, 961
- Buyers' merger, 965c
- Capital cost, 939, 949, 956
- Competition increased, 940, 946c5
- Competition lessened, 940, 941a
- Competitively preferable alternatives, 946-947, 961
- Complementary resources, 959
- Concentration inevitable, 940
- Concentration, relevance, 941a, 959-961
- Conclusions summarized, 939
- Conditions on availability, 939, 946c, 947, 948, 949
- Conglomerate merger compared, 1102-1103, 1149
- Cumulating small economies, 960
- "Defense" language explained, 941b
- Demand elasticity or trend, 939, 946
- Different market, 942
- Distribution, 939, 949, 953
- Economic performance, relevance, 941a
- Effects, 940
- Entry conditions, 939, 946
- Expansion required, 946
- Failing company defense, relation to, 945
- *General Dynamics* defense, relation to, 962b
- Integration economies required, 948c
- Internal expansion compared, 940, 946
  - capacity effect, 946c
  - conclusions, 946a, e
  - expansion barriers, 946c
  - likelihood in fact, 946c
  - preferability, 946b
  - product differentiation, 946c3
  - summary, 946a, e
- Joint venture compared
  - buying, 957
  - component production, 947
  - distribution, 953
  - generally, 947
  - procurement, 957
  - promotion, 954
  - research and development, 955
- Legislative history, 941b

Magnitude required, 939, 946e, 948c
Market expanding or not, 939, 946a, e
Multi-market mergers, 942, 953
Offsetting harm in different market, 942
One firm inefficient, 946c, 961
Overhead, 939, 949, 958
Pecuniary economies insufficient, 939
Plant size, 939, 949, 950
Plant specialization
complementary products, 949, 952
non-complementary products, 951
Practical difficulties. *See also* specific types (e.g., Research)
generally, 943, 948
Precedent, 941c
Preferred merger partner, 961
Presumptive illegality rules, relation to, 905e, 911c, 912e, 915, 945
Price rivalry, 940, 941, 946c5
Prices lower or higher, 940
Private economies insufficient, 939
Procurement, 939, 949, 957
Promotion, 939, 949, 954
Proofs. *See also* specific types (e.g., Distribution)
generally, 948d
high market shares, 962a
Rejection arguments, 941-948
summarized, 943
Rejection futile, 940-941
Research and development, 939, 949, 955
Resource savings only, 939f
Servicing, 953
Small economies, 939, 946c, 948c, 960
Statutory language, 941a
Substantial economies only, 939, 946e, 948c
Summary, 939
Types, generally, 949
Validity in principle, 940
Vertical effects also present, 1017
Vertical merger compared, 1016-1017
Welfare gains, 940
ECONOMIES OF SCALE. *See* EFFICIENCIES, GENERALLY; TYING
EFFICIENCIES, GENERALLY. *See also* DISTRIBUTION RESTRAINTS GENERALLY; ECONOMIES DEFENSE; PER SE RULE; RULE OF REASON; more particular topics (e.g., TYING VERTICAL INTEGRATION)
Advertising, 954, 1109
Allocative, 402b1
Antitrust objective, 103-112, 940
Capital costs, 408c3, 956, 1105-1106, 1135c, 1149c
Concentration, related to, 404d
Defined, 402b
Diseconomies, 1108e
Distribution, 953, 1109, 1149c

EFFICIENCIES, GENERALLY (*continued*)
Evidence, 404d
Finance, 956, 1105-1106, 1135c, 1149c
Legislative history, 106, 941
Management, 936, 1108
Marketing, 953-954, 1109
Monopoly, in, 403
Nature, 407
Oligopoly, in, 404b-c
Operating, 402b2, 951-952, 1108, 1149c
Overhead, 958
Pecuniary or private, contrasted, 939, 1103, 1104-1109
Plant economies, 408c1, 950, 1108, 1149c
Plant specialization, 408c2, 951-952, 1149c
Policy implications, 408d
Populist goals compared, 109-112
Precedent, 104
Procurement costs, 408c4, 957, 1104, 1149c
Promotion costs, 408c5, 954, 1109, 1149c
Research and development, 407, 955, 1108b, 1149c
Servicing, 408c6, 733c, 953, 1109c
Trends, 408c8
Vertical integration, 724a, 725
Warranties, 1109c2
Welfare gains, 940

EMPLOYEES
Acquisition as
attempted monopolization, 828f
monopolization, 702
Combinations. *See* LABOR UNIONS
Conspiracy among or with employer. *See* CONSPIRACY, INTRAENTERPRISE
Damages, 377b
Disloyal and tying, 1727g
Rival's, compromised, as monopolization, 738d, g
Standing, 377

EMPLOYER COMBINATION. *See* EMPLOYEES, STANDING; LABOR UNIONS

ENFORCEMENT. *See* more specific topics

ENTERPRISE, SINGLE. *See* CONSPIRACY, INTRAENTERPRISE

ENTRY BARRIERS OR CONDITIONS
Defined, 420a
Distribution restraints
increased by, 1612d-e, 1631c2, 1632c1
relevance to, 1604f8, 1606g4, 1631b, 1633
Economic and antitrust analysis of, 420c
Historical data, relevance of, 422d
Likelihood of entry, 422a
Potential competition and, 423
Predatory pricing and, 422

Proving, 420b
Sources of barriers to entry
access to inputs, 421e
access to customers, 421f
governmental constraints, 421h
high initial investment, 421b
low prices, 421d
product reputation, 421g
scale economies, 421a
unsalvageable investment, 421c
Sufficiency of entry, 422c
Timeliness of entry, 422b
Vertical integration and, 725h, 1011, 1103, 1135b
EQUITABLE RELIEF. *See also* DISSOLUTION AND DIVESTITURE; MERGER; PRIVATE ACTIONS; STANDING; specific substantive offenses (e.g., LEASE-ONLY)
Attempted monopolization, 837-838
Availability compared with damages or criminal penalties, 312, 346a
Change of law, 333
Content of offenses, bearing on
attempted monopolization, 837-838
monopolization, 623, 627
Fairness of, 620c
Foreign conduct, 238
Foreign governments, against, 239
Mistake of law, 217b, 332a
Modification of decree, 348b
Monopolistic practices
distribution restraints, 734f
generally, 621b, 627
lease-only, 735d
mergers
horizontal, 701i
vertical, 730d
patent acquisition, 705h
patent procurement impropriety, 707
resale restriction, 735d
supply preemption, 731f
tying, 733f
Oligopoly pricing, as sole remedy for, 850-851, 1432d5
Patent and trademark licensing, 621b
Preliminary injunction, 347
Private suits
availability, 346, 623, 851
government suit compared, 312d, 623, 851
scope, 346b
Restructuring of markets, generally, 346b, 627
Shared monopoly, 850-851
Standing to obtain, 346a
State government standing, 380
State officials, against, 217a
ESPIONAGE, INDUSTRIAL
Monopolization, 738f
ESSENTIAL FACILITY. *See also* ATTEMPTED MONOPOLIZATION; MONOPOLIZATION; CONCERTED REFUSAL TO DEAL; CONSPIRACY, INTRAENTERPRISE; JOINT VENTURE; RULE

ESSENTIAL FACILITY (*continued*)
OF REASON; TRADE ASSOCIATION
Arbitrary refusal to deal by monopolist, 736
Competitors create, 1478b4
Monopolist possesses. *See* Vertical integration
Non-cooperation with rivals, 738m
Vertical integration and refusal to deal, 728-729
EXAGGERATED CLAIMS
Monopolization, 738i
EXCLUSIONARY CONDUCT. *See* ATTEMPTED MONOPOLIZATION; MONOPOLIZATION; MONOPOLIZATION SHARED
EXCLUSIVE DEALING (Output or requirement contracts). *See also* FORECLOSURE ANALYSIS; MARKET PREEMPTION; MERGER, VERTICAL; SUPPLY PREEMPTION; TYING
Agreement. *See* CONSPIRACY, VERTICAL
Competitive effect. *See* FORECLOSURE ANALYSIS
Conditioned refusal to deal as conspiracy and
Clayton Act, 1460
Federal Trade Commission Act §5, 1461
Sherman Act. *See* CONSPIRACY, VERTICAL
Distribution restraint accompanies, 1610, 1632c2, 1646f, 1648c1
Monopolist, in favor of, 731-732
Standing to sue, 383a
EXCLUSIVE DISTRIBUTORSHIP OR OUTLET. *See* DISTRIBUTION RESTRAINTS GENERALLY; SOLE OUTLET; TYING
EXCLUSIVE LICENSE. *See* PATENTS
EXEMPTIONS AND IMMUNITIES. *See* AGRICULTURAL COOPERATIVES; EXPORT ASSOCIATIONS; FOREIGN COMMERCE; INSURANCE; LABOR UNIONS; NATIONAL DEFENSE; NEWSPAPERS; POLITICAL ACTION; REGULATED INDUSTRIES; SMALL BUSINESS; SPORTS; STATE ACTION
EXPORT ASSOCIATIONS, 230a
EXPORTS. *See* FOREIGN COMMERCE
EXTERNALITIES, 107, 414
EXTRATERRITORIALITY. *See* FOREIGN COMMERCE

FACILITATING PRACTICE. *See also* CONSPIRACY, GENERALLY; INTERDEPENDENT PARAL-

LELISM AS CONSPIRACY; RULE OF REASON
Advance price announcement, 1435d
Appraising impact and justification
  generally, 1436e
  more particularly, 1436f-j
Attempted monopolization, 1407f
Business functions, 1435. *See also* Intention; Legitimate objectives
Commitment distinguished, 1410
Concerted
  conspiracy equivalent on matter facilitated, 1407c
  conspiracy evidence on matter facilitated, 1407d
  illustrations, 1407, 1418, 1422-1423, 1435b
  unilateral (and interdependent) distinguished, 1407f, 1435-1436
  unreasonable restraint of trade, 1407e, 1435b. *See also* RULE OF REASON
Consequences. *See* Effects
Customer and territorial restraint vertical, 1606h, 1648c4
Defined, 1407b, 1435a
Delivered pricing, 1435f, 1436c
Discussions, 1406a, 1418
Distribution restraint, 1606c-e
du Pont case, 1435-1436
Effects. *See also* particular practices
  actual effects, 1436f-g, j
  generally, 1407b2-3, 1435, 1436e
  presumed from market structure, 1436f3-4
Ethyl case, 1435-1436
Exclusionary practices, 1435i
Federal Trade Commission Act §5, under, 1407b2, f, 1435-1436, esp. 1436c
Futility of condemning, 1435b
Generally, 1407a, 1435a, 1436a
Impact. *See* Effects
Information, 1406a, 1407a, e, 1417-1418, 1422-1423
Intention, 1436i
Interdependent and unilaterally adopted, 1435-1436
Jury role, 1405, 1407e, 1436e-j
Justifications. *See* Legitimate objectives
Legitimate objectives, 1435, 1436h. *See also* particular practices
  criterion, 1436h
  generally, 1407b, 1435
  less restrictive alternatives, 1436h3
  proof or presumptions, 1436h
  relevance, 1436h
Less restrictive alternatives, 1435, 1436h3
Meeting, 1406, 1417, 1418b

FACILITATING PRACTICE (*continued*)
Most favored buyer (or supplier or nation), 1435e
Parallel pricing compared, 1436c, b, d
Prerequisites for condemnation, 1436a, e-j
Presumptions, 1436e-j
Price formula, 1435h
Price manual, 1406c, 1435g
Price protection, 1435e
Proposals, 1436a, e-j
Reasonableness, 1407e, 1435. *See also* generally this title; RULE OF REASON
Remedy, 1407b3, 1436a-d
Resale price maintenance, 1606c-e
Restrains trade, 1407c
Sherman Act §1, under, 1407, 1435-1436, esp. 1436d
Speech, public, 1435c
Summary, 1407a, 1435a, 1436a
Tying, as, 1703d2, 1707, 1729f
Uncertainty reduced, 1407, 1435a
Unilaterally adopted
attempted monopolization, 1407f
conspiracy holding, implications for interdependent pricing, 1436a, b3, d
generally, 1407f, 1435-1436
legal treatment, 1436c-j
parallel pricing, implications for, 1436a-d
Vertical price fixing, 1606c-e
FAILING COMPANY DEFENSE
Absolute defense, 928
Buyers' merger, 965b
Competitive effects, 925a, c
Conglomerate merger compared, 1150
Disappearance from market, 925a
Divisions, 926d
Economies defense, relation to, 945
Failure defined
bankruptcy, 926c
divisions, 926d
impending exit, 926d
insolvency, 926c
subsidiaries, 926e
Failure preferred to merger, 925a
General issues, 924-925
Legislative history, 924
Preferred purchaser
alternative acquirer immune from this requirement, 928e
alternative acquirer itself subject to this requirement, 928f
conglomerate acquirer, 928e
continued operation, 928b
defined, 928
diligent search, 929
generally, 927a
insufficient, 927c
late offers, 929c

lawful acquirer, 928a
low offers, 930c
not required, 927b
piecemeal offer, 931
price, 930
price appraisals, 930e
price below value, 930b
price of only bidder, 930f
prices and private interests, 930d
prices disparate, 930c, e
price unreasonably low, 930b
ranking, 928e, f
required, 927c
search intensity, 929
significant difference required, 928c, d, e2
smaller rival, 928de
time-limited invitations, 929b
vertical acquirer, 928e
volunteered offers, 929c
Presumptive illegality rules, relation to, 925a, 927a
Private interests, 925
divergent interests, 925b
statutory recognition, 925c
Rationale, 925
Reorganization prospect and failure definition, 926b
high anticompetitive risk, 927c
liquidation probability, 927d
preferred to merger, 927c
Subsidiaries, 926e
Vertical merger compared, 1018
FAIR TRADE, 209-210

FALSE ADVERTISING
Attempted monopolizations, 828b
Monopolization, 738a
FEDERAL TRADE COMMISSION
Adjudication, 305d
Advisory opinions, 331
Cease and desist orders, 305e
Composition, 305c
Consent procedures, 305d
Enforcement guides, 331b
Expertness, 218, 305a
Harmonization with antitrust division, 305c
Informal procedures, 305d
Judicial review, 305f
Jurisdiction, 233a, 305c
Modification of orders, 305d
Preliminary injunctions, 305e
Remedial powers, 305e
Rule-making, 218, 305g, 307d
FEDERAL TRADE COMMISSION ACT. *See also* particular practices (*e.g.*, TYING)
Clayton Act, relation to, 307, 1719c
Conspiracy not required, and unilateral distribution restraints, 1461
facilitating practices, 1407f, 1435-1436, esp. 1436c
interdependent pricing, 1436c
solicitation, unsuccessful, of conspiracy, 1419
tying and exclusive dealing, 1461
Historical background, 305a
Interlocking directors, 1301b, 1302d-e, 1303

FEDERAL TRADE COMMISSION ACT (*continued*)
Market structure under §5, 306
Mergers conglomerate, 1145c
Patent procurement improper, 707c
Private remedies or intervention, 305e, 307c
Sherman Act, relation to, 307, 1719c
State law, relation to, 218
Text, *Appendix A*
FIRST AMENDMENT, 219b
FISHERMEN'S COOPERATIVES. *See* AGRICULTURAL COOPERATIVES
FORECLOSURE ANALYSIS. *See also* EXCLUSIVE DEALING; TYING
Absent, 1004b, c
Aggregations, 1011f1, 1014c, 1021
Analyzed, 1004
Assertions, general, 1000
Buyer choice reduced, 1010
Competition increased, 1004d, 1012
Competition reduced, 1004e-1011
Competitive markets, 1004c
Cumulations, 1011f1, 1014d, 1021
Defined, 1004
Destablization of rivals, 1009
Disruptive buyer eliminated, 1006
Entry barriers raised, 1011
Existence, 1004
Harmless, 1004c, 1012
Initial, 1014b
Measured, 570, 1013, 1015d, 1204d4-5
Realignment compared, 1004c, d
Scale, rivals deprived of, 1008
Second-level concentration raised, 1007
Self-dealing, 1004b-c
Trends, 1014e, 1021, 1022a
Vertical integration, 731-732. *See also* same
FOREIGN COMMERCE. *See also* FOREIGN GOVERNMENTS
Agents of foreign government, private party, 239b2
Basic issues, 234b
Comity, 239a
Compulsion by foreign state, 215b1, 239
Conflicting national interests. *See* generally this title
Diplomacy, 240
Effects, domestic
as statutory criteria, 236d
significance appraised, 237
significance criteria, 236f
Exports
export associations, 230a
restraints affecting, 236g, 237
Webb Act, 230a
Foreign conduct, 236-237. *See also* generally this title
Foreign governmental restraint induced, 239b1
Guidelines, Justice Department, 234

Imports restrained, 236-237, 608j, 703a
In rem jurisdiction, 235d
Intention to affect United States, 236e
Joint ventures, 237
Jurisdiction. *See* Personal jurisdiction; Statutory reach
Per se offenses, 237
Personal jurisdiction, 235a-c
Price fixing abroad, goods not exported to United States, 236f2
Remedial problems, 238
Significance of restraints, 236-237
Sovereign immunity, 239c
Statutory provisions, 230a, 234a, 239c
Statutory reach
Alcoa doctrine, 236c-f
American Banana rule, 236b
earlier (pre-*Alcoa*) precedents, 236b
effects tests, 236c-d, f, 237
summary, 236a
Substantiality of effects, 236f-g, 237
Summary, 234
Wilson Tariff Act, 235d, 311a

FOREIGN GOVERNMENTS. *See also* FOREIGN COMMERCE
Act of state, 215b1, 239b
Cause restraint, 239-240
Coercion or compulsion, 239
Cooperation on remedies, 238
Interests, 234b, 239-240
Sovereign immunity, 239c

FRANCHISE AGREEMENTS. *See* CONSPIRACY, VERTICAL; DISTRIBUTION RESTRAINT; EXCLUSIVE DEALING; POLITICAL ACTION; STATE ACTION; TYING.

GEOGRAPHIC MARKET. *See* MARKET POWER

GOALS OF ANTITRUST POLICY. *See* PUBLIC POLICIES

GOVERNMENT CONTRACTS OR FRANCHISES. *See* POLITICAL ACTION; STATE ACTION

GOVERNMENT, DEALING WITH, AS SHERMAN ACT VIOLATION. *See* POLITICAL ACTION; STATE ACTION

GOVERNMENT PROCEEDINGS, EFFECT ON PRIVATE SUITS. *See* LIMITATIONS; RES JUDICATA

GOVERNMENTS, FOREIGN. *See* FOREIGN GOVERNMENTS

GRANT-BACK. *See* PATENTS

GROUP BOYCOTT. *See* CONCERTED REFUSAL TO DEAL; CONSPIRACY, GENERALLY

GUIDELINES (issued by federal agency). *See also* particular topics
Generally, 234, 320
Intraenterprise conspiracy, 1467f2

GUIDELINES (*continued*)
Mergers, 909c
Vertical restraints, 1604c2, f3-5, 1606g3-6, 1633e

HARRASSMENT OF RIVALS. *See also* PREDATION; UNFAIR COMPETITION; particular practices
Attempted monopolization, 828b
Monopolization, 738
HEALTH CARE, HOSPITALS, AND INSURERS, 1402b, 1406f, 1409c, 1426a, d, 1471b, d-h, 1510c, 1622b, 1709c2, 1717f1, 1728f. *See also* PER SE RULE; RULE OF REASON
HERFINDAHL INDEX, 913a2, b2. *See also* CONCENTRATION; MERGER, HORIZONTAL AND GENERALLY; MARKET POWER
HORIZONTAL CONSPIRACY. *See* CONSPIRACY, GENERALLY

IMITATION, 209, 735, 829b, 1508c, 1613b, 1718f
IMMUNITIES. *See* EXEMPTIONS AND IMMUNITIES; POLITICAL ACTION; STATE ACTION
IMPORTS. *See* MARKET POWER
INCIPIENCY, 1709d3, 1720b3. *See also* EXCLUSIVE DEALING; all MERGER titles; TYING
INDIRECT PURCHASER RULE
Co-conspirators
exception to rule, 371h
Critique of rule, 371j
apportioning problems and suggestions, 371j2
lost profits as appropriate remedy for middlemen, 371j3
model of consumer as primary overcharge victim, 371j1
middlemen overcompensated, consumers undercompensated, 371j
protecting defendant from duplicate recovery if remote consumer gets standing, 371j1
variations on model of consumer as primary overcharge victim, 371j1
Equity suits and, 371d
Generally, 371a
Indirect sellers, 371g
Middleman's (direct purchaser's) standing, 371a
direct purchaser owned/controlled by indirect purchaser, 371f

direct purchaser
owned/controlled by defendant, 371f
"Pass on" defense of direct purchasers, 371a
Pre-existing, cost-plus contracts
exception to rule, 371e
fixed quantity requirement, 371e
Standing denied consumers for "pass on" damages, 371c
reasons for rule, 371a, c, e
state "parens patriae" suits no different, 371c, 380
State laws providing damages for indirect purchasers, 371i
effect of, 371i
not preempted by federal law, 371i
Tracing/measuring plaintiff's damages too complex
rule not applicable, 371h
Tying cases, 371h

INDIRECT SELLERS
Application of indirect purchaser rule, 371g
reasons for, 371g
Generally, 371g
Middleman's (direct seller's) standing, 371g

INDUSTRIAL ESPIONAGE, 738f

INDUSTRY SELF-REGULATION, 1477. *See also* PER SE RULE; RULE OF REASON

INFORMATION (Provided or exchanged). *See* COMPLAINT AGAINST RIVAL; all CONSPIRACY titles; FACILITATING PRACTICE; RULE OF REASON; TYING

INJUNCTION. *See* EQUITABLE RELIEF

INNOVATION. *See also* COMPETITION; MERGER; MONOPOLY; MONOPOLY SHARED; OLIGOPOLY; PATENTS; and particular restraints (such as VERTICAL INTEGRATION); TYING
Generally, 402b3, 407
Interindustry competition, 1115f
Multi-market interdependence, 1114c
Predatory, 738

IN PARI DELICTO. *See* PLAINTIFF'S VIOLATION

INSTITUTIONAL LIMITS, 113, 406b

INSURANCE, 210. *See also* HEALTH CARE

INTENTION. *See also* all CONSPIRACY titles; PER SE RULE; RULE OF REASON; particular substantive offenses
Attempted monopolizaiton, 821824
Distribution restraints generally. *See* same
Mergers
conglomerate, 1111

INTENTION (*continued*)
horizontal, 938
vertical, 1004
Monopolization, 626a
Predation, 711
Punitive sanctions, related to, 311
INTERDEPENDENCE. *See also* CONSPIRACY, GENERALLY; INTERDEPENDENT PARALLELISM AS CONSPIRACY; OLIGOPOLY
INTERDEPENDENT PARALLELISM AS CONSPIRACY. *See also* CONSPIRACY, GENERALLY; FACILITATING PRACTICE; FEDERAL TRADE COMMISSION ACT; OLIGOPOLY
Generally, 1428
Avoidable behavior, 1432d, h
Cartel (traditional conspiracy) compared
differences, 1432b, d
economic results, 1431
similarities, 1432b
Distribution restraints, and, 1604, 1606
Economic performance
measured, 1432b2
plus factor, as, 1434d
relevance, 1432f, 1434d
Express collusion compared, 1431a-b, 1432b
Facilitating practice. *See* same
Legal treatment generally, 1433. *See also* Plus factors
Marginal cost pricing compared, 1432d
Monopolist's behavior rules, consistency with, 1432d4
Non-price matters, 1425e, 1429c
Plus factors. *See also* CONSPIRACY, GENERALLY
defined, 1434a
facilitating practice. *See* same
motivation to conspire, 1412, 1434c
rationale, 1434a
required, 1433e, 1434
self-interest, acts against, 1415, 1434c
traditional conspiracy, 1434b
Policy reasons for, against, 1432
Power relevant, 1432b2, f
Remediable practices distinguished from price, 1432h, 1434e, 1436b
Remedies, 1435d5-g
Sanctions, relevance, 1432e
Statutory language, 1432c
Summary, 1432a, 1433a, 1434a, 1436a
Traditional conspiracy inferred, 1416-1427, esp. 1425
INTERFERENCE WITH RIVAL'S ADVANTAGEOUS RELATIONS
Monopolization, 7381

INTERINDUSTRY COMPETITION, 535d, 571a, 1115
INTERLOCKING DIRECTORATES
Banks, 1302d
Competitor defined, 1302b
Generally, 1300
Horizontal, 1302
Indirect, 1304
Management, 1302e
Mootness, 1305
Potential competitors, 1302c
Statutes, relevant, 1301
Vertical, 1303
INTERSTATE COMMERCE, 231-233
Affecting commerce, 232d
applications, 232e
inherent effects, 232b, e
minor effects, 232b
per se prohibitions, 232b-e
proofs, 232e
Antitrust purposes, 232b-c
"Any part of," 811
Clayton Act §§3 and 7, 233a, e
Flow of commerce, 232c, 233b
In commerce, 233a
Jurisdictional prerequisite, 231, 232c. *See also* generally this title
Robinson-Patman Act
§2(a), 233a, c
§§2(c)-(f), 233d
Sherman Act, 232
Statutes compared, 233a
Tying's per se rule, 1721b2-3
INTRABRAND COMPETITION. *See* DISTRIBUTION RESTRAINT
INTRACORPORATE CONSPIRACY. *See* CONSPIRACY, INTRAENTERPRISE
INTRAENTERPRISE CONSPIRACY. *See* CONSPIRACY, INTRAENTERPRISE

JOINT VENTURE. *See also* CONSPIRACY, INTRAENTERPRISE; RULE OF REASON
Alternative to merger, 947
Ancillary restraints, 947b
Anticompetitive effects illustrated, 1478, 1503a
Attempted monopolization, 829c
Buying, 957
Component production, 947
Conspiracy among creators, 1478b
Conspiracy, continuing among members, 1478c-d
Day-to-day operations as conspiracy of members, 1478c-d
Distribution, 953
Merger, as, 1202f2, h
Monopolization, 703c
Per se classification rejected although prices literally fixed, 1510c
Presumptions illustrated, 320
Procurement, 957, 1104b3
Promotion, 954, 1109
Reappraisal after error, success, or market changes, 1478b
Research and Development, 955, 1503a

JOINT VENTURE (*continued*)
Single entity, 1478c-d
Success hurts rivals, 1478b4
Summary disposition, 322
Transaction costs, 947b
JURY ROLE. *See also* all CONSPIRACY titles; RULE OF REASON; particular offenses
Issues for jury, 321
Relevance to summary disposition, 321, 322
JURY TRIAL
Advantages and disadvantages in antitrust suits, 321a
Allocating issues between judge and jury, 321b-c
implication of concurrent FTC enforcement, 321c
integrating the jury as fact-finder, 321c
Arguments against not allowing juries to apply reasonableness criteria to the facts, 321d
rejection of the arguments, 321d
Complexity, relevance of, 321e
arguments for and against a complexity exception to jury right, 321e
balancing right to a jury trial against right to due process, 321e
Generally, 321a
Inability of jury to set the appropriate standards, 321d
Inability of jury to understand technical meaning of "reasonable," 321d
Issues for judicial resolution, 321c
advantages of, 321c
assessing the reasonableness of a restraint, 321c
presumptions, 321c
Jury's role in summary judgment context, 322f
Need for uniformity and predictability in antitrust, 321d
Significance of avoiding submission of matters to the jury, 321d
JUSTICE DEPARTMENT
Consent decrees, 348
DOJ Clearances
as a defense to liability, 331c
bar to subsequent legal proceedings, 331c
completed conduct, 331c
effect of, 331c
generally, 331b, c
persuasive value, 331c
submissions of inaccurate information, 331c

LABOR UNIONS, 229
Background, 229a
Combinations with employers, 229e-f

"Employee" defined, 229c
Employer restraints, 229d
Entrepreneurs, 229c
Historical background, 229b
Independent contractors, 229c
Industry-wide wage determinations, 229e
"Non-statutory" exemption, 229b
Physicians' groups, 229c
Predatory agreements, 229e
Professional groups, 229c
Professional sports, 229d
Statutory basis, 229b
Strikes for forbidden agreements, 229b
Summary, 229a
Unilateral actions, 229f
relation to employer agreements, 229b
LACHES, 325e, 608h, 628
LEASE-ONLY
Attempted monopolization, 829b
Benefits, 735b
Damages, 337c
Evils, 735a
Monopolization, 735
relief scope, 735d
Shared-monopoly, 860
LESS RESTRICTIVE ALTERNATIVES. *See* ALTERNATIVES; particular restraints
LEVERAGE, 732c7, 1003, 1134c. *See also* RECIPROCITY; TYING
LIMIT PRICING
Generally, 1120b
Monopolist, by, 714b, 1120
Oligopolist, by, 1120
Potential competition, 116a, 1120
Predation as, 714b
Theory and weaknesses, 1120b
LITIGATION, IMPROPER. *See also* POLITICAL ACTION
Anticompetitive purpose, 202
Frivolous claims, 203b-c, 738j
Improper means, 204
Patent infringement actions, 708
Sham or bad faith, 203b, 738j
LOBBYING. *See* POLITICAL ACTION

MARKET DEFINITION. *See also* MARKET POWER; particular substantive offenses
Distribution restraints, 1604f2, 1606g7, 1648d
Tying, 1703d3, 1709c, 1729g
MARKET DIVISION. *See* DISTRIBUTION RESTRAINT; TERRITORIAL DIVISION BY COMPETITORS
MARKET POWER
Buyer response and, 506
differentiated products, 506c
duration of, 506d
identical products, 506b
Conduct as proof, 524
excluding rivals, 524b
facilitating practices, 524d
rigid prices, 524c
Costs, 712
Defined, 501

MARKET POWER (*continued*)
Direct computation from residual demand curves, 525
availability of data, 525f
assessed without market definition, 525c
firm-specific cost shocks and, 525e
limit pricing and, 525g
relation to market power, 525b
residual demand, defined, 525a
residual demand in practice, 525d
Durability and, 573a
leasing practices, 573b
Economic relationship with elasticities and, 507
Excess returns as proof of, 516
cost of capital and, 520b
persistence, 517
proving, 520
deficiencies in data, 520a
economic costs, 520a1
higher accounting profit, 520a2
lower accounting profit, 520a3
scarcity rents and, 518
sole producer and, 519
Formal price-cost measure of, 503
difficulties of, 504
Lerner index and, 503b
uncertain marginal cost, 504b
uncertain price, 504a
substantiality, 803, 805
variable cost surrogate for marginal cost, 805
Geographic markets
customer convenience and preference
limited common sellers and, 553d
stationary supply and, 553a
economics of, 551
foreign competition
actual imports and total output, 555c
international trade barriers, 555a
government guidelines and, 554
price relationships and, 550a
trading patterns and, 550b
transport costs
exceeding price difference, effect of, 552d
export seller cost advantage, 552c2
exporting region, 552c1
noncompetitive pricing by importer, 552c4
persistent one-way sales, 552d2
persistent two-way sales, 552d3
product differentiation, 552c6
price differences and, 552c
relationship to other costs, 552b

Geographic trade restraints, 556
Government regulation and, 572
  antitrust immunities and, 572d
  entry limitations, 572a
  fees and requirements, 572b
  price control, 572c
Intellectual property and, 523
Interindustry competition, 1115
Market definition and, 530
  boundaries and, 530d
  degrees of power and, 530b
  identifying future power, 531d
  identifying single firm power, 531c
  market, defined, 530a
  market structure and, 531e
  statutory requirement, 531b
  substitute for direct measurement, 531a
  time factor and, 530c
Market share
  capacity vs. output, 535c
  defined, 532
  internally used output and, 535e
  large shares, 532a
  low shares, 532b
  meaning, 847, 923, 925a, 932-938, 1151
  other market factors, 917-921
  partial inclusion and, 535f
  presumptions
    attempted monopolization, 835a
    monopolization, 803-808
    sharedmonopoly,846-849
  revenue and units sold, 535a
  sales and production, 535b
    orders exceed production, 535b1
    production exceeds sales, 535b2
  substantiality
    conduct, related to, 814-815
    general propositions, 802
    measurement crude, 814
    persistence, 807
    presumptions, 803
    proof level, 808
    purpose, 813
    reduced requirements, 809
    returns excessive, 806
Price increase methodology to define market, 536
  consumer impact of, 537d
  government guidelines, 538c
  impact of, 537c
    market size, 537c1
    relative profitability, 537c2
  objective data, 538a
  significance of increase, 537a
  subjective evidence, 538b
Price relationships and purchasing patterns
  absence of close price relationships, 534b
  buying-selling patterns, 534e
  close price relationships, 534c

MARKET POWER (*continued*)
distribution costs, 534f
historical trade patterns
competitive, 534a1
monopolistic, 534a2
market scope and, 534a
practical effect of, 534a3
price discrimination, 534d
Product market, 560
brand preferences and, 562e
cluster markets, 565
differentiated products
brand name and private labels, 563b
generally, 563a
incomplete interchangeability, 561b
perfect interchange-ability, 561a
price categories, 563c
price discrimination and, 562f
single brand within a product class, 563d
distribution modes, 564
ease of entry and, 561c
government guidelines and, 561d
user substitutes
generally, 562a
proximate substitutes and, 562d
similar products with differing prices, 562c
Structure tests, 804, 847, 854
"Submarket"
degrees of constraint and, 533b
demand substitution and, 533f
differentiated products and, 533e
geographic market and, 533g
price discrimination and, 533d
relation with "market," 533c
Vertical foreclosure, to assess
foreclosed market, effect of, 570b
competitor's market share and, 570b1
consumer's opportunities and, 570b2
limited markets and, 570e
proposed solution, 570e2
test case, 570e1
producer substitutes and, 570d
similar products and, 570c
supply foreclosure and, 570h
geographic market, 570h1
producer substitutes, 570h2
MARKET PREEMPTION. *See also* FORECLOSURE ANALYSIS; MERGER, VERTICAL; SUPPLY PREEMPTION; RECIPROCITY; TYING
Foreclosure assessed, 732c
Market definition, 570

Monopolization, 732
other antitrust statutes, relevance, 732b
relief scope, 732d
Reasonableness assessed, 732c, 1729b-f
Theory, 527a
Vertical integration compared, 732e

MAXIMUM PRICE FIXING. *See* DISTRIBUTION RESTRAINT; PRICE FIXING AMONG COMPETITORS; PER SE RULE; RULE OF REASON

MCGUIRE ACT, 210, 1629b

MEETINGS. *See* CONSPIRACY GENERALLY

MERGER, CONGLOMERATE. *See also* MERGER, HORIZONTAL AND GENERALLY. (Many conglomerate merger topics are indexed only there)
Acquisition
asset, 1202
defined, 1201-1202
investment only, 1204
partial, 1202-1203
Advertising economies, 1109a
Advertising, "wastefulness" of, 1109a
Aggregation of several effects, 1147
Approach, general, 1100
Asset aggregation, 1140-1143
criteria for controlling, 1143
data, 1141
social problem, as, 1142
statutory coverage, 1145
summary, 1140
Asset defined, 1202
Assets, large, 1135
Behavior, anticompetitive, increased opportunities for, 1127-1139
Benefits
absent, 1147c
generally, 1101-1112, 1149-1151
prohibitory rules, relation to, 1148
Brand recognition economies, 1109b
Capital cost savings, 1105-1106, 1135c
Cost savings, 1101, 1102-1109, 1149
Cross-market mergers, 1113-1115, 1147e4
Cumulation of several insubstantial effects, 1147
Defenses. *See* ECONOMIES; FAILING COMPANY; TOEHOLD; Weak firms
Defensive, 1110
Definition, 1100
Diseconomies of scale, 1108e
Diversification, 1105b
Dominant firms, 1103, 1134-1139
Economies defense, 1102, 1143e, 1149
Economies unlawful, 1103, 1104-1109
Effects, magnitude required, generally, 1146

MERGER, CONGLOMERATE (*continued*)
Entrenchment, 1103, 1104-1109
Entry barriers affected, 1103, 1135
Failing company defense, 1143e, 1150
Federal Trade Commission Act, 1145b
Financial savings, 1105-1106
General Dynamics defense, 1151
Horizontal mergers, compared and distinguished, 1115, 1117, 1152
Intent
anticompetitive, 1111
generally, 1101
Interdependence extended, 1114
Interindustry competition, 1115
Internal expansion compared, 1107, 1149d
Large companies, 1135
Large resources, 1135
Legislative history, 1145
Leverage, 1134
Limit pricing, 1116a, 1120b
Market definition uncertain, 1119d
Marketing economies, 1109
Motivations for, 1101-1112
relevance, 1101-1103, 1112
Multi-market merger, 1113-1115
One-stop service, 1109d
Operational economies generally, 1108
Package selling, 1109d, 1134
Partial acquisition, 1202-1204
Pecuniary savings, 1103, 1104-1109
Post-merger developments. *See* MERGER, HORIZONTAL AND GENERALLY
Potential competition. *See* same
Predatory activities, 1136
actual post-merger, 1136c
Price leadership, 1139
Prices, disciplinary, 1137
Prices, low, 1136-1137
Private savings, 1103, 1104-1109
Procurement savings, 1104
Proofs generally. *See also* more particular subtitles
magnitude required, 1146
modest shortfalls, 1147e
Prosecutorial discretion, 1146c
Protective, 1110
Purchasing economies, 1104
Purpose, anticompetitive, 1111
Reciprocity, 1128-1133
agreements, treatment and relevance, 1128, 1129h, 1130
coercive, 1128, 1129h
defined, 1128
economic effects, 1129
foreclosure magnitudes measured, 1132
invitational, 1128, 1129h
occurrence, likelihood, 1131

"reciprocity effect," 1128
substantiality standards, 1133
tying compared, 1133a
vertical merger compared, 1133b
Repair economies, 1109c1
Research and development economies, 1108b
Resources as such, 1135
Resource savings, 1103, 1104-1109, 1149
Scale economies, 1108a
Selling economies, 1109c1
Sherman Act, 1145b
Size disproportionate, 1103, 1135-1139, 1147e3
Specialized management, staff, 1108d
Statutory coverage, 1145
prophylactic purpose, 1130c, 1131
Structural alterations, 1113-1126
Subtle tying, 1134
Time of appraisal, 1205
Toehold acquisition. *See* same
Tying, 1134
Unfair advantages, 1103, 1127-1139
Unfair prices, 1136-1138
Vertical mergers compared and distinguished, 1133b, 1152
Warranty economies, 1109c2
Weak firms, 1151. *See also* ECONOMIES DEFENSE; FAILING COMPANY
Wide-line coverage, 1109d, 1114, 1115

MERGER, HORIZONTAL AND GENERALLY. *See also* MERGER, CONGLOMERATE; MERGER, VERTICAL
Acquisition defined, 1201
contract right, 1201
date of, 1201b, 1205g
lease, 1201
license, 1201d, 1202f
option, 1201
partial asset, 1202
partial stock, 1203
pledge, 1201
security interest, 1201
Administrative convenience and rule formulation, 905
Affiliated firms, 933
Agricultural cooperatives, 228b, d
Appraisal time, 1126c, 1205
Arbitrariness. *See* "Simple" rules
Asset acquisition. *See also* more particular subtitles (e.g., Patent acquired)
generally, 1202a
partial, 1202
Attempted monopolization, 829c
Basic concerns, 901, 903
Benefits, 901, 903, 939-940
Buyer concentration affecting seller power, 918
Buyers merge, 963-965
buyer collusion prospect, 964b

MERGER, HORIZONTAL AND GENERALLY (*continued*)
distinctive rules, rationale, 964
economies defense, 965c
failing company defense, 965b
presumptions proposed, 965
seller concentration compared, 964
seller shares compared, 963
supply cost curve relevant, 964a
Cases surveyed, 909a, b
Clayton Act §7
amended, 902c, Chs. 9-12 generally
original, 902b
Concealable price cuts, 918
Concentrated markets
collusion, relation to, 910b
competitive fringe, 910d
concentration ratios, 913a1, b1
critical degrees, 910
defined, 913
Herfindahl index, 913a2, b2
maximum for competition, 910d
measures of, 913
ratios, 913a1, b1
significance, 910
size disparities, 910d, 912b
substantiality, 910
defenses, relation to, 910
trends, 914
Conclusions summarized, 907c
Consummation date, 1201b, 1205g
Contract rights acquired, 1201d, 1202g
Copyright acquired, 1202f
Cost structures
differences, 920a
fixed, high, 920b
Criminal offense, as, 309b
Cumulating several insubstantial effects, 1147
Damages for
dealers, 381a
generally, 335d
rivals, 373b
suppliers, 375c
Defenses. *See also* ECONOMIES DEFENSE; FAILING COMPANY DEFENSE; Firm vitality; *General Dynamics* defense
preferred purchasers and other competitively preferable alternatives, 927, 934, 935b, 936, 946, 947, 961
Definitions, 900
Dissimilar-sized firms merge, 911f
Divestiture, 346b
du Pont time of suit rule, 1205
Economic values, 904
Economies defense. *See* same
Effects, adverse
cumulating insubstantial effects, 1147
magnitudes, 907c, 911-912, 915

modest shortfalls in proof, 1147e1
not implicit, 901
possibilities, 903
probabilities, 903
substantiality, 907c, 911-912, 915
Entrenchment, 1101, 1103
Entry barriers and
market definition, 917b
merger rules, 907c, 917
Equipment acquired, 1202d
Failing company defense. *See* same
Finance-deficient firms, 935
Firms' number
minimum for competition, 910c
number as such, 904
Firm vitality. *See also* *Generally Dynamics* defense
diseconomies of scale, 939, 962b
failure imminent, 925-926
financial difficulties, 935
generally, 932
management deficiencies, 936
market access inadequate, 934e
resources inadequate, 934a-d
special vitality or prospects, 937
Fishermen's cooperative, 228b, d
General Dynamics defense, 934-936, 961
competitively preferable alternatives, 934, 935b, 936, 961
economies defense, relation to, 962b
limited with respect to diseconomies, 962b
market access limited, 934e
"preferred purchaser" requirement, 934b, 935b, 961
resource deficient firms, 934
supply access limited, 934c, d
self-supply possibility, 934d
Government guidelines, 909c
Herfindahl index, 913a2, b2
Historical review, 902
Initial small merger, 911d
Intent, 938
Interpretive guides generally, 903-907
Intra-corporate mergers, 933
Inventory acquired, 1202c
Investment intent, 1204
Investment-only acquisition, 1204
Joint venture
merger alternative, 946
merger, as, 1202f2, h
Legislative history, 903
License as merger, 1202f
Management-deficient firm, 936
Marginal cases, 905f2
Market-deficient firm, 934e
Market definition uncertainties, 921

MERGER, HORIZONTAL AND GENERALLY (*continued*)
Market factors other than firm shares, 916-922
Market share(s)
aggregating several markets, 911
below-threshold merger, 912d
cases generally, in, 909b
competitive markets, 911
concentrated markets, 912
critical degrees, 910-912
disparate size
narowed, 912b
widened, 912c
government guidelines, in, 909c
market definition unclear, 921
presumptive proof of illegality, 907c, 908-915
significance
factors impeding oligopolistic collaboration, 404b2, 916-922
firm's peculiarities, 923, 925a, 932-938
affiliations, 933
diseconomies of scale, 939, 962b
failure imminent, 925-926
financial difficulties, 935
management deficiencies, 936
market access inadequate, 934e
resources inadequate, 934a-d
special vitality, 937
generally, 910-912
other general market factors, 916-922
overstated, 404, 520, 916-921, 925a, 932, 934-936, 962b
understated, 520, 937-938
substantiality
defenses, relation to, 910
generally, 907c, 910-912
small acquisitions, 911
Supreme Court cases, in, 909a
trends, 914
Merger defined, 1201
Mineral lease acquired, 1202e
Monopolization
diversification, 701e
efficiency, 701g
failing company, 701h
generally, 627b-c, 701a
monopoly achieved later, 817818
potential competition, 701c
progressiveness, 701f
related market, 701d
statutes, other antitrust, relevance, 701i
Newspapers, 230d
Order flow, 918
Overprohibition costs, 905d
Patent acquired, 1202f
Plant acquired, 1202d
Pledge acquired, 1201d
Political values, 904

Post-acquisition
  developments, 1131, 1136c, 1203e, 1204e, 1205
  evidence, 1205
Potential deconcentration, 912d
Predictability and rule formulation, 905
Pre-threshold condemnation, 911d
Price-fixing compared, 901
Product heterogeneity, 919
Private suits, 373b, 375c, 381, 905f1
Proofs. *See* more particular topics (e.g., ECONOMIES DEFENSE)
Prophylactic purpose, 903-905, 1130c, 1131
Prosecutorial discretion, 905f1, 1146c
Purpose, 938
Railroad cases, 902a
Real property acquired, 1202e
Regulated industries, 220-227
Related firms, 933
Resource-deficient firm, 934
Sellers merge, 900-962
  buyers' merger compared, 964
Shared monopoly, 860
Sherman Act, 902a, 906
"Simple" rules
  difficulties, 905a
  generally, 905
  interdependent subordinate rules, 905e
  legality, 905b
  need for, 905c
  structure, 905d
Smaller firms in concentrated market, 911d, 912b, c
Small mergers, 911d, f
Social values, 904
Stock acquisition
  generally, 1203
  partial, 1203
  solely for investment, 1204
Summary
  analysis, 907b
  conclusions, 907c
Supplies acquired, 1202c
Supreme Court cases, major, 902, 909a
Time of appraisal, 1126c, 1205
Time of suit rule, 1205
Toehold acquisition, 912d
Trademark acquired, 1202f
Trends in concentration or market share, 914, 1205f
Underprohibition costs, 905d
Weak firms, 932, 934-936. *See also* ECONOMIES DEFENSE; FAILING COMPANY DEFENSE
  "preferred purchaser" requirement, 934b, 935b, 961

MERGER, VERTICAL. *See also* MERGER, HORIZONTAL AND GENERALLY. (Many vertical merger topics are indexed only there)
  Acquisition
    asset, 1202
    defined, 1201

MERGER, VERTICAL (*continued*)
investment only, 1204
partial, 1202-1203
Aggregating foreclosures, 1014c-d
Assets acquisition defined, 1201-1202
Cases
generally characterized, 1000
generally surveyed, 1020
related to proposals, 1021
selectively discussed, 1022
Competitive effects. *See also* more particular headings (e.g., Disruptive buyer eliminated)
competition improved, 1004d, 1012
competition reduced
generally, 1004e, 1005
particulars, 1006-1011
summary, 1001
magnitude required, 1001, 1002, 1005-1011, 1012a, b, 1014d, 1015
Conclusions, 1001, 1015
Conglomerate advantages, 1003c
Consumer choice reduced, 1010
Cumulative foreclosure, 1014d
Date of, 1201, 1205
Defenses. *See* Economies; Failing company; *General Dynamics*
Destabilization of rivals, 1009
Disruptive buyer eliminated, 1006
Economic consequences, 1003-1014
Economies and
formulation of presumptions, 1001, 1012, 1014d2
internal expansion, 1000c, 1012a, 1016e
merger, 1012a, 1016
Economies defense
generally, 1016
one or both firms partially or wholly integrated, 1017
Effects, magnitude required, 1001, 1002, 1005-1011, 1012 a, b, 1014d, 1015
Efficient scale, rivals deprived of, 1008
Entrenchment, 1101, 1103
Entry barriers affected, 1011
Failing company defense, 1018. *See also* FAILING COMPANY DEFENSE
Foreclosure analysis
absent, 1004b, c
aggregations, 1011f1, 1014c, 1021
analyzed, 1004
assertions, general, 1000
buyer choice reduced, 1010
competition increased, 1004d, 1012
competition reduced, 1004e-1011
competitive markets, 1004c
cumulations, 1011f1, 1014d, 1021
defined, 1004

destabilization of rivals, 1009
disruptive buyer eliminated, 1006
entry barriers raised, 1011
existence, 1004
harmless, 1004c, 1012
initial, 1014b
measured, 527, 1013, 1015d, 1204d4-5
realignment compared, 1004c, d
scale, rivals deprived of, 1008
second-level concentration raised, 1007
self-dealing, 1004b, c
trends, 1014e, 1021, 1022a
tying law, and, 1700j2
vertical integration, 731-732. *See also* same

General Dynamics defense, 1019
General guidelines, 1001, 1002, 1012a-b, 1014d2, 1015
Input substitution ended, 1012c
Integration by internal growth compared. *See* Internal growth
Integration fallacies, 1003
Internal growth compared, 1000b-c
Legislative history, 1002
Market definition, 570, 1013
Market shares
measurement, 570, 1014
presumptive rules, 1015
significance, 1019

Monopolist's acquisition, 1015e
Multiple acquisitions, 1014c
Non-profit internal transactions, 1003a
Oligopolistic coordination impaired, 1012e
Partial acquisition, 1202-1204
Post-merger developments. *See* MERGER, HORIZONTAL AND GENERALLY
Precedents. *See* Cases
Presumptions proposed, 1015
Price discrimination, 1012c
Pricing more competitive, 1012
Problem defined, 1000a
Proofs, 1015
modest shortfalls, 1147e
Recoupment, 1003b
Rivals deprived of efficient scale, 1008
Rivals destabilized, 1009
Second-level market, concentration increased, 1007
Self-dealing
absent, 1004b
intention, relevance, 1004b
non-foreclosure, 1004c
presumed, 1004b
proof, necessity of, 1004b
rebuttable, 1004b
Small acquisitions, 1014d
Statutory language and history, 1002
Successive monopoly (oligopoly) ended, 1012b
Summary, 1001
Supply shortage, 1003d

MERGER, VERTICAL (*continued*)
Time of appraisal, 1205
Trends, foreclosure, 1014e
Tying compared, 1700j2
Weak firms. *See* Economies defense; Failing company defense; *General Dynamics* defense
MILLER-TYDINGS ACT
Implications of repeal, 1629c
Rationale, 1629b
Repeal, 1629
State law primacy, 210
MISREPRESENTATION. *See also* PATENTS, Procurement improprieties
Attempted monopolization, 828b
Evidence of conspiracy, 1417f
Monopolization, 738a
MISTAKE OF LAW DEFENSE
Action invited or directed by mistaken government agencies, 332a
Defense for reasonable mistake, 332a
Exemption orders for complying with regulations, 332b
Generally, 332
Interpretive regulations, 332b
Private persons, 332a
Regulations later held to be unauthorized, 332a
Statutory requirements, 332a
MONOPOLISTIC COMPETITION, 409
MONOPOLIZATION. *See also* ATTEMPTED MONOPOLIZATION; EQUITABLE RELIEF; MARKET POWER; MONOPOLY SHARED; specific practices (e.g., TYING)
Abuse, 626f, 736
Ancient acts, 628
Basic issues, 600
Blameless monopolists, 621-623
Change of law, 629
Conduct, exclusionary or monopolistic before monopoly attained, 816-819. *See also* ATTEMPTED MONOPOLIZATION
causation, 626c, 627
characteristics, 626
definitions, 626
degrees, generally, 814
deterrence rationale, 627b1-2
effects, 627
innocent behavior, 627b4
presumed present, 620b
relevance of, 614, 624-625, 627b
unconsummated, 627b, 630c3
"Defenses," 621, 622
Definitions, general, 601
Distribution restraints generally. *See* same title
Divisible resources, 621b
Equitable relief generally, 620c, 626-627
General rule, 624b, 700
Government equity actions, other suits

distinguished, 313-314, 623
Incentives, 622
Intention, 626a-b
Legal license, 621c
Legislative history, 617
Natural monopoly, 621a-b
Patent and trademark licensing, 621b
Persistence, 622e, 623, 624a
Persistent monopoly without exclusionary conduct, 623
Power requirement, 801-819
"any part of commerce," 811
monopoly later occurs, 816
presumptions, 802-809
reduced power arguments, 813
substantial power needed, 818
summary, 810
varied with conduct
conduct followed by monopoly, 816-819
grossly, 815
precisely, 814
Precedents, major, 602-613
Prevalence, 619
Prices, monopolistic, 710, 1636b
Private suits, government suits distinguished, 311, 312, 623
Remedies generally, 626-627, 849. *See also* particular exclusionary practices
Sanctions, relevance of, 620c, 623, 627
Self-correcting monopoly, 618
Skill, superior, 621-622, 849
Statutes, other antitrust, related to, 626e
Statutory language, 616
Wilfulness, 626a
MONOPOLY. *See also* EFFICIENCIES; MARKET POWER; MONOPOLIZATION; MONOPOLY SHARED; TYING; VERTICAL INTEGRATION
Benefits, 407-408
Cartels compared, 405
Defined, 403
Effects, 403
Efficiencies, 403, 408
Oligopoly compared, 404, 843
Pricing, 403a
Progressiveness, 407
Successive monopolies, 412, 725c
MONOPOLY POWER. *See* MARKET POWER
MONOPOLY PRICE, 710, 1636b, 1710
MONOPOLY SHARED. *See also* INTERDEPENDENT PARALLELISM AS CONSPIRACY; OLIGOPOLY
Attempted monopolization compared, 858
Basic issues, 840
Benefits, 843c-e
Conduct, exclusionary, 856-862
effects insubstantial, 860
private remedies, 858
relief scope, 857
shares redistributed, 861

MONOPOLY SHARED (*continued*)
Conspiracy or combination statutes compared, 841
Damages, 851, 858
Evils, 840a, 843a-b
Identifying, 846-851
Incentives, 844
Judicial mandate, 852, 855
Justifications, 843c-e, 844
Legislative history, 842a
Legislative proposals
illustration, 853
judicial approach compared, 854
Monopoly, single-firm, compared, 842-845
effects, 843-844
legal issues, 842
summarized, 845
Official discretion
implications, 851b
necessity, 851a
Performance tests, 849
Practical considerations, 842c-d
Price-cost tests, 848
Private actions, 851, 858
Profit tests, 848-849
Remedial problems, 850, 857
Self-defense, 859
Statutory language, 842a
Statutory purpose, 842b
Structural tests, 847
Summary, 840, 862
MONOPSONY, 574, 963-965
MOST FAVORED BUYER (or supplier or nation), 1435e. *See also* FACILITATING PRACTICE
NATIONAL DEFENSE, 230b
NATURAL MONOPOLY, 621
NEW PRODUCT. *See* INNOVATION
NEWSPAPERS, 230d
NOERR DOCTRINE. *See* POLITICAL ACTION
NON-PROFIT ENTITIES, 360c, 361, 1718j

OBJECTIVES. *See* PUBLIC POLICIES
OLIGOPOLY. *See also* COMPETITION; CONCENTRATION; CONSPIRACY, GENERALLY; EFFICIENCIES; INTERDEPENDENT PARALLELISM AS CONSPIRACY; MARKET POWER; MERGER; MONOPOLIZATION; MONOPOLY SHARED; TYING
Basic economic model, 404
"collective but non-collusive monopolization," 404b, 1429b, 1432b
evidence, 404d
express collusion
imperfect, 405b
interdependence compared, 405a, 1432b
innovation, 407
interdependence, 404b, 841a, 1429a
non-price competition, 405b2, 1429c
objectives of oligopolistic pricing, 405b1

predictability of response, 404b, 1425d
summary, 404b5
varieties, 404b
Basing point pricing, 1435f
Buyer concentration, 918
Buyer coordination, 963-965
Cartel compared, 405, 1429b, 1430-1431, 1432b
Competitive fringe, 910d
Competitiveness, 1430-1431
Concealed transactions, 404c3
Concentrated markets
coordination in, 404b, 841a, 910, 912
defined, 913, 1119, 1431a
measured, 913
Concentration
Herfindahl index, 404f2, 913a1, b1
measures, 913
ratios, 404f1, 913a1, b1, 1119
trends, 914
Conspiracy or combination, 841. *See also* CONSPIRACY GENERALLY; INTERDEPENDENT PARALLELISM AS CONSPIRACY
Coordination impeded, 404c, 917-920, 1012e, 1119g, 1430
Cost differences, 404c2, 920a
Defined, 404a
Efficiencies, 408
Facilitating practice. *See* same
Factors affecting performance, 1430
Firms' number, 910c
Fixed costs, 910c
Fringe firms, 404c6
Infrequent transactions, 404c4
Innovations, 407
Interdependence, 404b, 841, 910-912, 1410-1415, 1429-1432
Inter-industry competition, 1115
Knowledge, 404b, 406a
Legality
Federal Trade Commission Act, 1436
Sherman Act §1, 841a-b, 1433-1434
Sherman Act §2, 840-852
Legislative proposals, 853
Likelihood of coordination, 404d, 1430
Limit pricing, 1120b
Monopoly compared, 404, 842-845
Multi-market interdependence, 1114
Non-price competition, 405b2, c, 406a, 1425e, 1429c
Number of firms, 404e, f
Parallel pricing. *See also* INTERDEPENDENT PARALLELISM AS CONSPIRACY
economic analysis, 404b
legal analysis, 840-862, 1432-1434
Price discrimination, 404b3
Price leadership. *See* Parallel pricing
Product variety, 404c3, 919
Rate of return, 404d

OLIGOPOLY (*continued*)
Scale economies, 408
Signaling, 404c8
Tying, and. *See* same
Vertical integration effects, 1000b, 1004d, 1005-1012
Workable competition, 843-845
OLIGOPSONY, 963-965
OUTPUT AS MEASURE OF COMPETITIVE EFFECT, 1503b
OUTPUT CONTRACT. *See* EXCLUSIVE DEALING; FORECLOSURE ANALYSIS; MARKET PREEMPTION; SUPPLY PREEMPTION

PARALLELISM. *See* CONSPIRACY, GENERALLY; INTERDEPENDENT PARALLELISM AS CONSPIRACY; OLIGOPOLY
PARENS PATRIAE, 380
PARI DELICTO. *See* PLAINTIFF'S VIOLATION
PARKER v. BROWN DOCTRINE. *See* STATE ACTION
PATENTS
Accumulation, 705-706
Acquisitions from employees, 704e
Acquisitions generally, 705
competitive dangers, 705b
different technology, 705i
general rule, 705a
monopolistic intent, 705c
monopoly later achieved, 819
relief scope, 705h
shared monopoly, 860
Aggregation, 705-706
Assignment, 705
Attempted monopolization, 829c, 836b
Combination patent and tying, 1712g
Compulsory licensing, 705g, 706c3
Defense to monopolization, 621c2-7
Entry barrier, 421
Exclusion as monopolistic practice, generally, 704
Fraudulent procurement. *See* Procurement improprieties
Free riding prevented, 1613b
Grant-backs, 705e
Incentive to invest, 704c, 705d
Infringement suits, 708
Intention to exclude, 704a, 706b
Internal development, 706
Licensee estoppel, 209
Licenses
non-exclusive, 705d
restricted, 709
Misuse doctrine, 707b, d
Non-exclusive license for monopolist, 705d
Non-use, 706c
Procurement improprieties
attempted monopolization, 836b
candor lacking, 707i
defined, 707g-j

Federal Trade Commission Act, 707c
innocent holder, 707k
invalidity, 707b
materiality, 707g
misuse, 707b, d
monopolization, as, 707d-f
non-exclusionary, 707d
prior art representation, 707j
relief scope, 707l
wilfullness, 707h
Relevant interests, 704c-d, 705b-c
Resale prices on patented products, 1621
Restricted licenses, 709
Settlements, 709
Suppression, 706c
Threat to purchaser from infringer, as conspiracy, 1408f1
Tying, and. *See* same

PER SE RULE (generally). *See also* REGULATED INDUSTRIES; RULE OF REASON; STATE ACTION; particular substantive titles
Administrative convenience as sufficient rationale, 1509
Application, 1510-1511
Class application of rule of reason, 1509
Classification into, 1510b-c
Criminal sanctions, relevance to, 1509
Effects, market, uncertainty, 1509
Exceptions, 1510b-c
Inconsistencies explained, 1510
Legitimate objectives
absence of, 1509
exceptions to per se condemnation, 1510
"quick look," 1510c, 1511
rule application, 1510-1511
rule formulation, 1509
Meaning varies, 1510a
Naked restraint, 1504, 1509
Power, market
irrelevant, 1509
presumed, 1509, 1510b
proved easily, 1511
required sometimes, 1510a
Rationale for, 1509
Reasonableness of price irrelevant, 1509, 1510a
Rule of reason, similarities to
exceptions permitted, 1508
generally, 1511
legitimate objectives considered, 1509, 1510b-c
per se derived from, 1509
power sometimes required, 1510a
presumptions in both, 1508c
reasonableness summarily determined, 1507-1508, 1511
spectrum rather than dichotomy, 1511
Stare decisis compared, 1510
Tying's peculiar version, 1701c, 1720-1721, 1730

PERSONAL JURISDICTION, 235

PICK-BARTH DOCTRINE, 828b

PLAINTIFF'S VIOLATION OR PARTICIPATION
Damages, bearing on, 365c3, 390
Defense by participating defendant, 390, 1459c2
Defense to non-antitrust claim, 391
Defense to patent infringement, 707
In pari delicto, 390

PLEADINGS, 323

POLITICAL ACTION. *See also* STATE ACTION
Adjudication, 202b, 203b, 204c-d, e2
Administrative action, invalid 202b-c
Agency-court relation, 203b
Anticompetitive purpose, 202
Bad faith, 203
Bribery, 204
False information, 204
Frivolous claims, 203
Good faith efforts, 202c
Government contracts, franchises, leases, purchases, sales, 206
Improper means, 204
  adjudication, 204c-d, e2
  legislation, 204c-e1
More restriction than necessary, 205
Noerr rationale, 204b
Price agreements, 205
"Primary jurisdiction," 203b
Sham, 203
Statutes, invalid, 202b-c
Successful efforts, 202b, 203c, 204
Summary, 201

POTENTIAL COMPETITION, 1116-1126
Actual competition compared, 1117
Actual potential entrant, 1121. *See also* Future effect
Attractiveness of entry, 1121c2
Concentration, 1119-1120
Conclusions, 1116
Consistency in assessing probable entry, 1123d
Defendant's characteristics, 1121-1122
Definitions, 1116a
"Edge" effect. *See* Present effect
Effects. *See* Future effect; Present effect
Entry barriers, 1119f, 1120b, 1121c, 1123
Entry, probable, by others, 1123
Future effect
  conditions summarized, 1116b
  entrants, other, 1123
  entry probable, 1121
  generally, 1116
  market conditions needed, 1119
  prerequisites, 1116b, 1119, 1121, 1123
  proofs, 1116b, 1119, 1121, 1123
  summary, 1116
  toehold context, 1124-1125
  vertical context, 1126
Generally, 1116, 1147e5

Horizontal context, 1116-1125
Instability: concentration and market shares, 1119e
Legal barriers to entry, 1121c3
Market conditions, prerequisite
  future effect, 1119
  present effect, 1119-1120
Market definition, 1117b, 1119d
Market relations, existing and potential, 1121c5
Market structure, 1119-1120
"Most likely entrant," 1123
Perceived potential entrant, 1122. *See also* Present effect
Present effect
  conditions summarized, 1116b
  entrants, other, 1123
  entry probable, 1122
  generally, 1116
  market conditions needed, 1120
  prerequisites, 1116b, 1120, 1122, 1123
  proofs, 1116b, 1120, 1122, 1123
  summary, 1116
  toehold context, 1124-1125
  vertical context, 1126
Presumptive illegality proposals, 1116b
Probable entry
  burden of proof, 1121d, e
  objective likelihood, 1121c
  perceptions of others, 1122
  prerequisite, 1121a, 1122d
  proof, 1121-1122
  relation to other prerequisites, 1121e
  significance of scale, 1121d
  subjective intention, 1121b
Proofs summarized, 1116b
Proposals summarized, 1116b
Resources for entry, 1121c4
Scale of probable entry, 1121d
Significance, 1116. *See also* Scale of probable entry
Statutory coverage, 1118
Subjective intention to enter, 1121b
Summary, 1116
Toehold acquisitions. *See* same
Universe of potential entrants, 1123
  prerequisite, 1123
Vertical context, 1126
"Wings" effect. *See* Present effect

PREDATION IN
Advertising, 721
Innovation, 738
Investment, 718
Price discrimination. *See* same
Pricing. *See* PRICE PREDATION
Product variation, 722
Spending, 721

PREEMPTION OF MARKETS OR SUPPLIES. *See* FORECLOSURE ANALYSIS; MARKET PREEMPTION; SUPPLY PREEMPTION

PREEMPTION OF STATE LAW. *See* STATE ACTION

PRESUMPTIONS.*See also* PER SE RULE; RULE OF REASON
As a formal embodiment of a reasonableness standard, 320b
As guides for procedural matters, 320c
Dichotomy between per se rules and rule of reason, 320b
Generally, 320a-c
Judicial resolution of, 321c
Legal rules circumscribing fact-finding, 320b
Per se illegality as a presumption, 320b
Presumptively lawful conduct, 320b
Qualifications of, 320b
Reasons for, 320b, c
PRICE DISCIPLINE. *See also* OLIGOPOLY; PRICE PREDATION
Merger, after, 1137
Monopolist, by, 714c, 720
Oligopolist, by, 1137
PRICE DISCRIMINATION. *See also* CUSTOMER AND TERRITORIAL RESTRAINT VERTICAL; DISTRIBUTION RESTRAINTS GENERALLY; PRICE PREDATION; TYING
Allocative effects, 725e, 1711b-c
Alternative methods, 1703e1
Antitrust policy, and, 1710
Beneficial, 1711b-c
Buyer's cost saving, 957, 1104-1105
Cartel, by, 1710c2
Competitive outcome approached, 1711b
Distributional effects, 1711b4
Distribution restraints, through, 1616b, e, f, 1647c5-6, 1648c3
Effects, 1703e1, 1711b-c
First degree, 1711b4A
Illustration, 1711a2
Incremental exploitation as detriment, 1710
Independent demand function, 1711c
Independent demands, 1711c
Market power, bearing on, 522
Metering, 1711b
Non-exploitative, 1715c2
Non-use risk, 1711b
Output effects, 725e, 1711b-c
Perfect, 1711b41
Power needed, 1711a2
Predatory, 720
Prerequisite, 1711a2
Price squeeze by vertically integrated monopolist, 728c
precedent, 729
Regulated industries, 1715b
Robinson-Patman Act and tying, 1711g
Second degree, 1711b4B
Third degree, 1711c
Tying, 733d, 1703e1, 1711
damages, 347b
generally, 1703e1
precedent, 1710b
price competition, 1714e
Use intensity, 1711b

Vertical integration, 733d
Vertical merger, 1006, 1012c
PRICE FIXING AMONG COMPETITORS. *See also* FOREIGN COMMERCE; MONOPOLY SHARED; OLIGOPOLY; PER SE RULE; RULE OF REASON
Agreement. *See* CONSPIRACY, GENERALLY
Breakdowns, 405b2
Cartel defined, 405a
Departures from, 405b2
Divergent interests, 405b1
Employee competing with employer, 1471c
Interdependent parallelism as conspiracy. *See* same
Justifications, 413
Merger compared, 901
Non-price competition, 405b2
Oligopoly pricing compared, 405a
Output unchanged, 1710c2
Perfect price discrimination, 1710c2
Per se condemnation, rationale for, 1509
Productive joint venture, incident to, 1478a, 1510b-c
Purposes, 405b
Rigidity, 405b1
Various forms, 405b
PRICE FIXING VERTICAL. *See* RESALE PRICE, MAXIMUM; RESALE PRICE MINIMUM
PRICE FORMULA, 1435h. *See also* CONSPIRACY, GENERALLY; FACILITATING PRACTICE; OLIGOPOLY
PRICE, HIGH
Monopolization, 710
PRICE LEADERSHIP. *See* CONSPIRACY, GENERALLY; INTERDEPENDENT PARALLELISM AS CONSPIRACY
PRICE, LOW. *See also* PRICE DISCIPLINE; PRICE PREDATION
Conglomerate merger, after, 1138
PRICE MANUALS, 1406c-d, 1435g. *See also* CONSPIRACY, GENERALLY; FACILITATING PRACTICE
PRICE PREDATION
After merger, 1136c
Anticipated costs, 715d, 716
Attempted monopolization, 827, 835a, 836b
Average variable cost, 712, 715d
Conglomerate merger, 1136-1137
Costs, alternative measures of, 712
Differential returns on multiple products, 719
Discriminatory prices, 720
Full cost
below marginal cost, 715b2
below price, 714
defined, 712
Generally, 711
Intention, 715
Limit pricing, 714b

PRICE PREDATION (*continued*)
Loss leading compared, 1619
Marginal costs
anticipated vs. actual, 715d, 716
average variable cost surrogate, 715d
defined, 513b, 712, 715c
long-run standard, 715a (n.7)
prices above, 715a
prices below, 715b
short-run standard, 715a
Meeting competition defense, 717
Monopolization, 711-722
Post-merger, 1136c
Preconditions, 711b, 836b
Product variations excessive, 722
Promotional activities excessive, 721
Promotional pricing, 716
Resale price ceilings, 1637h
Robinson-Patman Act compared, 720c
Spending as predation, 721
Summary, 711
Temporary price reductions, 714c
Tying, and, 1711g, 1714e
PRICE PROTECTION CLAUSES. *See* FACILITATING PRACTICE
PRICE SQUEEZE. *See* VERTICAL INTEGRATION
PRIMARY JURISDICTION. *See* REGULATED INDUSTRIES
PRIVATE ACTIONS. *See also* ATTORNEY'S FEES; BUSINESS OR PROPERTY; CLASS ACTIONS; DAMAGES; DISSOLUTION AND DIVESTITURE; EQUITABLE RELIEF; JURY TRIAL; LIMITATIONS PERIOD; PLEADINGS; RES JUDICATA AND COLLATERAL ESTOPPEL; STANDING; SUMMARY DISPOSITION
Appropriateness
blameless monopoly, 623
generally, 312d, e
shared monopoly, 851, 858
Compensatory rationale, 355
Criminal suits compared, 312c
Damage and equity suits contrasted, 312d
Deterrence rationale, 355a, b
Government suits contrasted, 623, 851, 1640a
"Private attorney general," 355c, 365e, 1640
Public function, 355b
Public injury requirement, 355c
Resale price maximum, 1640
Resale price minimum, 1623f
PROCESS. *See* COMPETITION
PRODUCT DIFFERENTIATION. *See* DIFFERENTIATED PRODUCTS; DISTRIBUTION RESTRAINTS GENERALLY; PRODUCT VARIATIONS
PRODUCT MARKET. *See* MARKET POWER

PRODUCT VARIATIONS. *See also* MERGERS; OLIGOPOLY
Monopolization, 722
Vertical integration or merger, after, 1010
PROFESSIONAL ASSOCIATIONS. *See* CONSPIRACY, GENERALLY, Information, Meetings; CONSPIRACY, INTRAENTERPRISE, Rulemaking bodies; HEALTH CARE; JOINT VENTURES; RULE OF REASON; TRADE ASSOCIATION
PROMOTIONAL ACTIVITIES. *See also* EFFICIENCIES; all MERGER titles; OLIGOPOLY
Excessive, 721, 954a, 1109a
Monopolization, 721
Price predation, as, 716
Wastefulness, 954a, 1109a
PROOF, BURDEN OF. *See* all CONSPIRACY titles; RULE OF REASON; more particular titles
PUBLIC GOODS, 1613b
PUBLIC POLICIES GENERALLY, 103-113, 401. *See also* all CONSPIRACY titles; particular offenses
Competitive process, 1713c3
Consumer protection, higher prices, 1710
Departures from competitive model, implications, 406-415
Dispersed power, 100
Economic efficiency, 104-105, 408
Fairness, 109-112
Incentives, 1710c3
Income distribution, 108a, 1710c2
Mergers, in
conglomerate, 1142-1143, 1145
horizontal, 904
Output, 1703e4
Populist goals, 109b-112
Practical limitations, 113, 406b
Prices, 1703e4
Progressiveness, 407
Rivalry, 1703e4
Stabilization, 108b
PUBLIC SPEECH, 1435c. *See also* FACILITATING PRACTICE
PUBLIC UTILITIES. *See* REGULATED INDUSTRIES; STATE ACTION
PURPOSE. *See* INTENTION; PER SE RULE; RULE OF REASON

RECIPROCITY
Agreements, 1130
Competitive effects, 1129
Conglomerate merger, after, 1128-1133
Defined, 1128
Economic effects, 1129
Foreclosure magnitude measured, 1132
Occurrence likelihood, 1131
Substantiality standard, 1133
Tying compared, 1133a

RECIPROCITY (*continued*)
Vertical merger compared, 1133b

REFUSALS TO DEAL
Agreement implied. *See* CONSPIRACY, COERCED; CONSPIRACY, GENERALLY; CONSPIRACY, VERTICAL; TYING
Attempted monopolization, 729, 828c, e
Because of non-compliance with desires, suggestions, or conditions. *See* CONSPIRACY, COERCED; CONSPIRACY, VERTICAL
By a monopolist
arbitrary, 736
common law, 736c
legal theories, 736b
precedents, 729
supply squeeze, 728b
vertical integration, incident to, 728b, 729. *See also* VERTICAL INTEGRATION
vertical merger, after, 346, 375c, 381a, 1017c. *See also* MERGER, VERTICAL
Concerted refusal to deal. *See* same
Distribution limited. *See* DISTRIBUTION RESTRAINTS GENERALLY; particular restraints

REGULATED INDUSTRIES. *See also* AGRICULTURAL COOPERATIVES; BANKS; POLITICAL ACTION; STATE ACTION
Administrative agencies. *See* generally this title
Agency approval
not sought, 226
power, implications, 224e
required by statute, 224e
scope of, 225
Agency power
to prevent, implications, 224d, f
unexercised, 224d, f
Agency silence, 224d
Agency supervision
active, 223g
continuing, 225c
power, implications, 224d
Antitrust law enforces regulation?, 1712d2
Balancing functions, 223e, 226
Boycotts, 224d
Competition under regulation, 223c
Competitive premises, 221, 223c
Criminal sanctions, injunction distinguished, 226b-c
Damages, injunction distinguished, 226b-c
Exclusive jurisdiction, 223h. *See also* generally this title
Expertness, agency or court, 223g, 224d, 225d, 226b
Immunity, express, 224b

Immunity implied by
agency approval
requirement, 224e
agency power to prevent,
224f
assumptions of statute,
224d
pervasive regulation, 224e
requirements of statute,
224d
Inaction by agency, 224f, 226e
Industry domination, 223e
Injunction, damages
distinguished, 226b-c
Judicial competence, 223g,
224d, 225d, 226b
Judicial confidence in agency,
223g, 224e
Key issues, 222
Per se rules, 223d, 224d
Pervasive regulation, 223b,
224a, e
Post-approval acts, 225b
Pre-approval acts, 225b
Price
ceiling evaded via tie,
1712d1
fixing, 224b
floor evaded via tie,
1715b
Primary jurisdiction, 223h,
225d, 226b, 227
Prior resort, 225d, 226b, d,
227
Private complaints, 223c-e
Procedure is substance, 223e,
224e
Purposes and premises, 223b,
224a-e
Regulatory scope, 223b
Remedies, 223e
Reliance by private parties,
223f
Retroactive remedies,
223f
Rule-making, relevance of,
223f
Rule of reason, 223d, 226d
Scope of agency approval,
225
Silence by agency, 224d, 225,
226e
Standing before agency, 223c
Summary, 222, 227a
Supervision active, 223g
Supervision continuing,
225c
Terminated restraints, 223g
Unapproved conduct that
could have been
immunized, 226
REMEDIES
Criminal sanctions. *See*
CRIMINAL
SANCTIONS
Differentiating antitrust
offenses according to
remedy, 312, 312f
arguments against
differentiation, 312a
criminal offenses, 312c
expansion of definitions of
offenses, relation to
remedies, 312b
Gypsum decision, 312c
Public and private equity
suits compared, 312e
discretionary character of
equitable remedies,
312e4
distinctions between,
312e3

REMEDIES (*continued*)
equal treatment of public and private plaintiffs not compelled, 312e4
government suits coincide more with the public interest, 312e1-2
government suits more likely propose considered remedies, 312e1-2
limits on private relief for behavior-less monopoly, 312e4
remedies and proof distinctions, 312e3
Treble damages under the Clayton Act, 312d. *See also* PRIVATE ANTITRUST ACTIONS
REQUIREMENTS CONTRACTS. *See* EXCLUSIVE DEALING; FORECLOSURE ANALYSIS; MARKET PREEMPTION; SUPPLY PREEMPTION
RES JUDICATA AND COLLATERAL ESTOPPEL
Antitrust peculiarities, generally, 334a
Collateral estoppel, 336. *See also* COLLATERAL ESTOPPEL
Continuing conduct, 334c
changes in law or circumstances, 334c
successive causes of action for, 334c
Duplicate recovery barred, 335c2
First suit in federal court; second in state court, 335b
"artful pleading" rule, 335b
effect of dismissing federal claims, 335b
effect of state claims not included as pendent claims, 335b
federal court jurisdiction over state claims, 335b
First suit in state court; second in federal court, 335c
claim preclusion, generally, 335c2
"full faith and credit," 335c2
issue preclusion, generally, 335c1
preclusion determined by state law, 335c, c2
preclusive effect of state court judgments, federal court determination, 335c2
preclusive effect of state court judgments, state court determination, 335c2
Generally, 334a
Privity requirement, 334e
attorney abuse of, 334e
meaning of, 334e
Splitting the cause of action, 334b1
between federal and state courts, 335c2

government
monopolization suits, 334b3
ordinarily disallowed, 334b2
private equity suits before damages cause of action arises, 334b4
separate government suits for legal and equitable relief, 334b4
successive criminal and civil proceedings, 334b5
Successive federal and state suits, generally, 335a
effect of substantively similar laws, generally, 335a
factual determinations, generally, 335a
Successive private and public suits, 334d
Successive suits by different governmental agencies, 334d
RESALE PRICE MAINTENANCE. *See* RESALE PRICE MINIMUM
RESALE PRICE MAXIMUM. *See also* DISTRIBUTION RESTRAINTS GENERALLY
Advertised price, 1639d
Agents, 1473, 1622c
Agreement, 1623, 1639e. *See also* CONSPIRACY, VERTICAL
Albrecht case, 1450-1451, 1635, 1637g, 1640d
as applied by lower courts, 1639
critique, 1635-1637
monopoly inevitable, if, 1636b1
Antitrust injury by restrained or rival dealer, 1640
Appraised, 1636-1638a
Competitive price agreement, 1639b
Concern about, 1635, 1637
Conditioned allowances or reimbursements, 1626, 1639f-h
Consumer welfare, 1636-1637
Critique, 1636-1637, 1638a
Dealer autonomy limited, 1640d2
Dealer exploitation, 1637e1, 1638a
Dealer monopoly power, 1636a-b
Dealer number limited, 1637g
Dealer services effect, 1635, 1637f
Defined, 1634
Disguised minimum price, 1637c, 1638a, c, 1640d2
Dual distribution, 1605, 1639c, 1651d
Effects, 1638a
Evaded by tie, 1712e
Evils, 1637
Exploitation by sole outlets checked by, 1651c
Free ride on dealers' overhead, 1637i
Interbrand effect, 1640b2
Intrabrand competition effects, 1637a, 1638a, 1640

RESALE PRICE MAXIMUM (*continued*)
Introduction, 1634
Justifications for, 1636
Manufacturer allowances, 1626-1627
Manufacturers-consumer interests converge, 1636g
Minimum resale price distinguished, 1637a-b
Per se illegality, 1638a, 1651c
Per se legality?, 1637c
Pre-ticketed price, 1639d
Price discrimination, 1637f
Price erroneous, 1637e, 1638a, 1640d2
Price predation, 1637h-i
Recommendation, 1638a
Sales quota (minimum), 1639a
Sole outlet, and, 1651c
Standing to challenge, 1640
Suggested price, 1440, 1623c, 1639d
Temporary promotional price, 1639g
Wholesale price formulae, 1626, 1639f-h

RESALE PRICE MINIMUM. *See also* DISTRIBUTION RESTRAINTS GENERALLY
Agent, 1473, 1622c
Agreement, 1623, 1630D. *See also* CONSPIRACY, VERTICAL
Alienation restraint, 1620c1
Ancillary to non-price restraint, 1624c
Anticompetitive effects of, 1620c4
Availability of product, 1615d, 1631a3
Benefits to dealers, 1620c1-4, 1604
Brand significance, 1604f1, 1632c-d, 1633c
Burden of proof and persuasion, 1632e5, 1633
Business Electronics case, 1623a, e, 1624-1625
Buyer-seller price, 1622a
Classification disputes
conditional reimbursements to complying dealers, 1626
manufacturer allowances, 1626-1627
price vs. non-price restraints, 1624, 1625
resale prices vs. other prices, 1622
wholesale price formula, 1627
Common law, 1620c1
Conditional reimbursements, 1626, 1630d
conditions without agreements, 1626a
effects and justification, 1626a
non-price requirements, and, 1626d, 1639f
prices charged, 1626c, 1630d
prices in advertisements, 1626b
variations, 1626a
Dangers summarized and assessed, 1632, 1633c

Dealer coerces, 1632e. *See also* DEALER POWER
Dealer concentration, 1604fe, 1632d, 1633c
Dealer goodwill, 1614, 1631a4, 1647f
Dealer power, 1632e. *See also* DEALER POWER
Dealer services, 1611-1614, 1631c-d
Dealers preserved, 1615, 1631a3
Dealer warranty compensation, 1622a
De facto price restraint, 1624-1625, 1648e
Dr. Miles case, 1620a
Effects, 1630b, 1633
Entry barriers
  decreased, 1631b
  increased, 1631c
Entry facilitation, 1617a3, 1631b
Evaded by tie, 1715c
Evils summarized and assessed, 1632, 1633c
Excess service, 1612, 1631c2
Fashion signal, and, 1613d-g, 1631c3
Free riding remedied, 1611-1613, 1631c-d
Functional equivalents, legality of, 1626-1627
Horizontal dealer cartel, compared, 1603, 1604, 1620b, c2, 1630b. *See also* DEALER POWER
Image enhancement, 1613, 1631a1, 1633d
Indirect resale controls, 1623, 1626-1627. *See also* Agreement
Insurer payments distinguished, 1622b
Intrabrand competition. *See* generally this title
Justice Department guidelines, 1604c2, f3-5, 1606g3-6, 1628b; 1633e1
Justifications summarized and assessed, 1631, 1633d
Legality
  alternative legal rules, 1628b, 1633
  Dr. Miles rule, 1620. *See also* *Dr. Miles*
  indirect resale controls, 1623, 1626-1627
  legislative modifications, 1629
  recommendations, 1633
  reform impulses, 1628e, 1631e, 1632f
  stare decisis, 1628d, 1629c-d
Legislation, 1629
Legitimate objectives, 1623g
Lender sets borrower's selling price, 1622a
Lender sets lawyer charge, 1622a
Less restrictive alternatives, 1602c, 1631d4, 1633d. *See also* this title generally
Loss leading remedied, 1619, 1631a2, 1633d

RESALE PRICE MINIMUM (*continued*)
Manufacturer freedom to sell, implications, 1620b, 1623b. *See also* CONSPIRACY, VERTICAL
Manufacturer goodwill, 1613, 1631a1
Market coverage, 1604f4, 1606g5, 1632d-e, 1633c
Maximum resale price compared, 1637b
Non-price restraints compared and distinguished. *See also* CUSTOMER AND TERRITORIAL RESTRAINT, VERTICAL; SOLE OUTLET
ancillary to non-price restraints, 1624c
burden of proof, 1625c
content of, 1624, 1625a, c1
characterization as price restraint, 1624-1625, 1644, 1652b
distinction possible or justifiable, 1624-1625, 1630
intention to affect price, 1624-1625
legal treatment asymmetrical, 1630
presence of preexisting scheme, relevance, 1625a-c
price discounter disciplined, 1624-1625
Non-resale prices, 1620c1, 1622
Per se illegality challenged, 1628, 1630, 1631, 1632b, e5
Per se legality considered, 1628a, c, e
Price stability objective, 1604, 1606, 1631a5
Product image enhanced, 1613, 1631a1
Quality protection, 1619, 1631c2
Quality signal, 1613, 1631c3A
Quantity limits, 1627f
Recommendations, 1633
Reform impulses, 1628e, 1631e, 1632f
Role of jury, 1633d2
Stare decisis, 1628d, 1629c-d
Termination of discounting dealer: non-price grounds, 1624-1625
Business Electronics case, 1624a, 1625
Dr. Miles rule subverted?, 1625b, c2
inadequate service, 1624d2, 1625c1, e
mail order prohibition of, 1624d2
notorious termination, 1623d
proof of motivation, 1625c
sole outlet, desire for, 1624d3, 1625c3
territorial restraint, 1624d1, 1625c2
unauthorized dealer supplied, 1624d4
Wholesale price formula, 1627d-g

Colgate and *Monsanto* rules, distinguished from, 1627d1
dealer price discretion, 1627d1-2
exemplary termination, 1627e5
implied agreement, 1627d
temporary competitive allowance, 1627e
withdrawal from non-complying dealers, 1627e5
RESALE RESTRICTIONS. *See also* DISTRIBUTION RESTRAINTS GENERALLY
Agreement. *See* CONSPIRACY, VERTICAL
Attempted monopolization, 828d
Customer and territorial limits, Ch. 16D
Maximum prices generally, 1439, 1451c, Ch. 16c
Minimum prices generally, 1437, Ch. 16B
Monopolization, 626e, 735c
Price and non-price contrasted, 1453d, 1454c
Refusal to deal implements, as agreement. *See* CONSPIRACY, VERTICAL
Sole outlet, Ch. 16E
RESALE TO UNAUTHORIZED DEALERS, 1618d, 1624d4, 1647d3. *See also* CUSTOMER AND TERRITORIAL RESTRAINT, VERTICAL
RESTRAINT OF TRADE. *See* COLLABORATION AMONG COMPETITORS; all CONSPIRACY TITLES; DISTRIBUTION RESTRAINTS; FOREIGN COMMERCE; MARKET PREEMPTION; all MERGER titles; OLIGOPOLY; PATENTS; PER SE RULE; RULE OF REASON; SUPPLY PREEMPTION; TYING
ROBINSON-PATMAN ACT (Clayton Act §2)
Attempted monopolization compared, 828c
Competing buyers, 1711g
Concerns, 1711g
Disfavored buyers and tying, 1715c2
Distribution restraints, relevance to, 1613f
Package prices, 1711g
Predatory pricing
by monopolist compared, 720
via tying, 1711g, 1714e
Price differences, 1711g
package, 1711g
tying, 1711g
Price discrimination by monopolist compared, 720
Primary line injury, 1711g
profit maximization, 1711g
Procurement advantages, 1006f, 1104b2
Secondary line injury, 1711g

ROBINSON-PATMAN ACT (*continued*)
Technical requirements, 1711g
Text, *Appendix A*
Tying, 1703e1, 1707d, 1711g
Uniform prices, 1711g
RULE-MAKING ORGANIZATION, 1478
RULE OF REASON (generally). *See also* PER SE RULE; particular substantive titles
Administrative convenience, 1507a, 1508c, 1509
Ancillary restraint defined and illustrated, 1501
Application steps, 1511
Application summarized, 1633d
Arguments of parties decisive without detailed proofs, 1503a, 1504, 1508, 1510c
Burdens of persuasion and proof, 1508, 1633, 1649
Categorical rules within, 1508c
Competition made possible by restraint, 1504
Balancing, 1507, esp. c, 1511
Burdens of proof, 1503b, 1507b-c, 1508c, 1511
Common law illustrated and relevance, 1501
Constituent elements, 1502, 1511
Customer and territorial restraint vertical, 1649
Decisional process illustrated, 1507c, 1511
Distribution restraints, structured for, 1645, 1649, 1633, 1645a, 1649, 1654g
Economic theory, limitations and use, 1500
Effect, anticompetitive
determinative, 1500, 1502, 1511
intended, 1504, 1506
measuring, 1503b. *See also* Power
type, theory, illustrations, 1503a
uncertain, 1500, 1503b
"Every" restraint in Sherman Act §1 covers only unreasonable restraint, 1500, 1501
Facial unreasonableness, 1508b
Fact or law, 320, 321, 1507b
Fast applications, 1504, 1507c, 1508a, c, 1511
General formulae, 1502
History, 1501-1502
Indirect restraint, 1501
Intention. *See also* Competitive effect; Legitimate objective
anticompetitive, 1506
attribution to "the firm," 1506
conduct, substitute for analysis of, 1506
effects indicated, 1504, 1506
generally, 1502
inferred usually from conduct, 1506
interpretation, 1506

irrelevant, when, 1506
power inferred from, 1506
pro-competitive, 1504
relevance, 1502, 1506
superfluous, when, 1506
Jury role, 314-315, 1507b-c
Justification. *See* Legitimate objective
Legitimate objective. *See also* Less restrictive alternative
actually promoted by restraint, 1505a, 1633d, 1649d
alternative ways to achieve, 1505b, 1602, 1703c, 1711e
illustrations, 1504, 1511, 1633d, 1713-1718
legitimacy in principle, 1504
mixed functions, 1717f4
promotes competition, 1504
promotes general welfare, 1504
Less restrictive alternative, 1505, 1602, 1703c, 1711e. *See also* Legitimate objective
effectiveness, degrees of, 1505b, 1602c, 1611g
illustrations, 1505b, 1511, 1714-1718. *See* also generally particular restraints
least or merely less, 1505b
legal approaches, 1633d
relevance, 1505
restrictiveness, degrees of, 1505b
Market definition and shares, relevance, 1503b, 1511
Market failure, 1504
Methodology, 1502-1508, 1511
Naked restraint, 1504, 1511
Necessity, reasonableness, of restraint. *See also* Legitimate objective; Less restrictive alternative
degrees of, 1505
illuminates restraint, 1505
relevance, 1505
Objective of inquiry, 1501-1502, 1511
Output effects, measured and relevance, 1503b
Per se rule compared, 1628b
facial unreasonableness, 1508b
fast applications, 1504, 1597c, 1508a, c, 1511
generally, 1511
presumptions, 1507c, 1508c, 1511
spectrum rather than dichotomy, 1511
structured rule of reason, 1633d
Power, market
assumed or roughly gauged, 1503b, 1507c, 1511
substitute for effects, 1503b
Presumptions, 314, 1507a, c, 1508c, 1628b, 1633, 1649, 1654-1655
Privileged activities, 1508c

RULE OF REASON (*continued*)
Purpose, 1506. *See also* Intention; Legitimate objective
Reasonableness, relevance and meaning, 1500, 1633
Redeeming virtue. *See* Legitimate objective
Regulated industries, 223d, 226d
Restraint of trade required, 1502
Sliding scales, 1507c
State action and state law, 215c, 216b
Structured, detailed example, 1633c-e
Structured rule of reason analysis, 1633
in vertical distribution restraints, 1633, 1649, 1654-1655
Summarized, 1511
Summary disposition, 1508
Tying, and, 1728-1730
Uncertainty about general economy or case, 1500
Vertical-horizontal distinction, 1503a

SALES BELOW COST. *See* PRICE PREDATION
SALES QUOTA, 1616f, 1636g, 1639a, 1648d3f, 1651c
SCALE ECONOMIES. *See* EFFICIENCIES
"SECOND BEST," 411
SERVICES, REPAIR, AND INSTALLATION
Market definition, bearing on, 524
Scale economy, 408c6
Tie-in
attempted monopolization, 823, 829d
justification, 733c
monopolization, 733c
SHAM LITIGATION OR LOBBYING. *See* POLITICAL ACTION
SHERMAN ACT, GENERALLY. *See also* PER SE RULE; RULE OF REASON; more particular topics
Clayton Act, relation to,
generally, 303C, 304, 902, 906, 1145b
tying, 1719b
Common law, relation to, 302, 617
Federal Trade Commission Act, relation to,
generally, 305, 306, 1145
tying, 1719c
Focus, power or its fruits, 1710c3
Historical development generally, 304
Incentives, 1710c3
Judicial innovation, 852
Legislative history, 617, 811, 820, 842
Price control, 1710c1
Text, *Appendix A*
SIGNALING. *See* FACILITATING PRACTICE

SINGLE ENTERPRISE. *See* CONSPIRACY, INTRAENTERPRISE
SMALL BUSINESS. *See also* MERGER, HORIZONTAL AND GENERALLY; RULE OF REASON
- Preservation of, as antitrust objective, 108-112
- Special statutory provisions, 230c

SOCIAL AND POLITICAL VALUES. *See* Public policies generally
SOLE OUTLET
- Agreed or de facto, 1650, 1651f
- Burdens of proof and persuasion, 1653a, 1654g, 1655f1
- *Colgate* dictum, 1653a, d
- Control of needed distribution resources, 1654d
- Customer and territorial restraints compared, 1652d, 1654b
- Dealer autonomy unaffected, 1654b
- Dealer control over distribution resources vs. risk, 1655
  - checks on dealers, 1651
  - dealer initiatives, 1655g3
  - indicators, direct and indirect, 1655g
  - multi-brand sole outlet, 1655g7
  - multiple dealers replaced, 1655g4
  - multiproduct sole outlet for one manufacturer, 1655g6
  - relevance, 1655f-g
  - selective markets, 1655g5
- Dealer power
  - legitimacy, 1654e
  - remediable?, 1654f
- Dealer recommendations, 1654b
- Dealers acting collectively, 1655g3
- De facto vs. express, 1650, 1651f
- Definitions, 1650
- Desire for, and limiting or terminating other dealers, 1624d3, 1625c3
- Duration reasonable, 1651d-e, 1655a, f
  - persuasion and proof burden, 1655f1, 4
  - reasonableness criteria, 1655f3
  - risk reallocation, 1655f2
- Enhances resource value, 1655b
- Entry facilitation, 1655d-g
- Essential facility, 1652c2
- Evils, 1654
- Excessive service, 1654b
- Exclusion of would-be dealers, 1652c
- Exploitation of consumers, 1650, 1651, 1652c, 1654c, g
- Group boycotts compared, 1652b, 1653a

SOLE OUTLET (*continued*)
Horizontal restraint compared, 1652b
Intensity of restraint, 1651
Intrabrand effect, 1651, 1653b
Justifications, 1655
efficient scale, 1655c-d
new entry, 1655d-f
other, 1655c
Legality, 1650, 1652d, 1653, 1654g
Manufacturer-dealer share in sole outlet profits, 1654c1
Manufacturer error, 1654b, 1655d
Manufacturer monopoly not created by, 1653a
Manufacturer price coordination, 1654b
Manufacturer right to choose customers, 1652d, 1653a
Manufacturer self-distribution, 1651d, 1654g3
Many for one manufacturer, 1651b
Monopoly manufacturer, 1653d, 1654a, c2, d
Multiple manufacturers use same sole outlet, 1653e; 1654c1, g
Multiple sole outlets, 1650, 1651b1-2, 1655c
New entry facilitated, 1655d-f
One for many manufacturers, 1653e, 1654c1, g
One per manufacturer, 1650, 1651b
Output contracts compared, 1652c1
Pioneering dealer, 1655d
Presumptions re intensity of restraint, 1651c-e
Price discrimination, 1654b
Price fixing compared, 1652b, 1653a
Product class, 1653e
Product differentiation, 1654b
Product market, 1653e
Recommendations, 1654g
Refusal to deal, as, 1652a
Related legal concepts, 1652
Remedies, 1654f
damages,consumers,1654f3
damages, would-be dealers, 1654f3
invalidation of agreement, 1654f2
require dual outlet, 1654f2
Replacement of dealers
as violation, 1653
relevance of potential, 1651e
Resale price maintenance distinguished, 1625c3
Resale price maximum, 1651a. *See also* same title
Rule of reason governs, 1653a
Sales quota, 1651a, c
Schwinn dictum, 1653a, d
Scope and intensity, 1650, 1651, 1654g3
Single sole outlet, 1650, 1651b1, 1655c
Specialized dealer, 1655d
Substitution of dealers, 1653b
Tying, 1708

Unchecked sole outlet, 1654d-e
Vertical integration ability, relevance, 1651d

SOVEREIGN IMMUNITY, 239c

SPEECH, PUBLIC, 1435c. *See also* FACILITATING PRACTICE

SPORTS, PROFESSIONAL
Collective bargaining, 229d
Exemptions 230f
League as single entity vs. conspiracy among members, 1478
Typical analysis, 1478, 1511. *See also* RULE OF REASON

STANDING. *See also* DAMAGES
Antitrust injury
Brunswick case, basic doctrine, 360a, b, 362, 1640c-d
plaintiff deprived of monopoly profit, 1640d2-3
price fixing, financial losses from, 1640d2
profits lost from enhanced competition, distinguished, 1640c
Basic doctrine, 360
Business not yet in operation, 374
Business or property generally, 361
Citizen, 378b
Competitors vs.
unintegrated rivals, 373f
unlawful merger, 373b
Concept, 360
Consumers
generally, 370
resale price maintenance, 1459b, 1640a
Creditors, 378c
Damage and injunction actions compared, 312d
Damages
absent, 365c
doubtful, 365a, b
generally related to standing, 365
not within rationale of offense, 362
offset, 365c
Dealers vs.
rival's supplier, 383c
supplier, 335c. *See also* Terminated dealer
unlawful merger, 375c
Direct injury, 364g. *See also* generally this title
Employees, 377
labor market restrictions, 377c
other restraints, 377d
Equitable relief, for, 623, 851
Governments, state or foreign, 380
Illinois Brick doctrine, 371, 1459b
Key issues, 360
Landlords, 376
Licensors, 376
Manufacturer vs.
rival manufacturer misbehaving at different vertical level, 373f

STANDING (*continued*)
rival manufacturer using separate distribution channel, 373f
Maximum resale prices, 382a, 1459, 1640
Merger cases, 381
Middlemen, 371b
Minimum resale prices, 1459, 1623f
Nature of violation related to, 338c-d, 339c, 340, 346a
Non-profit plaintiffs, 370
Participant in unlawful agreement, 390, 1459c2
Property holder as defined by state law, 361
Prospective business, 374
Purchasers
direct, 361
indirect, 371
Resale prices, 1459, 1623f, 1640
Shareholders, 378
State officials, 380
Suppliers, 375. *See also* generally this title
Takeover target, 381b
Target area test, 364g. *See also* generally this title
Taxpayers, 378b
Terminated dealer and
Clayton Act §3, 1460c-f
maximum resale prices, 1459, 1640
non-compliance with condition, 1459d
own prior illegal agreement, 1459c1
supplier's illegal agreements with other dealers, 1459e
tying and exclusive dealing distinguished from resale price maintenance, 1459e3
umbrella theories, 1459b2
Unestablished business, 374

STANDARDIZATION, JOINT PRODUCT, 1503a

STATE ACTION; STATE LAW
Advertising limitation, 213d, 219b
Agency composition, 213b, 217a3, 219c
Apparent authority, 217b4
Approval by agency, 214b
Arbitration requirement, 213d, 216b
Authorized action, 214
Civil Rights Act, 219c
Clear statement of state purpose, 214e
Coexistence with federal law, 207
Commerce Clause, 220
Compulsion, 215b
necessity, 215b2
relevance, 215b3, 217b5
sufficiency, 215b1
Concurrent federal authority, 208
Court, as state agency, 213a
Criminal liability. *See* Damage immunity
Damage immunity, 217
government officials, 217a
private parties, 217b

Disclosure statutes, 214a
Equitable remedies against, 217a1-2
Entry limitations, 209, 216a, 220c
Federal regulation compared, 213f
Federal Trade Commission Act, 218
Foreign regulation compared, 215b1
Franchises, 214b
Free speech, 219b
General view, 207
Government contracts, franchises, leases, purchases, sales, 216a
Implied immunity, general rule, 212c
Inaction by supervising agency, 213f, 214c, 217b4
Indispensability to state purpose, 214a-b
Informal action, 217b4
Initiative from private party, 213e, 214b1, 215b, 217b3. *See also* POLITICAL ACTION
Injunction, damages distinguished, 217a
Insurance, 210
Interstate burden, 220c
Interstate commerce impaired, 220
Licensee estoppel, 209
Liquor trade, 210
Merger approval, 214a-b, 215b2
Mistake of law, 217
Officials, immunity from damages, 217a
Parker v. Brown doctrine, 210, 212c. *See also* generally this title
Participation by state officials, 214c
Preempted by federal law, 208-209. *See also* generally this title
Price fixing unsupervised, 209, 213b
Primacy accorded by federal law, 210
"Primary jurisdiction" for state agency, 213f
Private parties protected
  immunity, 212b, 215d
  liability, 213f, 217b
Purpose to displace antitrust law, 214. *See also* generally this title
Reasonableness of state decisions, 215c, 216b. *See also* generally this title
Regulation, 213-214
Rule of reason, 215c
Self-executing statutes, 209, 213d
Self-regulation, private, 213b
State agencies and instrumentalities, against, 217a. *See also* generally this title
Summary, 207
Supervision of private parties, 213. *See also* generally this title
  by whom, 213b, 219c
  intensity, 213c
  requirement, 213

STATE ACTION; STATE LAW (*continued*)
Utilities
equipment restrictions, 214b4, 215b2, 220c
installation charges, 214
tie-ins, 214
Voluntary compliance, 217b
STATES. *See* STANDING; STATE ACTION
STATES, FOREIGN. *See* FOREIGN COMMERCE; FOREIGN GOVERNMENTS; STANDING
STATUTE OF LIMITATION
Accrual of cause of action, 338b
administrative prerequisites to antitrust suit, 338e
continuing violation, 338b
defendant's initiation of a prior lawsuit, 338b
indefinite future damages, 338c
plaintiff's injury from defendant's illegal act, 338b
refusal to deal, 338b
restarting the limitations period, 338b
termination of relations, 338b
Zenith exception, 338c
Clayton Act §4B, 338a
limitation period for damage actions, 338a
Clayton Act §5(i), 339a
administrative proceedings, 339b
applicability of, generally, 339a
FTC proceedings, 339b
government action tolls statute of limitation for private action, 339a
multiple defendants, 339a
overlapping tolling periods, 339a
private action based "in whole or in part" on prior governmental action, 339a
purposes of, 339b
Damage actions, 338a, 338f
Equity actions, 338f
Delay in suing, 338f
justifiable, 338f
unjustifiable, 338f
Estoppel defense, 338f
Evidence, stale or lost, 338f
Fraudulent concealment, 338d
burden of proof, 338d
class actions, 338d
elements of, 338d
self-concealing conspiracies, 338d
Function of, 338a
Generally, 338a
Governmental delay in suing, 338f
Laches defense, 338f
against the government, 338f
illustrations of, 338f
Prior administrative or judicial proceedings, 338e
Prior federal suits, 338e

Prior state antitrust suits, 338e

SUMMARY JUDGMENT
- Award in favor of party with burden of persuasion, 322f
- Awards turning on legal doctrine rather than facts, 322e
- Appropriateness of, 322c
- Burdens of proof, 322c
- Causation requirements, 363
- Conduct ostensibly warranting summary judgment, 322f
  - horizontal conspiracies, 322f
  - manufacturer conspires with dealers against plaintiff dealer, 322f
  - manufacturer replaces one sole-outlet dealer with another, 322f
  - oligopolistic coordination, 322f
  - parallel conduct, 322f
  - per se offenses, 322f
  - proof of each element of violation required, 322f
- Directed verdict and JNOV requirements compared, 322c
- Direct evidence of conspiracy, 322i
- Establishing a genuine issue of fact, 322c
- Evidence in equipoise, 322c, f
- Expert affidavits, 322j
  - creating a genuine issue of fact, 322j
  - requirement of support for opinion, 322j
- Generally, 322a
- Importance of in antitrust cases, 322a
- Intent and credibility issues, 322c
- Judgments about conduct affect formulation of legal doctrine, 322f
- Jury's role, 322f
- *Kodak* case, 322e
- *Matsushita* case, 322c
  - direct evidence of conspiracy, 322i
  - limits, 322e
  - lower court treatment, 322c
- More probable than not requirement, 322c
- Motivation and rationality of conspiracy, 322g
  - evidence that alleged conspiracy would harm conspirators, 322g
  - necessary for inferring conspiracy, 322g
  - not necessary to support a conspiracy finding, 322g
- Obstacles to, 322b
  - affidavits, depositions, etc. may not survive cross-examination, 322b
  - deprive plaintiff of jury trial, 322b
  - doubt about nature and content of substantive offenses, 322b

SUMMARY JUDGMENT (*continued*)
exposure of defendant's wrongs, 322b
summary judgment should be used sparingly, 322b-c
Prediscovery summary disposition, 323. *See also* PREDISCOVERY SUMMARY DISPOSITION
Rule of reason cases, 322h
Standards for awarding summary judgment, generally, 322a, c, f
Summary judgment on a single issue, 322d
SUPPLIERS OF RIVALS COMPROMISED
Monopolization, 734e
SUPPLY PREEMPTION. *See also* EXCLUSIVE DEALING; FORECLOSURE ANALYSIS; MARKET PREEMPTION; MERGER, VERTICAL; RECIPROCITY; TYING
Duration, 731c
Exclusive dealing, output and requirements contracts, 731b, e
Market definition, 570h
Merger compared, 731h
Monopolization, 731
relief scope, 731f
Purchases excessive, 731d
Theory, 570a
Vertical integration compared, 731g

TERRITORIAL DIVISION BY COMPETITORS. *See also* PER SE RULE; RULE OF REASON
Agreement, 1424d4. *See also* CONSPIRACY, GENERALLY
Monopolization, 703
TERRITORIAL LIMITATION, VERTICAL. *See* CONSPIRACY, COERCED; CONSPIRACY, VERTICAL; CUSTOMER AND TERRITORIAL RESTRAINT, VERTICAL; DISTRIBUTION RESTRAINTS GENERALLY
TOEHOLD ACQUISITION
Alternatives, preferred, 1124
Beneficial, 1124b, 1125
Defense, class, 1125, 1143e, 1149b
Defined, 1124c, 1125d
Economies defense, relation to, 1125c, 1149b
Exclusive merger route, 1124
Likelihood, 1124d
Offensive-defensive uses interrelated, 1125c
Permitted, 1125
Potential acquirers, other, 1124e
Preconditions, summarized, 1124a

Premises, 1124
Required, 1124
Statutory provisions, 1124g
TORTS. *See also* UNFAIR COMPETITION
Attempted monopolization, 828b
Monopolization, 626d, 737-739
TRADE ASSOCIATION. *See also* CONSPIRACY, INTRAENTERPRISE; JOINT VENTURE; RULE OF REASON
Conspiracy among creators, 1477
Conspiracy, continuing among members, 1477
Day-to-day operations as members' conspiracy, 1477
Dealers. *See* DEALER POWER
Liability for unauthorized acts, 1477
Liability of members, 1477
Single entity, 1477
TRADEMARK
Acquired, 1202f
Tying product. *See* TYING
TRADE SECRET, and tying, 1716e1, f
TREBLEDAMAGES. *See*DAMAGES; PRIVATE ACTIONS
TYING
Access fee, 1716e4, 1727d
Access to supplies, 1703f6, 1708
Administrative convenience, 1730
Advantage over rivals, 1700d2, 1707e4, 1713c3, 1714b, 1715d
Agreement, 1700i, 1702, 1709d1. *See also* CONSPIRACY, COERCED; CONSPIRACY, VERTICAL; Coercion
Alien factor, 1700d2, 1707e4
Allocations based on past sales, 1725e
Alternatives. *See also* Defenses
alternate source. *See* Approved source
approved source. *See* same this title
condemn restraint, 1703c1
cost, 1703c1
customer option. *See* same this title
education. *See* Specifications
effectiveness, 1703c1
implications, 1703c, 1711e
less restrictive, 1703c1
lump-sum payment, 1712c4
package discount. *See* same this title
prove intent?, 1703c2
relevance, 1703c2, 1711e
save restraint, 1703c1, 1711e
specifications. *See* same this title
substitute restrained, 1712c4
surrender trade secret, 1716f

TYING (*continued*)
two-tier pricing. *See* Customer option; Package discount
vertical integration, 1712c4
warranty disclaimer, 1716c1
Anticompetitive effect required, 1722c
Antitrust goal
output, 1703e4, 1710, 1729b-f
price, 1703e4, 1710, 1729i1
rivalry, 1703e4, 1710, 1729b-f
Antitrust injury
substitute's producers or customers, 1705f3
Approved source, 1716e, 1726e
approval fee, 1716e4
buyer choice, 1716e1
charade, 1716e2, 1727b2
effects negated, 1716e1
efficiency, 1716e2
efficient quality protection, 1716e1
fee
access, 1716e4, 1727d
approval, 1716e4, 1727d
inspection, 1716e3, 1727d
patent, 1716f3, 1727d1
royalties, 1716f3, 1727d1
trade secret, 1716f3, 1727d1
few, 1716e5, 1726e4
fictional, 1716e2, 1727b2
good faith, 1716e2, 1726e
inspection fee, 1716e3
abusive, 1716e3
permissible, 1716e3
reasonable, 1716e3
legal relevance, 1716e1, 1726e
less restrictive alternative, as, 1716e1
many, 1716e5
monitoring, 1716e1
more qualified, 1716e2
more sought, 1716e2
number of approvals, 1716e5, 1726e
practicality, 1716e2
recognizing vs. creating equivalent product, 1716f4
royalty, 1716f3, 1727d1
disguised approval fee, 1716f3
permissibility, 1716f3
reasonableness, 1716f3, 1727d1
"too high", 1716f3
sham, 1716e2, 1727b2
specifications compared, 1716e1
tie negated, 1716e1, 1726e
trade secret, 1716e1, 1727d1
disclosure limited, 1716e1
non-disclosure, 1716e1
universal, 1726e1
unreasonably withheld, 1716e2
widespread, 1726e2
Attempted monopolization, 829d
Autonomy of buyer, 1700d3, 1703f5, 1710, 1718c, 1724b, 1729i3

Average pricing, 1703g2, 1717e
Bargain ties, 1715
Benefits. *See also* generally this title and these specific topics
  allocative efficiency and
    input substitution, 1712c
    price discrimination, 1711
    sequential monopoly, 1712b
  combination patent rewarded, 1712g
  convenience, 1717
  costs lowered, 1717
  efficiency increased generally, 1717b1, 1718b
  entry aided, 1713
  equalize customers, 1718d
  historically unclaimed, 1703b1
  paternalism, 1716c, 1718j
  price
    competition, 1714-1715
    cuts indirect or selective, 1714-1715
    floors evaded, 1715b-c
    transparency, 1718g
  profit increased generally, 1717b1, 1718b
  promotions, 1714
  quality protected, 1716
  summarized, 1703
  value increased, 1717b2, 1718i
Blanket license, 1717f3
Block booking, 1717c1
Bundled products
  generally, 1716c2, 1717f1
  price comparison aided, 1712f
Buyer
  autonomy. *See* same this title
  choice, 1703d1, 1703f5, 1718c, 1729i3
  damage, 1701c2
  defined, 1700fi
  exploitation. *See* same this title
  foreclosed from supply, 1703f6, 1708
  foreclosure. *See* same this title
  indifferent, 1707e
  non-tied, 1706b2, 1709c3, 1721d, 1729h
  oppression. *See* Autonomy; Exploitation
Cartel
  downstream, 1712b
  evaded, 1715c1
Charity, 1718j
Cheating supplier, 1718e
Choice. *See* Autonomy
Choice, customer, 1718c
Clayton Act §3
  Sherman Act compared, 1719b
  text, 1700e, 1719b, 1726b
Coercion, 1700i, 1702, 1714b1, 1717c1, 1717d2, f2, 1721d3B. *See also* CONSPIRACY COERCED
Combination customary, 1717b2
Combination patent rewarded, 1712g

TYING (*continued*)
Commodity, 1700f
Competition. *See also* generally this title
effects on, 733, 1134b. *See also* Effects
increased tying market, 1715
process impaired, 1713c3
protected, 1700d, 1703d, 1709c1, 1729
with buyer, 1708
Competitive conditions clause, 1707e, 1707e3, 1715f, 1729f3
Competitor. *See also* Competition
Clayton Act §3 language, 1726b
in tied market, defined, 1727
or competition affected, 1709c1, 1729g
Complementary products, 1726dB-C, 1729b
fixed proportion, 1706
variable proportion, 1706, 1711
Compulsory vs. voluntary, 1714b1. *See also* Coercion
Concentration
proof, 1729e1
results, 1704, 1729d-e
threshold, 1729e1
tied market, 1703d3, 1704c, 1707, 1709b1-2, e1, 1713-1715, 1729d-f
tying market, 1704c, 1714-1715, 1729b-c
Concerns generally, 1700d, 1703, 1729
Condominium, 1717f4
Conglomerate merger, after, 1134
Convenience of buyer, 1703g2, 1717
Coordination impediments
proof, 1729e1
relevance, 1729e1
Copying obstructed, 1703f4, 1718f, 1729i2
Copyright, 1700f, 1717f3
Costs saved, 1703g2. *See also* Efficiency
entry aided, 1713b2
scale economics, 1717b12
varieties, 1717b
Cumulative foreclosure, 1703d3, 1709d2, 6, 1721c3, 1729e-f
Custom, 1703b2, 1717
Customer
autonomy. *See* same this title
choice. *See* Autonomy
convenience, 1717b2, 1717f2, 4. *See also* Efficiency
costs, 1717b2
deceived, 1712f, 1729i2
option, 1717c1, 1717d. *See also* Package discount
appeal, 1717d1
copyright package, 1717f3
de facto tie, 1717d2
no less restrictive, 1717d2

patent package, 1717f3
practicality, 1717b2, 1717d2, 1717f2
same price for one product, 1717b2, 1717d2, 1717f3
turnkey franchise, 1717f2
preference. *See* convenience
utility. *See* convenience; Efficiency
Damages, 365c, 1702
Dealer
freedom. *See* Autonomy
full-line force, 1725c-d
incentives, 1725e, 1725g
monopoly, 1709c3
rewards, 1725g
ties generally, 1709e6, 1725b, 1729h
Deceive customers, 1712f
Defenses, 1701c2. *See also* generally this title
costs saved, 1717
customer convenience, 1717
efficiency, 1717, 1718b
entry aided. *See* Entry
equalize buyers, 1718d
goodwill, 1716
liability interconnected, 1700c, 1716a2, 1728c
mixed functions, 1717f4
paternalism, 1718j
profit, 1718b
quality, 1716
reasonability vs. per se standards, 1728c
reputation, 1716
risk reduction, 1713b2
safety, 1716
weak firm. *See* same this title
Definition and variations, 733a, 1700a-b
Designated supplier pays fee. *See* Approved source
Detrimental effects. *See also* generally this title
cumulative, 1729a
dealer rewards, 1725g
dealers tied, 1725b
filters, 1729
foreclosure, intrinsically minor, 1725
foreclosure zero, 1724
full-line force, 1725c
generally, 1703d-f, 1729
non-foreclosure based proofs, 1729i
presumptions, 1729
proof burden, 1722e
proofs, 1729
reasonability and per se compared, 1728e
results, 1729d, e2
sales quota, 1725f
summarized, 1703d-f, 1729
temporary promotions, 1725h
tests
foreclosure zero, 1723
per se rule, under, 1721b, 1722-1727
reform proposed, 1730
rule of reason, 1729
without foreclosure, 1703e-f, 1729i
Detriments. *See* Detrimental effects

TYING (*continued*)
Disapproved supplier, 1726e3. *See also* Approved source
Discount, 1700i, 1714-1715, 1717
Discrimination, 1715c2
Disguised discount, 1714-1715
Disguised price, 1703f1-3, 1703g3
Disloyal employee, 1727g
Disruptive buyer eliminated, 1707d, 1729f2
Disrupt oligopoly pricing, 1707e4, 1714-1715
Distribution restraint accompanies, 1610, 1632c2, 1646f, 1648c1
Doctrinal elements interdependent, 1700c
Doctrine
black letter, 1702
effects required, 1719-1730
expansion, 1701c1
over-extension, 1701c1
retraction, 1701c2
summarized, 1702
Dollar volume test, 1721, 1721b1
allocations based on past sales, 1725e
all tied purchasers, 1721c2
approvals, 1726e
coerced package, 1721d3
competitor not foreclosed. *See* Economic interest in tied product
dealer incentives or rewards, 1725e, g
dealers tied, 1725b
disapprovals, 1726e
exclusions, 1722-1727
exiting from tied market, 1727f
financial interest in tied product. *See* Economic interest in tied product
foreclosure
minor, intrinsically, 1725
share ignored, 1721b1
zero, 1723, 1724
fractional requirement, 1725i
full-line force, 1725c
indirect effects test, 1722-1727
inflation, 1721b3
intrastate sales, 1721b3
irrelevant foreclosure, 1721d, 1726-1727
jurisdiction, 1721b2
magnitude, 1721b4
meaning, 1720a, 1721
measurement, 1721
multi-year, 1721b3
new user, 1724d2
non-foreclosing sales, 1721d, 1722-1724
package, 1721d3
partial tie, 1721d3
policy relevance, 1721b2
positive foreclosure required, 1722
pre-tie customers, 1721d2
promotion, temporary, 1725h
qualitative test, 1722c
relevant foreclosure required, 1722, 1726-1727

rival sellers absent, 1723
sales quota, 1725f
single-brand buyer, 1724c
single purchaser, 1721c1
specifications, 1726e
threshold requirement, 1722
unfinanced user, 1724d1
unwanted product, 1724b
value added, 1721b3
yearly, 1721b3
zero foreclosure, 1721d, 1722, 1723-1724
Downstream concentration increased, 1703f6, 1708
Duration, 1707d, 1709e3, 7
Early cases, 1720b2
Economic interest in tied product, 1703d3, 1709e5, 1726, 1727
access fee, 1727d
creditor, 1727c
defined, 1727
exiting from tied market, 1727f
"family" interest, 1727c
fee for service, 1727g
fee from seller of tied product, 1727d
inspection fee, 1727d
kickback to employee, 1727g
license fee, 1727d
partial equity, 1727c
presence in tied market, 1727b
quality in tied market, 1727g
relevance, 1726
reselling goods purchased from others, 1727e
Effects, 733. *See also* Defenses; Detrimental effects; generally this title
downstream, 1708, 1712c4
economic interest in tied product, relevance, 1716-1727
entry and, 1713d1
generally, 1134b, 1146, 1703
miscellaneous, 1718
non-tied buyers, 1703d1, 1721d, 1729h
summarized, 1703
tests under
per se rule, 1721-1727
rule of reason, 1729
tied buyers, 1703d1
tied product, 733c
tying product, 733e
Efficiency. *See also* generally this title
alternatives, 1717d1
alternatives as, 1717b1D
average pricing, 1717e
bundled products, 1717f1
copyright package, 1717f3
costs, which, 1717c2
discounts and, 1717d3
efficient pricing tying product, 1712c3
enhanced, 1703h1
enhanced revenue as, 1717c3
guaranteed market as, 1717c3
input substitution. *See* same this title
legitimacy, 1717c
enhanced revenue, 1717c3

TYING (*continued*)
guaranteed market, 1717c3
which costs, 1717c2
less restrictive alternative. *See* Alternatives
monitoring infringement, 1717f3
patent package, 1717f3
pecuniary savings, 1717f1
proof degrees, 1717c4, 1717f
proof difficulties, 1717c4
recognized, 1717c
revenue enhancement as, 1717b13
risk reduced, 1717b13, 1717c2
scale
tied product, 1717b1B
tying product, 1717b1B
scale economics, 1717b12, 1717c2
seller savings, 1717b11
tie needed?, 1717d1
turnkey franchise, 1717f2
two products, and, 1717
varieties, 1717b
vertical integration, 1717f1
Employee vs. contractor services, 1717f1
Enhanced price competition, 1714-1715
Entry
aided, 1703g4, 1713
alien factor, 1713c3
approving dicta, 1713c2
barriers overcome, 1713c2
benefits, 1713d
by tying monopolist, 1713d
competitive process and, 1713c3
competitive process distorted, 1713c3
conditions, 1729e1
defense, 1713
defense expires, 1713d2
duration, 1713d2
effects test and, 1713d1
foreclosure, 1713d2
foreclosure large but brief, 1713d6
full-line force, 1713c2, 1725c-d
Griffith formula, 1713c3
illustrated, 1713c2
justification, 1713
legitimate, 1713c2
market performance unchanged, 1713d4
permanent small foreclosure, 1713e
potential reduced, 1705c-e, 1729b, d-e
power test and, 1713b1
pre-existing competition, 1713d5
process objection, 1713c3
pro-competitive, 1713c2, 1713d
related market, 1713d7
related product, 1713c2
rival complaint, 1713c3
rival reaction, 1713d4
slothful entrant, 1713d4
tied market, into, 1713b1, 1729d-e
tie's necessity, 1713d3
tying market, into
consumer value, 1713b3
necessity, 1713b3

obstructed, 1705c-e, 1729b
revenue up, 1713b3
tying monopolist, by, 1713c2
Entry barriers raised. *See* Entry
Equalize dealers, 1718d
Equivalent product absent, 1716d1
Evils. *See* Detrimental effects
Exclusive
dealing, 1700j3, 1709e8, 1724c, 1729h
distributor or outlet, 1708
Exit from tied market, 1727f
Exploitation (of tying market power), 1703e, 1710-1712, 1727d3, 1729i
frequency, 1710a
incremental, 1710a, 1711e
net, 1710a
precedent, 1710b
relevance, 1703e4, 1710, 1729i1
Facilitate oligopolistic coordination, 1707, 1729f
Federal Trade Commission Act, 1702, 1719c
Fee for service in tied market, 1727g
Fee from seller of tied product, 1716e3-4, f3, 1727d
Financial interest in tied product. *See* Economic interest in tied product
Financing as tying product, 1724d1
Foreclosure, 1700d1, 1703d3. *See also* Detrimental effects; generally this title
adding rivals, 1709d6
aggregating all ties, 1709d2, 1729h
allocations based on past sales, 1725e
all sellers, 1703d3, 1729e1-2, h
anticipated, 1709d3, 1729h
approved suppliers, 1729h. *See also* same this title
assessed, 1703d3, 1729a-f
buyers from supplies, 1703f6, 1708
coerced purchase, 1721d3, 1729h. *See also* Coercion
competitor not foreclosed, 1723-1724. *See also* Economic interest in tied product
complaining customers, 1709d1, 1729h
concentrates tied market, 1703d, 1704c, 1729d-e
concentration, 1703e, 1709b1-2, e1, 1729e. *See also* same this title
cumulative, 1703d3, 1704c4, 1709d2, 6, 1721c3, 1729e2, 1729h
dealer incentives, 1725e-g
dealers tied, 1703d3, 1725b-d, 1729h. *See* Dealer
dealer stimulation, 1729e-g
designated supplier pays fee, 1709e4, 1727d

TYING (*continued*)
disapproved supplier, 1726e
dollar-volume test. *See* same this title
duration, 1703d3, 1709e3, 7, 1714. *See also* New user
economic interest in tied product. *See* same this title
entry potential mitigates, 1709e6
exclusions, 1729h. *See also* Dollar-volume test
exclusive dealer, 1724c, 1729h
exiting from tied market, 1727f, 1729h
financial interest in tied sale. *See* Economic interest in tied product
first step, 1709d4-6, 1729h
fractional requirement, 1721d3, 1725i, 1729h
full-line force, 1729h
imminent tied sales, 1709d4-6, 1729h
incipient, 1709d3-6, 1729
inclusions, 1729h. *See also* Dollar-volume test
indirect, 1705f, 1729c, h
industry-wide. *See* cumulative
market relevant, 1709c, 1714c, 1715e, 1721b1, 1728, 1729g
meaning and measurement, 1703d3, 1709c-e, 1729h. *See also* Dollar-volume test
mechanism, 1704
medical specialists, 1709c2
middlemen tied. *See* Dealer
minor, intrinsically, 1725
mitigating factors, 1709e
monopoly both markets, 1704c1
more ahead, 1709d3-6
new user, 1703d3, 1724d2, 1729h
non-tied sales, 1721d, 1729h
old customer, 1704b1, 1709d1, 1721d2, 1729h
overstated, 1703d3
packages, 1709e3, 1721d3, 1729h
partial tie, 1709d1, 1721d3, 1725i, 1729h
per se rule, under, 1722-27. *See also* Dollar-volume test
practical effect, 1709e3
presumptions, 1729e2
pre-tie customer. *See* old customer
price stabilization, and, 1703d2, 1707, 1729f
prospective, 1709d3-6
requirements contracts, 1703d3, 1709d2, 1729h
reseller of tied product, 1709e4, 1727e, 1729h
rivals. *See* same this title
sales quota, 1725f
scale inefficiency, 1704b2, 1729, 1729e3
significance generally, 1703d, 1729

single-brand buyer, 1724c, 1729h
specifications, 1726e
stable buyer, 1704b3
sub-optimal scale, 1704b2, 1729, 1729e3
substantiality, 1705e2, 1729e2
substitute rather than tied product, 1705f3
temporary promotions, 1714, 1725h
threshold of significance, 1729e2
tied product market, 527, 1709c1, 1714c, 1715e, 1729g
turnkey franchise, 1717f2
tying product. *See also* generally this title
if none, 1709e8
widely purchased separately, 1703d3
tying seller. *See also* generally this title
buys tied product, 1709e4, 1727e, 1729h
middleman, as, 1709e4, 1727e, 1729h
sales, 1709d1
unaffected purchasers, 1706b2, 1709c3, d1, 1721d, 1729h
unfinanced user. *See* New user
untied sales, 1709d1, 1721d, 1729h
unwanted product, 1724, 1729h
vertical integration included, 1703d3, 1709d2
volatile buyer, 1704b3
voluntary tie, 1709e7
zero, 1723, 1724
Forms, 1134a, 1700f-g, i
Fractional requirement, 1725i
Fraud on principal or supplier, 1703f3, 1718e, 1729i2
Full-line force, 1713c2, 1725c-d
Functions. *See also* generally this title
custom, 1703b2
generally, 1704-1718
miscellaneous, 1718
summarized, 1703
Generally, 316d, 1134, 1146. *See also* generally this title
Goodwill. *See* Quality
Government price ceilings or floors, 1703e3, f1, 1712d, 1715b, 1729i2
Griffith formula, 1713c3
Guidelines, 1707d, 1729
Harmless?, 1703a, 1729a, 1730c
Higher price for tying product. *See* Exploitation
Historical sketch, 1701, 1720
Hospital services, 1709c2, 1717f1, 1728f
Hostility, 1701c1, 1720b-c
Identifying tying-tied product, 1709c, 1714c, 1715e, 1729g

TYING (*continued*)
Imitation, 1709d2, 6, 1729h. *See also* Copying obstructed
Incentives, 1710c3. *See also* Dealer
Incipiency, 1709d3. *See also* Foreclosure, cumulative
Income distribution, 1710c2
Incremental exploitation. *See* Exploitation
Incremental value, 1718h-i
Indirect
  foreclosure, 1705f, 1729c, h
  price cut, 1714-1715
  price rise, 1712
Inefficient substitution limited, 1712c3
Inferior tied product, 1713e
Information. *See* Price
Input substitution, 1703e2, h2, 1712c, 1729i1
Inspection fee, 1716e3, 1727d
Intangible, 1700f
Intention, 1703b. *See also* Motive
Interdependence of issues, 1703g
Intrabrand distribution restraint compared, 1700j4
Issues interdependent, 1703g
Justice Department guidelines, 1700j4, 1705e2, 1709b, 1729e1
Justification. *See* Defenses
Land, 1700f
Large buyer removed from contention, 1703d2, 1707d, 1729f2
Lease, 1700f
Legality generally, 1133a, 1134c. *See also* generally this title
Legitimate purpose or function. *See also* generally this title
  partial or sale objective, 1717f4
  summarized, 1703g-h
Less restrictive alternative, 1703c. *See also* Alternatives; specific functions
Leverage, 1700d, 1701b, 1703d, 1704, 1729b-e
License, 1700f
License fee, 1716f, 1727d1
Limited distribution, and, 1700j4, 1708
Limited purpose sale, 1718k
Linguistic
  conventions, 1700b
  elasticity, 1701c1
Lock-in, 1709c5
Long-run dangers, 1705
Manager beliefs, 1703b1
Market definition. *See also* same; MARKET POWER
  generally, 527, 1703d3, 1709c
  geographic, 1703d3, 1709c
  guides, 1729g
  rivals absent, 1723c
  single brand, 1729g
  which tied or tying, 1703d3, 1714c, 1715e
Metering, 1711b
Middlemen tied. *See* Dealer
Misleading prices, 1712f

Models
 limits, 1703b1
 vs. intent, 1703b
Monitoring rivals, 1703d2, 1707e3, 1729f3
Monopolization, 626e, 733
 relief scope, 733f
 statutes, other antitrust, relevance, 733f
Monopoly
 both markets, 1704c1
 causation, 1729d
 created, 1703d1, 1704b, c1-2, 1729d
 downstream, 1712b
 effects, 1703d1, 1705b-c, e, 1706b
 foreclosure relevance, 1703d1, 1704b, 1729d
 non-tied purchasers, if none, 1729d
 presumptions, 1729d
 price for tying product. *See* Exploitation
 sequential, 1703h4, 1712b
 stranger, for, 1726d2
Motion Picture Patents Company, 1701b, 1720b1
Motive. *See also* generally this title
 effect, vs., 1704d
 generally, 1703a-b
 long-run, 1704d
 non-economic, 1704d
Movie industry, 1701b, 1717f3, 1720b1
Necessity. *See* Alternatives; Defenses; specific functions
New entry. *See* Entry
New product, 1716c2
New user, 1724d, 1729h
Non-market transaction, 1703h5, 1718j
Non-tied purchasers, 1706b2, 1729a, d, e4
Non-tying foreclosures, 1700j
Non-use risk, 1711b
Not insubstantial commerce. *See* Dollar-volume test
Oligopoly. *See also* same; Concentration
 causation, 1729e2
 coordination facilitated, 1703d2, 1707, 1729f
 created, 1703d1m, 1704c3-4, 1729e
 downstream market, in, 1712b
 effects, 1703d1, 1705d, 1706c-d, 1707
 foreclosure relevance, 1703d1, 1704b, 1707, 1729e-f
 impaired, 1715c1
 monitoring, 1707e3, 1729f3
 result, 1704c3-4
 strangers, created for, 1726d2
 tying market, in, 1704c4, 1705f, 1729c
 tying monopolist's incentive, 1704c3
Output contracts, and, 1708
Package customary, 1717b2
Package discount, 1717c1, d. *See also* Promotion
 as tie, 1717d3C
 customers reject, 1717d3C
 enhanced price competition, 1715c2

TYING (*continued*)
exceeds savings, 1717d3A
manipulated, 1717f2
none, 1717f3
practicality, 1717d2
savings relation uncertain, 1717d3D
savings unrealized, 1717d3C
turnkey franchise, 1717f2
tying product power, 1711a2
under savings, 1717d32
which product tying or tied, 1709c4, 1714c, 1715e
Paradigm, 1700a
Partial substitute tied, 1703d1, 1705f, 1729c
Partial tie, 1709d1, 1721d3, 1725i
Patent, 1700f
combination, 1703g5, 1712g
constant value with or without tie, 1703g2, 1718h
infringement, 1701a, 1720b1
regimenting industry, 1701b
reward, 1703g5, 1712g
misuse, 1701ab, 1720b1
package, 1717fc
Paternalism, 1703h5, 1718j
Per se, 1701c2
Per se rule
anticompetitive effect meaning, 1722c
clarity absent, 1730
created, 1720b3
critique, 1730
detrimental effects required. *See* Dollar-volume test; Economic interest in tied product
foreclosure
share ignored, 1721b1
some required, 1722
zero, 1723, 1724
full-line force, 1725c
history, 1720b
history summarized, 1720c
indirect effects test, 1722-1727
meaning, 1720a, 1721
not literal, 1728, 1730
power in tying market required, 1720b4
premises unmet, 1730
qualitative, 1722c
rationale, 1720c
reasonability considered indirectly, 1728
reform proposed, 1730
relevant foreclosure required, 1722
rule of reason compared, 1728, 1730
simplicity absent, 1730
social impact, 1730b
specifications, 1726e
threshold requirement, 1722
tied market power requirement?, 1722d
unusual version, 1730
Pioneering product, 1716c2, 4
Power in tied market. *See* Detrimental effects
Power in tying market
entry and, 1713b1

reasonability and per se compared, 1728d
required, 1701c2, 1702, 1720b4
Practical effect, 1700g, 1709d1, 1709e3
Predation on tying product, 1714e
Pre-tied customers, 1709d1, 1721d2, 1729h
Price
antitrust policy, and, 1710c1
better information, 1703h4, 1718g
ceiling evaded
government, 1703e3, 1712d, 1729i2
private, 1703e3, 1712e
comparison simplified, 1718g
competition
arena narrowed, 1707c. *See also* Disruptive buyer
disguised, 1715
incentive, 1707
increased, 1703g3, 1713-1715
partial vs. general, 1715c2
selective, 1715c1
tied market, 1715d, f
tying monopolist, 1715d2
concealed, 1703f2, 1712d
cut indirect on tying product, 1715a, c1
disguised, 1703e3, f1-2, g3, 1712d-e, 1715b-c, 1718e
effects when
ineffective tying oligopoly, 1706d
input substitution limited, 1705f, 1712c
monopoly, 1706b1
non-tied users. *See* same this title
oligopoly, 1706c, d, 1707
price discrimination. *See* same this title
floor evaded
benefit, as, 1703h3
government, 1703f1, 1715b, 1729i2
private, 1703f1, 1715c
indirect. *See* disguised
revealed, 1718g
selective cut, 1703g3, 1714-1715
stabilized, 1707e3
transparent, 1703h4, 1718g
Price discrimination, 1703e1, 1710-1711, 1729i1
alternatives and relevance, 1703c, 1711e
benefit, as, 1703h2, 1711b, f
condemnation ground, 1711f1
effects, 1703e1, 1711b4
allocative, 1711b4
ambiguous, 1711c
distributional, 1711b4
independent demands, 1711c
entry aided, 1713b2
first degree, 1711b4A
foreclosure not required, 1711a1
illustration, 1711a2

TYING (*continued*)
independent demand function, 1711c
innocent explanation, 1710a
metering, 1711b
more competitive result, 1711b
motivation, 1710a
non-exploitative, 1715c2
non-leverage explanation, 1711a1
non-use risk, 1711b
output-expanding illustration, 1711a2
perfect, 1711b4A
per se rule and, 1711f3
precedent, 1710b
prerequisites, 1711a2
proof, 1729i1
proposal, 1711f
recommendation, 1711f
redemption ground, 1711f2
relevance, 1703e, 1710, 1729i1
second degree, 1711b4B
third degree, 1711c
tied power immaterial, 1703e1
tied product price, 1711b3
use intensity, 1711b
Prima facie illegality
defined, 1716a2
per se rule, 1720-1721
rule of reason, 1729
Process, 1700f, 1713c3
Product
defined, 1700f
quality, 1703g1, 1716
variety, 1703d1, 1718c
Profit
economic vs. accounting, 1704d
enhanced, 1703h1, 1718b
maximization goal, 1704d
Promotions
advertising alternative, 1714b2
alternatives, 1714b2
duration, 1714d
foreclosure, 1714b3
general price cut alternative, 1714b2
predation compared, 1714e
price, 1714
temporary, 1725h
tie-in motive, 1714b2, 1718k
Proof, 1703b2
Proof and presumptions, 1729
Proposals, detrimental effect proof, 1729-1730
Quality, 1716
alternative. *See* same this title
approved source. *See* same this title
auto dealer, 1716c3
buyer alone at risk, 1716c1
customer interest, 1716c
defined, 1716c
distribution limited, 1716c4
entry aided, 1713b2
equivalent product absent, 1716d1
examining tied, 1716g
"gold plating", 1716c3
immediate buyer vs. consumer, 1716c3

intermediate buyer vs. consumer, 1716c3
legitimacy, 1716a3
less restrictive alternative. *See* Alternatives
new product, 1716c2, 1716c4
past failure, 1716d2
pioneer, 1716c2, 1716c4
price trade-off, 1716c
self-protecting, 1716c
seller interest, 1716, 1716c2
specifications. *See* same this title
summary, 1703g1
warranty disclaimed, 1716c1
Realignment merely, 1704b1
Reasonability: effects and criteria, 1729
Reduce costs, 1717. *See also* Efficiency
Reformed effect test, 1729-1730
Reform proposal, 1729-1730
Refusal to deal to enforce. *See also* CONSPIRACY, VERTICAL
Clayton Act, under, 1460
Federal Trade Commission Act §5, under, 1461
Sherman Act, under. *See* CONSPIRACY, VERTICAL
Regulated prices evaded, 1712d, 1715b
Regulation vs. antitrust domain, 1712d2
Repair parts, 1711b3
Reputation, 1716. *See also* Quality
Requirements contract, 1700j3, 1707c, 1709d2, e8
Resale price
evaded, 1712e, 1715c
irrelevant, 1703e1
Reselling goods purchased from others, 1709e4, 1727e, 1729h
Resource allocation improved, 1711b, 1712c3
Resource savings, 1717. *See* Efficiency
Results, actual, 1729d, e2
Revenue maximization goal, 1704d
Risk reduced, 1717b1C. *See also* Entry
Rivals. *See also* Concentration
absent, 1723, 1729h
buyers foreclosed from supply, 1708
complaints, 1715f
destabilized, 1009, 1704b3
inefficient scale, 1704b2, 1729, 1729e3
inferior, 1723e
insufficient patronage, 1704b2, 1729, 1729e3
marketing options, 527, 1709c2, 1729g
numerous, 1704c4
reaction, 1713c3, 1714-1715
Robinson-Patman Act, 1707d, 1711g
Rule of reason. *See also* same
competitor not foreclosed, 1723-1724, 1726-1727
detrimental effects proved, 1729

TYING (*continued*)
generally, 1729a
per se rule
substitute, 1729-1730
supplement, 1728
proof of harm, 1729
relevant inquiries, 1729a
structured, 1729a
uncertainty, 1729a
usual applications, 1728f
Safety. *See* Quality
Sales
defined, 1700f
maximization goal, 1704d
quota, 1725f
Scale economics, 1704b2, 1729b-e
Selective discount
alternative, 1715c2
rival choices, 1715c2
tying product, 1715c1
Seller defined, 1700f
Separate availability, 1715c3
Sequential monopoly, 1703h4, 1712b
Service, 733c, 823, 829d. *See also* Quality
condominium and, 1717f4
coverage, 1700f
innovation aided, 1716g
reasonable duration, 1717f4
reasonable price, 1717f4
tie limits copying, 1718f
Sherman Act
relevance, 1700e
test, 1719b
Single
brand buyer, 1724c
brand market, 1729g
monopoly profit, 725b, 1706b1
product, 1701c2
purchaser, 1721c1
Specifications, 1726e
adequacy, 1716d2, 1716d3
adequacy presumption, 1716d1
administration, 1716d4
approved source compared, 1716e1
as alternative, 1716d
auto parts, 1716d4
brand uniformity, 1716d2
complex, 1716d2
compulsory, 1716d3
consumer complaint, 1716d4
costs, 1716d4
delivery service, 1716d2
detailed, 1716d2
food, 1716d2
graves, 1716d2, 1716d4
impractical, 1716d2
jury role, 1716d2
luxury auto parts, 1716d4
manual incomplete, 1716d2
monitoring, 1716d4
preferable, 1716d1
reseller, 1716d2
taste involved, 1716d2
trade secret at stake, 1716f
voluntary, 1716d3
Stable buyer, 1704b3
Stagnation result
monopoly, 1705b
oligopoly, 1705d
Standing, 1702
Stare decisis, 1730c

Statutes relevant, 1700e, 1719b
Statutory coverage, 1719b
Substantial commerce. *See* Dollar-volume test
Substitute for tying product weakened, 1703d1, 1705f, 1729c
Substitution limited, 1712c
Successive monopolies avoided, 1712b
Summary, 1703
Supplier cheated, 1718e
Tacit coordination facilitated, 1703d2, 1707, 1729f
Temporary price, 1714, 1725h
Test
  detrimental effects. *See* same this title; Per se rule; Rule of reason
  generally, 1701c1
Threshold requirement, 1722b
Tied market. *See* Concentration; Detrimental effects; Entry; Market definition; Monopoly; Oligopoly; Per se rule; Rule of Reason; Price; generally this title
Tied product
  identified, 1708, 1709c4, 1714c, 1715e
  installation, 1716
  service, 1716
  substitute for tying product, 1705f, 1712c, 1729c
  valueless, 1718h
Trademark, 1700f, 1717f2
Trade secret, 1700f, 1716f
  actual, 1716f2
  already surrendered, 1716f2
  continuing secret, 1716f2
  no disclosure obligation, 1716f4
  product structure, 1716f1
  protective covenant, 1716f2
  recipe, 1716f1
  royalty, 1716f3, 1727d1
  service manual, 1716f1
  significance, 1716f2
Turnkey franchise, 1703g2, 1717f2
  coercion, 1717f2
  foreclosure, 1717f2
  legitimacy, 1717f2
  two products, 1717f2
Two
  level entry, 1703d1, 1705c-e, 1729b
  products. *See also* Defenses
    generally, 1700h, 1702, 1713d7, 1717e-f
    illustrations, 1701c1, 1709e5, 1717c-f, 1718j
  tier pricing. *See* Customer option; Package discount
Tying market. *See* Concentration; Detrimental effects; Entry; Market definition; Monopoly; Oligopoly; Per se rule; Price; Rule of Reason; Substitute; generally this title

TYING (*continued*)
Tying product
defined, 1700a, 1712d1, 1714c, 1715e
distribution limited, 1708
identified, 1708, 1709c4, 1715e
if none, 1709e8
power
indirectly exploited. *See* Exploitation
required. *See* Per se rule
when measured, 1709c5
price. *See* Exploitation; Package discount; Price
Tying seller buys tied product, 1709e4, 1727e, 1729h
Unfair market advantage, 1707e4, 1713c3, 1714d, f
Unfair to other oligopolists, 1707e4, 1713c3, 1714d, f
Unfinanced user, 1724d1
Uniform test, all statutes, 1719b
Unwanted product, 1724b
Use intensity, 1711b
Value
increased, 1703g2, 1718i
unaffected, 1703g2, 1718h
Vertical integration, 1700j1, 1707c, 1709d2, 1717f1
Vertical merger, and, 1700j2
Volatile buyer, 1704b3
Voluntary, 1700i. *See also* Coercion; Package discount
Warranty, 1700a
claim fraudulent, 1716c1
disclaimer, 1716c1
Weak tied product supported, 1713e

"UMBRELLA" TRANSACTIONS, 372
Damages for the umbrella plaintiff, 372
Standing for the umbrella plaintiff, 372
UNCLEAN HANDS. *See* PLAINTIFF'S VIOLATION
UNFAIR COMPETITION
Attempted monopolization, 828b
Compromise rival's employee or supplier, 738d-e, g
Concealment, 738k
Disparage rival, 738c
Espionage, industrial, 738f
Impulse for intraenterprise conspiracy. *See* CONSPIRACY, INTRAENTERPRISE
Influence buyers, 738a, b, i
Interfere with rival's advantageous relation, 738l
Misrepresentation or exaggeration, 738a, i
Monopolization, 737
Refusal to deal. *See* same
Sham litigation, 738j. *See also* POLITICAL ACTION
State law preempted, 209

UNILATERAL ACTIVITY. *See* ATTEMPTED MONOPOLIZATION; all CONSPIRACY titles; REFUSAL TO DEAL
UNIONS. *See* LABOR UNIONS
UNREASONABLY LOW PRICES. *See* PRICE PREDATION

VERTICAL CONSPIRACY. *See* CONSPIRACY, VERTICAL
VERTICAL INTEGRATION. *See also* DISTRIBUTION RESTRAINTS; FORECLOSURE ANALYSIS; LEASE-ONLY; MERGER, VERTICAL; MARKET PREEMPTION; SUPPLY PREEMPTION; REFUSALS TO DEAL; RESALE RESTRICTIONS; TYING
- Alternative to distribution restraint, 1608, 1612e, 1616e, 1636g
- Attempted monopolization, 828c
- Benefits
  - efficiencies, 724a, 725d
  - input substitution eliminated, 725f
  - no benefit situations, 726d
  - output effects, 725e
  - successive monopolies, 725c
- Definition, 723
- Distribution restraint compared, 1608
- Evils
  - double monopoly profit, 725b
  - efficiency reduced, 725g, 1636g
  - entry barriers increased, 725h
  - innovation reduced, 725g
  - output effects, 725e
  - price manipulation, 724b
  - recoupment, 724b
  - transfers, internal, at cost, 724b
- Exceptional rules, 726d-e
- Franchised, regulated monopoly, 726e
- General rule, 726b-c
- Market power absent, 724
- Monopolist, by, 725-726, 1000b, 1015e, 1017c
- Non-monopolist, by, 724, 1003-1012
- Oligopolist, by, 1000b, 1003-1012
- Partial integration, 725a, h-i, 726d
- Per se approaches, 726b
- Precedents
  - vertical integration as such, 727
- Presumptions, 726
- Price discrimination, 725e, 1616b, e, f; 1647c5-6; 1648c3

VERTICAL INTEGRATION (*continued*)
  Price squeeze, 728a, c
  Refusal to deal
    arbitrary, 736
    merger, after, 1017c
    supply squeeze, 728a, b
  Remedies, administrability, 729e, 736e, 1507a
  Successive monopolies, 725c, 725h2
  Tying compared, 1700j1
  Varieties, 723

VERTICAL RESTRAINT. *See* DISTRIBUTION RESTRAINTS GENERALLY; TYING; particular restraints

WEBB ACT, 230a
  Text, *Appendix A*

WILSON TARIFF ACT, 235d, 311a
  Text, *Appendix A*